Himalaya's

Objectives and MCQs in

MARKETING MANAGEMENT

Features

- Summary
- Fill in the Blanks
- True/False
- Multiple Choice Questions
- Match the Following

AF798806

Himalaya Publishing House
ISO 9001:2015 CERTIFIED

© No part of this publication may be reproduced, stored in a retrieval system, or transmitted in any form or by any means, electronic, mechanical, photocopying, recording and/or otherwise without the prior written permission of the author and the publisher.

First Edition : 2019

Published by : Mrs. Meena Pandey for **Himalaya Publishing House Pvt. Ltd.**,
"Ramdoot", Dr. Bhalerao Marg, Girgaon, Mumbai - 400 004.
Phone: 022-23860170, 23863863; **Fax:** 022-23877178
E-mail: himpub@bharatmail.co.in; **Website:** www.himpub.com

Branch Offices :

New Delhi : "Pooja Apartments", 4-B, Murari Lal Street, Ansari Road, Darya Ganj, New Delhi - 110 002. Phone: 011-23270392, 23278631; Fax: 011-23256286

Nagpur : Kundanlal Chandak Industrial Estate, Ghat Road, Nagpur - 440 018. Phone: 0712-2738731, 3296733; Telefax: 0712-2721216

Bengaluru : Plot No. 91-33, 2nd Main Road, Seshadripuram, Behind Nataraja Theatre, Bengaluru - 560 020. Phone: 080-41138821; Mobile: 09379847017, 09379847005

Hyderabad : No. 3-4-184, Lingampally, Besides Raghavendra Swamy Matham, Kachiguda, Hyderabad - 500 027. Phone: 040-27560041, 27550139

Chennai : New No. 48/2, Old No. 28/2, Ground Floor, Sarangapani Street, T. Nagar, Chennai - 600 017. Mobile: 09380460419

Pune : "Laksha" Apartment, First Floor, No. 527, Mehunpura, Shaniwarpeth (Near Prabhat Theatre), Pune - 411 030. Phone: 020-24496323, 24496333; Mobile: 09370579333

Lucknow : House No. 731, Shekhupura Colony, Near B.D. Convent School, Aliganj, Lucknow - 226 022. Phone: 0522-4012353; Mobile: 09307501549

Ahmedabad : 114, "SHAIL", 1st Floor, Opp. Madhu Sudan House, C.G. Road, Navrang Pura, Ahmedabad - 380 009. Phone: 079-26560126; Mobile: 09377088847

Ernakulam : 39/176 (New No. 60/251), 1st Floor, Karikkamuri Road, Ernakulam, Kochi - 682 011. Phone: 0484-2378012, 2378016; Mobile: 09387122121

Cuttack : New LIC Colony, Behind Kamala Mandap, Badambadi, Cuttack - 753 012, Odisha. Mobile: 09338746007

Kolkata : 108/4, Beliaghata Main Road, Near ID Hospital, Opp. SBI Bank, Kolkata - 700 010. Phone: 033-32449649; Mobile: 07439040301

DTP by : Nilima Jadhav / Pravin

Printed by : M/s. Aditya Offset Process (I) Pvt. Ltd., Hyderabad. On behalf of HPH.

Contents

Chapter 1

Overview of Marketing

SUMMARY

Marketing is the process used to determine what products or services may be of interest to customers and the strategy to use in sales, communications and business development. It generates the strategy that underlies sales techniques, business communication and business developments.

Marketing deals with customers' creating customer value and satisfaction are the heart of modern marketing thinking and practice. Traditional view of the marketing asserts that the customer will accept whatever product the seller presents to them. In this way, the main concern of the producer is to produce without considering the choice or the behavior of the customer. But this point of view of marketing has now changed.

The term marketing concept holds that achieving organizational goals depends on knowing the needs and wants of target markets and delivering the desired satisfactions. It proposes that in order to satisfy its organizational objectives, an organization should anticipate the needs and wants of consumers and satisfy these more effectively than competitors.

Marketing is used to identify the customer, satisfy the customer, and keep the customer. With the customer as the focus of its activities, marketing management is one of the major components of business management.

A seller's market is one in which the demand for goods and services exceeds the supply. In such a situation there is tendency of growing monopolies. On the other hand, buyer's market is one in which the supply of goods exceeds the demand.

The systems approach in business was an idea born in 1960s. This was designed to utilize scientific analysis in complex organizations for developing and managing operating systems and designing information system for decision making. A tenet of systems theory is that every system is held together by information exchange.

A successful marketer is akin to a successful hitter in baseball. Even the greatest batters of all time got out more often than they got a hit. In the major leagues, if you get three hits for every ten throws you are considered as a highly successful hitter.

Buying is the first step in the process of marketing. A manufacturer has to buy raw materials for production; a wholesaler has to buy goods to be sold to the consumer. Buying involves transfer of ownership of goods from seller to the buyer. Assembling means creation and maintenance of the stock of goods, purchased from different sources. Branding is the management process by which a product is branded. It is a general term covering various activities such as giving a brand name to a product, designing a brand mark and establishing and popularizing it.

Salesmanship is neither an art nor is it completely based on scientific principles. It is a combination of both. A salesman must possess inborn talents and must have a real interest in the profession. Salesman comes in contact with any number of persons, guides and advises them to purchase goods of the producer to whom he represents, convinces them, describes the attractive and positive features of the products and pre-sale and after sale services and thus makes a sale.

Sales promotion and personal selling are parts of promotional mix. Sales promotion techniques are indirect and non-personal. While personal selling is quite direct and personal. The main purpose of the sales promotion activities is to stimulate consumers and dealers effectively. Sales promotion directed at consumers may be done with a view to increase the products rate of use among existing consumer products.

The nature of marketing requires marketing managers and professionals to work together on all aspects of marketing. It is common for the marketing manager to be at the center of a set of activities being worked on by people within the company sales force, promotion manager, product development teams, etc., and outside the company, ad agencies, consultants, marketing research firms, etc. Thus, marketing managers must spend considerable time in consultation and collaboration with other people.

The services described in the second half of the definition are those included in the sale of goods to the customer, viz., pre-sale and after-sale services, e.g., services of installation of machinery, its maintenance and repairs, credit and delivery services, etc.

Marketing is the function by which a marketer plans, promotes and delivers goods and services for customers and clients. In the context of marketing of services, we can say that marketing is the creation and delivery of customer-satisfying services at a profit to the supplier or provider of service.

The term marketing concept holds that achieving organizational goals depends on knowing the needs and wants of target markets and delivering the desired satisfactions. It proposes that in order to satisfy its organizational objectives, an organization should anticipate the needs and wants of consumers and satisfy these more effectively than competitors. The spirit of market is exchange of products and services to satisfy human needs, wants, demand, utility, exchange, etc.

1. **Needs:** A human need is a state of self deprivation of some basic satisfaction. People require food, clothing, shelter, safety and a few other things for survival. These needs exist in the very texture of human biology.
2. **Wants:** Wants are specific satisfier of these deeper needs, e.g., an individual needs food and wants cake. Human wants are continuously shaped and reshaped by social forces and institutions.
3. **Demand:** Demands are wants for specific products that are backed by an ability and willingness to buy. Wants become demands when supported by purchasing power, e.g., many people want a Mercedes, but only if you have ability and willingness to purchase it.
4. **Utility:** It is expected satisfaction from the product.
5. **Exchange:** It is an act of obtaining a desired product from someone by offering something in return. A product is anything that can be offered to satisfy a need or want.

Marketing is helpful not only to plan the production but it is also helpful in business planning and in taking various decisions regarding the business. In today's economy, production is planned according to the sales forecasts and not according to the production capacity of the firm. A firm will produce what it can sell or as much quantity it can sell and not what and how much it can produce. Thus, marketing decisions affect the business decisions. All other activities such as planning, production, purchase, finance revolve around the marketing decisions.

Every business is carried on with a profit motive. Marketing helps in increasing the business profits by reducing the selling costs on one hand and by increasing the demand of the product through advertising and sales promotion activities on the other hand.

Business collects various information regarding consumers' behaviour and the changes in their behaviors from time to time through marketing. Marketing also provides information to the firm about the competitors, prices, policies and distribution policies. Marketing provides extensive information of the product regarding its quality, price, utility and place of availability to the society. Thus, society comes to know about the new products.

Traditional concept of marketing includes the activities which are involved in the physical transfer and ownership of goods form part and parcel of marketing. In other words, marketing is concerned with handling and transportation of goods from the point of production to the point of consumption.

On the other hand, modern concept of marketing discuss the process of planning and executing the conception, pricing, promotion, and distribution of ideas, goods and services to create exchanges that satisfy individual and organizational goals. It includes production-oriented marketing, sales-oriented marketing, customer-oriented marketing and social-oriented marketing. It also implies that management firmly believes that if we have a good product, the customer's response will be favorable. The sales-oriented concept, points out that we cannot have enough customer response without promotion efforts. Customer-oriented concept approach takes the primary task and values of the potentials customers. Social-oriented marketing concept implies environmental trends like public welfare, concern for better living environment as qualify of life, etc. Marketing is the function by which a marketer plans, promotes and delivers goods and services to customers and clients. In the context of marketing of services, we can say that marketing is the creation and delivery of customer-satisfying services at a profit to the supplier or provider of service. When marketing is defined as the creation and delivery of standards of living to the society, the role of customer-satisfying services assumes unique importance in the customer-oriented marketing approach. In the sales of services to customers, what is important is that customers are satisfied, that their needs and wants are fulfilled by the providers of services.

FILL IN THE BLANKS

1. Market is a _______, _______ and _______ concept.
2. On the basis of selling area, the types of markets are ________, ________ and ________ markets.
3. On the basis of article of trade, the types of markets are ________ markets.
4. On the basis of nature of exchange dealings, the types of markets are ________ and ________ markets.
5. On the basis of nature of goods sold, the types of markets are ________ and ________ goods market.
6. On the basis of period, the types of markets are ________ and ________ term markets.
7. On the basis of nature and magnitude of selling, the types of markets are ________ and ________ markets.
8. The kinds of goods are _______, _______ and ________.
9. ________ goods may be consumer goods needed for use by consumer.
10. ________ goods may be in the form of raw materials for industry or consumer goods for immediate consumption.
11. ________ are the free gifts of nature and they are the raw materials for industry.
12. The categories of consumer goods are ________, ________ and ________ goods.
13. Marketing aims at _______ and ________.

14. ________ covers seeking, matching and programming.

15. Manufacturer is required to buy raw materials for ________ purposes.

16. Wholesaler has to buy goods from ________ for purposes of sales.

17. ______ has to sell the goods to consumers.

18. JIT stands for ________.

19. ________ can plan for short-term, medium-term and long-term finances.

20. Open system has its own environment giving the ________ and accepting the ________.

21. The output of ________ system is sales of goods.

22. The flow of information required to check performance is called ______ information.

23. ________ system provides data for decision making in all marketing areas or problems.

24. Marketing environment affects ________ and ________.

25. Producer gets the surplus value in the form of ________.

26. ________ gets the surplus value in the form of utility satisfaction.

27. The marketing process involves the activities of ______, ______ and ______.

28. Supply of goods has to be adjusted to demand on the basis of ______, ______ and ________.

29. Concentration, dispersion and equalization constitute the heart of ________.

30. Demand for a product starts with ______.

31. Marketing management ends with ______.

32. The price is based on ______ and ______ cost.

33. ________ is adopted only to give emphasis on product features, quality and price.

34. ________ and ________ of the company activities rotate around the primary goal of satisfying customer needs.

35. The entire marketing mix will be formulated on the basis of marketing ________ and ________.

36. Corporate plans, programmes and operations must have focused around customer ________ and ________.

37. ________ is a vital resource in planning action control process of management.

38. Selling focuses on the ________.

39. Marketing focuses on the ________.

40. Selling aims at profit through ________ volume.

41. ________ aims at profit through serving customer demand.

42. Product gives ________, ________ and ________ satisfactions.

43. Under marketing concept, supply becomes the function of ________.

44. Demand is the ________ factor.

45. Demand analysis becomes the foundation of a ________.

46. ________ and ________ should achieve consumer protection and environment protection.

47. In a business firm, marketing generates revenues that are managed by the ________ people.

48. In a business firm, marketing generates revenues that are used by the ________ people.

49. In ________, goods are purchased from various sources and assembled at one place to suit the requirement of the buyer.

50. The social marketing concept is known as the ________ and ________ concept.

Answers for Fill in the Blanks

1.	Place; Area; Demand	26.	Consumer
2.	Local; international; National	27.	Concentration; dispersion; equalization
3.	Product	28.	Time, quantity; quality
4.	Cash; Forward	29.	Marketing
5.	Consumer; Industrial	30.	Needs and wants of buyer
6.	Short-term; long-term	31.	Customer satisfaction
7.	Wholesale; retail	32.	Production; distribution
8.	Manufactured; agricultural; natural raw material	33.	Promotion
		34.	Planning; coordination
9.	Manufactured	35.	Information; research
10.	Agricultural	36.	Needs; desires
11.	Natural raw material	37.	Information
12.	Convenience; shopping; specialty	38.	Seller's needs
13.	Customer satisfaction, customer service	39.	Buyer's needs
14.	Marketing	40.	Sales
15.	Production	41.	Marketing
16.	Manufacturer	42.	Economic; social; psychological
17.	Retailer	43.	Demand
18.	Just in time	44.	Controlling
19.	Marketer	45.	Marketing functions
20.	Inputs; outputs	46.	Consumer; government
21.	Marketing	47.	Finance
22.	Feedback	48.	Production
23.	Marketing information	49.	Assembling
24.	Producer; consumer	50.	Human; ecological
25.	Profit		

TRUE / FALSE

1. Marketing refers to all activities to identify the customer, satisfy the customer and keep the customer. (True / False)

2. Efficiency is a productivity metrics meaning how fast one can do something. (True / False)

3. Marketing concepts are broadly classified into two types such as traditional concept and modern concept. (True / False)

4. The exchange orientation is the modern concept of marketing. (True / False)

5. Segmentation is the identifying the target customers. (True / False)

6. On the basis of nature and magnitude of selling, the type of markets is short-term and long-term markets. (True / False)

7. On the basis of period, the types of market are wholesale and retail markets. (True / False)

8. The kinds of goods are manufactured, salutary and agricultural, goods, natural raw material. (True / False)

9. Agricultural goods can be consumer goods needed for use by consumers. (True / False)

10. Manufactured goods may be in the form of raw materials for industry or consumer goods for consumption. (True / False)

11. Natural raw materials are the free gifts of nature and they are the raw material of industry. (True / False)

12. The categories of consumer goods are convenience shopping and specialty goods. (True / False)

13. Marketing is process of creating customer demand only. (True / False)

14. Marketing covers seeking, matching and programming. (True / False)

15. Agents are required to buy raw materials for production purposes. (True / False)

16. Wholesaler generally buy goods from manufacturer for purpose of sales. (True / False)

17. Retailer has to sell the goods to consumers. (True / False)

18. JIT stands for justification in technology. (True / False)

19. The company can plan for short-term, medium-term and long-term finances. (True / False)

20. Process system has its own environment giving the inputs and accepting the outputs. (True / False)

21. The output of marketing system is sales of goods. (True / False)

22. The flow of information required to check performance is called feedback information. (True / False)

23. Marketing research involves systematic study of marketing problem. (True / False)

24. Marketing environment affects both producer and consumer. (True / False)

25. Manager gets the surplus value in the form of profit. (True / False)

26. Consumers get the surplus value in the form of utility satisfaction. (True / False)

27. The marketing mix involves the activities of concentration, dispersion and equalization. (True / False)

28. Supply of goods has to be adjusted to demand on the basis of time, quantity and quality. (True / False)

29. Concentration, dispersion and equalization constitute the heart of marketing. (True / False)

30. Discussion on marketing process starts with market management. (True / False)

31. Discussion on marketing process ends with market demand. (True / False)

32. The price is based on production and distribution cost. (True / False)

33. Product is adopted only to give emphasis on product features, quality and price. (True / False)

34. Planning and co-ordination of the company activity rotate around the primary goal of satisfying customer needs. (True / False)

35. The entire marketing mix will be formulated on the basis of marketing management and channels. (True / False)

36. Corporate plans and programmes must be focused around customer needs and desires. (True / False)

37. Product is a vital resources in planning action control process of management. (True / False)

38. Selling focuses on the seller's needs. (True / False)

39. Marketing focuses on the profitability needs. (True / False)

40. Selling aims at profit through sales volume. (True / False)

41. Marketing aims at profit through serving customer demand. (True / False)

42. Product gives only economic satisfactions. (True / False)

43. Under marketing concept, supply becomes the function of demand. (True / False)

44. Demand is the controlling factor. (True / False)

45. Place analysis becomes the foundation of a marketing function. (True / False)

46. Consumerism and government should achieve consumer protection and environmental protection. (True / False)

47. In a business firm, marketing generate revenues that are managed by the finance people. (True / False)

48. In a business firm, marketing generates revenues that are used by the finance people. (True / False)

49. In assembling, goods are purchased from various sources and assembled at one place to suit the requirements of the buyer. (True / False)

50. The social marketing concept is known as the human and ecological concept. (True / False)

Answers for True / False

1.	True	11.	True	21.	True	31.	False	41.	True
2.	True	12.	True	22.	True	32.	True	42.	False
3.	True	13.	False	23.	True	33.	False	43.	True
4.	False	14.	True	24.	True	34.	True	44.	False
5.	False	15.	False	25.	False	35.	False	45.	False
6.	False	16.	True	26.	True	36.	True	46.	True
7.	False	17.	True	27.	False	37.	False	47.	True
8.	True	18.	False	28.	True	38.	True	48.	False
9.	True	19.	True	29.	True	39.	False	49.	True
10.	True	20.	False	30.	False	40.	True	50.	True

MULTIPLE CHOICE QUESTIONS

1. Which of the following is (are) the related concept of marketing?

(a) Place concept
(b) Area concept
(c) Demand concept
(d) All the above

2. Which of the following is (are) the type(s) of market, on the basis of selling area?

(a) Local markets
(b) International markets
(c) National markets
(d) All the above

3. Which of the following is (are) the type(s) of market, on the basis of article of trade?

(a) Product markets
(b) Price markets
(c) Promotion markets
(d) Distribution markets

4. Which of the following is (are) the type(s) of market, on the basis of nature of exchange dealings?

(a) Spot and cash market
(b) Futures and forward market
(c) Cash and forward market
(d) Deficit and desirable market

5. Which of the following is (are) the type(s) of market, on the basis of nature of goods sold?

(a) Consumer goods market
(b) Industrial goods market
(c) Both (a) and (b)
(d) None of the above

6. Which of the following is (are) the type(s) of market, on the basis of period?

(a) Short-term and medium-term markets
(b) Short-term and long-term markets
(c) Medium-term and long-term markets
(d) None of the above

7. Which of the following is (are) the type(s) of market, on the basis of nature and magnitude of selling?

(a) Manufacture and wholesale markets
(b) Wholesale and retail markets
(c) Manufacture and retail markets
(d) Retail and agent markets

8. Which of the following is not related to marketing?

(a) Sales
(b) Promotion
(c) Production
(d) Plant layout

9. Which goods may be consumer goods needed for use by consumers?

(a) Manufactured goods
(b) Salutary goods
(c) Agricultural goods
(d) Natural raw materials

10. Which goods may be in the form of raw materials for industry or consumer goods for immediate consumption?

(a) Manufactured goods
(b) Natural raw materials
(c) Agricultural goods
(d) Salutary goods

11. Which are the free gifts of nature and they are the raw materials of industry?

(a) Manufactured goods
(b) Salutary goods
(c) Agricultural goods
(d) Natural raw materials

12. The categories of consumer goods are __________.

(a) Convenience goods
(b) Shopping goods
(c) Specialty goods
(d) All the above

13. Marketing is used for __________.

(a) Customer satisfaction
(b) Customer service
(c) Both a and b
(d) None of the above

14. Marketing covers __________.

(a) Seeking
(b) Matching
(c) Programming
(d) All the above

15. Who is required to buy raw materials for production purposes?

(a) Manufacturer
(b) Wholesaler
(c) Retailer
(d) Agents

16. Who has to buy goods from manufacturer for purpose of sales?

(a) Manufacturer
(b) Wholesaler

(c) Retailer
(d) Agents

17. Who has to sell the goods to consumers

(a) Manufacturer
(b) Wholesaler
(c) Retailer
(d) Agents

18. JIT stands for __________.

(a) Justification information technology
(b) Just in time
(c) Justification in technology
(d) Just information time

19. Who can plan for short-term, medium-term and long-term finances?

(a) Retailer
(b) Consumer
(c) Manufacturer
(d) All the above

20. Which system has its own environment giving the inputs and accepting the outputs?

(a) Marketing
(b) Information
(c) Open
(d) Process

21. The output of which system is sales of goods?

(a) Marketing
(b) Information
(c) Open
(d) Process

22. The flow of information required to check performance is called __________.

(a) Flow of products
(b) Flow of money
(c) Market communications
(d) Feedback information

23. Which system provides data for decision-making in all marketing areas or problems?

(a) Marketing research
(b) Marketing information
(c) Management research
(d) Management information

24. Marketing environment affects __________.

(a) Producer
(b) Consumer
(c) Both a and b
(d) None of the above

25. Who gets the surplus value in the form of profits?

(a) Producer
(b) Consumer
(c) Manager
(d) Wholesaler

26. Who gets the surplus value in the form of utility satisfaction?

(a) Producer
(b) Consumer
(c) Manager
(d) Wholesaler

27. The marketing process involves the activities of __________.

(a) Concentration
(b) Dispersion
(c) Equalization
(d) All the above

28. Supply of goods has to be adjusted to demand on the basis of __________.

(a) Time
(b) time and quality
(c) Time, quantity and quality
(d) Time, place, quantity and quality

29. What constitute the heart of marketing?

(a) Concentration
(b) Dispersion

(c) Equalization
(d) All the above

30. Discussion on marketing process starts with ________.

(a) Market channels
(b) Market demand
(c) Market functions
(d) Market management

31. Discussion on marketing process ends with ________.

(a) Market management
(b) Market channels
(c) Market functions
(d) Market demand

32. The price is based on ________.

(a) Production cost
(b) Distribution cost
(c) Both a and b
(d) None of the above

33. Which is adopted only to give emphasis on product features, quality and price?

(a) Product
(b) Promotion
(c) Price
(d) Place

34. Which of the company activities rotate around the primary goal of satisfying customer needs?

(a) Planning
(b) Coordination
(c) Both a and b
(d) None of the above

35. The entire marketing mix will be formulated on the basis of ________.

(a) Marketing information and research
(b) Marketing management and channels
(c) Marketing information and functions
(d) Marketing management and demand

36. What must be focused around customer needs and desires?

(a) Corporate plans
(b) Programmers
(c) Operations
(d) All the above

37. Which is a vital resource in planning-action control process of management?

(a) Product
(b) Information
(c) Demand
(d) Process

38. Selling focuses on the ________.

(a) Sellers needs
(b) Buyer's needs
(c) Profitability
(d) Utility satisfaction

39. Marketing focuses on the ________.

(a) Seller's needs
(b) Buyer's needs
(c) Profitability
(d) Utility satisfaction

40. Selling aims at profit through ________.

(a) Sales volume
(b) Profit volume
(c) Cost volume
(d) None of the above

41. Marketing aims at profit through ________.

(a) Serving sellers demand
(b) Serving customer demand
(c) Both a and b
(d) None of the above

42. Product gives ________.

(a) Economic satisfactions
(b) Social satisfactions
(c) Psychological satisfactions
(d) All the above

43. Under marketing concepts, supply becomes the function of __________.

(a) Demand
(b) Market
(c) Profit
(d) Satisfaction

44. Demand is the __________.

(a) Uncontrolling factor
(b) Controlling factor
(c) Formal factor
(d) Informal factor

45. Which becomes the foundation of a marketing function?

(a) Market analysis
(b) Place analysis
(c) Demand analysis
(d) Time analysis

46. Who should achieve consumer protection and environmental protection?

(a) Capitalism and consumerism
(b) Consumerism and government
(c) Socialism and consumerism
(d) Communism and consumerism

47. In a business firm, marketing generates revenues that are managed by the

(a) Production people
(b) Distribution people
(c) Finance people
(d) Accounts people

48. In a business firm, marketing generates revenues that are used by the __________.

(a) Production people
(b) Distribution people
(c) Finance people
(d) Accounts people

49. In which, goods are purchased from various sources and assembled at one place to suit the requirements of the buyer?

(a) Warehousing
(b) Inventory management
(c) Material Handling
(d) Assembling

50. The social marketing concept is known as the __________.

(a) Human concept
(b) Ecological concept
(c) Both a and b
(d) None of the above

Answers for MCQ

1.	(d)	**10.**	(c)	**19.**	(c)	**28.**	(c)	**37.**	(b)	**46.**	(b)
2.	(d)	**11.**	(d)	**20.**	(c)	**29.**	(d)	**38.**	(a)	**47.**	(c)
3.	(a)	**12.**	(d)	**21.**	(a)	**30.**	(b)	**39.**	(b)	**48.**	(a)
4.	(c)	**13.**	(c)	**22.**	(d)	**31.**	(a)	**40.**	(a)	**49.**	(d)
5.	(c)	**14.**	(d)	**23.**	(b)	**32.**	(c)	**41.**	(b)	**50.**	(c)
6.	(b)	**15.**	(a)	**24.**	(c)	**33.**	(b)	**42.**	(d)		
7.	(b)	**16.**	(b)	**25.**	(a)	**34.**	(c)	**43.**	(a)		
8.	(d)	**17.**	(c)	**26.**	(b)	**35.**	(a)	**44.**	(b)		
9.	(a)	**18.**	(b)	**27.**	(d)	**36.**	(d)	**45.**	(c)		

MATCH THE FOLLOWING

1.	Demand	(a)	Target customers
2.	Selling	(b)	Motor car
3.	Marketing	(c)	Profits through sales volume
4.	Segmentation	(d)	Worth of the offer
5.	Value	(e)	Customers satisfaction and profit
6.	High involvement goods	(f)	Ability and willingness to buy

Answers for Match the Following

1.	(f)	2.	(c)	3.	(e)	4.	(c)	5.	(d)	6.	(b)

Chapter 2

Marketing Management

SUMMARY

Marketing Management is the activity of planning and executing the conception, pricing, promotion and distribution of ideas, goods, and services to create exchanges that satisfy individual and organizational goals.

Marketing management includes those activities by which management is able to satisfy customers with a view to earn profits. The main principles of marketing management are as follows:

(i) **Sound Planning:** Planning is essential to achieve the three important goals of marketing (i) Growth of the organization, (ii) Improves the sales volume and (iii) Increase in net profit.

(ii) **Effective Organization:** The marketing manager has to organize its division on the basis of modern principles of the organization. He should clearly understand the duties and functions of the personnel engaged in the responsible task.

(iii) **Proper Directions:** The management executive issues necessary directions to his subordinate and coordinate all the activities under different departments.

(iv) **Decision Making:** All the activities of marketing decisions are directed towards achieving the overall goals of the management. A market needs to take careful decisions.

(v) **Sales Promotion:** The ultimate objective of the enterprises is to maximize sales volume. The marketing executive should make all possible efforts to promote the sales of the company.

(vi) **Motivation:** The success of a executive can be judged by his ability to motivate the staff under him to maximize its efforts and to achieve the target of the enterprises.

(vii) **Research and Development:** Change in the tastes, preferences of the consumers takes place all the time. The marketing manager has to study and carry on research and adopt the product in conformity to the preferences of the final consumers.

Management Guru Philip Kotler defines marketing as "Marketing Management is the analysis, planning, implementation and control of programmes designed to bring about the desired exchanges with target audiences for the purpose of personal and mutual gain. It relies heavily on adoption and coordination of the product, price, promotion and place for achieving response". In other words, a business discipline, which is focused on the practical application of marketing techniques and the management of a firm's marketing resources and activities is Marketing Management.

Marketing Management focuses upon the psychological and physical factors of marketing. The marketing managers are responsible for influencing the level, timing, and composition of customer demand is the accepted definition of the term. While the psychological factors focus upon discovering the needs and wants of the consumer and the changing patterns of buying behavior, habit, etc., the physical factors focus upon fulfilling those needs and demands by better product design, channel of distribution and other functions.

Marketing in action is marketing management. Marketing management has the responsibility to perform many functions in the field of marketing such as planning, organizing, directing, motivating, coordinating and controlling. All these function aim to achieve the marketing goals.

Marketing management determines the marketing objectives. The marketing objectives may be short-term or long-term and need a clear approach. They have to be in coherence with the aims and objectives of the organization.

Planning: After objectively determining the marketing objectives, the important function of the marketing management is to plan how to achieve those objectives. This includes sales forecast, marketing programme's formulation, marketing strategies.

Organization: A plan once formulated needs implementation. Organizing functions of marketing management involves the collection and coordination of required means to implement a plan and to achieve predetermined objectives. The organization involves structure of marketing organization, duties, responsibilities and powers of various members of the marketing organization.

Coordination: Coordination refers to harmonious adjustment of the activities of the marketing organization. It involves coordination among various activities such as sales forecasting, product planning, product development, transportation, warehousing, etc.

Direction: Direction in marketing management refers to development of new markets, leadership of employees, motivation, inspiration, guiding and supervision of the employees.

Control: Control refers to the effectiveness with which a marketing plan is implemented. It involves the determination of standards, evaluation of actual performance, adoption of corrective measures,

Staffing: Employment of right and able employees is very crucial to success of a market plan. The market manager coordinates with the human resource manager of an organization to hire staff with desired capabilities.

Analysis and Evaluation: The marketing management involves the analysis and evaluation of the productivity and performances of individual employees.

FILL IN THE BLANKS

1. _______ approach is an important tool for understanding marketing management process.
2. The primary function of a business is to create and maintain a _______.
3. No longer is _______ the operational goal of effective marketing performance.
4. _______ is the task of designing and controlling an industrial system.
5. Marketing concept demands customer-oriented marketing _______, _______ and _______.
6. Marketing management has to formulate sound marketing _______ and _______.
7. Marketing management has to implement marketing _______, _______ and _______.
8. Opportunity to create competitive difference is a big challenge in all means of _______.
9. _______ and _______ can create competitive difference.
10. _______ enable the selection of marketing targets and the development of marketing programme.
11. Marketing deals with customers. Creating customer value and satisfaction are the heart of modern marketing _______ and _______.
12. Marketing plan is the main operational and control document of _______.

13. ________ and ________ form the basis of effective distribution in mass markets.

14. Corporate ________ and ________ are considerably influenced by power of consumer in the market.

15. ________ process begins with a review of current market situation through situation analysis.

16. Productivity and profitability without sacrificing social responsibilities are main ends in marketing ________ and ________.

17. A successful marketing strategy must have a marketing mix and a ________ market.

18. Product mix, price mix, promotion mix and distribution mix are ________.

19. ________ are optimum productivity and satisfaction.

20. Product range, service after sale, brand and package are the four components of ________.

21. Marketing is centered on the ________.

22. ________ has to cover pricing, discounts, allowances and terms of credit.

23. Price deals with ________ competition.

24. ________ includes channels of distribution, transportation, and warehousing and inventory control.

25. ________ is the persuasive communication about the product by the company to the prospect.

26. Place is the delivery of the ________ and right to consume it.

27. ________ covers advertising, personal selling, sales promotion, publicity, public relations, exhibition and demonstrations.

28. Promotion deals with ________ competition.

29. The four elements of marketing mix are co-equal, ________ and ________.

30. The additional ingredients in the formula of marketing mix are ________, ________ and ________.

31. ________ is a faculty of insight enabling to discover and seize the hidden marketing opportunity.

32. In the evaluation of modern marketing philosophies, the three areas are ________, ________ and ________ area.

33. Gradually emerging competition due to overproduction of machine-made goods introduced ________ area.

34. With the emergence of marketing concept, ________ area began.

35. Marketing area began around the year ________.

36. ________ is responsible to coordinate, integrate and control the competing functional specialists.

37. Marketing in action is ________.

38. Under the marketing concept, all the marketing staff must have ________ oriented approach.

39. ________ is the chief executive in charge of planning, implementation and evaluation.

40. ________ is in charge of marketing plan preparations, marketing intelligence service, marketing information and research.

41. The advent of a strong buyer's market created the need for a ________.

42. ________ is one of the four components of promotion-mix.

43. ________-oriented marketing organization is the best medium to practice marketing concept.

44. Socially responsible marketing firm should have a separate ________ department.

45. In ________ marketing organization there are zonal sales or marketing managers.

46. The modern marketing philosophy stresses the ________ concept and not the ________ concept.

47. Mass marketing techniques were invented to sell the ________ goods when industrial revolution took off.

48. Mass marketing tools are ______, ______ and ________.

49. ________ is a decision making process that involves the analysis of internal capabilities and external environments of a firm.

50. In strategic marketing, various models and strategies are used for ________.

Answers for Fill in the Blanks

1.	Systems	26.	Product
2.	Satisfied customer	27.	Promotion
3.	Profit	28.	Non-price
4.	Management	29.	Essential; Interdependent
5.	Plans; programmes; policies	30.	Packaging; perception; persistence
6.	Policies; programmes	31.	Perception
7.	Strategies; programmes; campaigns	32.	Production; sales; marketing
8.	Promotion	33.	Sales
9.	Branding; advertising	34.	Marketing
10.	Marketing opportunities	35.	1960
11.	Thinking, practice	36.	Marketing manager
12.	Marketing department	37.	Marketing management
13.	An implementation; planning	38.	Customer
14.	Plans; policies	39.	Marketing manager
15.	Planning	40.	Marketing service manager
16.	Planning; management	41.	Customer orientation
17.	Target	42.	Advertising
18.	Marketing mix	43.	Customer
19.	Output	44.	Public relations
20.	Product	45.	Geographical
21.	Customer	46.	Profit: volume
22.	Price	47.	Mass produced
23.	Price	48.	Advertising; promotion; distribution
24.	Place	49.	Strategic marketing
25.	Promotion	50.	Decision making

TRUE / FALSE

1. Traditional approach is an important tool for understanding marketing management process. (True / False)

2. The primary function of a business is to create and maintain a satisfied customer. (True / False)

3. No longer is sales the operational goal of effective marketing performance. (True / False)

4. Management is the task of designing and controlling an industrial system. (True / False)

5. Marketing concept demands customers-oriented marketing plans, programmes and policies. (True / False)

6. Marketing channel has to formulate sound marketing policies and programmes. (True / False)

7. Marketing management has to implement marketing strategies, programmes and campaigns. (True / False)

8. Opportunity to create competitive difference is a big change in all means of product. (True / False)

9. Branding and advertising create competitive difference. (True / False)

10. Marketing opportunities enables the selection of marketing targets and the development of marketing information. (True / False)

11. Marketing research and information service alone can act as effective tool in all decisions of marketing management. (True / False)

12. Marketing strategy is the main operational and control document of marketing department. (True / False)

13. Research and planning activities from the basis of effective distribution in mass markets. (True / False)

14. Corporate plans and policies are considerably influenced by power of consumers in the market. (True / False)

15. Staffing process begins with a review of current market situation through situation analysis. (True / False)

16. Productivity and profitability without sacrificing social responsibilities are main ends in marketing planning and management. (True / False)

17. A successful marketing strategy must have a marketing mix and a dynamic market. (True / False)

18. Product mix, price mix, promotion mix and distribution mix are marketing mix. (True / False)

19. Output is optimum productivity and satisfaction. (True / False)

20. Product range, service after sales, brand and package are the four components of place. (True / False)

21. Product is the valuation placed upon the product by the offerer. (True / False)

22. Price has to cover pricing, discounts, allowances and terms of credit. (True / False)

23. Price deals with product competition. (True / False)

24. Place includes channels of distribution, transportation and warehousing and inventory control. (True / False)

25. Place is the persuasive communication about the product by the offerer to the prospect. (True / False)

26. Promotion is the delivery of the product and right to consume it. (True / False)

27. Promotion covers advertising, personal selling sales promotion, publicity, public relation, exhibition and demonstrations. (True / False)

28. Promotion deals with non-price competition. (True / False)

29. The two elements of marketing mix are co-equal, interdependent and essential. (True / False)

30. The additional ingredients in the formula of marketing mix are packaging, perception and persistence. (True / False)

31. In marketing mix, perception is a faculty of insight enabling to discover and size the hidden marketing opportunity. (True / False)

32. In the evaluation of modern marketing philosophy, the areas are production, sales and marketing area. (True / False)

33. Gradually emerging competition due to overproduction of machine-made goods introduced marketing area. (True / False)

34. With the emergence of marketing concept sales area began. (True / False)

35. Marketing area began around 1960. (True / False)

36. Brand manager is responsible to coordinate, integrate and control the competing functional specialists. (True / False)

37. Marketing manager ensure unity, harmony and team spirit. (True / False)

38. Under the marketing concept, all marketing staff must have sales-oriented approach. (True / False)

39. Marketing manager is the chief executive in charge of planning, implementation and evaluation. (True / False)

40. Marketing service manager is in charge of marketing plan preparations, marketing intelligence service, marketing information and research. (True / False)

41. Marketing research covers each elements of marketing planning. (True / False)

42. Advertising is one of the four components of promotion-mix. (True / False)

43. Customer-oriented marketing organization is the best medium to practice marketing concept. (True / False)

44. Economical responsible marketing firm should have a separate public relations department. (True / False)

45. In geographical marketing organization there are zonal sales or marketing manager. (True / False)

46. Modern marketing philosophy stresses the volume concept and not the profit concept. (True / False)

47. Mass marketing technique was invented to sell the mass produced goods when industrial revolution took off. (True / False)

48. The mass marketing tools are mass advertising, promotion and distribution. (True / False)

49. Strategic marketing is a decision making process that involves the analysis of internal capabilities of a firm only. (True / False)

50. In strategic marketing, various models and strategies are used for decision making. (True / False)

Answers for True / False

1.	False	**11.**	True	**21.**	False	**31.**	True	**41.**	False
2.	True	**12.**	False	**22.**	True	**32.**	True	**42.**	True
3.	False	**13.**	True	**23.**	False	**33.**	False	**43.**	True
4.	True	**14.**	True	**24.**	True	**34.**	False	**44.**	False
5.	True	**15.**	False	**25.**	False	**35.**	True	**45.**	True
6.	False	**16.**	True	**26.**	False	**36.**	False	**46.**	False
7.	True	**17.**	False	**27.**	True	**37.**	True	**47.**	True
8.	False	**18.**	True	**28.**	True	**38.**	False	**48.**	True
9.	True	**19.**	True	**29.**	False	**39.**	True	**49.**	False
10.	False	**20.**	False	**30.**	True	**40.**	True	**50.**	True

MULTIPLE CHOICE QUESTIONS

1. Which is an important tool for understanding marketing management process?
   (a) Systems approach
   (b) Traditional approach
   (c) Functional approach
   (d) Institutional approach
2. The primary function of a business is to create and maintain a ________.
   (a) Satisfied seller
   (b) Satisfied customer
   (c) Satisfied product
   (d) Satisfied environment
3. Which is the operational goal of effective marketing performance?
   (a) Sales
   (b) Cost
   (c) Profit
   (d) Loss
4. Which is the task of designing and controlling an industrial system?
   (a) Organization
   (b) Management
   (c) Market
   (d) Programmes
5. Marketing concept demands customer-oriented marketing ________.
   (a) Plans
   (b) Programmes
   (c) Policies
   (d) All the above
6. Which has to formulate sound marketing policies and programmes?
   (a) Marketing management
   (b) Marketing Research
   (c) Marketing channel
   (d) Marketing strategy
7. Marketing management has to implement marketing ________.
   (a) Strategies
   (b) Programmes
   (c) Campaigns
   (d) All the above
8. Opportunity to create competitive difference is a big challenge in all means of ________.
   (a) Product
   (b) Price
   (c) Promotion
   (d) Place
9. Which can create competitive difference?
   (a) Product line and branding
   (b) Branding and advertising
   (c) Design and package
   (d) Packaging and advertising
10. Marketing opportunities enable the selection of marketing targets and the development of ________.
    (a) Marketing organization
    (b) Marketing information
    (c) Marketing programme
    (d) Marketing activities
11. Which service alone can act as effective tool in all decisions of marketing management?
    (a) Marketing research
    (b) Marketing information
    (c) Both a and b
    (d) None of the above
12. Which is the main operational and control document of marketing department?
    (a) Marketing plan
    (b) Marketing research

(c) Marketing strategy
(d) Marketing process

13. Which activities form the basis of effective distribution in mass markets?

(a) Planning and organizing
(b) Organizing
(c) Research and planning
(d) Controlling and planning

14. Which are considerably influenced by power of consumers in the market?

(a) Corporate plans
(b) Corporate policies
(c) Both a and b
(d) None of the above

15. Which process begins with a review of current market situation through situation analysis?

(a) Controlling
(b) Planning
(c) Organizing
(d) Staffing

16. Productivity and profitability without sacrificing social responsibilities are main ends in ________.

(a) Marketing planning
(b) Marketing management
(c) Both a and b
(d) None of the above

17. A successful marketing strategy must have a marketing mix and a ________.

(a) Target market
(b) Potential market
(c) Dynamic market
(d) Social market

18. Product mix, price mix, promotion mix and distribution mix are ________.

(a) Marketing plan
(b) Marketing mix
(c) Marketing channel
(d) Marketing strategy

19. Which are optimum productivity and satisfaction?

(a) Output
(b) Input
(c) Process
(d) Programme

20. Product range, service after sale, Brand and package are the four components of ________.

(a) Product
(b) Price
(c) Place
(d) Promotion

21. Which is the valuation placed upon the product by the offerer?

(a) Product
(b) Place
(c) Price
(d) Promotion

22. Which has to cover pricing, discounts, allowances and terms of credit?

(a) Product
(b) Price
(c) Place
(d) Promotion

23. Which of the following deals with price competition?

(a) Product
(b) Price
(c) Place
(d) Promotion

24. Which of the following includes channels of distribution, transportation, warehousing and inventory control?

(a) Product
(b) Price
(c) Place
(d) Promotion

25. Which is the persuasive communication about the product by the offerer to the prospect?

(a) Product
(b) Price
(c) Place
(d) Promotion

26. Which is the delivery of the product and right to consume it?

(a) Product
(b) Price
(c) Place
(d) Promotion

27. From the following which covers advertising, personal selling, sales promotion, publicity, public relations, exhibition and demonstrations?

(a) Product
(b) Promotion
(c) Price
(d) Place

28. Which of the following deals with non-price competition?

(a) Product
(b) Promotion
(c) Price
(d) Place

29. Which of the following is (are) the element(s) of marketing mix?

(a) Product
(b) Price
(c) Promotion
(d) All the above

30. The additional ingredients in the formula of marketing mix are ________.

(a) Packaging
(b) Perception
(c) Persistence
(d) All the above

31. In marketing mix, which is a faculty of insight enabling to discover and seize the hidden marketing opportunity?

(a) Packaging
(b) Perception
(c) Persistence
(d) Promotion

32. In the evaluation of modern marketing philosophy, the areas are ________.

(a) Production areas
(b) Sales areas
(c) Marketing areas
(d) All the above

33. Gradually emerging competition due to over- production of machine - made goods introduced which areas?

(a) Sales areas
(b) Production areas
(c) Marketing areas
(d) None of the above

34. With the emergence of marketing concept, which areas began?

(a) Sales areas
(b) Production areas
(c) Marketing areas
(d) None of the above

35. Marketing areas began around ________.

(a) 1950s
(b) 1960s
(c) 1970s
(d) 1980s

36. Who is responsible to coordinate, integrate and control the competing functional specialists?

(a) Marketing manager
(b) Sales manager
(c) Brand manager
(d) Advertising manager

37. Marketing manager ensure _________.

(a) Unity

(b) Harmony

(c) Team spirit

(d) All the above

38. Under the marketing concept, all marketing staff must have _________.

(a) Product-oriented approach

(b) Customer-oriented approach

(c) Market-oriented approach

(d) Sales-oriented approach

39. Who is the chief executive in charge of planning, implementation evaluation?

(a) Marketing manager

(b) Product manager

(c) Marketing service manager

(d) Physical distribution manager

40. In the functional marketing organization, who is in charge of marketing plan preparations, marketing intelligence service, marketing information and research?

(a) Marketing manager

(b) Product manager

(c) Marketing service manager

(d) Physical distribution manager

41. Marketing research covers each elements of _________.

(a) Marketing planning

(b) Marketing mix

(c) Marketing strategy

(d) Marketing channels

42. Which is one of the four components of promotion-mix?

(a) Advertising

(b) Branding

(c) Pricing

(d) Packaging

43. Which oriented marketing organization is the best medium to practice marketing concept?

(a) Product

(b) Customer

(c) Market

(d) Sales

44. Which responsible marketing firm should have a separate public relation department?

(a) Socially

(b) Economically

(c) Legally

(d) Politically

45. Generally, how many zonal sales or marketing managers are there in geographical marketing organization?

(a) Two

(b) Three

(c) Four

(d) Five

46. Modern marketing philosophy stresses _________.

(a) The profit concept, not the volume concept

(b) Not the profit concept, not the volume concept

(c) Not the profit concept, the volume concept

(d) None of the above

47. Which techniques were invented to sell the mass produced goods when Industrial Revolution took off?

(a) Mass production

(b) Mass marketing

(c) Mass advertising

(d) Mass promotion

48. What are tools of mass marketing?

(a) Mass advertising

(b) Mass promotion

(c) Mass distribution

(d) All the above

49. Strategic marketing is a decision making process that involves the analysis of ________.

(a) Internal capabilities of a firm

(b) External environments of a firm

(c) both a and b

(d) None of the above

50. In strategic marketing, various models and strategies are used for ________.

(a) Decision making

(b) Production

(c) Planning

(d) Distribution

Answers for MCQ

1.	(a)	**10.**	(c)	**19.**	(a)	**28.**	(b)	**37.**	(d)	**46.**	(a)
2.	(b)	**11.**	(c)	**20.**	(a)	**29.**	(d)	**38.**	(b)	**47.**	(b)
3.	(c)	**12.**	(a)	**21.**	(c)	**30.**	(d)	**39.**	(a)	**48.**	(d)
4.	(b)	**13.**	(b)	**22.**	(b)	**31.**	(b)	**40.**	(c)	**49.**	(c)
5.	(d)	**14.**	(c)	**23.**	(b)	**32.**	(d)	**41.**	(b)	**50.**	(a)
6.	(a)	**15.**	(b)	**24.**	(c)	**33.**	(a)	**42.**	(a)		
7.	(d)	**16.**	(c)	**25.**	(d)	**34.**	(c)	**43.**	(b)		
8.	(c)	**17.**	(a)	**26.**	(c)	**35.**	(b)	**44.**	(a)		
9.	(b)	**18.**	(b)	**27.**	(b)	**36.**	(a)	**45.**	(c)		

MATCH THE FOLLOWING

1.	Measurement of sales progress	**(a)**	Branding
2.	Marketing plan	**(b)**	Focus of marketing
3.	Customer satisfaction profitability	**(c)**	Sales volume and profit
4.	Product demand	**(d)**	Marketing operation and control
5.	Traditional selling	**(e)**	Against set goals
6.	Competitive differences	**(f)**	Needs and wants of consumer

Answers for Match the Following

1.	(e)	**2.**	(d)	**3.**	(b)	**4.**	(f)	**5.**	(c)	**6.**	(a)

Chapter 3

Marketing Environment

SUMMARY

Marketing Environment refers to the encompass of the marketing team within an organization and includes all of the outside factors of marketing that affect the team's ability to develop and maintain successful customer relationships with their targeted customer group.

The internal environment of an organization consists of such factors such as the financial and non-financial factors, production and human resource capabilities, that influence its marketing decisions to a great extent. Marketing sales forces such as promotion, the marketing managers in consultation with the top management and keeping in view the company's internal environment, i.e., its own capacity in terms of production, finance, R&D, purchase, sales, and development should make decisions regarding their market proposals.

Even regarding the suppliers the organization can think of availing the required material or labor according to its manufacturing programme. It can adopt a purchase policy which gives bargaining power to the organization.

Normally, every producer has to appoint a number of intermediaries in assisting him in promoting, selling, and distributing the goods and services to ultimate consumers. The intermediaries are middlemen (Wholesalers, retailers and agents), distributing agencies, market service agencies and financial institutions.

The customers of a company may be of five kinds – ultimate consumers, industrial consumers, Government and other non-profit customers, international customers. It must not be forgotten that the satisfaction of customer and consumer is the main motto of every business firm. The population also contains the prospective consumers of company's products and the company has to identify them which are not easy. Goodwill built up by the company sometimes influences the consumers to become the customer of the company.

Competitors are those who sell the goods and services of the same and similar description, in the same market. Apart from this competition, there are other forms of competition like product differentiation. It is therefore, necessary to build an efficient system of marketing. This will arouse confidence and with better results. For this purpose, first of all, competitors are to be identified and closely monitored.

Companies are not alike in terms of their mix of resources, namely, people, finances, and facilities. Many executives believe that a firm's most important asset is its employees and that success is highly influenced by the quality of company management and the skills of its marketing, R&D and production personnel. For some types of industries, success is heavily dependent on the competence of the people in particular functional areas, engineering for capital goods industries such as tooling and production, machinery finance for capital intensive industries such as steel and petroleum, and marketing for consumer packaged goods companies.

Marketing strategies that differ greatly from top management's philosophy have little chance of being approved or of receiving enthusiastic support if they are accepted. Management's with a more conservative philosophy feel more comfortable with steady but unspectacular growth, maximization of cash flow from current business, high dividends and investment.

It is the duty of the company to satisfy the people at large along with its competitors and the consumers. It is necessary for future stay and growth. The actors of the company do influence the other groups forming the general public for the company. A public is defined as "Any group that has an actual or potential interest in or in part on a company's ability to achieve its objectives.

Macro-environment refers to those factors which are not concerned with the immediate environment. These factors are external to the company and are quite uncontrollable. These factors do not affect the marketing ability of the concern directly but it indirectly influences the marketing decision of the company. As against this, micro-environmental factors directly affect the company's marketing activities and these forces are internal and controllable to some extent. The following are the factors that affect the company's marketing decisions:

Marketers are keenly interested in the size and growth rate of population in different cities, regions and nations, age distribution, ethnic mix, educational levels, household patterns, regional characteristics and movements. The effect of all these changes is to fragment the mass market into numerous micro markets, differentiated by age, sex, education, geography, and lifestyle and so on. Each group has strong preferences and consumer characteristics and is reached through increasingly targeted communication and distribution channels.

Global environment helps the cause of business by making the businessmen come out of their shell ad see beyond physical boundaries of the country. It helps them to explore overseas markets in a big way. It is the global environment that helps in integration with the world economy through unification calls for removal of all the trade business among countries.

Components of physical forces are earth's natural renewal and non-renewal resources. Marketers need to be aware of the threats and opportunities associated with four trends in the natural environment.

Technological Developments are uncontrollable environmental factors and important for marketing. They affect the market plans in two ways, Firstly, they are quite unpredictable and secondly, the adoption of new technology is prevented by many internal and external constraints. It's also true that technical progress and at the same time it poses threat to individual companies. As an opportunity, technology is a source of new and improved product. As a threat, technological development by competitors may result in loss of markets. The technological changes result in changes in consumption pattern and marketing systems. A market may find out new challenges and opportunities by appropriating more budgets for research and development activities.

Developments in political and legal field greatly affect the marketing decisions. Sound marketing decisions cannot be taken without taking into account the government agencies, political party in power and in opposition and their ideologies. These variables create tremendous pressures on marketing management. Laws affect production capacity, capability, product designs, pricing, and promotion.

Social responsibility concept has crept into marketing literature as an alternative to the marketing concept. The social forces attempt to make the marketing socially responsible. It means the business firms should take a lead in eliminating socially harmful products (e.g., cigarettes or alcohol) and produce only what is beneficial to the society. There are some core-cultural values which are found in our society which is deep-rooted and stable and hence, change very little. There are also secondary cultural values which are susceptible to fast changes. Some of them are like hairstyles, clothing, etc. Even in a given culture, the entire population doesn't adopt the changes, there are different degrees with which people adopt them.

Micro-environment factors are the company's immediate environment that affects its ability to serve its markets, suppliers, market intermediaries, customers, competitors and publics. The main objective of the company is to profitably serve and satisfy specific needs of chosen target market.

Macro-environment: Macro-environment forces include demographic, economic, natural, technological, political and cultural forces. These forces represent uncontrollable factors, which the company must monitor and respond to. The major components of micro-environment are the company and its suppliers, marketing intermediaries, customers, competitors and public that shape opportunities and pose threat to company.

The concept of market segment is based on the fact that the markets of commodities are not homogeneous but they are heterogeneous. Market represents a group of customers having common characteristics but two customers are never common in their nature, taste, habit, hobbies, income and purchasing styles. There exists a lot of difference in their buying behaviour and buying decisions. On the basis of these characteristics, customers having similar qualities are grouped in segments. The characteristics of customers of one segment differ with those of other segments. In this way, market segmentation refers to various segments of the market based on the common characteristics of the customers.

FILL IN THE BLANKS

1. The marketing environment surrounds and impacts upon the ________.
2. ________includes suppliers that deal directly or indirectly, consumers and customers, and other local stakeholders.
3. The ________ includes all factors that can influence and organization, but that are out of their direct control.
4. Natural environmental factors include the weather and ________
5. ________ is the area of applied ethics which deals with the moral principles behind the operation and regulation of marketing.
6. System elements operate on input such as ________, ________ and ________.
7. A system consists of ________ and ________, ________, ________.
8. A system is always ________-oriented.
9. Processor transforms ________ into ________.
10. When the process is designed by the manager, it is termed as a ________.
11. When the transformation process is not known in details and it is too complicated, then the process is called a________.
12. Resources received by the organization from the environment are ______ variable.
13. Environment provides ______ and ______.
14. Output of an organization is in the form of ______, ________ and ________.
15. The environment reacts to the ________ of an organization.
16. A ________ is an interacting set of institution, activities and flows.
17. External uncontrollable and partially controllable forces, and internal controllable forces are the types of forces of the dynamic ________.
18. The customers or market, suppliers and market intermediaries are ________ forces.
19. Corporate resources and marketing mix are ________ forces.
20. ________ is the heart of a marketing system.
21. Corporate resources are ______ and ______ resources.

22. ________ include money, machinery, materials and management.

23. The marketing management has to assess the ________.

24. The ________ must keep close contact with many uncontrollable.

25. The uncontrollable forces are known as the ________.

26. ________ is becoming increasingly important to marketing decision process.

27. Consumer legislation tries to protect ________.

28. ________ cannot ignore the legislation regulating competition and protecting consumers.

29. ________ is the science dealing with living things and their environment.

30. Ecology, economic development and marketing economy are not ________.

31. Nature can fulfill human ________ and not human ________.

32. Customer demand is ________, ________ and ________.

33. Under ________-oriented marketing philosophy, customer needs and desires act as the as the centre of the marketing universe.

34. Marketing policies, programmes and strategies are planned, organized and executed with the main objective of customer ________ and ________.

35. Repeat sales are possible only on ________.

36. The environment of business is not ________.

37. Many firms are still production-oriented and not ________.

38. ________ has definite control over product, place, price and promotion mixer.

39. ________ firms are affected more by changing environmental considerations.

40. ________ firms are likely to be less constrained by environmental forces.

41. The marketing manager's major task is that of ________ and ________.

42. Marketing has to design his marketing strategies based on the current ________.

43. The components of marketing environment are ________ and ________.

44. ________ is concerned with matching of the organization with the demands of the business environment.

45. ________ is a set of objects, elements or components that are interrelated and interact with one another.

Answers for Fill in the Blanks

1.	Organization	11.	Black box
2.	Micro-environment	12.	Controllable
3.	Macro-environment	13.	Resources; opportunities
4.	Climate change	14.	Products; services; information
5.	Marketing ethics	15.	Output
6.	Physical resource; human resources; information	16.	Marketing system
		17.	Marketing environment
7.	Inputs; outputs; processor; feedback	18.	External partially controllable
8.	Goal	19.	Internal controllable
9.	Input; output	20.	Marketing mix
10.	White box	21.	Human; non-human

22.	Non-human resources	34.	Satisfaction; service
23.	Marketing opportunity	35.	Customer satisfaction
24.	Marketing management	36.	Static
25.	Macro-environmental forces	37.	Market-oriented
26.	Consumerism	38.	Marketing manager
27.	Consumer interests	39.	Adaptive
28.	Marketing management	40.	Innovative
29.	Ecology	41.	Trend trackers; opportunity seekers
30.	Inconsistent	42.	Marketing environment
31.	Needs; greed	43.	Micro-environment; macro-environment
32.	Ever changing; unpredictable; unmeasurable	44.	Marketing management
		45.	System
33.	Market		

TRUE / FALSE

1. The marketing manager's major task is that of trend trackers and opportunity seekers. (True / False)
2. A marketer has to design his marketing strategies based on the current marketing plans. (True / False)
3. The components of marketing environment are micro and macro- environment. (True / False)
4. Marketing programmes is concerned with matching of the organization with the demands of the business environment. (True / False)
5. System is a set of objects, elements or components that are interrelated and interact with one another. (True / False)
6. System elements operate on inputs of physical resources only. (True / False)
7. A system consists of inputs and outputs, processor, feedback. (True / False)
8. A system is always product-oriented. (True / False)
9. Processor transforms, input into output. (True / False)
10. When the process is designed by the manager, is termed as a white box. (True / False)
11. When the transformation process is not known in details and it is too complicated, then the process is called a black box. (True / False)
12. Resources received by the organization from the environment are uncontrollable variable. (True / False)
13. Environment provides resources and opportunities. (True / False)
14. Output of an organization is in the form of services only. (True / False)
15. The environment reacts to the input of an organization. (True / False)
16. A marketing system is an interacting set of institutions, activities and flows. (True / False)
17. External controllable force is the types of marketing environment. (True / False)
18. The customer or market, suppliers and market intermediaries are external partially controllable forces. (True / False)

19. Corporate resources and marketing mix are internal controllable forces. (True / False)

20. Marketing plan is the heart of a marketing system. (True / False)

21. Corporate resources are human and non-human resources. (True / False)

22. Major resources are called 5Ms, that is men, money, machinery, materials and management. (True / False)

23. The marketing management has to assess the marketing policies. (True / False)

24. The marketing management must keep close contact with many controllable forces. (True / False)

25. The uncontrollable forces are parameters of the market. (True / False)

26. Consumerism is becoming increasingly important to marketing decision process. (True / False)

27. Consumer plan tries to protect consumer interests. (True / False)

28. Marketing management cannot ignore the legislation regulating competition and protecting consumers. (True / False)

29. Social science is the science dealing with living things and their environment. (True / False)

30. Ecology, economic development and market economy are not inconsistent. (True / False)

31. Nature can fulfill human greed and not human needs. (True / False)

32. Customer demand is ever changing, unpredictable and unmeasurable. (True / False)

33. Under sales-oriented marketing philosophy, customer needs and desires act as the centre of the marketing universe. (True / False)

34. Marketing polices, programmes and strategies are not planned with the main objective of customer satisfaction and service. (True / False)

35. Repeat sales are possible only on customer satisfactions. (True / False)

36. The environment of business is static. (True / False)

37. Many firms are still production or sales oriented and not market oriented. (True / False)

38. Brand manager has definite control over product, place, price and promotion mixes. (True / False)

39. Adaptive firms are affected more by changing environmental considerations. (True / False)

40. Innovative firms are likely to be less constrained by environmental forces. (True / False)

Answers for True / False

1.	True	9.	True	17.	False	25.	True	33.	False
2.	False	10.	True	18.	True	26.	True	34.	False
3.	True	11.	True	19.	True	27.	False	35.	True
4.	False	12.	False	20.	False	28.	True	36.	False
5.	True	13.	True	21.	True	29.	False	37.	True
6.	False	14.	False	22.	False	30.	True	38.	False
7.	True	15.	False	23.	False	31.	False	39.	True
8.	False	16.	True	24.	False	32.	True	40.	True

MULTIPLE CHOICE QUESTIONS

1. Which of the following is not related to Economic environment?

(a) GDP
(b) Profit
(c) Income
(d) Gender

2. Which of the following is not related to Technological environment?

(a) Innovation
(b) Creativity
(c) Research and Development
(d) Population

3. Which of the following is under Natural environment?

(a) Production
(b) Raw material
(c) Age
(d) None of the above

4. Which marketing approaches a business enterprise is to study their customers and offer products which will give the desired satisfaction and services to the customers?

(a) Potential marketing
(b) Customer concept marketing
(c) Social marketing
(d) None of them

5. ________ refers to mixing and matching marketing activities to maximize their individual and collective effects.

(a) Social marketing
(b) Potential marketing
(c) Integrated marketing
(d) None of them

6. System elements operate on inputs such as ________.

(a) Physical resources
(b) Human resources
(c) Information
(d) All the above

7. A system consists of ________.

(a) Inputs and outputs
(b) Processor
(c) Feedback
(d) All the above

8. A system is always ________.

(a) Product-oriented
(b) Goal-oriented
(c) Market-oriented
(d) Sales-oriented

9. Processor transforms ________.

(a) Input into outputs
(b) Outputs into inputs
(c) Input into feedback
(d) Feedback into inputs

10. When the process is designed by the manager, it is termed as a ________.

(a) Black box
(b) White box
(c) Green box
(d) Red box

11. When the transformation process is not known in details and it is too complicated, then the process is called as ________.

(a) Black box
(b) White box
(c) Green box
(d) Red box

12. Resources received by the organization from the environment are ________.

(a) Uncontrollable variable
(b) Controllable variable

(c) Both a and b
(d) None of the above

13. Which of the followings provides resources and opportunities?

(a) Environment
(b) Ecology
(c) Economic
(d) social

14. Output of an organization is in the form of ________.

(a) Products
(b) Services
(c) Information
(d) All the above

15. The environment reacts to the ________ of an organization.

(a) Output
(b) Input
(c) Process
(d) Feedback

16. A marketing system is an interacting set of ________.

(a) Institutions
(b) Activities
(c) Flows
(d) All the above

17. What are types of forces of the dynamic marketing environment?

(a) External uncontrollable forces
(b) External partially controllable forces
(c) Internal controllable forces
(d) All the above

18. The customers or market, suppliers and market intermediaries are ________.

(a) External uncontrollable force
(b) External partially controllable forces
(c) Internal controllable forces
(d) All the above

19. Corporate resources and marketing mix are ________.

(a) External uncontrollable forces
(b) External partially controllable forces
(c) Internal controllable forces
(d) Internal partially controllable forces

20. Which is the heart of a marketing system?

(a) Marketing mix
(b) Marketing plan
(c) Marketing programmes
(d) Marketing policies

21. Corporate resources are ________.

(a) Human resources
(b) Non-human resources
(c) Both a and b
(d) None of the above

22. Which is called as 5Ms that are men, money, machinery, materials and management?

(a) Human resources
(b) Non-human resource
(c) Marketing resources
(d) Non-marketing resource

23. The marketing management has to assess the ________.

(a) Marketing programmes
(b) Marketing policies
(c) Marketing opportunity
(d) Marketing plan

24. The marketing management must keep close contact with many ________.

(a) Uncontrollable forces
(b) Controllable forces
(c) Formal forces
(d) Informal forces

25. The uncontrollable forces are the parameters of the ________.

(a) Organization
(b) Market

(c) Management
(d) Production

26. What is becoming increasingly important to marketing decision process?

(a) Capitalism
(b) Socialism
(c) Consumerism
(d) Communism

27. Consumer legislation tries to protect ________.

(a) Consumer interests
(b) Consumer policies
(c) Consumer plan
(d) Consumer needs

28. Who cannot ignore the legislation regulating competition and protecting consumers?

(a) Marketing organization
(b) Marketing management
(c) Marketing strategies
(d) Marketing decisions

29. Which is the science dealing with living things and their environment?

(a) Ecology
(b) Demography
(c) Social
(d) Political

30. What are not inconsistent?

(a) Ecology
(b) Economic development
(c) Market economy
(d) All the above

31. Nature can fulfill ________.

(a) Human greed and human needs
(b) Human needs and not human greed
(c) Human greed and not human needs
(d) None of the above

32. Customer demand is ________.

(a) Ever changing
(b) Unpredictable
(c) Immeasurable
(d) All the above

33. Under which oriented marketing philosophy, customer needs and desires act as the centre of the marketing universe?

(a) Product
(b) Customer
(c) Market
(d) Sales

34. What are planned, organized and executed with the main objective of customer satisfaction and service?

(a) Marketing policies
(b) Marketing programmes
(c) Marketing strategies
(d) All the above

35. Repeat sales are possible only on ________.

(a) Customer satisfaction
(b) Seller satisfaction
(c) Production
(d) Advertising

36. The environment of business is ________.

(a) Static
(b) Not statics
(c) Consistent
(d) Inconsistent

37. Many firms are still production or sales oriented and not ________.

(a) Customer-oriented
(b) Market-oriented
(c) Project-oriented
(d) Action-oriented

38. Who has definite control over product, place, price and promotion mixes?

(a) Product manager
(b) Marketing service manager
(c) Marketing manager
(d) Physical distribution manager

39. Which firms are affected more by changing environmental considerations?

(a) Adaptive
(b) Innovative
(c) Corporative
(d) None of the above

40. Which firms are likely to be less constrained by environmental forces?

(a) Adaptive
(b) Innovative
(c) Corporative
(d) None of the above

41. The marketing manager's major task is that of ________.

(a) Trend trackers
(b) Opportunity seekers
(c) Both a and b
(d) None of the above

42. A marketer has to design his marketing strategies based on the current ________.

(a) Marketing environment
(b) Marketing plans
(c) Marketing programmes
(d) Marketing analysis

43. What are the components of marketing environment?

(a) Micro-environment
(b) Macro-environment
(c) Both a and b
(d) None of the above

44. Which is concerned with matching of the organization with the demands of the business environment?

(a) Marketing environment
(b) Marketing management
(c) Marketing programmes
(d) Marketing planning

45. Which is a set of objects, elements or components that are interrelated and interact with one another?

(a) System
(b) Process
(c) Output
(d) Input

Answers for MCQ

1.	(d)	9.	(a)	17.	(d)	25.	(b)	33.	(c)	41.	(c)
2.	(d)	10.	(b)	18.	(b)	26.	(c)	34.	(d)	42.	(a)
3.	(b)	11.	(a)	19.	(c)	27.	(a)	35.	(a)	43.	(c)
4.	(b)	12.	(b)	20.	(a)	28.	(b)	36.	(d)	44.	(b)
5.	(c)	13.	(a)	21.	(c)	29.	(a)	37.	(b)	45.	(a)
6.	(d)	14.	(d)	22.	(b)	30.	(d)	38.	(c)		
7.	(d)	15.	(a)	23.	(c)	31.	(b)	39.	(a)		
8.	(b)	16.	(d)	24.	(a)	32.	(d)	40.	(b)		

MATCH THE FOLLOWING

1.	A business organization	**(a)**	Competition
2.	Macro-environment	**(b)**	Man and environment
3.	Micro-environment	**(c)**	Company image
4.	Ecology	**(d)**	Marketing-mix
5.	Internal environment	**(e)**	Largely uncontrollable by management
6.	Marketing strategy	**(f)**	Socio-economic system

Answers for Match the Following

1.	(f)	**2.**	(e)	**3.**	(a)	**4.**	(b)	**5.**	(c)	**6.**	(d)

Chapter 4

Customer Demand and Marketing Segmentation

SUMMARY

Customer Demand Planning is a business-planning process that enables sales teams to develop demand forecasts as input to service-planning processes, production, inventory planning and revenue planning.

Market segmentation is the process of defining and subdividing a large homogeneous market into clearly identifiable segments having similar needs, wants or demand characteristics. Its objective is to design a marketing mix that precisely matches the expectations of customers in the targeted segment. Few companies are big enough to supply the needs of an entire market; most break down the total demand into segments and choose those company that is best equipped to handle.

The concept of market segment is based on the fact that the market of commodities are not homogeneous but they are heterogeneous. Market represents a group of customers having common characteristics but two customers are never common in their nature, taste, habit, hobbies, income and purchasing styles. There exists a lot of difference in their buying behaviour and buying decisions. On the basis of these characteristics, customers having similar qualities are grouped in segments. The characteristics of customers of one segment differ with those of other segments. In this way, market segmentation refers to various segments of the market based on the common characteristics of the customers.

Segmentation is the process of defining and subdividing a large homogeneous market into clearly identifiable segments having similar needs, wants, or demand characteristics. Its objective is to design a marketing mix that precisely matches the expectations of customers in the targeted segment.

Whenever a market for a product or service consists of two or more buyers, the market is capable of being segmented, that is divided into meaningful buyer groups. The purpose of segmentation is to determine differences among buyers which may be consequential in choosing away them or marketing to them.

Market segmentation consists of taking the total heterogeneous market for a product and dividing it into several sub-markets or segments, each of which tends to be homogeneous in full significant aspects.

Benefits of Market Segmentation

1. **Adjustment of product and marketing appeals:** Market segmentation presents an opportunity to understand the nature of the market. The seller can adjust his thrust to attract the maximum number of the market. The seller can adjust his product to attract the maximum number of customers by various publicity media and appeals. More resources may be allocated to market segment where sales opportunities are better.
2. **Better position to spot marketing opportunities:** The producer can make a fair estimate of the volume of his sales and the possibilities of furthering

his sales. In the regions where response of the consumers is poor, the strategy of approach can be readjusted accordingly to push the sales on the basis of marketing research. On the basis of research, habits, tastes, hobbies and nature of consumers of different markets can be understood deeply to harness marketing opportunities.

3. **Allocation of marketing budget:** It is on the basis of market segmentation than the marketing budget is adjusted for a particular region or locality. In the place where the sales opportunities are limited, it is no use of allocating a huge budget there.
4. **Making the competition effective:** It helps the producer to face the competition of his rivals effectively. The producer can adopt different policies, program, and strategies for different markets taking into account the rival's strategies, policies, and programmes.
5. **Effective marketing programme:** It also helps the producer to adopt an effective marketing programme and serve the consumer better at comparatively low cost. Different marketing programme can be attached for different segments.
6. **Evaluation of marketing activities:** Thus, market segmentation helps the manufacturer to find out and compare the marketing potentialities of the products. It helps to adjust production and in using his resources in the most profitable manner. As soon as the product becomes obsolete, the product line could be diversified or discontinued.
7. **Increase in sales volume:** By segmenting the market, the producer can increase his sales volume. As we know, each segment has demand pattern and the producer satisfies the demand of each segment, by improving his product. The total sales volume for the enterprise increases. It is based on the fact that the multiple demand curves in a market are better than a single demand curve.

Customer-based Segmentation

1. **Geographic location of customers:** The starting point of all market segmentation is the geographic location of customers. It helps the firm in planning the marketing offer. The common method is to classify according to rural and urban, metro or non-metro markets. There are also other classifications like district and block markets. We all know that there was the perception that the rural markets are different from urban markets and naturally the product promotion, pricing and distribution were accordingly designed to meet those markets. But now with the development of technology and the advent of various modes of communication like TV, the customers in the rural areas are much exposed and are more aware of the availability. Today, the rural customer buys the same branded product which is purchased by the urban customer.
2. **Demographic characteristics:** Factors like age, sex, income, occupation, family size, education, marital status are used singly or in combination to segment the market. Age is one of the most important factors for segmenting the market. The producer should know for what age group his product could be most suited so that he can plan his pricing policy, advertisement policy, marketing policy and strategy accordingly.
3. **Psychographics variables:** No two consumers act in the same manner though the two may be of the same age, from the same profession, same education and have same income. Each of the customers may have different attitudes because of personality and

lifestyle differences. Markets are using psychographic variables to segment their market For e.g., Citibank, Diners Card, Titan Watch, Savvy has used psychographic variables to segment its market and distance itself from all others, including Femina savvy women is identified as the highly liberated independent strong women, who have a definite plan in society and to whom career would be extremely important.

4. **Buyer readiness:** Buyers are at different stages of readiness. People may be unaware, people who are aware but are not interested, people who are interested and desires to buy and those who will buy the product. The relative proportion of buyers at different stages will affect the marketer's tasks.

Estimation of Market Segments

Any organization takes into account three factors in evaluating different market segments. These are segment size and growth, segment structural attractiveness and company objectives and resources.

(a) **Segment Size and Growth:** An organization first determines segment size and growth. It collects and analyses data on current segment sales, growth rates and expected profitability for various segments. The company will be concerned with segments that have the right size and growth characteristics. But the idea of right size and growth is relative. Some companies will want to choose segments with large current sales, a high growth rate and a high profit margin. However, every company may not find the largest, fastest-growing segments attractive ones. Smaller companies may feel that they don't have the skills and resources needed to serve the large segments, or that these segments are too competitive. These companies may select segments that are apparently smaller and less attractive, but that are potentially more profitable for them.

(b) **Segment Structural Attractiveness:** Subdivision with desirable size and growth may not have strong profit potential. For assessing long run segment attractiveness in terms of profit, the company must examine several major structural factors. For instance, a segment is less attractive if it is composed of many strong and aggressive competitors. If there are many substitute products, they may restrict prices and profits. The relative power of buyers also influences segment attractiveness.

FILL IN THE BLANKS

1. Market consists of ________ and ________ of people and ________ bodies.
2. When a want is supported by purchasing power it is called________.
3. Customer demand is a very important element in the________.
4. ________ and ________ are the dimensions of sound marketing system.
5. Demographic variables and lifestyle patterns are the variable factors of ________.
6. ________ is the variable factor of market demand.
7. Demand for product begins with ______ of buyers.
8. Purchasing power has two aspects ______.
9. ________ is the study of population structure and process.
10. Demographic variables are most widely employed in ________.

11. Family size and income will indicate ________ purchasing patterns.

12. The physical distribution of population indicates ________ markets regionally.

13. Income levels are analyzed on the basis of ________ income and ________ purchasing power.

14. ________ income is our take home pay (income less taxes).

15. ________ income is the income left after paying taxes and after necessary items.

16. ________ implies that consumption is a function of available income.

17. ________, ________ and ________ are the objective elements of our purchasing power.

18. Economic ability to buy must be combined with ________ to buy.

19. ________ is the key to the level of consumer spending.

20. Demand, buyer behaviour and market segmentation are the building blocks of any ________.

21. ________ consists of a large identifiable group within a market.

22. ________ helps in designing the marketing mix as per the requirements of customers.

23. ________ must be able to focus its marketing efforts on the chosen segment.

24. Segment must be large enough to be a ________ target.

25. Segmentation is required only if there are market differentiation in terms of ________.

26. The purpose of segmentation is to measure the changing behaviour pattern of ________.

27. In reality market demand is ________ and not ________.

28. Segmentation strategy is a ______-oriented philosophy.

29. ________ can maximize the impact of company strengths and minimize the exposure of its weakness.

30. Marketer has three strategic options are ________, ________ and ________ marketing.

31. Market segmentation enables the firm to select one or a few segments which act as ________ market.

32. ________ task is simple for a mass market strategy but in keen competition market it becomes necessary.

33. ________ and ________ factors are accepted criteria for market segmentation.

34. Geographical and socio-economic factors are objective and tend to be ________ measurable factors.

35. ________ and ________ factors are used for market segmentation.

36. The main approaches to identify market segments are ________ and ________-oriented market segmentation.

37. ________ approach is also called customer personal characteristic approach.

38. Product-oriented approach is also called ________.

39. In the case of frequently bought consumer goods, ________ and ________ variables is used in segmenting the markets.

40. Social class is also a ________ variable.

41. Social classes are ________, ________ and ________ class.

42. ________, ________ and ________ can explain regularities and diversities in human behaviour.

43. ________ and ________ influence buyer behaviour indirectly.

44. ________ concept as a basis for segmentation is quite reasonable and desirable.

45. AIO stands for ________.

46. ________ shows lifestyle of consumers.

47. ________ is interested in regional distribution of population and urban, suburban and rural population.

48. ________, ________ and ________ characteristics are easy to apply but cannot offer real reasons of buyer behaviour.

49. If segmentation is identified, if should be within reach through suitable means of ________ and ________.

50. ________ class is based on income, occupation, education and place of residence.

Answers for Fill in the Blanks

1.	Individuals; groups; corporate	26.	Consumer
2.	Demand	27.	Heterogeneous; homogeneous
3.	Marketing system	28.	Customer
4.	Demand analysis; competitions	29.	Segmentation
5.	Market demand	30.	Concentrated; differentiated; undifferentiated
6.	Demographic variable	31.	Target
7.	Wants and desires	32.	Marketing management
8.	Ability to buy and willingness to buy	33.	Geographical; socio-economic
9.	Demography	34.	Quantitative
10.	Marked segmentation	35.	Demographic; socio-economic
11.	Household	36.	People; product
12.	Potential	37.	People-oriented
13.	Disposal; discretionary	38.	Customer response approach
14.	Disposable	39.	Demographic; socio-economic
15.	Discretionary	40.	Complex
16.	Effective demand	41.	Upper; middle; lower
17.	Income; credit; assets	42.	Religion; race; culture
18.	Willingness	43.	Demographic; socio-economic
19.	Consumer confidence	44.	Lifestyle
20.	Marketing programme	45.	Activities, interests, opinions
21.	Marketing segment	46.	AIO
22.	Segmenting	47.	Marketers
23.	Organization	48.	Geographic; demographic; socio-economic
24.	Profitable	49.	Communication; distribution
25.	Demand	50.	Social

TRUE / FALSE

1. Market consists of individuals and groups of people and corporate bodies. (True / False)

2. When a want is supported by purchasing power it is called supply. (True / False)

3. Customer demand is a very important element in the marketing strategy. (True / False)

4. Demand analysis and the competition are the dimensions of sound marketing system. (True / False)

5. Demographic variable, effective demand and lifestyle patterns are the variable factors of market demand. (True / False)

6. Effective demand is the variable factors of market demand, to ascertain size of demand. (True / False)

7. Demographic variable is the variable factors of market demand, to ascertain potential demand. (True / False)

8. Lifestyle pattern is the variable factory of market demand that reflects the purchasing propensity and indicating customer behaviour. (True / False)

9. Geography is the study of population structure and process. (True / False)

10. Demographic variables are most widely employed in market segmentation. (True / False)

11. Market is a place, area and demand concept. (True / False)

12. The physical distribution of population indicates dynamic markets regionally. (True / False)

13. Income levels are analyzed on the basis of disposable income and discretionary purchasing power. (True / False)

14. Discretionary income is our take home pay (income less taxes). (True / False)

15. Disposable income is the income left after paying taxes and after necessary items. (True / False)

16. Effective demand implies that consumption is a function of available income. (True / False)

17. Income credit and assets are the objective elements of our purchasing power. (True / False)

18. Social ability to buy most be combined with or willingness to buy. (True / False)

19. Consumer confidence is the key to the level of consumer spending. (True / False)

20. The building blocks of any marketing programme are demand, buyer behaviour and market segmentation. (True / False)

21. Marketing research consists of a large identifiable group within a market. (True / False)

22. Segmenting helps in designing the marketing mix as per the requirements of customers. (True / False)

23. Marketer must be able to focus its marketing efforts on the chosen segment. (True / False)

24. Segment must be large enough to be a profitable target. (True / False)

25. Segmentation is required only if there are market differentiation in terms of demand. (True / False)

26. The purpose of segmentation is to measure the changing behaviour pattern of sellers. (True / False)

27. In reality market demand is heterogeneous and not homogeneous. (True / False)

28. Segmentation strategy is a product-oriented philosophy. (True / False)

29. Segmentation can maximize the impact of company strengths and minimize the exposure of its weaknesses. (True / False)

30. Marketer has three strategic options are concentrated, differentiated and undifferentiated marketing. (True / False)

31. Market opportunities enable the firm to select one or a few segments which act as target market. (True / False)

32. Marketing management task is simple for a mass market strategy but in keen competition market it becomes necessary. (True / False)

33. Demographic factors are accepted criteria for market segmentation. (True / False)

34. Geographical and socio-economic factors are objective and tend to be qualitative measurable factors. (True / False)

35. Demographic factors are used for market segmentation. (True / False)

36. The main approaches to identify market segments are people and product-oriented market segmentation. (True / False)

37. Sales-oriented approach is also called customer personal characteristic approach. (True / False)

38. Product-oriented approach is also called customer response approach. (True / False)

39. In case of frequently bought consumer goods, only demographic variables is used in segmenting the markets. (True / False)

40. Social class is also a complex variable. (True / False)

41. Social class is upper, middle and lower class. (True / False)

42. Political class can explain regularities and diversities in human behaviour. (True / False)

43. Demographic and socio-economic influence buyer behaviour indirectly. (True / False)

44. Personality concept as a basis for segmentation is quite reasonable and desirable. (True / False)

45. AIO stands for Activities, Interests, and Options. (True / False)

46. AIO statements show the lifestyle of consumers. (True / False)

47. Marketers are interested in regional distribution of population only. (True / False)

48. Geographic, demographic and socio-economic characteristics are easy to apply but cannot offer real reasons buyer behaviour. (True / False)

49. If segmentation is identified, it should be within reach through suitable means of communication and distribution. (True / False)

50. Economic class is based on income, occupation, education and place of residence. (True / False)

Answers for True / False

1.	True	11.	True	21.	False	31.	False	41.	True
2.	False	12.	False	22.	True	32.	True	42.	False
3.	False	13.	True	23.	True	33.	False	43.	True
4.	True	14.	False	24.	True	34.	False	44.	False
5.	True	15.	False	25.	True	35.	True	45.	True
6.	False	16.	True	26.	False	36.	True	46.	True
7.	False	17.	True	27.	True	37.	False	47.	False
8.	True	18.	False	28.	False	38.	True	48.	True
9.	False	19.	True	29.	True	39.	False	49.	True
10.	True	20.	True	30.	True	40.	True	50.	False

MULTIPLE CHOICE QUESTIONS

1. Customer Demand Planning is a business-planning process that enables sales teams to develop demand forecasts as input to ________.

(a) Service-planning processes
(b) Inventory planning
(c) Revenue planning
(d) All the above

2. When a want is supported by purchasing power it is called________.

(a) Demand
(b) Supply
(c) Resource
(d) system

3. Customer demand is a very important element in the________.

(a) Marketing environment
(b) Marketing system
(c) Marketing management
(d) Marketing strategy

4. What are the dimensions of sound marketing system?

(a) Demand analysis
(b) Competition
(c) Both (a) and (b)
(d) None of the above

5. What are the variable factors of market demand?

(a) Demographic variable
(b) Effective demand
(c) Lifestyle patterns
(d) All the above

6. Which is the variable factors of market demand, to ascertain size of demand?

(a) Demographic variable
(b) Effective demand
(c) Lifestyle patterns
(d) All the above

7. Which is the variable factors of market demand, to ascertain potential demand?

(a) Demographic variable
(b) Effective demand
(c) Lifestyle patterns
(d) None of the above

8. Which is the variable factors of market demand that reflects the purchasing propensity and indicating customer behaviour?

(a) Demographic variable
(b) Effective demand
(c) Lifestyle patterns
(d) None of the above

9. Which is the study of population structure and process?

(a) Demography
(b) Geography
(c) Market research
(d) Market information

10. Demographic variables are most widely employed in

(a) Market information
(b) Market segmentation
(c) Market programmes
(d) Market process

11. Which will indicate household purchasing patterns?

(a) Family size
(b) Income
(c) Both (a) and (b)
(d) None of the above

12. The physical distribution of population indicates________.

(a) Potential markets regionally
(b) Dynamic markets regionally
(c) Target markets regionally
(d) Strategic markets regionally

13. Income levels are analyzed on the basis of________.

(a) Disposable income
(b) Discretionary purchasing power
(c) Both (a) and (b)
(d) None of the above

14. Which income is our take home pay (income less taxes)?

(a) Disposable income
(b) Discretionary income

(c) Distribution income
(d) Demand income

15. Which income is the income left after paying taxes and after necessary items?
(a) Disposable income
(b) Discretionary income
(c) Distribution income
(d) Demand income

16. Which implies that consumption is a function of available income?
(a) Demographic variable
(b) Effective demand
(c) Lifestyle patterns
(d) All the above

17. What are the objective elements of our purchasing power?
(a) Income
(b) Credit
(c) Assets
(d) All the above

18. Which must be combined with willingness to buy?
(a) Social ability to buy
(b) Economic ability to buy
(c) Political ability to buy
(d) Legal ability to buy

19. Which is the key to the level of consumer spending?
(a) Consumer confidence
(b) Consumer needs
(c) Consumer wants
(d) Consumer desire

20. What are the building blocks of any marketing programme?
(a) Demand
(b) Buyer behaviour
(c) Market segmentation
(d) All the above

21. What consists of a large identifiable group within a market?
(a) Marketing programmes
(b) Marketing segment
(c) Marketing management
(d) Marketing research

22. What helps in designing the marketing mix as per the requirements of customers?
(a) Accessibility
(b) Identity
(c) Segmenting
(d) Responsiveness

23. Who must be able to focus its marketing efforts on the chosen segment?
(a) Organization
(b) Management
(c) Market
(d) Production

24. Which must be large enough to be a profitable target?
(a) Accessibility
(b) Segment
(c) Identity
(d) Responsiveness

25. Segmentation is required only if there are market differentiation in terms of________.
(a) Demand
(b) Supply
(c) Status
(d) Quality

26. The purpose of segmentation is to measure the changing behaviour pattern of ________.
(a) Sellers
(b) Economy
(c) Consumer
(d) Status

27. In reality market demand is________.

(a) Heterogeneous and not homogeneous
(b) Homogeneous and not heterogeneous
(c) Not heterogeneous and not homogeneous
(d) None of the above

28. Segmentation strategy is a________.

(a) Market-oriented philosophy
(b) Customer-oriented philosophy
(c) Product-oriented philosophy
(d) Sales-oriented philosophy

29. Which can maximize the impact of company strengths and minimize the exposure of its weaknesses?

(a) Market opportunities
(b) Market programmes
(c) Corporate resources
(d) Segmentation

30. What are the strategic options?

(a) Concentrated marketing
(b) Differentiated marketing
(c) Undifferentiated marketing
(d) All the above

31. Which enables the firm to select one or a few segments which act as target market?

(a) Market segmentation
(b) Market opportunities
(c) Market programmes
(d) Market strategy

32. Which task is simple for a mass market strategy but in keen competition market it becomes necessary?

(a) Marketing segmentation
(b) Marketing management
(c) Marketing opportunities
(d) Marketing strategy

33. What are accepted criteria for market segmentation?

(a) Geographical factors
(b) Socio-economic factors
(c) Both a and b
(d) None of the above

34. Geographical and socio-economic factors are objective and tend to be

(a) Qualitative measurable factors
(b) Quantitative measurable factors
(c) Qualitative immeasurable factors
(d) Quantitative immeasurable factors

35. Which factors are used for market segmentation?

(a) Demographic
(b) Socio-economic
(c) Both (a) and (b)
(d) None of the above

36. The main approaches to identify market segments are________.

(a) People-oriented market segmentation
(b) Product-oriented market segmentation
(c) Both (a) and (b)
(d) None of the above

37. Which approach is also called customer personal characteristic approach?

(a) people-oriented
(b) product-oriented
(c) sales-oriented
(d) Market-oriented

38. Which approach is also called customer response approach?

(a) People-oriented
(b) Product-oriented
(c) Sales-oriented
(d) Market-oriented

39. In case of frequently bought consumer goods, which is used in segmenting the markets?

(a) Demographic variables
(b) Socio-economic variables

(c) Both (a) and (b)
(d) None of the above

40. Which class is also a complex variable?
(a) Social
(b) Economic
(c) Political
(d) Legal

41. Social classes are ________.
(a) Upper class
(b) Middle class
(c) Lower class
(d) All the above

42. Which of the following can explain regularities and diversities in human behaviour?
(a) Religion
(b) Race
(c) Culture
(d) All the above

43. Which influence buyer behaviour indirectly?
(a) Demographic
(b) Socio-economic
(c) Both (a) and (b)
(d) None of the above

44. Which concept as a basis for segmentation is quite reasonable and desirable?
(a) Demography
(b) Lifestyle
(c) Personality
(d) Social class

45. AIO stands for________.
(a) Activities, Interests, Opinions
(b) Activities, Information, Opinions
(c) Activities, Information, Organization
(d) Approach, Information, Organization

46. Which statements are the hearts of the survey?
(a) CAC
(b) AIO
(c) UNO
(d) WTO

47. Who is interested in regional distribution of population and urban, suburban and rural population?
(a) Marketers
(b) Managers
(c) Manufactures
(d) Distributors

48. What characteristics are easy to apply but cannot offer real reasons of buyer behaviour?
(a) Geographic
(b) Demographic
(c) Socio-economic
(d) All the above

49. If segmentation is identified, it should be within reach through suitable means of________.
(a) Communication
(b) Distribution
(c) Both (a) and (b)
(d) None of the above

50. Which class is based on income, occupation, education and place of residence?
(a) Social
(b) Economic
(c) Political
(d) Legal

Answers for MCQ

1.	(d)	**10.**	(b)	**19.**	(a)	**28.**	(b)	**37.**	(a)	**46.**	(b)
2.	(a)	**11.**	(c)	**20.**	(d)	**29.**	(d)	**38.**	(b)	**47.**	(a)
3.	(b)	**12.**	(a)	**21.**	(b)	**30.**	(a)	**39.**	(c)	**48.**	(d)
4.	(c)	**13.**	(c)	**22.**	(c)	**31.**	(a)	**40.**	(a)	**49.**	(c)
5.	(d)	**14.**	(a)	**23.**	(a)	**32.**	(b)	**41.**	(d)	**50.**	(a)
6.	(a)	**15.**	(b)	**24.**	(b)	**33.**	(c)	**42.**	(d)		
7.	(b)	**16.**	(b)	**25.**	(a)	**34.**	(b)	**43.**	(c)		
8.	(c)	**17.**	(d)	**26.**	(c)	**35.**	(c)	**44.**	(b)		
9.	(a)	**18.**	(b)	**27.**	(a)	**36.**	(c)	**45.**	(a)		

MATCH THE FOLLOWING

1.	Social class	**(a)**	Lifestyle
2.	Geographical location	**(b)**	Beliefs, Traditions
3.	Demographic factors	**(c)**	Middle class
4.	Psychography	**(d)**	Purchasing power
5.	Culture	**(e)**	Rural market
6.	Economic factor	**(f)**	Population

Answers for Match the Following

1.	(c)	**2.**	(e)	**3.**	(f)	**4.**	(a)	**5.**	(b)	**6.**	(d)

Chapter 5

Buyer Behaviour

SUMMARY

Buyer behaviour is the study of when, why, how, and where people do or do not buy a product. It blends elements from psychology, sociology, social anthropology and economics. It attempts to understand the consumer decision making process, both individually and in groups. It studies characteristics of individual consumers such as demographics and behavioral variables in an attempt to understand people's wants. It also tries to assess influences on the consumer from groups such as family, friends, reference groups, and society in general.

Buyer behaviour study is based on consumer buying behaviour, with the customer playing the three distinct roles of user, payer and consumer. Relationship marketing is an influential asset for customer behaviour analysis as it has a keen interest in the re-discovery of the true meaning of marketing through the re-affirmation of the importance of the customer or consumer. A greater importance is also placed on consumer retention, customer relationship management, personalization, customization and one-to-one marketing. Social functions can be categorized into social choice and welfare functions.

Consumer behaviour is a comparatively new field of study. It is the attempt to understand and predict human actions in the buying role. It has assumed growing importance under market-oriented or customer-oriented marketing planning and management. Consumers' market for many products and the growth of consumerism and consumer legislation since 1960 have created special interest in consumer behaviour and the formulation of marketing mixes to respond favorably to consumer behaviour in the market place.

Consumer behaviour is defined as "all psychological, social and physical behaviour of potential customers as they become aware of, evaluate, purchase, consume, and tell others about products and services." Each element of this definition is important:

(1) Consumer behaviour involves both individual (psychological) processes and group (social) processes.

(2) Consumer behaviour is reflected from awareness right through post-purchase evaluation indicating satisfaction or non-satisfaction, from purchases,

(3) Consumer behaviour includes communication, purchasing and consumption behaviour,

(4) Consumer behaviour is basically social in nature. Hence, social environment plays an important role in shaping consumer behaviour, and

(5) Consumer behaviour includes both consumer and business consumer behaviour.

Consumer behaviour includes the acts of individuals directly involved in obtaining and using economic goods and services including sequence of decision processes that precede and determine these acts. Actual purchase is only a part of the decision process. In consumer behaviour we consider not only why, how, and what people buy but other factors such as where, how often, and under what conditions the purchase is made. An understanding of consumer behaviour is essential in marketing planning and programmes. In the final analysis consumer behaviour is one of the most important keys to successful marketing.

Determinants or Influencing Factors of Consumer Behaviour

1. **Cultural Factor:** Cultural factor divided into three sub factors: (i) Culture, (ii) Subculture and (iii) Social Class.

   (i) Culture: The set of basic values perceptions, wants, and behaviors learned by a member of society from family and other important institutions. Culture is the most basic cause of a person's wants and behaviour. Every group or society has a culture, and cultural influences on buying behaviour may vary greatly from country to country.

   (ii) Subculture: A group of people with shared value systems based on common life experiences and situations. Each culture contains smaller subcultures a group of people with shared value system based on common life experiences and situations. Subculture includes nationalities, religions, racial groups and geographic regions. Many subcultures make up important market segments and marketers often design products.

   (iii) Social Class: Almost every society has some form of social structure, social classes are society's relatively permanent and ordered divisions whose members share similar values, interests and behaviour.

2. **Social Factors:** A consumer's behaviour also is influenced by social factors, such as the (i) Groups, (ii) Family and (iii) Roles and status.

   (i) Groups: Two or more people who interact to accomplish individual or mutual goals. A person's behaviors are influenced by many small groups. Groups that have a direct influence and to which a person belongs are called membership groups. Some are primary groups includes family, friends, neighbors and coworkers. Some are secondary groups, which are more formal and have less regular interaction. These include organizations like religious groups, professional associations and trade unions.

   (ii) Family: Family members can strongly influence buyer behaviour. The family is the most important consumer buying organization society and it has been researched extensively. Marketers are interested in the roles, and influence of the husband, wife and children on the purchase of different products and services.

   (iii) Roles and Status: A person belongs to many groups, family, clubs, and organizations. The person's position in each group can be defined in terms of both role and status. For example: "X" plays the role of father, in his family, he plays the role of husband, in his company he plays the role of manager, etc. A role consists of the activities people are expected to perform according to the persons around them.

3. **Personal Factors:** It includes: (i) Age and life cycle stage, (ii) Occupation, (iii) Economic situation, (iv) Lifestyle and (v) Personality and self concept.

   (i) Age and Life Cycle Stage: People change the goods and services they buy over their lifetime. Tastes in food, clothes, furniture, and recreation are often age related. Buying is also shaped by the stage of the family life cycle.

   (ii) Occupation: A person's occupation affects the goods and services bought. Blue collar workers tend to buy more rugged work clothes, whereas white-collar workers buy more business suits. A Co., can even specialize in making products needed by a given occupational group. Thus, computer software companies will design different products for brand managers, accountants, engineers, lawyers and doctors.

(iii) **Economic Situation:** A person's economic situation will affect product choice.

(iv) **Lifestyle:** Lifestyle is a person's pattern of living, understanding these forces involves measuring consumer's major AIO dimensions, i.e., activities (Work, hobbies, shopping, support etc.) interest (Food, fashion, family recreation) and opinions (About themselves, business, products)

(v) **Personality and Self Concept:** Each person's distinct personality influences his or her buying behaviour. Personality refers to the unique psychological characteristics that lead to relatively consistent and lasting responses to one's own environment.

4. **Psychological Factors:** It includes these factors: (i) Motivation, (ii) Perception, (iii) Learning and (iv) Beliefs and attitudes.

(i) **Motivation:** Motive (drive) a need that is sufficiently pressing to direct the person to seek satisfaction of the need.

(ii) **Perception:** The process by which people select, organize, and interpret information to form a meaningful picture of the world.

(iii) **Learning:** Changes in an individual's behaviour arising from experience.

(iv) **Beliefs and Attitudes:** Belief is a descriptive thought that a person holds about something. Attitude of a person is consistently favourable or unfavourable evaluations, feelings, and tendencies towards an object or idea.

Buying decisions may be made by individuals or a group such as a family or a committee within a commercial or industrial organization. Where a group is involved, the term Decision Making Unit (DMU) is commonly used. Marketers are interested in identifying all of the parties involved in the decision making process and are careful to distinguish between buyers and users. The farmer may make the final decision as to whether a given piece of agricultural equipment is purchased but his/her decision could well be influenced by the views, attitudes and aptitudes of the farm worker who will operate the machine. Moreover, the subsequent experience of the operator will play a major role in determining whether or not the decision to buy is positively reinforced. Similarly, the mother in the family may be the chief buyer of household foods but children may have a major influence on the purchase of those food items of which they are the main consumers.

Behaviouralists have used empirical evidence to develop models of the buying process. These models usually portray the buying decision as having several discrete stages. It should be emphasized that these models have been developed in the context of buying decisions in which there is a high level of involvement on the part of the potential buyer, that is, where the item under consideration is expensive and purchased infrequently. Typically, the buying decision models comprised five stages: problem recognition, information search, evaluation of alternatives, purchase decision and post-purchase behaviour. Such models underline the fact that the actual decision to purchase is but a single event in a process which begins sometimes beforehand and continues after the item is bought. The marketer is encouraged to think about influencing a buying process rather than a buying decision.

FILL IN THE BLANKS

1. ________ is the attempt to understand and predict human actions in the buying role.
2. Buyer behaviour has assumed growing importance under market-oriented marketing ________ and ________.
3. Buyer behaviour involves ________ and ________ process.
4. Buyer behaviour includes ________, ________ and ________ behaviour.
5. Consumer behaviour is basically ________ in nature.
6. ________ environment plays an important role in shaping buyer behaviour.
7. Inputs include ________, ________ and other factors.
8. ________ of the marketing mix appeals are through advertising, salesmen, reference groups and sales promotion.
9. ________ influence is reflected in motivation, perception, learning, attitudes and personality of buyers.
10. ________ influence is represented by family, social class, reference groups and culture.
11. ________ factors are economics, technological, legal and political factors.
12. Buyer's mind is called the ________.
13. ________ and ________ stimuli enter the buyer's mind through cultural, social, personal and psychological factors.
14. ________ is the first essential step to understand consumer behaviour.
15. Buyers characteristics are ________, ________ and ________.
16. The firm's ________ are designed to positively expose, inform and influence consumer.
17. ________ model of consumer behaviour is one-dimensional.
18. Economics model centre on the ________ and not on the ________.
19. Consumption behaviour is ________ behaviour.
20. Marketing communications are influenced totally by ________.
21. Consumer needs may be ________, ________ and ________.
22. Any usage moving or prompting a person to purchase decision is called as ________ motive.
23. ________ gives the direction or path to be taken by the behaviour.
24. ________ refers to changes in behaviour brought about by practice or experience.
25. The learning of links between ________, ________ and ________ results in habits.
26. ________ affect both perception and behaviour.
27. ________ is a complex psychological concept.
28. Personality's primary features are ________, ________ and ________ of consciousness.
29. ________ marketing is a new technique for analyzing and predicting consumer behaviour.
30. ________ regarding product, promotion and channels of distribution are influenced by the family members making actual purchases.
31. The concept of reference group is borrowed from ________ and ________.
32. Group influence is seen in brand ________ and ________.
33. Sociology points out the relationship between ________ and ________ pattern.

34. ________ class act as one criterion for market segmentation.

35. ________ class consumers want products and brands that are clear symbols of their social status.

36. ________ class consumers shop carefully and read advertisements and compare prices before they buy.

37. ________ class consumers buy usually on impulse and should be influenced by point of purchase materials.

38. Cultural institutions provides guidelines to ________.

39. The interrelation between person-centered factors and the situation- centered factors indicates the transaction nature of ________.

40. ________ should offer appropriate cues in the communications which can promote the sales of products.

41. ________ and ________ can help in the evaluation of alternative.

42. ________ risk may influence the decision to purchase.

43. Higher priced products involve higher ________.

44. Sophisticated products involve ________ risk.

45. Buying process is also influenced by ________ factors.

46. The Howard-Sheth model of buyer behaviour emphasizes three key variables and they are ________, ________ and ________.

47. The two sources of information are ________ and ________.

48. Marketer also consider various buying motives which are ________, ________ and ________ motives.

49. Marketer considers buying habits for ________, ________ and ________ goods while offering the marketing mix to a target market.

50. ________ is a consumer commitment for a product.

51. ________ is a person who first suggests or thinks of the idea of buying the particular product.

52. ________ is a person who explicitly or implicitly has some influence on the final buying decision of other.

53. ________ is a person who ultimately determines any part of the buying decision.

54. ________ is the person who actually purchases.

55. ________ is the person who actually uses or consumers the services or products.

56. The consumer behaviour regarding marketing decisions is influenced by a variety of ________ and ________ factors.

57. Marketing mix for consumer markets will be dominated by ________, ________ and ________.

58. Culture is ________, ________ and ________.

59. Ego is the rational control centre acting as a mediator between them ________ and the ________.

60. Human behaviour is ________ and ________.

61. In the ________ market, all types of consumable goods are available for consumption.

62. ________ is regarded as a black box as we cannot see what is going on in his mind.

63. Consumer buying process includes: (i) recognition of an unsatisfied need (ii) Search for relevant information (iii) Evaluation of alternatives (iv) Purchase decision and ________.

64. ________ groups are the social, economic or professional groups and a consumer uses to evaluate his or her opinions and beliefs.

65. Consumer and user is the realm of ________.

Answers for Fill in the Blanks

1.	Buyer behaviour	34.	Social
2.	Planning; management	35.	Upper
3.	Psychological; social	36.	Middle
4.	Communication; purchasing; consumption	37.	Lower
5.	Social	38.	Marketer
6.	Social	39.	Buyer behaviour
7.	Buying power; marketing mix	40.	Marketing management
8.	Promotion	41.	Brand images; brand concepts
9.	Intrapersonal	42.	Perceived
10.	Interpersonal	43.	Degree of risk
11.	Environmental	44.	Performance
12.	Black box	45.	External
13.	Marketing; environmental	46.	Perception; learning; attitude information
14.	Consumer buying process	47.	Social sources; commercial sources
15.	Cultural; personal; psychological	48.	Emotional, rational; specialty
16.	Marketing efforts	49.	Convenience; shopping; specialty
17.	Economic	50.	Purchase
18.	Product; consumer	51.	Initiator
19.	Goal directed	52.	Influencer
20.	Culture	53.	Decider
21.	Physiological; social; psychological	54.	Buyer
22.	Buying	55.	User
23.	Perception	56.	Organizational; environmental
24.	Learning	57.	Sales promotion; advertising; distribution
25.	Stimulus; cue; response	58.	Alive; moving; ever changing
26.	Attitudes	59.	Id; superego
27.	Personality	60.	Ever changing; unpredictable
28.	Self-concept; role; levels	61.	Consumer
29.	Psychographics	62.	Consumer
30.	Marketing policies	63.	Post-purchase behavior
31.	Sociology; psychology	64.	Reference
32.	Preference; choices	65.	Consumer behaviour
33.	Social class; consumption		

TRUE / FALSE

1. Buyer behaviour is the attempt to understand and predict human actions in the buying role. (True / False)

2. Buyer behaviour has assumed growing importance under market-oriented marketing opportunities and management. (True / False)

3. Buyer behaviour involves psychological and social process. (True / False)

4. Buyer behaviour includes communication, purchasing and consumption behaviour. (True / False)

5. Consumer behaviour is basically political in nature. (True / False)

6. Social environment plays an important role in shaping buyer behaviour. (True / False)

7. Inputs include buying power, marketing mix and other factors. (True / False)

8. Promotion appeals are through advertising, salesmen, reference groups and promotion. (True / False)

9. Interpersonal influence is reflected in motivation, perception, learning, attitudes and personality of buyers. (True / False)

10. Intrapersonal influences are represented by family social class, reference groups and culture. (True / False)

11. Internal factors are economics, technological, legal and political factors. (True / False)

12. Buyer's mind is called the black box. (True / False)

13. Marketing and environmental stimuli enter the buyer's mind through cultural, social, personal and psychological factors. (True / False)

14. Consumer protection process is the first essential step to understand consumer behaviour. (True / False)

15. Buyers characteristics are cultural, personal and psychological. (True / False)

16. The firm's marketing efforts are designed to positively influence consumers only. (True / False)

17. Economic model of consumer behaviour is one-dimensional. (True / False)

18. Economic model centres on the consumer and not on the product. (True / False)

19. Consumption behaviour is goal directed behaviour. (True / False)

20. Marketing communications are influenced totally by culture. (True / False)

21. Consumer needs may be physiological, social and psychological. (True / False)

22. Any urge moving or prompting a person to purchase decision is called a learning motive. (True / False)

23. Perception gives the direction or path to be taken by the behaviour. (True / False)

24. Learning refers to changes in behaviour brought about by practice or experience. (True / False)

25. The learning of links between stimulus, cue and response results in habits. (True / False)

26. Personality affects both perception and behaviour. (True / False)

27. Perception is a complex psychological concept. (True / False)

28. Personality primary features are self-concept, role and levels of consciousness. (True / False)

29. Psychographics marketing is a new technique for analyzing and predicting consumer behaviour. (True / False)

30. Marketing mix regarding product, promotion and channels of distribution are influenced by the family members making actual purchases. (True / False)

31. The concept of reference group is borrowed from sociology and psychology. (True / False)

32. Culture influence is seen in brand preference and choices. (True / False)

33. Sociology points out the relationship between social class and consumption pattern. (True / False)

34. Social class act is one criterion for market segmentation. (True / False)

35. Middle class consumers want products and brands that are clear symbols of their social status. (True / False)

36. Upper class consumers shop carefully and read advertisements and compare prices before they buy. (True / False)

37. Lower class consumers buy usually on impulse and should be influenced by point of purchase materials. (True / False)

38. Cultural institutions provide guidelines to marketers. (True / False)

39. The interrelation between person-centered factors and the situation-centered factors indicates the transactional nature of buyer-process. (True / False)

40. Marketing management should offer appropriate cues in the communications which can promote the sales of products. (True / False)

41. Brand images and concepts can helps in the evaluation of alternative. (True / False)

42. Degree of risk influences the decision to purchase. (True / False)

43. Higher priced products involve higher perceived risk. (True / False)

44. Sophisticated products involve performance risk. (True / False)

45. Buying process is also influenced by internal factors. (True / False)

46. The Howard-Sheth model of buyer behavior emphasizes three key variables are perception learning and attitude information. (True / False)

47. The sources of information are social and commercial sources. (True / False)

48. Marketer considers only the emotional motives. (True / False)

49. Marketer consider buying habits for convince, shopping and specialty goods while offering the marketing mix to a target market. (True / False)

50. Evaluation is a consumer commitment for a product. (True / False)

51. Initiator is a person who first suggests or thinks of the idea of buying the particular product. (True / False)

52. Decider is a person who explicitly or implicitly has some influence on the final buying decision of others. (True / False)

53. Influence is a person who ultimately determines any part of the buying decision. (True / False)

54. Buyer is the person who actually purchases. (True / False)

55. User is the person who actually uses or consumer the services or products. (True / False)

56. The consumer process regarding marketing decisions is influenced by organizational factors. (True / False)

57. Marketing mix for consumer markets will be dominated by sales promotion only. (True / False)

58. Culture is alive, moving and ever-changing. (True / False)

59. Personality is the rational control centre acting as a mediator between the id and the superego. (True / False)

60. Human behaviour is ever changing and unpredicted table. (True / False)

Answers for True / False

1.	True	5.	False	9.	False	13.	True	17.	True
2.	False	6.	True	10.	False	14.	False	18.	False
3.	True	7.	True	11.	False	15.	True	19.	False
4.	True	8.	True	12.	True	16.	False	20.	True

21.	True	**29.**	True	**37.**	True	**45.**	False	**53.**	False
22.	False	**30.**	False	**38.**	True	**46.**	True	**54.**	True
23.	True	**31.**	True	**39.**	False	**47.**	True	**55.**	True
24.	True	**32.**	False	**40.**	True	**48.**	False	**56.**	False
25.	True	**33.**	True	**41.**	True	**49.**	True	**57.**	False
26.	False	**34.**	True	**42.**	False	**50.**	False	**58.**	True
27.	False	**35.**	False	**43.**	False	**51.**	True	**59.**	True
28.	True	**36.**	False	**44.**	True	**52.**	False	**60.**	True

MULTIPLE CHOICE QUESTIONS

1. Which is the attempt to understand and predict human actions in the buying role?

(a) Buyer behaviour
(b) Buyer protection
(c) Buyer legislation
(d) Buyer process

2. Who contracts to acquire an asset in return for some form of consideration?

(a) Seller
(b) Manufacturer
(c) Consumer
(d) Both i and ii

3. Which of the following is not related to consumer behaviour?

(a) Searching
(b) Purchasing
(c) Using
(d) Supplying.

4. Which of the following is not related to consumer buying process?

(a) Problem identification
(b) Search for relevant information
(c) Evaluation of alternatives
(d) Exchanging

5. Which are the goods available in consumer market?

(a) FMCG
(b) Raw materials
(c) Shopping goods
(d) Only (a) and (c)

6. Which environment plays an important role in shaping buyer behaviour?

(a) Social
(b) Economic
(c) Political
(d) Legal

7. Which of the following factors include buying power, marketing mix and other factors?

(a) Outputs
(b) Inputs
(c) Process
(d) Feedback

8. Which of the marketing mix appeals are through advertising, salesmen, reference groups and sales promotion?

(a) Product
(b) Price
(c) Place
(d) Promotion

9. Which influences are reflected in motivation, perception, learning, attitudes and personality of buyers?

(a) Intrapersonal
(b) Interpersonal

(c) Other environmental factors
(d) None of the above

10. Which influences are represented by family, social class, reference groups and culture?

(a) Intrapersonal
(b) Interpersonal
(c) Other environment
(d) All the above

11. What factors are economics, technological, legal and political?

(a) Environmental
(b) Social class
(c) Internal
(d) External

12. Buyer's mind is called the ________.

(a) White box
(b) Black box
(c) Green box
(d) Red box

13. Which stimuli enters the buyer's mind through cultural, social, personal and psychological factors?

(a) Marketing stimuli
(b) Environmental stimuli
(c) Both a and b
(d) None of the above

14. Which is the first essential step to understand consumer behaviour?

(a) Consumer protection process
(b) Consumer buying process
(c) Consumer legislation process
(d) Consumer behaviour process

15. Buyers characteristics are ________.

(a) Cultural
(b) Personal
(c) Psychological
(d) All the above

16. The firm's marketing efforts are designed to positively ________.

(a) Expose consumers
(b) Inform consumers
(c) Influence consumers
(d) All the above

17. Which model of consumer behaviour is one-dimensional?

(a) Social
(b) Economic
(c) Political
(d) Legal

18. Which model centres on the product not on the consumer?

(a) Social
(b) Economic
(c) Political
(d) Legal

19. Consumption behaviour is ________.

(a) Goal directed behaviour
(b) Goal satisfying behaviour
(c) Goal object behaviour
(d) Goal profit behaviour

20. Marketing communications are influenced totally by ________.

(a) Social
(b) Culture
(c) Business
(d) Economic

21. Consumer needs may be ________.

(a) Physiological
(b) Social
(c) Psychological
(d) All the above

22. Any urge moving or prompting a person to purchase decision is called a ________.

(a) Buying motive
(b) Selling motive

(c) Learning motive
(d) Perception motive

23. Which gives the direction or path to be taken by the behaviour?

(a) Perception
(b) Learning
(c) Personality
(d) Attitudes

24. Which refers to changes in behaviour brought about by practice or experience?

(a) Perception
(b) Learning
(c) Personality
(d) Attitudes

25. The learning of links between which results in habits?

(a) Stimulus
(b) Cue
(c) Response
(d) All the above

26. Which of the psychological model of consumer affect both perception and behaviour?

(a) Learning
(b) Attitudes
(c) Personality
(d) Perceived want

27. Which is a complex psychological concept?

(a) Perception
(b) Attitudes
(c) Personality
(d) Learning

28. Personality primary features are _________.

(a) Self-concept of consciousness
(b) Role of consciousness
(c) Level of consciousness
(d) All the above

29. Which marketing is a new technique for analyzing and predicting consumer behaviour?

(a) Psychographics
(b) Economic model
(c) Social class
(d) Culture

30. Marketing policies regarding which are influenced by the family members making actual purchases?

(a) Product
(b) Promotion
(c) Channels of distribution
(d) All the above

31. The concepts of reference group is borrowed from _________.

(a) Sociology
(b) Psychology
(c) Both a and b
(d) None of the above

32. Which influence is seen in brand preferences and brand choices?

(a) Family
(b) Group
(c) Social
(d) Culture

33. Sociology points out the relationship between _________.

(a) Social class
(b) Consumption pattern
(c) Both a and b
(d) None of the above

34. Which class act is one criterion for market segmentation?

(a) Social
(b) Economic
(c) Legal
(d) Political

35. Which consumers want products and brands that are clear symbols of their social status?

(a) Upper class
(b) Middle class
(c) Lower class
(d) All the above

36. Which consumers shop carefully and read advertisements and compare prices before they buy?

(a) Upper class
(b) Middle class
(c) Lower class
(d) None of the above

37. Which consumers buy usually on impulse and should be influenced by point of purchase materials?

(a) Upper class
(b) Middle class
(c) Lower class
(d) None of the above

38. Which institutions provided guidelines to marketers?

(a) Social
(b) Cultural
(c) Environmental
(d) Economical

39. The interrelation between person-centered factors and the situation-centered factors indicates the transactional nature of ________.

(a) Buyer behaviour
(b) Buyer process
(c) Buyer decision
(d) Buyer preference

40. What should offer appropriate cues in the communications which can promote the sale of products?

(a) Marketing management
(b) Marketing opportunities
(c) Marketing programme
(d) Marketing strategy

41. What can help in the evaluation of alternative?

(a) Brand images
(b) Brand concepts
(c) Both a and b
(d) None of the above

42. Which may influence the decision to purchase?

(a) Perceived risk
(b) Degree of risk
(c) Performance risk
(d) Evaluation risk

43. Higher priced products involve higher ________.

(a) Perceived risk
(b) Degree of risk
(c) Performance risk
(d) Evaluation risk

44. Sophisticated products involve ________.

(a) Perceived risk
(b) Degree of risk
(c) Performance risk
(d) Evaluation risk

45. Buying process is also influence by ________

(a) Internal factors
(b) External factors
(c) Social factors
(d) Economic factors

46. The Howard-Sheth model of buyer behaviour emphasizes the key variables of ________.

(a) Perception
(b) Learning
(c) Attitude information
(d) All the above

47. The sources of information are ________.

(a) Social sources
(b) Commercial sources
(c) Both a and b
(d) None of the above

48. What are the buying motives that marketer also considers?

(a) Emotional motives
(b) Rational motives
(c) Speciality motives
(d) All the above

49. While offering the marketing mix to a large market, the marketer also considers buying habits for ________.

(a) Convenience goods
(b) Shopping goods
(c) Speciality
(d) All the above

50. Which is a consumer commitment for a product?

(a) Purchase
(b) Evaluation
(c) Purchase decision
(d) Intention

51. Who is a person who first suggests or thinks of the idea of buying the particular product?

(a) Initiator
(b) Influencer
(c) Decider
(d) Buyer

52. Who is a person who explicitly or implicitly has some influence on the final buying decision of others?

(a) Initiator
(b) Influencer
(c) Decider
(d) Buyer

53. Who is a person who ultimately determines any part of the buying decision?

(a) Influencer
(b) User
(c) Decider
(d) Buyer

54. Who is the person who actually purchases?

(a) Influencer
(b) User
(c) Buyer
(d) Decider

55. Who is the person who actually uses or consumer the services or products?

(a) Influencer
(b) User
(c) Buyer
(d) Decider

56. The consumer behaviour regarding marketing decision is influenced by a variety of ________.

(a) Organizational factors
(b) Environmental factors
(c) Both a and b
(d) None of the above

57. Marketing mix for consumer markets will be dominated by ________.

(a) Sales promotion
(b) Advertising
(c) Distribution
(d) All the above

58. Culture is ________.

(a) Alive
(b) Moving
(c) Ever changing
(d) All the above

59. Which is the rational control centre acting as a mediator between the id and the super ego?

(a) Ego

(b) Attitudes

(c) Personality

(d) Perception

60. Human behaviour is ________.

(a) Ever changing

(b) Unpredictable

(c) Both a and b

(d) None of the above

Answers for MCQ

1.	(a)	11.	(a)	21.	(d)	31.	(c)	41.	(c)	51.	(a)
2.	(c)	12.	(b)	22.	(b)	32.	(b)	42.	(a)	52.	(b)
3.	(d)	13.	(c)	23.	(b)	33.	(c)	43.	(b)	53.	(c)
4.	(d)	14.	(b)	24.	(c)	34.	(a)	44.	(c)	54.	(c)
5.	(d)	15.	(d)	25.	(d)	35.	(a)	45.	(b)	55.	(b)
6.	(a)	16.	(d)	26.	(b)	36.	(b)	46.	(d)	56.	(c)
7.	(b)	17.	(b)	27.	(c)	37.	(c)	47.	(c)	57.	(d)
8.	(d)	18.	(b)	28.	(d)	38.	(b)	48.	(d)	58.	(d)
9.	(a)	19.	(a)	29.	(a)	39.	(a)	49.	(d)	59.	(a)
10.	(b)	20.	(b)	30.	(d)	40.	(a)	50.	(a)	60.	(c)

MATCH THE FOLLOWING

1.	Buyer's mind	(a)	Lower class
2.	Reference group	(b)	Lifestyle
3.	Consumer market	(c)	Motivation
4.	Social class	(d)	Fast moving goods
5.	Personal factor	(e)	Members of social club
6.	Psychological factor	(f)	Black box

Answers for Match the Following

1.	(f)	2.	(e)	3.	(d)	4.	(a)	5.	(b)	6.	(c)

Chapter 6

Demand and Sales Forecasting

SUMMARY

Demand forecast is the forecast that is actually needed by the customer or by market. It will reflect the actual demand situation in the market. Demand forecasting is based on the statistical data about past behavior and empirical relationships of the demand determinants. Demand forecasting is not a speculative exercise into the unknown. It is essentially a reasonable judgement of future probabilities of the market events based on scientific background. Demand forecasting is an estimate of the future demand. It cannot be hundred per cent precise. But, it gives a reliable approximation regarding the possible outcome, with a reasonable accuracy. It is based on the mathematical laws of probability.

Importance of Demand Forecasting

1. **Important for production planning:** Demand forecasting is a prerequisite for the production planning of a business firm. Expansion of output of the firm should be based on the estimates of likely demand, otherwise there may be overproduction and consequent losses may have to be faced.
2. **Sales forecasting:** Sales forecasting is based on the demand forecasting. Promotional efforts of the firm should be based on sales forecasting.
3. **Control of business:** Demand forecasting is important for controlling the business on a sound footing, it is essential to have a well conceived budgeting of costs and profits that is based on the forecast of annual demand/sales and prices.
4. **Inventory control:** A satisfactory control of business inventories, raw materials, intermediate goods, semi-finished product, finished product, spare.
5. **Growth and long-term investment programmes:** Demand forecasting is necessary for determining the growth rate of the firm and its long-term investment programmes and planning.
6. **Stability:** Stability in production and employment over a period of time can be made effective by the management in the light of the suitable forecasting about market demand and other business variables and smoothening of the business operations through counter-cyclical and seasonally adjusted business programmes.

Short-term forecasting normally relates to a period not exceeding a year. Some writers like Professor E.J. Douglas, prefers to use the term demand estimation for short-term demand forecasting. To him demand estimation refers to the determination of the volume of current demand for a firm's product, for a short period say over a month or a year.

Short-term forecasts relate to the day to day particulars which are concerned with tactical decisions under the given resource constraints; as in the short run, the available resources, scale of operations, etc., are fixed or unalterable, by and large. In short-term forecasting, a firm is primarily concerned with the optimum utilization of its existing production capacity.

Long-term forecasting refers to the forecasts prepared for long period during which the firm's scale of operations or the production capacity may be expanded or reduced.

Long-term forecasts are normally for the periods exceeding a year, usually 3-5 years or even a decade or more. Functionally, the long periods which permit alternations in the scale of production differ from industry to industry and firm to firm.

Prediction markets (also known as predictive markets, information markets, decision markets, idea futures, event derivatives, or virtual markets) are speculative markets created for the purpose of making predictions. The current market prices can then be interpreted as predictions of the probability of the event or the expected value of the parameter. For example, a prediction market security might reward a dollar if a particular candidate is elected; such that an individual who thinks the candidate had a 70% chance of being elected should be willing to pay up to 70 cents for such a security.

People who buy low and sell high are rewarded for improving the market prediction, while those who buy high and sell low are punished for degrading the market prediction. Evidence so far suggests that prediction markets are at least as accurate as other institutions predicting the same events with a similar pool of participants.

The Delphi method is a structured communication technique, originally developed as a systematic, interactive forecasting method which relies on a panel of experts. The experts answer questionnaires in two or more rounds. After each round, a facilitator provides an anonymous summary of the experts' forecasts from the previous round as well as the reasons they provided for their judgments. Thus, experts are encouraged to revise their earlier answers in light of the replies of other members of their panel. It is believed that during this process the range of the answers will decrease and the group will converge towards the "correct" answer. Finally, the process is stopped after a pre-defined stop criterion (e.g., number of rounds, achievement of consensus and stability of results) and the mean or median scores of the final rounds determine the results.

Sales forecast is the forecast actually made by the sales based on the company's current position based on its budget, current financial situation, current profit margin, etc., which will be decided by sales team and sales team management personnel which will be fixed and forecast will be made accordingly. Both sales forecast and demand forecast may or may not be same for a typical condition. In general, sales forecast can be adjusted to reduce or exceed the demand forecast based on the performance of the company.

Sales forecast is the projection of achievable sales revenue, based on historical sales data, analysis of market surveys and trends, and salespersons' estimates. Also called sales budget, it forms the basis of a business plan because the level of sales revenue affects practically every aspect of a business.

FILL IN THE BLANKS

1. Modern markets first resort to market segmentation on the basis of ________, ________ and ________.
2. Demand in a segment is based on the factors of ________, ________ and ________.
3. Effective demand for a product needs ________ and ________.
4. ________ is a function of three variable factors: aggregate power, environmental variables and marketing efforts.
5. Purchasing power has the aspects of ________ and ________ to buy.
6. ________ to buy is represented by national per capita income and disposable income of buyers.

7. ________ to buy is influenced by environmental factors and marketing effort of the industry.

8. ________ demand is also called sales possibilities.

9. ________ is the company's share of the market demand.

10. ________ is the foundation of all budgeting and corporate operational plans.

11. ________, ________ and ________ are the forecasts at level of activity.

12. Forecasts are different from ________.

13. Forecasts are the cornerstone of the ________.

14. Budgeting is also closely related to ________.

15. ________ is a blueprint of the financial aspects.

16. ________ term forecasting may cover a period of three months, six months and one year.

17. Short-term forecast is one which provides information for ________ decisions.

18. Long-term forecast is one which provides information for major ________ decisions.

19. Sales forecasting may be undertaken at three different levels are ________, ________ and ________ level.

20. ________ and ________ of forecasting are usually different for new products.

21. The purpose of forecasting differs according to types of forecasting: ________ and ________ forecasting.

22. Sales forecast are useful to the ________, ________ and ________.

23. Sales forecast and demand measurement constitute the building blocks of ________.

24. There can be no effective business planning without estimates of ________.

25. ________ forecast is the starting point in customer-oriented business planning.

26. Sales forecast is the keystone of ________.

27. Entire marketing mix revolves around the ________.

28. Sales forecasting acts as the basis not only of production planning and marketing planning but also of ________ and ________ planning.

29. Sales forecasts are made from ________, ________ and ________ factors.

30. ________ decisions in any area of business without sales volume are impossible.

31. ________ is the oldest type of sales forecasting.

32. ________ managers can evaluate and merge individual estimates into an overall production for the territory.

33. ________ analysis involves the projection of sales trends into the future.

34. A high correlation means that the extrapolated index values will indicate future ________.

35. Sales forecasts form the basis of all ________ by the company.

36. Adequate market planning will become the foundation for integrated ________.

37. Marketing information system or data base is naturally a must for reliable ________ and ________.

38. Test market approach is suitable for ________.

39. Regression analysis can be used only when we have necessary ________ data and ________ conditions.

40. The first step in systematic forecasting is determining the kind of estimate ________.

41. ________ term is concerned with day to day operations within the limits of resources currently available.

42. ________ is concerned with extending or reducing the limits of resources.

43. Cash-requirements depend on ________ and ________.

44. The key figure of ________ is the basis of integrated customer-oriented business planning and corporate operating plans.

45. ________, ________ and ________ are ultimately based on sales forecasts.

46. Sales forecasts provide a reliable basis for ________ and ________ in all areas of business.

47. We have to adjust our sales forecasts on the basis of ________ buying.

48. Sales forecast of present product plus sales estimate of a new product indicate a ________ gap.

49. ________ gives the direction or path to be taken by the behaviour.

50. Both ________ and ________ may or may not be same for a typical condition.

Answers for Fill in the Blanks

1.	Demography; socio-economic factors; behaviour of buyers	26.	Marketing management
2.	Purchasing power; market potential; sales potential	27.	Sales forecast
3.	Purchasing power; buying motives	28.	Financial; manpower
4.	Market potential	29.	Uncontrollable; partially controlled; controllable
5.	Ability; willingness	30.	Rational
6.	Ability	31.	Opinion of executive
7.	Willingness	32.	Sales
8.	Company	33.	Time-series
9.	Company demand	34.	Sales volume
10.	Sales forecast	35.	Planning
11.	Economy; market; sales	36.	Marketing action
12.	Plans	37.	Sales forecasts; business planning
13.	Planning process	38.	New product
14.	Planning	39.	Historical; business
15.	Budget	40.	Desired
16.	Short	41.	Short
17.	Tactical	42.	Long-term
18.	Strategic	43.	Sales level; production operations
19.	Macro; industry; firm	44.	Sales forecast
20.	Problems; methods	45.	Master plan; functional plan; budget
21.	Short-term; long-term	46.	Plans; operations
22.	Industry; government, company	47.	Current customer
23.	Marketing planning	48.	Planning
24.	Sales	49.	Perception
25.	Sales	50.	Sales forecast, demand forecast

TRUE / FALSE

1. Modern marketers first resort to market segmentation on the basis of demography, socio-economic factors and behaviour of buyers. (True / False)
2. Demand in a segment is based on purchasing power only. (True / False)
3. Effective demand for a product needs purchasing power and buying motives. (True / False)
4. Market programme is a function of three variable factors; aggregate power, environmental variable and marketing efforts. (True / False)
5. Purchasing power has the aspects of ability to buy only. (True / False)
6. Ability to buy is represented by national per capita income and disposable income of buyers. (True / False)
7. Willingness to buy is influenced by environmental factors and marketing efforts of the industry. (True / False)
8. Company demand is also called sales volume. (True / False)
9. Company demand is the company's share of the market. (True / False)
10. Sales volume is the foundation of all budgeting and corporate operational plans. (True / False)
11. Sales planning is a part of marketing planning. (True / False)
12. Forecasts are different from plans. (True / False)
13. Forecast is the cornerstone of the management process. (True / False)
14. Budgeting is also closely related to planning. (True / False)
15. Budget is a blueprint of the financial aspects. (True / False)
16. Long-term forecasting may cover a period of three months, six months and one year. (True / False)
17. Short-term forecasting is one which provides information for strategic decisions. (True / False)
18. Long-term forecast is one which provides information for major tactical decisions. (True / False)
19. Sales forecasting may be undertaken at macro, Industry, firm level. (True / False)
20. Problems and methods of forecasting are usually different for new products. (True / False)
21. The purpose of forecasting differ according to types of forecasting; of long-term for casting only. (True / False)
22. Sales forecast are useful to the industry and government. (True / False)
23. Sales forecast and demand measurement constitute the building blocks of marketing opportunities. (True / False)
24. There can be no effective business planning without estimates of sales. (True / False)
25. Sales forecast is the starting point in customer-oriented business planning. (True / False)
26. Sales forecast is the keystone of marketing programmes. (True / False)
27. Entire marketing mix revolves around the sales forecast. (True / False)
28. Sales forecasting acts as the basis of only financial planning. (True / False)
29. Sales forecasts are made from uncontrollable, partially controllable and controllable factors. (True / False)

30. Rational decisions in any area of business without sales volume are impossible. (True / False)

31. Opinion of executive is the latest type of sales forecasting. (True / False)

32. Sales managers can evaluate and merge individual sales estimates into an overall sales estimate. (True / False)

33. Correlation analysis involves the projection of sales trends into the future. (True / False)

34. A high correlation means that the extrapolated index values will indicate future sales volume. (True / False)

35. Sales forecasts form the basis of all planning by the company. (True / False)

36. Adequate market planning will become the foundation for integrated marketing mix. (True / False)

37. Marketing information system or data base is naturally a must for reliable sales forecasts and business planning. (True / False)

38. Test market approach is suitable for present product only. (True / False)

39. Regression analysis can be used only when we have necessary historical data and business conditions. (True / False)

40. The first step in systematic forecasting is determining the kind of estimate desired. (True / False)

41. Long-term is concerned with day to day operations within the limits of resources currently available. (True / False)

42. Long-term is concerned with extending or reducing the limits of resources. (True / False)

43. Cash requirements depend on sales level and production operations. (True / False)

44. The key figure of sales volume is the basis of integrated customer-oriented business planning and corporate operating plans. (True / False)

45. Master plan, functional plan and budget are ultimately based on sales forecasts. (True / False)

46. Sales forecasts provide a reliable basis for operations in all areas of business only. (True / False)

47. We have to adjust our sales forecasts on the basis of current customer buying. (True / False)

48. Sales forecast of present product plus sales estimate of a new product indicates a planning gap. (True / False)

49. Attitude gives the direction or path to be taken by the behaviour. (True / False)

50. Long-term forecasts are normally for the periods exceeding a year, usually 3-5 years or even a decade or more. (True / False)

Answers for True / False

1.	True	11.	True	21.	False	31.	False	41.	False
2.	False	12.	True	22.	True	32.	True	42.	True
3.	True	13.	False	23.	False	33.	False	43.	True
4.	False	14.	True	24.	True	34.	True	44.	False
5.	False	15.	True	25.	True	35.	True	45.	True
6.	True	16.	False	26.	False	36.	False	46.	False
7.	True	17.	False	27.	True	37.	True	47.	True
8.	False	18.	False	28.	False	38.	False	48.	True
9.	True	19.	True	29.	True	39.	True	49.	False
10.	False	20.	True	30.	False	40.	False	50.	True

MULTIPLE CHOICE QUESTIONS

1. Modern marketers first resort to market segmentation on the basis of ________.

(a) Demography
(b) Socio-economic factors
(c) Behaviour of buyers
(d) All the above

2. Demand in a segment is based on the factors of ________.

(a) Purchasing power
(b) Market potential
(c) Sales potential
(d) All the above

3. Effective demand for a product needs ________.

(a) Purchasing power
(b) Buying motives
(c) Both a and b
(d) None of the above

4. Market potential is a function the variable factors of ________.

(a) Aggregate power
(b) Environmental variables
(c) Marketing efforts
(d) All the above

5. Purchasing power has the aspects of ________.

(a) Ability to buy
(b) Willingness to buy
(c) Both a and b
(d) None of the above

6. What is represented by national per capita income and disposable income of buyers?

(a) Ability to buy
(b) Willingness to buy
(c) Marketing efforts
(d) Environmental variables

7. What is influenced by environmental factors and marketing effort of the industry?

(a) Ability to buy
(b) Willingness to buy
(c) Marketing efforts
(d) Environmental variables

8. Company demand is also called ________.

(a) Sales possibilities
(b) Sales demand
(c) Sales forecast
(d) Sales volume

9. What is the company's share of the market demand?

(a) Company demand
(b) Company supply
(c) Company forecast
(d) Company sales

10. What is the foundation of all budgeting and corporate operational plans?

(a) Sales possibilities
(b) Sales demand
(c) Sales forecast
(d) Sales volume

11. What are the forecast at level of activity?

(a) Economy
(b) market
(c) Sales
(d) All the above

12. Forecasts are different from ________.

(a) Plans
(b) Process
(c) Programme
(d) Production

13. Forecasts is the cornerstone of the ________.

(a) Planning process
(b) Business process
(c) Marketing process
(d) Management process

14. Which is also closely related to planning?

(a) Profit
(b) Budgeting
(c) Costing
(d) Sales

15. Which is a blueprint of the financial aspects?

(a) Budget
(b) Planning
(c) Sales
(d) Profit

16. Short-term forecasting may cover a period of ________.

(a) Three months
(b) Six month
(c) One year
(d) All the above

17. Which forecast is one which provides information for tactical decisions?

(a) Short-term
(b) Medium-term
(c) Long-term
(d) None of the above

18. Which forecast is one which provides information for major strategic decisions?

(a) Short-term
(b) Medium-term
(c) Long-term
(d) None of the above

19. Sales forecasting may be undertaken at ________.

(a) Macro-level
(b) Industry-level
(c) Firm-level
(d) All the above

20. Which of forecasting are usually different for new products?

(a) Problems
(b) Methods
(c) Both a and b
(d) None of the above

21. The purposes of forecasting differ according to

(a) Short-term forecasting
(b) Long-term forecasting
(c) Both a and b
(d) None of the above

22. Which are useful to the industry and the government?

(a) Sales forecast
(b) Sales demand
(c) Sales volume
(d) Sales possibility

23. Sales forecast and demand measurement constitute the building blocks of ________.

(a) Marketing strategy
(b) Marketing planning
(c) Marketing management
(d) Marketing opportunities

24. There can be no effective business planning without estimates of ________.

(a) Sales
(b) Profits
(c) Cost
(d) Demand supply

25. Which forecast is the starting point in customer-oriented business planning?

(a) Sales
(b) Profits
(c) Cost
(d) Supply

26. Sales forecast is the keystone of ________.

(a) Marketing strategy
(b) Marketing planning
(c) Marketing management
(d) Marketing opportunities

27. Entire marketing mix revolves around the ________.

(a) Sales demand
(b) Sales forecast
(c) Sales possibility
(d) Sales volume

28. Sales forecasting acts as the basis not only of production planning and marketing planning but also of ________.

(a) Financial planning
(b) Manpower planning
(c) Both a and b
(d) None of the above

29. Sales forecasts are made from ________.

(a) Uncontrolled factors
(b) Partially controllable factors
(c) Controllable factors
(d) All the above

30. Which decisions in any area of business without sales forecasts are impossible?

(a) Tactical
(b) Rational
(c) Strategic
(d) Product

31. Which is the oldest type of sales forecasting?

(a) Opinion of executives
(b) Sales forces estimates
(c) Customer's expectations
(d) Statistical sampling

32. Who can evaluate and merge individual estimates into an overall production for the territory?

(a) Brand managers
(b) Sales managers
(c) Advertising managers
(d) Product managers

33. Which involves the projection of sales trends into the future?

(a) Estimate analysis
(b) Time-series analysis
(c) Correlation analysis
(d) Sampling analysis

34. A high correlation means that the extra-polated index values will indicate future ________.

(a) Sales volume
(b) Sales possibilities
(c) Sales forecast
(d) Sales demand

35. Sales forecasts form the basis of all ________ by the company?

(a) Organizing
(b) Staffing
(c) Planning
(d) Controlling

36. Adequate market planning will become the foundation for integrated ________.

(a) Marketing management
(b) Marketing action
(c) Marketing strategy
(d) Marketing process

37. Marketing information system or data base is naturally a must for reliable ________.

(a) Sales forecasts
(b) Business planning
(c) Both a and b
(d) None of the above

38. Test market approach is suitable for ________.

(a) Old product
(b) Present product
(c) New product
(d) All the above

39. Regression analysis can be used only when we have necessary ________.

(a) Historical data
(b) Business conditions
(c) Both a and b
(d) None of the above

40. The first step in systematic forecasting is determining the kind of ________.

(a) Estimate desired
(b) Estimate wants
(c) Estimate needs
(d) Estimate profit

41. Which is concerned with day to day operations within the limits of resources currently available?

(a) Short-term
(b) Medium-term
(c) Long-term
(d) None of the above

42. Which is concerned with extending or reducing the limits of resources?

(a) Short-term
(b) Medium-term
(c) Long-term
(d) None of the above

43. Cash requirements depend on ________.

(a) Sales level
(b) Production operations
(c) Both a and b
(d) None of the above

44. The key figure of which is the basis of integrated customer-oriented business planning and corporate operating plans?

(a) Sales volume
(b) Sales forecast
(c) Sales possibilities
(d) Sales demand

45. Which are ultimately based on sales forecasts?

(a) Master plan
(b) Functional plan
(c) Budget
(d) All the above

46. Sales forecasts provide a reliable basis for which in all areas of business?

(a) Plans
(b) Operations
(c) Both a and b
(d) None of the above

47. We have to adjust our sales forecasts on the basis of ________.

(a) Current customer buying
(b) Future customer buying
(c) Past customer buying
(d) None of the above

48. Sales forecast of present product plus sales estimate of new product indicate a ________.

(a) Planning gap
(b) product gap
(c) Distribution gap
(d) promotion gap

Answers for MCQ

1.	(d)	9.	(a)	17.	(a)	25.	(a)	33.	(a)	41.	(a)
2.	(d)	10.	(c)	18.	(c)	26.	(c)	34.	(a)	42.	(c)
3.	(c)	11.	(d)	19.	(d)	27.	(b)	35.	(c)	43.	(c)
4.	(d)	12.	(a)	20.	(c)	28.	(c)	36.	(b)	44.	(b)
5.	(c)	13.	(a)	21.	(c)	29.	(d)	37.	(c)	45.	(d)
6.	(a)	14.	(b)	22.	(a)	30.	(b)	38.	(c)	46.	(c)
7.	(b)	15.	(a)	23.	(b)	31.	(a)	39.	(c)	47.	(a)
8.	(a)	16.	(d)	24.	(a)	32.	(b)	40.	(a)	48.	(a)

MATCH THE FOLLOWING

1.	Sales forecast	(a)	Independent experts
2.	Short-term sales forecast	(b)	New products
3.	Time-series	(c)	Sales, selling expenses
4.	Delphi method	(d)	Post sales trend
5.	Test marketing	(e)	One year period
6.	Sales budget	(f)	Estimation of future sales

Answers for Match the Following

1.	(f)	2.	(e)	3.	(d)	4.	(a)	5.	(b)	6.	(c)

Chapter 7

Marketing Information and Research

SUMMARY

Marketing Information Systems involves the people, equipment, and procedures to gather, sort, analyze, evaluate and distribute with, timely and accurate information to marketing decision makers. Marketing intelligence system is a set of procedures and sources used by executives to obtain their everyday information about pertinent developments in the marketing environment.

Importance of Marketing Information System

1. **MIS helps Large-scale Production:** Industrial revolution led to the invention of new method of production with the help of plant and machinery. This resulted in mass production by industrial units. To sell the goods in large quantities, it is necessary for a manufacturer to know the potential areas where his goods could be marketed, the probable demand for the same and the extent of profitability and competition. This is possible only with the establishment of marketing information system.
2. **Change in the Market Forces:** Over a period with the increase in the competition, there has been a shift from sellers to buyers markets. This necessitates the understanding of consumer behavior which is possible by gathering information about market and consumers.
3. **Change in Consumers' Choice:** As the income of consumers increase they become more selective in their choice of goods. Firms find it difficult to predict consumer's response to different product features, package, price, shape, and other attributes. These things make firms to depend on marketing information system.
4. **From Price to Non-price Competition:** Sellers are increasingly using branding to distinguish their products from other goods. Marketing tools like product differentiation, advertising and sales promotion require marketing information to be effective.
5. **Improved Understanding:** Marketing Information System, by providing the current information about markets, competitors and consumers, helps to establish a better understanding with the firm and the consumers. It establishes two way communication with the firm and the consumers.
6. **Market Coverage:** As firms expand their activities geographically the gap between the firm and markets widens. This necessitates a system which supplies marketing information to the managers to take decisions.

Components of Marketing Information System

1. **Internal Accounting System:** This is a subsystem which collects the information about the various aspects of the firm. The information regarding order on hand, actual sales, inventory levels of raw materials, work-in-progress, finished products, order processing procedure, time taken to accomplish the orders, etc. This information would help marketing

department to know how these things are dealt with. By analyzing this information it can spot the strength and weakness and take corrective action to set the things right.

2. **Marketing Intelligence System:** Information about current happenings in the marketing environment is vital to a firm. The marketing strategies are formulated based on what is happening in the environment. This information is collected by marketing intelligence system.
3. **Marketing Research System:** This subsystem exists to work on a definite problem entrusted by the marketing division. Marketing research system provides special information on request when unexpected, unique problems are encountered by the marketing department. It may be requested to collect information regarding consumers' opinion about the products offered by the company, effectiveness of advertisement, trends in the market etc.
4. **Analytical Marketing System:** The main task of this subsystem is to analyze the data supplied by the accounting system, market intelligence system and marketing research system. Statistical tools are extensively used to find out the relationship between various variables, to forecast the trends, to build the models which are useful in assessing the situations and help managers to develop better marketing alternatives. Thus, from foregoing explanations it may be observed that the subsystem marketing information, the accounting system provides internal information. Market intelligence system collects current market information and marketing research operates to gather data to solve specific marketing problems and analytical system analyses the data and establishes logical and meaningful relationships suggesting the possible alternative remedies.

The process of gathering, analyzing and interpreting information about a market, about a product or service to be offered for sale in that market, and about the past, present and potential customers for the product or service.

Marketing Research Approach refers to the approach that has been adopted to conduct the research for supporting of marketing activities. It involves the selection of research questions, the conceptual framework that has to be adopted, the selection of appropriate research method such as primary research, secondary research etc.

Approaches to Marketing Research

Marketing Research Approach refers to the approach that has been adopted to conduct the research for supporting of marketing activities. It involves the selection of research questions, the conceptual framework that has to be adopted, the selection of appropriate research method such as primary research, secondary research, etc.

A. Quantitative Research Approach: Quantitative research refers to the systematic experimental investigation of quantitative properties and their relationships. The objective of quantitative research is to develop and employ mathematical models, theories and/or hypotheses pertaining to properties.

1. **Descriptive research:** Descriptive research involves collecting data in order to test hypotheses or answer questions concerning the current status of the subjects of the study. It determines and reports the way things are.
2. **Correlation research:** Correlation research attempts to determine whether and to what degree a relationship exists between two or more quantifiable variables. However, it never establishes a cause-effect relationship. The relationship is expressed by correlation

coefficient, which is a number between .00 and 1.00.

3. **Causal-comparative research:** Causal-comparative research: establishes the cause-effect relationship, compares the relationship, but the cause is not manipulated, such as "gender."

4. **Experimental:** Experimental research establishes the cause-effect relationship and does the comparison, but the cause is manipulated. The cause, independent variable makes the difference. The effect, dependent variable is dependent on the independent variable.

B. Qualitative Research Approach: Qualitative research is a method of inquiry employed in many different academic disciplines, traditionally in the social sciences, but also in market research and further contexts. Qualitative researchers aim to gather an in-depth understanding of human behaviour and the reasons that govern such behaviour.

Ethnographic approach to qualitative research comes largely from the field of anthropology. The emphasis in ethnography is on studying an entire culture. The idea of culture was tied to the notion of ethnicity and geographic location. It has been broadened to include virtually any group or organization. That is, we can study the "culture" of a business or defined group (e.g., a Rotary club).

Phenomenology is considered a philosophical perspective as well as an approach to qualitative methodology. It has a long history in several social research disciplines including psychology, sociology and social work. Phenomenology is a school of thought that emphasizes a focus on people's subjective experiences and interpretations of the world. That is, the phenomenologist wants to understand how the world appears to others.

Observation is the act of seeing from a distance. As the name suggests, the research is carried out by observation. The respondents are neither contacted nor questioned. But their behavior is observed. Field surveys are commonly used in marketing research to collect primary data from the respondents. This technique intends to secure a broad range of information from the respondents. Surveys can bring out information about socio-economic characteristics of a particular market.

FILL IN THE BLANKS

1. Information system is an organized way of ________, ________ and ________ messages.
2. ________ system includes both formal flow of information as well as informal flow of information.
3. Information is a critical or crucial resource both in ________ and ________.
4. A system means ________, ________ and ________.
5. ________ system is an organized, ongoing system for providing information to decision makers at all levels of management.
6. Effective planning and control depends on new way of ________ information.
7. Marketing decisions influence ________ and ________ environment.
8. The real power of information is just like the power of ________.
9. ________ and ________ are energy sources that can be harnessed for useful purposes.
10. ________ energy can be harnessed through organization wide reporting system.
11. ________ is the power of harness information energy.
12. MIS stands for ________.
13. EIS stands for ________.
14. DSS is________.

15. Expansion of EDI is ________.

16. BPR stands for ________.

17. To mobilize all resource to 'master change' is called as ________.

18. ________ system is the greatest asset of the enlightened and innovative markets.

19. ________ is information that flow into the firm from environment.

20. ________ is information that flows from the firm outward to the environment.

21. ________ is a information that is gathered with in the firm.

22. We can define a marketing information system as a ________ system.

23. Marketing information system consists of ________, ________ and ________.

24. The overall objective of ________ system is to provide input from target markets, marketing channels, competitors, consumers and other forces.

25. ________ is one of the marketing management decisions.

26. ________ is not the marketing management decisions.

27. ________ is one of the marketing information systems.

28. ________ is not the marketing information system.

29. Marketing levels are ________ and ________.

30. The strategic level is the ________ level of management.

31. Under the strategic level, the decisions are established for the organization in the ________ range plans.

32. The tactical level is the ________ level of management.

33. Under the tactical level, the decisions made mainly for the ________ activities.

34. The basic purpose of ________ and ________ data is to produce information.

35. ________ and ________ are key ingredients.

36. There is an unlimited amount of data from sources both ________ and ________ to the organization.

37. ________ method guarantees that data will be processed in accordance with the needs of the user.

38. The primary function of information is to increase the ________ of the user.

39. ________ refers to the ease and speed with which the particular information could be obtained.

40. ________ and ________ access will have more value as compared to difficult access.

41. If the information is being generated from a formal information system it is authentic and could be ________.

42. Marketing information system has two formats they are ________ and ________ sheet.

43. ________ sheet contains information like marketing decision, parameters, frequency, source and the format code.

44. ________ sheet of marketing information system will contain the items, relationship, standard, actual, variance and reason.

45. The research assessment sheet format is useful from the ________ point of view.

46. ________ sheet of marketing information system could be used for control.

47. ________ manager uses the MKIS to learn about consumer needs and wants.

48. Marketing information is the ________ blood of marketing.

49. ________ and ________ in ever expanding markets are based on anticipation of consumer demand.

50. Under ________ oriented marketing approach, every marketer needs up to date knowledge about consumer needs and wants.

51. In a dynamic economy, consumer________, ________ and ________ constantly changing.

52. Forces of ________ and ________ are constantly changing.

53. In a wider and complex economy, fluctuations in ________, ________ and ________ are tremendous.

54. ________ must have latest information on the changing trends of supply, demand and price.

55. Modern markets are ________.

56. ________ is the slogan in the existing marketing environment.

57. In an ever widening market there is a communication gap between ________, ________ and ________.

58. The communication gap between consumers, users and marketers is responsible for ________ marketing plans and programmes.

59. Marketing data received from any components of the MIS is systematically ________, ________ and ________.

60. Internal marketing information, marketing intelligence and marketing research projects are the major components of ________.

61. The four major strategic area of marketing mix are ________, ________, ________ and ________.

62. ________ men can supply current information on buyer behaviour, dealer behaviour and also on competitors.

63. Marketing intelligence acts as a mirror of ________.

64. ________ system is the third component of the marketing information system.

65. Marketing research studies are ________ oriented.

66. Marketing information system stands between ________ and ________.

67. Marketing decisions influence ________ and ________ environment.

68. Marketing programme starts from ________ idea.

69. Alpa and omega of marketing is consumer ________.

70. Research is the process of ________, ________ and ________ of critical and relevant facts.

71. Marketing research is only ________ branch of the marketing information system.

72. ________ means actual and potential customers.

73. ________ is the systematic and intelligent investigator that study of the "Who, What, Where, When, Why and How of actual and potential buyers".

74. Size of the market items of study and analysis are included in ________.

75. The basic resource or input in the management is ________.

76. ________ is the fourth subsystem of marketing management.

77. Information is the lifeblood of ________, ________ and ________ any enterprise.

78. The marketing research played a minor role under ________ oriented approach.

79. Research task is purely a ________ function.

80. The major components of a special marketing information and analysis centre are information ________, ________ and ________.

81. In ________ year the marketing concept was first articulated.

82. Change means ________.

83. In ________ year marketing research has recorded fast growth and development.

84. Marketing environment was described as ________ market.

85. Only ________ marketing took some interest in using marketing information and research for decisions on marketing mix.

Answers for Fill in the Blanks

1.	Sending, receiving, recording	39.	Accessibility
2.	Information	40.	Faster; easier
3.	Planning, control	41.	Measurable
4.	Order, arrangement, purpose	42.	Research assessment sheet; marketing activity evaluation
5.	Information management		
6.	Managing	43.	Research assessment
7.	Internal; external	44.	Marketing activity evaluation
8.	Wind	45.	Information
9.	Wind; information	46.	Marketing activity evaluation
10.	Information	47.	Marketing
11.	Information management	48.	Life
12.	Management information system	49.	Mass production; mass distribution
13.	Executive information system	50.	Customer-
14.	Decision support system	51.	Tastes; fashions; liking
15.	Electronic data interchange	52.	Demand; supply
16.	Business process re-engineering	53.	Demand; supply; prices
17.	Marketers	54.	Marketing
18.	Modern information	55.	Competitive
19.	Marketing intelligence	56.	Innovate or perish
20.	Marketing communication	57.	Consumers; users; marketers
21.	Internal marketing information	58.	Unrealistic
22.	Computer-based	59.	Analyzed; evaluated; processed
23.	People; equipment; procedure	60.	Marketing information system
24.	Marketing information	61.	Product; price; promotion; distribution
25.	Product	62.	Sales
26.	Internal Records	63.	Marketing environment
27.	Marketing research	64.	Marketing research
28.	External records	65.	Project-
29.	Strategic level; practical level	66.	Marketing environment; marketing decision makers
30.	First		
31.	Long	67.	External; internal
32.	Second	68.	Product
33.	Short-term	69.	Satisfaction
34.	Capturing; processing	70.	Gathering ; recording ; analyzing
35.	Data	71.	One
36.	Internal; external	72.	Market
37.	Data processing	73.	Market research
38.	Knowledge	74.	Market research

75.	Information	**81.**	1952
76.	Controlling	**82.**	Progress
77.	Planning; directing; controlling	**83.**	1960
78.	Sales-	**84.**	Seller's
79.	Staff	**85.**	National
80.	Gathering; processing; utilization		

TRUE / FALSE

1. Information system is an organized way of sending, receiving and recording and recording messages. (True / False)

2. Marketing system includes both formal flow of information as well as informal flow of information. (True / False)

3. Information is a critical or crucial resource both in planning and control. (True / False)

4. A system means order, change and purpose. (True / False)

5. Information marketing system is an organized, ongoing system for providing information to decision makers at all level of management. (True / False)

6. Effective planning and control depends on new ways of managing information. (True / False)

7. Marketing decisions influence only external decision. (True / False)

8. The real power of information is just like the power of wind. (True / False)

9. Wind and information are energy sources that can be harnessed for useful purposes. (True / False)

10. Marketing energy can be harnessed through organization wide reporting system. (True / False)

11. Information management is the power of to harness information energy. (True / False)

12. MIS stands for management information system. (True / False)

13. EIS stands for executive information system. (True / False)

14. DSS stands for direct support system. (True / False)

15. Expansion of EDI is electronic data information. (True / False)

16. BPR stands for business process re-engineering. (True / False)

17. Marketing is called upon to mobilize all resources to 'master change'. (True / False)

18. Marketing information system is the greatest assets of the enlightened and innovative markets. (True / False)

19. Marketing intelligence is a information that flows into the firm from the environment. (True / False)

20. Internal marketing information is a information that flows from the firm outwards to the environment. (True / False)

21. Marketing communication is a information that is gathered within the firm. (True / False)

22. We can define a marketing information system as a computer-based system. (True / False)

23. Marketing information system consists of marketer, sort and procedure. (True / False)

24. Marketing information system objects is to provide input from target markets, competitors, marketing channels, consumers and other forces. (True / False)

25. Pricing is one of the marketing management decisions. (True / False)

26. Internal records is also one of the marketing management decisions. (True / False)

27. Marketing research is one of the marketing information system. (True / False)

28. Marketing intelligence is one of the marketing information system. (True / False)

29. Strategic level and traction level are the marketing levels. (True / False)

30. The strategic level is the first level of management. (True / False)

31. The decision is established for the organization in the short-range plans under strategic level. (True / False)

32. The tactical level is the third level of management. (True / False)

33. The decisions made mainly for the short term activities, under tactical level. (True / False)

34. Capturing and processing data is the basic purpose to produce information. (True / False)

35. Disk is key ingredient. (True / False)

36. There is an unlimited amount of data from sources both internal and external to the organization. (True / False)

37. No disk processing method guarantees that data will be processed in accordance with the needs of the user. (True / False)

38. The primary function of information is to increase the knowledge of the user. (True / False)

39. Accessibility refers to the ease and speed with which the particular information could be obtained. (True / False)

40. Only easier access will have more value as compared to difficult access. (True / False)

41. If the information is being generated from a formal information system it is authentic and could be measurable. (True / False)

42. Research assessment sheet and marketing activity evaluation sheet are the two important formats of marketing information system. (True / False)

43. Planning assessment sheet contains information like marketing decisions, parameters, etc. (True / False)

44. Research assessment sheet will contain the items, relationship, standard, actual, etc. (True / False)

45. The research assessment sheet format is useful from the information point of view. (True / False)

46. Marketing activity evaluation sheet could be used for control. (True / False)

47. Sales manager uses the MKIS to learn about consumer needs and wants. (True / False)

48. Marketing information is the lifeblood of marketing. (True / False)

49. Mass promotion and mass distribution in ever expanding markets are based on anticipated of consumer demand. (True / False)

50. Under customer-oriented marketing approach, every marketing needs up to date knowledge about consumer needs and wants. (True / False)

51. In a dynamic economy, consumer tastes, fashions and liking are constant. (True / False)

52. Forces of demand and supply are constant. (True / False)

53. In a wider and complex economy, fluctuations in demand, supply and prices are tremendous. (True / False)

54. Sales manager must have latest information on the changing trends of supply, demand and prices. (True / False)

55. Modern marketing are competitive. (True / False)

56. Innovate or perish is the slogan in the existing marketing environment. (True / False)

57. In an ever expanding marketing there is a communication gap between consumers, users and marketers. (True / False)

58. The communication gap between consumers, users and marketers is responsible for unrealistic marketing plans and programmes. (True / False)

59. Marketing data received from any components of the MIS is systematically analyzed only. (True / False)

60. The three major components of marketing information system are internal marketing information, marketing intelligence and marketing research project. (True / False)

61. The four major strategic areas of marketing mix are product, price, promotion and distribution. (True / False)

62. Marketing can supply correct information on buyer behaviour, dealer behaviour and also on competitors. (True / False)

63. Marketing research acts as a minor of marketing environment. (True / False)

64. Marketing research is the third component of the marketing information system. (True / False)

65. Marketing research studies are customer oriented. (True / False)

66. Marketing information system stands between the marketing environment and marketing decision makers. (True / False)

67. Marketing decision influence only internal environment. (True / False)

68. Marketing programme starts from promotion idea. (True / False)

69. Alpa and omega of marketing is consumer satisfaction. (True / False)

70. Research is the process of gathering only critical and relevant facts. (True / False)

71. Marketing research is only two branch of the marketing information system. (True / False)

72. Market means actual and potential customer. (True / False)

73. Market research is the systematic and intelligent investigation that study of the "Who, What, Where, When, Why and How of actual and potential buyers". (True / False)

74. Size of market item of study and analysis are not included in market research. (True / False)

75. Information is the basic resource or input in the management. (True / False)

76. Controlling is the third subsystem of marketing management. (True / False)

77. Management is the life blood of planning, directing and controlling any enterprise. (True / False)

78. Intensive study, scientific approach and decision tool are the elements of marketing research. (True / False)

79. Research is purely a control function. (True / False)

80. Information gathering, processing and utilization are the major components of a special marketing information and analysis centre. (True / False)

81. In the year 1962 the marketing concept was first articulated. (True / False)

82. Change means analyze. (True / False)

83. Since from the year 1960 marketing research has recorded fast growth and development. (True / False)

84. Marketing environment was described as buyer's market. (True / False)

85. Only national marketing took some interest in using marketing information and research for decisions on marketing mix. (True / False)

86. Under sales - oriented marketing approach the marketing research played a minor role. (True / False)

87. Marketing research is the poor cousin of sales promotion. (True / False)

88. Advertising agencies have now turned to marketing research. (True / False)

Answers for True / False

1.	True	**19.**	True	**37.**	False	**55.**	True	**73.**	True
2.	False	**20.**	False	**38.**	True	**56.**	True	**74.**	False
3.	True	**21.**	False	**39.**	True	**57.**	False	**75.**	True
4.	False	**22.**	True	**40.**	False	**58.**	True	**76.**	False
5.	False	**23.**	False	**41.**	True	**59.**	False	**77.**	False
6.	True	**24.**	True	**42.**	True	**60.**	True	**78.**	True
7.	False	**25.**	True	**43.**	False	**61.**	True	**79.**	False
8.	True	**26.**	False	**44.**	False	**62.**	False	**80.**	True
9.	True	**27.**	True	**45.**	True	**63.**	False	**81.**	False
10.	False	**28.**	True	**46.**	True	**64.**	True	**82.**	False
11.	True	**29.**	True	**47.**	False	**65.**	False	**83.**	True
12.	True	**30.**	False	**48.**	True	**66.**	True	**84.**	False
13.	True	**31.**	False	**49.**	False	**67.**	False	**85.**	True
14.	False	**32.**	False	**50.**	True	**68.**	False	**86.**	True
15.	False	**33.**	True	**51.**	False	**69.**	True	**87.**	False
16.	True	**34.**	True	**52.**	False	**70.**	False	**88.**	True
17.	True	**35.**	False	**53.**	True	**71.**	False		
18.	False	**36.**	True	**54.**	False	**72.**	True		

MULTIPLE CHOICE QUESTIONS

1. Information system is organized way of __________.

(a) Sending message
(b) Receiving messages
(c) Recording messages
(d) All the above

2. Which system includes both formal and informal flow of information?

(a) Marketing
(b) Information
(c) Business
(d) None of the above

3. Information is a critical or crucial resource both in __________.

(a) Planning and organizing
(b) Organizing and planning
(c) Planning and controlling
(d) Organizing and controlling

4. A system means __________.

(a) Order
(b) Arrangement
(c) Purpose
(d) All the above

5. Which system is an organized, ongoing system for providing information to decision making at all levels of management?

(a) Information management
(b) Information marketing
(c) Information business
(d) Information technology

6. Which depends on new ways of managing information?

(a) Effective planning and control
(b) Effective organizing and planning
(c) Effective planning and staffing
(d) Effective organizing and staffing

7. Marketing decisions influence ________.

(a) Internal environment
(b) External environment
(c) Both a and b
(d) None of the above

8. The real power of information is just like the power of ________.

(a) Wind
(b) Water
(c) Fire
(d) Energy

9. Which are the energy sources that can be harnessed for useful purposes?

(a) Energy and information
(b) Wind and information
(c) Market and information
(d) Power and information

10. Which energy can be harnessed through organization wide reporting system?

(a) Marketing
(b) Business
(c) Information
(d) Management

11. Which is the power to harness information energy?

(a) Information marketing
(b) Information Business
(c) Information management
(d) Information technology

12. MIS stands for ________.

(a) Marketing information system
(b) Management information system
(c) Marketing and information system
(d) Management and information system.

13. EIS stands for ________.

(a) Executive information system
(b) Effective information system
(c) External information system
(d) Excellent information system

14. Expansion of DSS is ________.

(a) Direct support systems
(b) Director support system
(c) Decision support system
(d) None of the above

15. EDI stands for ________.

(a) Electronic Decision Interchange
(b) Electronic Data Information
(c) Electronic Decision Information
(d) Electronic Data Interchange

16. BPR is ________.

(a) Business process re-engineering
(b) Business planning re-engineering
(c) Business pricing re-engineering
(d) Business promotion re-engineering

17. Who are called upon to mobiles all resources to 'master change'?

(a) Suppliers
(b) Customers
(c) Business partners
(d) Marketers

18. Which system is the greatest asset of the enlightened and innovative markets?

(a) Marketing information
(b) Modern information
(c) Management information
(d) None of the above

19. Which of the following is a information that flows into the firm form the environment?

(a) Marketing intelligence
(b) Marketing communication
(c) Internal marketing information
(d) External marketing information

20. Which of the following is a information that is gathered within the firm?

(a) Marketing intelligence
(b) Internal marketing information

(c) External marketing information
(d) Marketing communication

21. Which of the following is a information that flows from the firm outward to the environment?

(a) Marketing communication
(b) Marketing intelligence
(c) External marketing information
(d) Internal marketing information

22. Marketing information system as a ________.

(a) Functional information system
(b) Problem solving system
(c) Fast changing system
(d) Computer-based system

23. Marketing information system consists of ________.

(a) People
(b) Equipment
(c) Procedure
(d) All the above

24. What is the main object of marketing information system (MIS)?

(a) To provide input from target markets
(b) To provide input from marketing channels and competitors.
(c) To provide input from consumers and other forces
(d) All the above

25. Which one of the following is not marketing management decisions?

(a) Product
(b) Pricing
(c) Evidence
(d) None of the above

26. Which one of the following is not is not marketing management decisions?

(a) Physical
(b) Internal Records
(c) Marketing intelligence
(d) Marketing Research

27. Which one of the following is marketing information system?

(a) External records
(b) Internal records
(c) Marketing strategy
(d) Marketing information

28. Which one of the following is not marketing information system?

(a) Internal records
(b) Marketing Research
(c) External records
(d) Marketing intelligence

29. Which are the levels of marketing?

(a) Strategic level
(b) Practical level
(c) Both a and b
(d) None of the above

30. The strategic level is the ________ level of management.

(a) First
(b) Second
(c) Third
(d) Fourth

31. Under the strategic level, the decisions are established for the organization in the ________.

(a) Long-range plans
(b) Medium-range plans
(c) Short-range plans
(d) None of the above

32. The tactical level is the ________ level of management.

(a) First
(b) Second
(c) Third
(d) Fourth

33. Under the tactical level, the decisions made are mainly for the ________ activities of the organization.

(a) Long-term
(b) Medium-term
(c) Short-term
(d) None of the above

34. Which is the basic purpose of data to produce information?

(a) Capturing and processing data
(b) Recording and processing data
(c) Sending and receiving data
(d) Recording and receiving data

35. Which is called as key ingredient?

(a) Data
(b) Process
(c) Drive
(d) Disk

36. From which sources there is an unlimited amount of data to the organization?

(a) Internal
(b) External
(c) Both a and b
(d) None of the above

37. Which method does not guarantees that data will be processed in accordance with the needs of the user?

(a) Central processing method
(b) Data processing method
(c) Random processing method
(d) Multiprocessing method

38. The primary function of information is ________.

(a) to increase the input from target markets.
(b) to increase the input from competitors
(c) to increase the knowledge of the user.
(d) to increase the uncertainty of the user

39. Which refers to the ease and speed with which the particular information could be obtained?

(a) Accuracy
(b) Comprehensive
(c) Authenticity
(d) Accessibility

40. Which access will have more value as compared to difficult access?

(a) Faster
(b) Easier
(c) Both a and b
(d) None of the above

41. If the information is being generated from a formal information system it is authentic and could be ________.

(a) Measurable
(b) Immeasurable
(c) Certain
(d) Uncertain

42. Which is the important format of marketing information system (MIS)?

(a) Research assessment sheet
(b) Marketing activity evaluation sheet
(c) Both a and b
(d) None of the above

43. Which sheet of marketing information system contains information like marketing decisions parameters, frequency, source and the format code?

(a) Research assessment sheet
(b) Marketing activity evaluation sheet
(c) Marketing system evaluation sheet
(d) Planning assessment sheet

44. Which sheet of marketing information system will contain the items, relationship, standard, actual, variance and reason?

(a) Research assessment sheet
(b) Marketing activity evaluation sheet

(c) Marketing system evaluation sheet
(d) Planning assessment

45. From which point of view the research assessment sheet format is useful

(a) Planning
(b) Organizing
(c) Controlling
(d) Information

46. Which sheet of marketing information system could be used for control?

(a) Research assessment sheet
(b) Planning assessment sheet
(c) Marketing activity evaluation sheet
(d) Marketing system evaluation sheet

47. The steps needs for implementing the newly designed marketing information system could be ___________.

(a) Prepare marketing research plan and operating schedule
(b) Train the research staff
(c) Evaluate and modify the research system
(d) All the above

48. Which manager uses the MKIS to learn about consumer needs and wants?

(a) Marketing
(b) Brand
(c) Sales
(d) Advertising

49. Which one of the following is not a reason for considering marketing information as the lifeblood of marketing?

(a) Significance of competition
(b) Marketing planning
(c) Consumerism
(d) Evaluation of alternatives

50. Which one of the following is a reason for considering marketing information as the lifeblood of marketing?

(a) Information search
(b) Complexity of marketing
(c) Purchase decision
(d) Evaluation of alternatives

51. Which of the two in ever expanding markets are based on anticipation of consumer demand?

(a) Mass product and mass distribution
(b) Mass promotion and mass distribution
(c) Mass product and mass promotion
(d) None of the above

52. Under which marketing approach, every market needs up to date knowledge about consumer needs and wants?

(a) Project-oriented
(b) Action-oriented
(c) Customer-oriented
(d) Sales-oriented

53. What is constantly changing in the customer in a dynamic economy?

(a) Tastes
(b) Fashions
(c) Liking
(d) All the above

54. Forces of which are constantly changing?

(a) Demand
(b) Supply
(c) Both a and b
(d) None of the above

55. Fluctuation which are tremendous in a wider and complex economy?

(a) Demand
(b) Supply
(c) Prices
(d) All the above

56. Who must have latest information on the changing trends of supply, demand and prices?

(a) Marketer
(b) Sales manager
(c) Brand manager
(d) Advertising manager

57. Modern markets are ________.

(a) Accurate
(b) Competitive
(c) Free from bias
(d) Authenticity

58. Marketing Information Systems involves ________.

(a) The people
(b) Equipment
(c) Procedures
(d) All the above

59. In an ever widening market there is a communication gap between ________.

(a) Consumers
(b) Users
(c) Marketers
(d) All the above

60. The communication gap between consumer's users and marketers is responsible for which marketing plans and programmes?

(a) Innovatory
(b) Unrealistic
(c) Insulated
(d) Strategic

61. Marketing data received from any components of the MIS is systematically ________.

(a) Analyzed
(b) Evaluated
(c) Processed
(d) All the above

62. Which are the major components of marketing information system?

(a) Internal marketing information
(b) Marketing intelligence
(c) Marketing research projects
(d) All the above

63. Which one of the following is not a marketing mix?

(a) Production mix
(b) Promotion mix
(c) Distribution mix
(d) None of the above

64. Salesmen can supply current information on ________.

(a) Buyer behaviour
(b) Dealer behaviour
(c) Competitors
(d) All the above

65. Which of the following acts as a minor of marketing environment?

(a) Marketing intelligence
(b) Marketing research
(c) Marketing information
(d) Marketing system

66. Which system is the third component of the marketing information system?

(a) Marketing intelligence
(b) Internal marketing information
(c) Marketing research
(d) Marketing environment

67. Marketing research studies are ________.

(a) Decision-oriented
(b) Project-oriented
(c) Action-oriented
(d) Customer-oriented

68. Marketing information system stands between the ________.

(a) Marketing environment
(b) Marketing decision makers
(c) Both a and b
(d) None of the above

69. Marketing decisions influence ________.

(a) External environment
(b) Internal environment

(c) Both a and b
(d) None of the above

70. From which idea marketing programme starts?

(a) Product
(b) Price
(c) Promotion
(d) Distribution

71. Alpa and omega of marketing is ________.

(a) Consumer wants
(b) Consumer satisfaction
(c) Consumer needs
(d) Consumer delight

72. Research is the process of ________.

(a) Gathering
(b) Recording
(c) Analyzing
(d) All the above

73. Market research is only ______ branch of the marketing information system.

(a) One
(b) Two
(c) Three
(d) Four

74. Which means actual and potential customers?

(a) Marketing research
(b) Marketing segmentation
(c) Market
(d) Business

75. Which is the systematic and intelligent investigator that study of the "Who, What, Where, When, Why and How of actual and potential buyers"?

(a) Marketing segmentation
(b) Marketing research
(c) Marketing information
(d) Marketing inventory

76. From the following which items of study and analysis are not included in market research?

(a) Size of the market
(b) Geographic location of customers
(c) Dealers wants and preferences
(d) Significance of economic indicators

77. Which is the basic resource or input in the management?

(a) Finance
(b) Information
(c) Research
(d) Decision

78. Controlling is the________ subsystem of marketing management.

(a) First
(b) Second
(c) Third
(d) Fourth

79. Which is the lifeblood of planning, directing and controlling any enterprise?

(a) Information
(b) Marketing
(c) Management
(d) Segmentation

80. From the following which are the elements of marketing research?

(a) Intensive study
(b) Scientific Approach
(c) Decision
(d) All the above

81. Research task is purely a ________.

(a) Plan function
(b) Staff function
(c) Control function
(d) Direct function

82. Which are the major components of a special marketing information and analysis centre?

(a) Information gathering
(b) Information processing
(c) Information utilization
(d) All the above

83. In which year the marketing concept was first articulated ___________.

(a) 1942
(b) 1952
(c) 1962
(d) 1972

84. Change means ___________.

(a) Progress
(b) Constant
(c) Analyze
(d) Gathering

85. Since from which year marketing research has recorded fast growth and development?

(a) 1940
(b) 1950
(c) 1960
(d) 1970

86. Marketing environment is described as ___________.

(a) Buyer's market
(b) Retailer's market
(c) Seller's market
(d) Wholesaler's market

87. Which marketers take interest nowadays in using marketing information and research for decision on marketing mix?

(a) Only national
(b) Only multinational
(c) Only international
(d) All of the above

88. Under which marketing approach the marketing research played a minor role?

(a) Project
(b) Sales
(c) Action
(d) decision

89. Marketing research is the poor cousin of___________.

(a) Sales promotion
(b) Personal selling
(c) Advertising
(d) publicity

90. Which agencies have now turned to marketing research?

(a) Selling
(b) Advertising
(c) Manufacturing
(d) None of the above

Answers for MCQ

1.	(d)	**9.**	(b)	**17.**	(d)	**25.**	(d)	**33.**	(c)	**41.**	(a)
2.	(b)	**10.**	(c)	**18.**	(b)	**26.**	(a)	**34.**	(a)	**42.**	(c)
3.	(c)	**11.**	(c)	**19.**	(a)	**27.**	(b)	**35.**	(a)	**43.**	(a)
4.	(d)	**12.**	(b)	**20.**	(b)	**28.**	(c)	**36.**	(c)	**44.**	(b)
5.	(a)	**13.**	(a)	**21.**	(a)	**29.**	(c)	**37.**	(b)	**45.**	(d)
6.	(a)	**14.**	(c)	**22.**	(d)	**30.**	(a)	**38.**	(c)	**46.**	(c)
7.	(c)	**15.**	(d)	**23.**	(d)	**31.**	(a)	**39.**	(d)	**47.**	(d)
8.	(a)	**16.**	(a)	**24.**	(d)	**32.**	(b)	**40.**	(c)	**48.**	(a)

49.	(d)	**56.**	(a)	**63.**	(d)	**70.**	(a)	**77.**	(b)	**84.**	(a)
50.	(b)	**57.**	(b)	**64.**	(d)	**71.**	(b)	**78.**	(d)	**85.**	(c)
51.	(a)	**58.**	(d)	**65.**	(a)	**72.**	(d)	**79.**	(a)	**86.**	(a)
52.	(c)	**59.**	(d)	**66.**	(c)	**73.**	(a)	**80.**	(d)	**87.**	(d)
53.	(d)	**60.**	(b)	**67.**	(b)	**74.**	(c)	**81.**	(b)	**88.**	(b)
54.	(c)	**61.**	(d)	**68.**	(c)	**75.**	(b)	**82.**	(d)	**89.**	(c)
55.	(d)	**62.**	(d)	**69.**	(c)	**76.**	(d)	**83.**	(b)	**90.**	(b)

MATCH THE FOLLOWING

1.	Marketing research	**(a)**	Accounting system
2.	Tactical decisions	**(b)**	Human behaviour
3.	Marketing intelligence	**(c)**	Input-process-output
4.	Internal marketing information	**(d)**	Information about changing conditions in the market
5.	Quantitative research	**(e)**	Short-term activities
6.	Marketing research process	**(f)**	Problems in field of marketing

Answers for Match the Following

1.	(f)	**2.**	(e)	**3.**	(d)	**4.**	(a)	**5.**	(b)	**6.**	(c)

Chapter 8

Marketing Research Process

SUMMARY

The marketing research process involves a round of separate stages of data interpretation, organization and collection. These stages could be considered as a benchmark of market research, but it depends on an organization on how they have encapsulated their strategies to follow this process. Hence, some of the interlinked stages could be conducted repeatedly and some of the stages can also be omitted. Given below is a typical market research process which is depicted stage-wise:

Stage-1: Defining the problem or need: The starting phase is always identifying the reason or problem for which research is to be conducted. This includes collecting of relevant initial information and how this information will affect decision making process. It also includes defining problems after discussing with decision makers of the organization. Once the problem is defined precisely and the need of research is discussed, the further process could be conducted in an efficient manner.

Stage-2: Determining who will do the research: Once the initial stage of defining the problem and the need of research is done, it is important to determine who will do the research and what will be the approaches to resolve these problems. This involves creating a problem solving framework and analytical models after discussing it organization experts. In this sample case studies are created according to the defined framework by enforcing the relevant information and secondary data.

Stage-3: Picking out the appropriate methodology: A specific methodology is entailed by the research professional after identifying the specific needs and exploring the case studies. It may include a combination of specific approaches like telephone survey, web or email survey, one-to-one interviews, secondary research, etc.

Stage-4: Data collection process: This process includes field work and desk work for collecting all relevant data and information. Field work includes interviewing the personals by interacting them face to face by visiting them in homes or offices or arranging group meetings at any preferred place. Desk work includes contacting personals over telephone or via series of emails and web meetings. This could take comparatively more time as compared to the field work. Involving experienced and trained executive for this helps in reducing data collection errors.

Stage-5: Data preparation, tabulation and analysis of results: After the data collecting stage the collected data is edited, corrected, if required and validated. This process is the most important process in the research as the results are generated on the basis of data preparation. So it is required for an organization to verify the authenticity of the collected data and edit or correct it if needed. The final data is then segmented according to the business standards and inserted into the CRM database in a more tabulated form so that search or combination could be made easily.

Stage-6: presentation and report generation: The entire process is properly documented with respect to organizational standards so that it can be referred in future for decision making process or to change or modify any specific processor module. This document contains overall architecture of the project depicting all the processes with the help of tables, graphs and figures to provoke impact and clarity.

Techniques of Marketing Research

1. Observation: Observation is the act of seeing from a distance. As the name suggests, the research is carried out by observation. The respondents are neither contacted nor questioned. But their behavior is observed. In this method, the services of an observer are used. The observer would observe the relevant factors and settings carefully and record the events as they happen. The recording may be done in writing or by some mechanical device, e.g., camera, audio meter, etc. If the happenings are to be recorded manually by writing down what would happen, then observers are to be trained as to how and what to record the events or happenings.

A firm which wants to study buyers' behavior in respect of a particular product may deploy trained observers at strategic retail outlets. They observe the purchase behavior of consumer without making known to them that their behavior is being observed. Conversation held during the purchase and their non-verbal expressions are noted. Later on, the behaviors are analyzed to arrive at conclusions.

The advantages of this method are its objectivity and accurate results. The respondents are not questioned but their behavior is observed. There are all possibilities that a respondent may give a false or biased reply. But there is no chance of deceiving the observer because he would not know that his behavior is being observed. Hence, the observer gets the right clues.

The main limitation of this method is the observer himself. The quality of observation depends on the level of the competence of the observer and his bias. Secondly, all problems cannot be reached by observation method.

2. Survey: Field surveys are commonly used in marketing research to collect primary data from the respondents. This technique intends to secure a broad range of information from the respondents. Surveys can bring out information about socio-economic characteristics of a particular market. They throw light on the knowledge, expectations, beliefs, preferences, satisfaction of consumers. They are useful for conducting research, related to planning product features, advertising copy, advertising media, pricing, planning new products, product modifications, sales promotion, etc. To conduct the survey, first the sample design is to be finalized and questionnaire with appropriate questions has to be prepared. Then sample respondents are contacted and answers are sought to the questions in the questionnaire. The administration of questionnaire to sample respondent is called interview. Based on the structure of the questionnaire interviews are classified into structured interviews, semi-structured interviews and unstructured interviews.

(i) **Structured Interviews:** In structured interviews, the questionnaire will contain specific questions for which the answers are sought. The interviewer just administers the questionnaire and the respondent is supposed to fill the answer. If the respondent is illiterate or not interested in writing the answer, the answers are recorded by the interviewer. The interviewer will not ask any questions other than the questions that are there in the questionnaire nor interferes in the answers.

Structural interviews are conducted when the information is to be collected from a very large sample. Majority of the questions will have multiple choice answers or 'yes' or 'no' type answers. This is what makes the questionnaire structured.

(ii) **Semi-structured Interviews:** In semi-structured interviews, the questionnaire is prepared as in case of structured interviews but the difference lies in the administration of questionnaire. Here, the interviewer will have the flexibility and freedom to begin with any question which suits the circumstance. He may not ask questions as in the questionnaire. He may jump questions and return to them later. He may re-form the questions to make the respondents understand the questions. However, there is always a danger that the interpretations of the questions and answer will differ with the interviewers. There is the need to train the researcher as to conduct the interview and record the same without any bias. Semi-structured interviews can be employed when the sample size is small.

(iii) **Unstructured Interviews:** In this type of interviews the checklist is designed by the interviewer of researcher. The interview is conducted with the help of checklist which would be unstructured. The information is elicited through discussions rather than through questions and answers. It should be remembered in all cases that the questions asked should be simple and clear. Otherwise, respondents would give evasive answers or avoid answering questions. The questions asked should be neither too personal nor offend the feelings of the respondents.

3. Telephonic and Mail Surveys: Surveys may also be conducted over phone or by mail. Under telephonic surveys, the interviewer contacts sample respondents over phone and elicits the answers. This is costly and only few respondents may be covered. Detailed investigation is not possible. Questionnaires are sent to respondents by mail in case of mail survey. First, the address of the respondents is prepared. Printed copy of the questionnaire is posted along with the reply envelope. Gifts and incentives are offered to get the co-operation of the respondents. The success of this method depends on the response of the respondents.

4. Experiments: Normally, scientific experiments are conducted under controlled conditions within the four walls of the laboratory. Such experiments may be useful in developing new products or product modifications. But this cannot be called market research. Experiment in marketing research. Experiment in marketing research would mean exploring the cause and effect relationship in a market situation.

A firm which is interested in knowing the effect of change in price on sales or effect of advertising on sales or effect of change in package on sales, etc., can take up marketing research using experimental method. The cause and effect relationship is studied by selecting a representative market. The changes are introduced into the variables and their effects are studied. Such experiments in a selected market would give small-scale experience which would be useful in determining large-scale action.

Observations, surveys and experimental methods are used both in carrying out quantitative and qualitative researches. But there are techniques used exclusively in qualitative research. These are depth interviews and projective techniques. They are discussed in brief.

5. Depth Interviews: Depth interviews are one of the methods of qualitative research. In this method the questions are administered to respondents in a free and released environment where in the respondents is free to express them without any fear of disapproval. Respondents are encouraged to talk about the subject rather than answering 'Yes' or 'No' to the questions. The relaxed atmosphere can be used creatively by the investigator to explore the hidden motivations and attitudes. An attempt is made to go deep into the mind of the respondent so that the unconscious feelings, needs, fears, conflicts and the like can be unearthed. The whole interview would be in the form of conversation and the respondent is made to talk freely. The job of the interviewer is only to see that the topic of discussion does not go out of track. Depth interviews may be done taking a group of people or a single individual. The conversations/discussions are recorded using tape recorders and analyzed at a later date.

6. Projective Techniques: In order to overcome the limitations of depth interviews wherein respondents may not reveal their true attitudes, feelings and opinions about matters which they consider socially unacceptable, projective techniques have been used by market researchers. Projective techniques are borrowed from clinical psychology which is administered to sample respondents in which respondents are asked and encouraged to reveal their feelings, attitudes, etc., towards a third person or an object. Some of the commonly used projective techniques are word association test, sentence completion test, thematic appreciation test, third person test and balloon test.

FILL IN THE BLANKS

1. Marketing research studies an ________ unit.
2. ________, ________ and ________ are the various constituents of marketing research process.
3. Marketing research is a systematic of ________, ________ and ________ of data.
4. Marketing research is the branch of ________.
5. AMA stands for ________.
6. There is a change from a seller's market to a ________ market.
7. The basic aim of marketing research is to formulate a ________ oriented long-term strategy.
8. For longer firms, market research would facilitate the laying out of ________ and ________ strategies.
9. For smaller and medium firms marketing research can reveal its various ________.
10. In non-profit institutions, marketing research come out with ______ information.
11. ________ information is presently is very much lacking and hampers the growth of non-profit institutions.
12. ________ research gives valuable insight, generates ideas and hypotheses.
13. The major benefits of exploratory research are that is ________ and ________.
14. Descriptive research is concerned with ________ and ________ the frequencies with which things occur.
15. ________ reports are often descriptive.
16. Descriptive research measure market ________, ________ and ________ of consumers in the market place.
17. Causal research is concerned with establishing ________ and ________ relationship and an attempt to explain why things happen.
18. ________ and ________ conditions are the important aspects of causal research.
19. ________ condition means that the caused events cannot occur in the absence of the causative event.
20. ________ condition means that the causative event is all that is needed to bring about the caused event.
21. The main purpose of ________ research is to arrive to a forecast, prediction and some measurement to the researcher.
22. The ultimate target of predictive research is the ________ of the firm.
23. ________ research is used to measure market potential, characteristics of the market and share of markets for a particular brand or company.
24. Marketing research helps to make better ________ decisions.

25. Marketing research uses the techniques of science but it it is not an ________.
26. The marketing research results obtained are not accurate as compared to ________ and ________ science.
27. In India, marketing research is considered to be a ________ activity.
28. ________ and ________ still remain limitations with all types of marketing research.
29. Marketing research requires the application of the ________ approach.
30. Each step in the research process must be ________ and ________.
31. The basic characteristics of the process of marketing research are ________, ________ and ________.
32. Input is a ________.
33. The called data is processed by ________.
34. ________, ________ and ________ operations involved in data processing.
35. Information is ________.
36. The characteristics of good output are it should be ________, ________ and ________.
37. Output should not be ________ but ________.
38. The information is the processed data in the form of ________, ________ and ________.
39. Information is the processed data act as the basis for ________ and ________ decisions.
40. Marketing research process provides ________ to marketing executives.
41. Marketing research process do not provide ________ to marketing executives.
42. The main aim of ________ analysis is to define and analyze the marketing problem to be solved.
43. Research design is a ________ plan.
44. A ________ design is a master plan for the conduct of formal investigation.
45. The ________ plan will concentrate on the selection of sources of information and methods and procedures for gathering data.
46. Under the formal investigation plan, data gathering forms are ________.
47. Questionnaires and other forms are ________, under the formal investigation plan.
48. Under the formal investigation plan, samples for investigation are ________.
49. A research study requires both ________ and ________ data.
50. ________ data must be assembled by the researcher for the first time.
51. ________ data is already available for processing.
52. Primary data is gathered through the use of ________.
53. Collected data must be ________, ________ and ________.
54. Under the marketing research report, the recommendations must be ________, ________ and ________.
55. The style of courting report must be ________ and ________.
56. A small number of items are called as ________.
57. A large number of items are called as ________.
58. ________ is a selection of units from the entire group called the population or universe of interest.
59. ________ plan is a vital element of research design.
60. The sampling plan indicates sampling ________, ________ and ________.
61. A number is drawn at random, usually between ________.
62. Stratified random sample is a sample in which the population is divided into ________.

63. A ______ is a set of questions with or without a blank space for recording answers.

64. The types of questions are ______, ______ and ______.

65. In case of unstructured questions and answers, ______ and ______ have freedom to communicate information.

66. ______ questions are more formalized and the respondent can answer the questions in his or her own words.

67. ______ questions are also called as closed-ended questions.

68. ______, ______ and ______ provides sources of primary data.

69. ______ and ______ sources are the two sources of data for investigation in the marketing researches.

70. Research starts with ______ data.

71. The limitations of secondary data are it must be ______, ______ and ______.

72. Examination of secondary data is the ______ and ______ procedure of research.

73. Entire preliminary investigation is based on ______ data.

74. In secondary data, information relates to ______ period.

75. Primary data is more useful as it gives ______ information.

76. Secondary data is available ______, ______ and ______.

77. The information is recorded on a form known as ______.

78. ______, ______ and ______ are the three alternative ways to communication with the informant under questionnaire method.

79. Higher rate of refusal and lower degree of accuracy are the important weaknesses of the ______ survey.

80. ______ survey is quick and lower at cost.

81. ______ is the act of recognizing and noting facts or occurrences.

82. ______ are not asked in data collection.

83. Respondents may be individual ______, ______ and ______.

84. ______ research enables the researcher to measure small changes in purchases, habits and other activities.

85. Panels are made up of respondents who regularly and routinely report their ______ behaviour.

86. ______ audit of a sample of retailers will point out the measurement of flow of goods at ______ levels.

87. ______ method is an important tool to find out causal relationship.

88. The controlled experiment gives ______ experience.

89. Small-scale experience is useful to determine the ______ action in any branch of marketing mix.

90. Lessons learnt from experimental method can be employed for making the large-scale activity more ______ and ______.

91. ______ method can be applied in testing advertising, sales, products etc.

Answers for Fill in the Blanks

1.	Economic	6.	Buyer's
2.	Consumers; buyers; sellers	7.	Customer
3.	Gathering; recording; analyzing	8.	Planning; corporate
4.	Marketing information system	9.	Weaknesses
5.	American marketing association	10.	Automatic

11.	Automatic	52.	Sampling
12.	Exploratory	53.	Edited; tabulated; analyzed
13.	Less expensive; less time-consuming	54.	Precise; clear-cut; feasible
14.	Measuring; estimating	55.	Interesting; stimulating
15.	Market research	56.	Sample
16.	Size; structure; behaviour	57.	Population
17.	Cause; effect	58.	Sample
18.	Necessary; sufficient	59.	Sampling
19.	Necessary	60.	Unit; size; procedure
20.	Sufficient	61.	1 to 10
21.	Predictive	62.	Group
22.	Future sales level	63.	Questionnaire
23.	Marketing	64.	Structured; semi-structured; unstructured
24.	Advertising	65.	Investigator; respondent
25.	Exact science	66.	Semi-structured
26.	Physical; chemical	67.	Structured
27.	Wasteful	68.	Observation; survey; experiments
28.	Time, money	69.	Internal; external
29.	System	70.	Internal
30.	Carefully planned; effectively coordinated	71.	Sufficiently current; reliable; impartial
31.	Input; process; output	72.	Simplest; earliest
32.	Data	73.	Secondary
33.	Researchers	74.	Past
34.	Editing; classification; analysis	75.	Latest
35.	Power	76.	Easily; quickly; cheaply
36.	Timely; sufficient; reliable	77.	Questionnaire
37.	Data; information	78.	Mail; telephone; personal interview
38.	Interpretations; inferences; conclusions	79.	Mail
39.	Sound; prompt	80.	Phone
40.	Information	81.	Observation
41.	Data	82.	Questions
42.	Situation	83.	Consumers; retailers; wholesalers
43.	Master	84.	Panel
44.	Research	85.	Buying
45.	Formal investigation	86.	Shop; retail
46.	Prepared	87.	Experimental
47.	Tested	88.	Small-scale
48.	Planned	89.	Large-scale
49.	Primary; secondary	90.	Effective; profitable
50.	Primary	91.	Experimental
51.	Secondary		

TRUE / FALSE

1. Marketing research studies a social unit. (True / False)
2. The various constituents of marketing research process are consumers, buyers and sellers. (True / False)
3. Marketing research is a systematic of gathering, recording and analyzing data. (True / False)
4. Marketing research is the branch of marketing information. (True / False)
5. AMA stands for American Marketing Accuracy. (True / False)
6. There is a change of area from a seller's market to a buyer's market. (True / False)
7. The basic aim of marketing research is to formulate a future-oriented long-term strategy. (True / False)
8. For longer firms, market research would facilitate the laying out of planning and corporate strategies. (True / False)
9. Marketing research can reveal its various weaknesses, for small and medium firms. (True / False)
10. In non-profit institutions, marketing research come out with economic information. (True / False)
11. Automatic information is presently very much lacking and hampers the growth of non-profit institutions. (True / False)
12. Causal research gives valuable insight, generates ideas and hypotheses. (True / False)
13. Exploratory research major benefit is that is it less expensive and less time-consuming. (True / False)
14. Descriptive research is concerned with measuring and estimating the frequencies with which things occur. (True / False)
15. Market information reports are often descriptive. (True / False)
16. Descriptive research measure only market size and structure in the market place. (True / False)
17. Causal research is concerned with establishing cause and effect relationship and an attempt to explain why things happen. (True / False)
18. Necessary and sufficient condition is the important aspects of causal research. (True / False)
19. A necessary condition means that the caused events can occur in the absence of the causative event. (True / False)
20. Limited condition means that the causative event is all the is needed to bring about the caused event. (True / False)
21. The main purpose of predictive research is to arrive to a forecast, prediction and some measurement to the researcher. (True / False)
22. Future project level is the ultimate target of the firm, under predictive research. (True / False)
23. Marketing research is used to measure only market potential. (True / False)
24. Marketing research helps to make better advertising decisions. (True / False)
25. Marketing research uses the techniques of science but it it is an exact science. (True / False)
26. The results obtained by marketing research are not accurate as compared to physical and chemical science. (True / False)
27. Marketing research is considered to be a wasteful activity in India. (True / False)
28. Buyers and sellers still remain the main limitations with all types of marketing research. (True / False)

29. Marketing research requires the application of commodity approach. (True / False)

30. Each step in the research process must be carefully planned and effectively co-ordinated. (True / False)

31. Input is the only basic characteristics of the process of marketing research. (True / False)

32. Input is a data. (True / False)

33. The collected data is processed by executives. (True / False)

34. In data processing the operations involved are editing, classification and analysis. (True / False)

35. Information is power. (True / False)

36. The characteristics of good output is that it should be timely, sufficient and reliable. (True / False)

37. Output should not be information but data. (True / False)

38. Information is the processed data in the form of interpretations, inferences and conclusions. (True / False)

39. Information is the processed data act as the basis for sound and prompt decisions. (True / False)

40. Marketing research process provides data to marketing executives. (True / False)

41. Market is a place, area and demand concept. (True / False)

42. To determine the proper sample size is the main aim of situation analysis. (True / False)

43. Research design is a master plan. (True / False)

44. A research design is a master plan for conduct of informal investigation. (True / False)

45. The formal investigation plan concentrate on the selection of sources of information and methods and procedures for gathering data. (True / False)

46. Under formal investigation plan, data gathering forms are planned. (True / False)

47. Under formal investigation plan, questionnaires and other forms are tested. (True / False)

48. Under formal investigation plan, samples for investigation are prepared.(True / False)

49. A research study requires both primary and secondary data. (True / False)

50. Internal data must be assembled by the researcher for the first time. (True / False)

51. Secondary data is already available for processing. (True / False)

52. Primary data is gathered through the use of distributing. (True / False)

53. Collected data must be edited, tabulated and analyzed. (True / False)

54. Under the marketing research report, the recommendations must be precise, clear-cut and feasible. (True / False)

55. Experimental method can be applied in testing advertising, sales, products, etc. (True / False)

56. A small number of items are called samples. (True / False)

57. A large number of items are called population. (True / False)

58. Area is a selection of units from the entire group called the population or universe of interest. (True / False)

59. Sampling plan is a vital element of research design. (True / False)

60. The sampling media indicate sampling unit, size and procedure. (True / False)

61. A number is drawn at random, usually between 0 to 10. (True / False)

62. Stratified random sample is a sample in which the population is divided into groups. (True / False)

63. A questionnaire is a set of questions with or without a blank space for recording answers. (True / False)

64. Structured and Unstructured questions are the two types of questions. (True / False)

65. Investigator and respondent have freedom to communicate information, in the case of unstructured questions. (True / False)

66. Unstructured questions are more formalized and the respondent can answer the questions in his or her own words. (True / False)

67. Structured questions are also called as closed-ended questions. (True / False)

68. Observation, survey and experiments provide sources of primary data. (True / False)

69. Formal and informal sources are the two sources of data for investigation in the marketing researchers. (True / False)

70. Research starts with internal data. (True / False)

71. The limitation of secondary data is that it must be accurate, reliable and impartial. (True / False)

72. Primary data of examination is the simplest and easiest procedure of research. (True / False)

73. Entire preliminary investigation is based on secondary data. (True / False)

74. In primary data, information relates to past period. (True / False)

75. Primary data is more useful as it gives latest information. (True / False)

76. Secondary data is available easily, cheaply and quickly. (True / False)

77. The information is recorded on a form known as records. (True / False)

78. Through mail or post office, telephone and personal interview are the three alternative ways to communicate with the information under questionnaire method. (True / False)

79. Higher rate of refusal and lower degree of accuracy are the important weaknesses of the mail survey. (True / False)

80. Mail survey is quick and lower at cost. (True / False)

81. Observation is the act of recognizing and noting facts or occurrences. (True / False)

82. In data collection no questions are asked. (True / False)

83. Respondents may be only consumers. (True / False)

84. Panel research enables researcher to measure small change in purchases, habits and other activities. (True / False)

85. Panels are made up of respondents who regularly and routinely report their selling behaviour. (True / False)

86. Shop audit of a sample of retailers will point out the measurement of flow of goods at retail levels. (True / False)

87. Experimental method is an important tool to find out causal relationship. (True / False)

88. The controlled experiment gives large-scale experience. (True / False)

89. Small-scale experience is useful to determine the large-scale action in any branch of the marketing mix. (True / False)

90. Lessons learnt from experimental method can be employed for making the small-scale activity more effective and profitable. (True / False)

Answers for True / False

1.	False	3.	True	5.	False	7.	False	9.	True
2.	True	4.	False	6.	True	8.	True	10.	False

11.	False	27.	True	43.	True	59.	True	75.	True
12.	False	28.	False	44.	False	60.	False	76.	True
13.	True	29.	False	45.	True	61.	False	77.	False
14.	True	30.	True	46.	False	62.	True	78.	True
15.	False	31.	False	47.	True	63.	True	79.	True
16.	False	32.	True	48.	False	64.	False	80.	False
17.	True	33.	False	49.	True	65.	True	81.	True
18.	True	34.	True	50.	False	66.	False	82.	True
19.	False	35.	True	51.	True	67.	True	83.	False
20.	False	36.	True	52.	False	68.	True	84.	True
21.	True	37.	False	53.	True	69.	False	85.	False
22.	False	38.	True	54.	True	70.	True	86.	True
23.	False	39.	True	55.	True	71.	True	87.	True
24.	True	40.	False	56.	True	72.	False	88.	False
25.	False	41.	True	57.	True	73.	True	89.	True
26.	True	42.	False	58.	False	74.	False	90.	False

MULTIPLE CHOICE QUESTIONS

1. Marketing research studies an ________.

(a) Economic unit
(b) Social unit
(c) Marketing unit
(d) Research unit

2. What are the various constituents of marketing research process?

(a) Consumers
(b) Buyers
(c) Sellers
(d) All the above

3. Marketing research is a systematic of ________.

(a) Gathering of data
(b) Recording of data
(c) Analyzing of data
(d) All the above

4. Marketing research is a systematic of ________.

(a) Gathering of data
(b) Recording of data
(c) Analyzing of data
(d) All the above

5. AMA stands for ________.

(a) American Mathematical Accuracy
(b) American Marketing and Accuracy
(c) American Marketing Association
(d) American Marketing Accuracy

6. There is a change of area from a seller's market to a ________.

(a) Competitive market
(b) Buyer's market
(c) Trend market
(d) Public market

7. The basic aim of marketing research is ________.

(a) To formulate a customer-oriented long-term strategy
(b) To identify and define the problem including causes

(c) To suggest reasonable and profitable alternative courses of action
(d) To test the feasibility of alternative course of action.

8. For which firms, market research would facilitate the laying out of planning and corporate strategies?
(a) Larger firms
(b) Small firms
(c) Medium firms
(d) None of the above

9. For small and medium firms, marketing research can reveal it's various ______.
(a) Strengths
(b) Weaknesses
(c) Plans
(d) Information

10. In non-profit institutions marketing research come out with what information?
(a) Marketing
(b) Economic
(c) Automatic
(d) Social

11. Which information is presently very much lacking and hampers the growth of non-profit institutions?
(a) Marketing
(b) Economic
(c) Automatic
(d) social

12. Exploratory research gives ______.
(a) Valuable insight
(b) Generates ideas
(c) Hypotheses
(d) All the above

13. The major benefit of exploratory research is that it is ______.
(a) Less expensive
(b) less time-consuming
(c) Both a and b
(d) None of the above

14. Which research is concerned with measuring and estimating the frequencies with which things occur?
(a) Exploratory
(b) Descriptive
(c) Casual
(d) Predictive

15. Market research reports are often ______.
(a) Exploratory
(b) Descriptive
(c) Causal
(d) predictive

16. In the market place what are measures done under descriptive research?
(a) Market size and structure
(b) The behaviour of consumers
(c) The attitudes
(d) All the above

17. Which research is concerned with establishing cause and effect relationship and an attempt to explain why things happen?
(a) Exploratory
(b) Descriptive
(c) Causal
(d) Predictive

18. The important aspects of causal research ______.
(a) Necessary condition
(b) Sufficient condition
(c) Both a and b
(d) None of the above

19. Which condition means that the caused events cannot occur in the absence of the causative event?
(a) Necessary
(b) Sufficient

(c) Limited
(d) Extra

20. Which condition means that the causative event is all that is needed to bring about the caused event?

(a) Necessary
(b) Sufficient
(c) Limited
(d) Extra

21. The main purpose of predictive research is ________.

(a) To arrive at a forecast
(b) To arrive at a prediction
(c) To arrive at a some measurement to the researcher
(d) All the above

22. What is the ultimate target of the firm, under predictive research?

(a) Future-oriented level
(b) Future project level
(c) Future sales level
(d) Future marketing level

23. Marketing research is used ________.

(a) To measure market potential
(b) To measure characteristics of the market
(c) To measure share of markets for a particular brand or company
(d) All the above

24. Marketing research helps to make better ________.

(a) Advertising decisions
(b) Sales decisions
(c) Marketing decisions
(d) Brand decisions

25. Which research uses the techniques of science but it itself is not an exact science?

(a) Causal
(b) Marketing
(c) Exploratory
(d) Descriptive

26. The results obtained by marketing research are not accurate as compared to ________.

(a) Physical science
(b) Chemical science
(c) Both a and b
(d) None of the above

27. In India, marketing research is considered to be a ________.

(a) Useful activity
(b) Necessary activity
(c) Wasteful activity
(d) None of the above

28. Which still remain limitations with all types of marketing research?

(a) Time
(b) Money
(c) Both a and b
(d) None of the above

29. Marketing research requires the application of the ________.

(a) System approach
(b) Commodity approach
(c) Functional approach
(d) Institutional approach

30. What must be in each step in the research process?

(a) Carefully planned
(b) Effectively coordinated
(c) Both a and b
(d) None of the above

31. What are the basic characteristics of the process of marketing research?

(a) Input
(b) Process
(c) Output
(d) All the above

32. Input is ________.

(a) Progress
(b) Data
(c) Unit
(d) Source

33. The collected data is processed by ________.

(a) Researchers
(b) Marketers
(c) Managers
(d) Executives

34. What are the operations involved in data processing?

(a) Editing
(b) Classification
(c) Analysis
(d) All the above

35. Information is ________.

(a) Efforts
(b) Loyal
(c) Power
(d) Energy

36. What are the characteristics of good output?

(a) It should be timely
(b) It should be sufficient
(c) It should be reliable
(d) All the above

37. Output should not be ________.

(a) Data
(b) Information
(c) Investigation
(d) Sufficient

38. In what form us the information a processed data?

(a) Interpretations
(b) Inferences
(c) Conclusions
(d) All the above

39. Information is the processed data which act as the basis for ________.

(a) Sound decisions
(b) Prompt decisions
(c) Both a and b
(d) None of the above

40. What does marketing research process provides to marketing executives?

(a) Data
(b) Information
(c) Source
(d) Unit

41. What does marketing research process do not provides to marketing executives?

(a) Data
(b) Information
(c) Source
(d) Unit

42. The main aim of situation analysis is ________.

(a) To formulate a customer-oriented long-term strategy
(b) To define and analyses the marketing problem to be solved
(c) To determine the proper sample size
(d) To analyze objectively the data collected

43. Which design is a master plan?

(a) Product
(b) Marketing
(c) Research
(d) Packing

44. A research design is a master plan for the conduct of ________.

(a) Formal investigation
(b) Informal investigation
(c) External investigation
(d) Internal investigation

45. The formal investigation plan will concentrate on ________.

(a) The selection of sources of information
(b) The selection of methods and procedures
(c) Both a and b
(d) None of the above

46. Under formal investigation plan, data gathering forms are ________.

(a) Tested
(b) Prepared
(c) Planned
(d) Analyzed

47. Under formal investigation plan, questionnaires and other forms are ________.

(a) Tested
(b) prepared
(c) Planned
(d) Analyzed

48. Under formal investigation plan, samples for investigation are ________.

(a) Tested
(b) Prepared
(c) Planned
(d) Analyzed

49. A research study require ________.

(a) Primary data
(b) Secondary data
(c) Both a and b
(d) None of the above

50. Which data must be assembled by the researcher for the first time?

(a) Primary data
(b) Secondary data
(c) Internal data
(d) External data

51. Which data is already available for processing?

(a) Primary data
(b) Secondary data
(c) Internal data
(d) External data

52. Primary data is gathered through the use of ________.

(a) Advertising
(b) Sampling
(c) Labeling
(d) Distributing

53. Collected data must be ________.

(a) Edited
(b) Tabulated
(c) Analyzed
(d) All the above

54. Under the marketing research report, the recommendations must be ________.

(a) Precise
(b) Clear-cut
(c) Feasible
(d) All the above

55. The style of courting report must be ________.

(a) Interesting
(b) Stimulating
(c) Both a and b
(d) None of the above

56. A small number of items are called as ________.

(a) Sample
(b) Units
(c) Size
(d) Area

57. A large number of items are called as

(a) Population
(b) Area
(c) Size
(d) Unit

58. Which is a selection of units from the entire group called the population or universe of interest?

(a) Random
(b) Sample
(c) Size
(d) Area

59. Which plan is a vital element of research design?

(a) Sampling
(b) Formal
(c) Master
(d) Marketing

60. The sampling plan indicate ________.

(a) Sampling unit
(b) Sampling size
(c) Sampling procedure
(d) All the above

61. A number is drawn at random, usually between ________.

(a) 0 to 10
(b) 1 to 10
(c) 0 to 9
(d) 1 to 9

62. Stratified random sample is a sample in which the population is divided into ________.

(a) Groups
(b) Populations
(c) Units
(d) Size

63. A questionnaire is a set of questions with or without a blank space for ________.

(a) Recording answers
(b) Analyzing answers
(c) Collecting answers
(d) None of the above

64. What are the types of questions?

(a) Structured questions
(b) Sem-structured questions
(c) Instructed questions
(d) All the above

65. In case of instructed questions and answers, who have freedom to communicate information ________.

(a) Investigator
(b) Respondent
(c) Both a and b
(d) None of the above

66. Which questions are more formalized and the respondent can answer the questions in his or her own words?

(a) Structured
(b) Semi-structured
(c) Unstructured
(d) None of the above

67. Which questions are also called as closed-ended questions?

(a) Structured
(b) Semi-structured
(c) Unstructured
(d) None of the above

68. What provides sources of primary data?

(a) Observation
(b) Survey
(c) Experiments
(d) All the above

69. What are the sources of data for investigation in the marketing researchers?

(a) Internal sources
(b) External data
(c) Both a and b
(d) None of the above

70. With which data the research starts?

(a) Internal data
(b) External data
(c) Formal data
(d) Informal data

71. The limitations of secondary data are ________.

(a) It must be sufficiently current
(b) It must be relevant and valid
(c) It must be impartial
(d) All the above

72. Which data of Examination is the simplest and easiest procedure research?

(a) Primary
(b) Secondary
(c) Internal
(d) External

73. Entire preliminary investigation is based on ________.

(a) Primary data
(b) Secondary data
(c) Internal data
(d) External data

74. In secondary data, information relates to ________.

(a) Past period
(b) Present period
(c) Future period
(d) None of the above

75. Primary data is more useful as it gives ________.

(a) Past information
(b) Latest information
(c) Future period
(d) None of the above

76. Secondary data is available ________.

(a) Easily
(b) quickly
(c) Cheaply
(d) All the above

77. The information is recorded on a form known as ________.

(a) Sampling
(b) Records
(c) Questionnaire
(d) Collection

78. In the questionnaire method, communication with the informant alternative ways through ________.

(a) Mail or post office
(b) Telephone
(c) Personal interview
(d) All the above

79. The important weakness of the mail survey is ________.

(a) Higher rate of refusal
(b) Both a and b
(c) Lower degree of accuracy
(d) None of the above

80. Which survey can be quick and at a lower cost?

(a) Mail
(b) Post
(c) Phone
(d) Personal interview

81. Which is the act of recognizing and noting facts or occurrences?

(a) Observation
(b) Experiment
(c) Survey
(d) Panel research

82. No questions are asked in ________.

(a) Data process
(b) Data collection
(c) Data analyses
(d) Data progress

83. Respondents may be individual ________.

(a) Consumers
(b) Retailers
(c) Wholesalers
(d) All the above

84. Which research enables researcher to measure small change in purchases, habits and other activities?

(a) Panel
(b) Marketing
(c) Managerial
(d) Dealer panel

85. Panels are made up of respondents who regularly and routinely report their ______.

(a) Selling behaviour
(b) Buying behaviour
(c) Sellers behaviour
(d) Buyers behaviour

86. Which audit of a sample of retailers will point out the measurement of flow of goods at retail levels?

(a) Shop
(b) Consumer
(c) Purchase
(d) Selling

87. Which method is an important tool to find out causal relationship?

(a) Survey
(b) Observation
(c) Experimental
(d) Interview

88. What experience does the controlled experiment gives?

(a) Large-scale
(b) Small-scale
(c) Medium-scale
(d) None of the above

89. In any branch of the marketing mix, small-scale experience is useful to determine the ________.

(a) Large-scale action
(b) Small-scale action
(c) Medium-scale action
(d) All the above

90. Lessons learnt from experimental method can be employed for making the large-scale activity more ________.

(a) Effective
(b) Profitable
(c) Both a and b
(d) None of the above

Answers for MCQ

1.	(a)	16.	(d)	31.	(d)	46.	(b)	61.	(b)	76.	(d)
2.	(d)	17.	(c)	32.	(b)	47.	(a)	62.	(a)	77.	(c)
3.	(d)	18.	(c)	33.	(a)	48.	(c)	63.	(a)	78.	(d)
4.	(d)	19.	(a)	34.	(d)	49.	(a)	64.	(d)	79.	(c)
5.	(c)	20.	(b)	35.	(d)	50.	(a)	65.	(c)	80.	(c)
6.	(b)	21.	(d)	36.	(d)	51.	(b)	66.	(b)	81.	(a)
7.	(a)	22.	(c)	37.	(a)	52.	(b)	67.	(a)	82.	(b)
8.	(a)	23.	(d)	38.	(d)	53.	(d)	68.	(d)	83.	(d)
9.	(b)	24.	(a)	39.	(c)	54.	(d)	69.	(c)	84.	(a)
10.	(c)	25.	(b)	40.	(b)	55.	(c)	70.	(a)	85.	(b)
11.	(c)	26.	(c)	41.	(a)	56.	(a)	71.	(d)	86.	(a)
12.	(d)	27.	(c)	42.	(b)	57.	(a)	72.	(b)	87.	(c)
13.	(c)	28.	(c)	43.	(c)	58.	(b)	73.	(b)	88.	(b)
14.	(b)	29.	(a)	44.	(a)	59.	(a)	74.	(a)	89.	(a)
15.	(b)	30.	(c)	45.	(c)	60.	(d)	75.	(b)	90.	(c)

MATCH THE FOLLOWING

1.	Consumer research	(a)	Not an exact science
2.	Primary data	(b)	Personal interview
3.	Field survey	(c)	Consumer needs, motives and buying behaviour
4.	Shop audit	(d)	Data from original sources
5.	Exploratory research	(e)	Retailer information
6.	Marketing research	(f)	Identify nature of problems

Answers for Match the Following

1.	(c)	2.	(d)	3.	(b)	4.	(e)	5.	(f)	6.	(a)

Chapter 9

Marketing Planning/Strategy

SUMMARY

Marketing planning is the process of analyzing one or more potentially interesting marketplace in order to determine how a business can optimally compete in them. The market planning process typically results in a marketing strategy that can be used to enhance sales for the business producing it.

Marketing planning process is a logical sequence and series of activities leading to the setting of strategic planning objectives for an enterprise, and the formulation of strategic plans for achieving them. It involves creating a plan for an organization's marketing activities. It may pertain to a specific product or the overall marketing strategy of an organization. It is derived from the organization's overall business strategy.

A marketing plan is a business document written for the purpose of describing the current market position of a business and its marketing strategy for the period covered by the marketing plan. Marketing plans usually have a life of one to five years.

Purpose of a Marketing Plan

The purpose of creating a marketing plan is to clearly show what steps will be undertaken to achieve the business' marketing objectives. While some small business owners include their marketing plan as part of their overall business plan, if a business owner follows the recommended SBA format, parts of the marketing plan will be included in the various areas of the business plan. As an alternative, the marketing plan may be attached in its entirety as an appendix to a business plan.

A typical small business marketing plan might include a description of its competitors, the demand for the product or service, and the strengths and weaknesses from a market standpoint of both the business and its competitors. Description of the product or services including special features. Marketing budget includes the advertising and promotional plan. Description of the business location includes advantages and disadvantages for marketing.

Market segmentation specializing in specific niche markets or, if mass marketing, how marketing strategy might differ between different segments, such as age groups. Like a business plan, a marketing plan is an important document that needs to be updated on a regular basis. Even five year marketing plans should be revisited periodically at least once each year - to address changes in market conditions, demands, pricing issues, etc.

Behind the corporate objectives, which in themselves offer the main context for the marketing plan, will lay the "corporate mission," which in turn provides the context for these corporate objectives. In a sales-oriented organization, the marketing planning function designs incentive pay plans to not only motivate and reward frontline staff fairly but also to align marketing activities with corporate mission. The marketing plan basically aims to make the business provide the solution with the awareness with the expected customers.

Marketing is the process of developing and implementing a plan to identify, anticipate and satisfy consumer demand, in such a way as to make a profit. The two main elements of this plan are market research to identify and anticipate customer requirements and the planning of an appropriate marketing mix to meet these requirements. Market research involves gathering and recording information about consumers, market, product, and the competition in an organized way. The information is then analyzed and used to form marketing decisions.

Steps for Preparing Marketing Plan

Step-1: The Executive Summary: A high-level summary of the marketing plan as a whole, and a paradox on paper: this is the last section that you should write, but the first section that should be in the finished report. It's best to keep the Executive Summary as short and sweet as possible — just a couple of sentences to sum everything up. While writing it, imagine that you're going to present this summary "elevator pitch" style. Once you've finished it, read it out loud. If it takes you longer than ten seconds to read it all, it probably needs to be simplified even further.

Step-2: The Challenge: This section should contain a brief description of the product(s) and/or product line(s) that your company offers. With each description, include goals that you want to set for each product and product line (sales figures, strategic and company-wide goals, etc.). Keep the number and complexity of your goals at a maximum of three per product/product line, and remember that they need to be concise, measurable, and moderately easy to achieve.

Step-3: Situation Analysis: This section contains a snapshot of your company, your customer base, and your market at large.

Step-4: Market Segmentation: Each market has its own different segments. Understanding the relevant segments for your product(s) in your market is important, for they allow you to adjust your "marketing mix" (the "Four Ps" discussed later) to better adapt to the different needs of each segment. Segments should be measurable, accessible, different from other segments in response to a marketing mix, durable (not constantly changing), substantially large enough to produce a profit, and homogeneous.

Step-5: Alternative Marketing Strategies: Write down details about any alternatives that you and your team considered before arriving at your current strategy. These may include eliminating a particular product or line, changing the price point of a product or line, etc.

Step-6: Selected Marketing Strategy: Explain the strategy that you and your team have developed and agreed upon. Why did you choose this strategy? Why do you feel that it's the best possible strategy for the near future? Once that's on paper, put your "Four Ps" down for each product.

Step-7: Short and Long-term Projections: This section should include forecasts of revenues and expenses, your break-even analysis, and any changes or adjustments that you predict you'll need to make in the future.

Step-8: The Conclusion: This is an expanded version of your Executive Summary. You should include all specific numbers (projected costs, revenues, profits, etc.).

Marketing strategy is an organization's strategy that combines all of its marketing goals into one comprehensive plan. A good marketing strategy should be drawn from market research and focus on the right product mix in order to achieve the maximum profit potential and sustain the business. The marketing strategy is the foundation of a marketing plan.

The benefits of a planned marketing strategy are numerous. Business owners often rely solely on their intuition to make business decisions. While this informal knowledge is important in the decision making process, it may not provide you with all the facts you need to achieve marketing results. A marketing strategy will help you in defining business goals and develop activities to achieve them.

Relationship marketing is a strategy designed to foster customer loyalty, interaction and long-term engagement. This customer relationship management (CRM) approach focuses more on customer retention than customer acquisition.

Relationship marketing is designed to develop strong connections with customers by providing them with information directly suited to their needs and interests and by promoting open communication. This approach often results in increased word-of-mouth activity, repeat business and a willingness on the customer's part to provide information to the organization.

Relationship marketing contrasts with transactional marketing, an approach that focuses on increasing the number of individual sales. Most organizations combine elements of both relationship and transaction marketing strategies.

Many companies focus on building relationships with their customers instead of always exclusively trying to sell them something (transactional marketing). Customers who love your brand more will also spend more money with your brand. Many traditional retailers have found this to be true. Walgreens has seen that customers who buy from all of their purchasing channels (store, web, mobile, etc.) buy up to six times more than the average customer that only buys in their store.

Transactional marketing is a business scheme that centres on single, point of sale transactions. It places prominence on getting the customer to purchase a certain product and walk away. This way, there is maximization of the efficiency and volume of individual sales.

Driving sales can be challenging, especially for retailers that have to consistently sell products in high volume to consumers. In order to stay with the demands of investors, retailers have to encourage consumers to buy using coupons, discounts, liquidations, and sales events. High volume big-box retailers like Target are constantly running promotional events in order to get interested consumers into their stores.

Scarcity in marketing means to use the fear of shortage to sell more. In some markets it's important to control how much product is available at one time. In many cases this is done because of the difficulty of acquiring raw materials or higher quality of the product. A company may choose to make their products accessible to only a few customers. Rolls-Royce's release of their Chinese edition car called Phantom sold quickly. While the cost of the car was higher than most cars the scarcity drove the desire and the price.

Word-of-mouth Marketing is the passing of information from person to person by oral communication. Customers are very excited to share with the world the brands they love. Many consumers find meaning in sharing stories of their favorite products and services. Word-of-mouth is one of the ancient ways people learned about what to purchase. Modern marketers have learned how to create authentic word-of-mouth for their companies and the products they represent.

Call to Action (CTA) Marketing is a part of inbound marketing used on websites in the form of a banner, text or graphic, where it is meant to prompt a person to click it and move into the conversion funnel, that is, from searching to navigating an online store to converting it to a sale.

Viral marketing is a marketing strategy that focuses on spreading information and opinions about a product or service from person to person, especially by using unconventional means such as the Internet or e-mail. Cult Brand marketers are constantly creating new business ideas that keep their products in the heart and minds of the global consumer. Each time a new product is created, customers have to be given a reason to dream about their future purchase. Sometimes marketers of Cult Brands hit on something so great that people can't help but share with others. Getting your customers talking about your products and services is very important to growing awareness for your business.

FILL IN THE BLANKS

1. In a customer-centered enterprise, ______ management is called upon to assess marketing opportunity.
2. The _______ has to motivate the personnel, evaluate and adjust marketing effort to achieve the set goals.
3. Planning execution-control is an ________ process.
4. ________ provides the basis for integrated marketing strategy.
5. ________ input provides situation analysis which answers the questions.
6. Setting mission and objectives is the first step in ________.
7. Planning is the first management function to be performed in the process of _______.
8. A business enterprise is an ________, ________ and ________ system living in a dynamic environment.
9. Situation analysis reveals the ________ and ________ factors.
10. ________ and ________ are the twin management functions acting as the two sides of the same coin.
11. ________, ________, ________ is a continuing cycle and these functions are difficult to separate.
12. Greater emphasis on ecology and human resources are the significant reasons accounting for the growing importance and popularity of business ________.
13. _______ approach to ______ management demands synthesis, coordinates and integrates.
14. The systems approach views a business enterprise as a _______ system of business operating in a dynamic environment.
15. The customer-citizen ________, ________ and ______ are dynamic and ever changing.
16. ________, ________ and _______ customer needs alone can assure profitable growth of any business.
17. ________ needs are the probable market opportunities.
18. ________ executives have to evolve marketing strategies to overcome competition in the market.
19. ________ is a key element in a company's marketing opportunity.
20. ________ planning is always based on the assessment of competition.
21. Customer needs are also influenced by ________, ________, ________ and ________ environment.
22. ________ are subject to deterioration.
23. Availability of resources clearly limits the range of ________ and ________.
24. IBP stands for ________.
25. ________ opportunities are seen in terms of unsatisfied customer needs.
26. ________ planning of an organization is planning for the organization's revenue earning activities.
27. The first step in the marketing planning process is setting down marketing ________ and ________.
28. In marketing planning process, the objectives must be the _______ objectives.
29. The marketing planning process can be fixed interims of ________.
30. The second step in the marketing planning process is designing the ________.
31. In ________ system, a company has to design/define each function with its contribution.
32. The third step in the marketing planning process is to develop separate ________, ________ and ________.

33. The fourth step is drawing of detailed plans for each function for a ________ period under marketing planning process.

34. The fifth step in marketing planning process is merging the marketing plans into ________.

35. The fourth step in marketing planning process is helpful in defining ________, ________ and ________.

36. Marketing planning is indispensable in the field of ________.

37. Without planning, ________ become random in nature.

38. Without planning, ________ become meaningless.

39. Marketing planning helps in ________, ________ and ________.

40. ________ involves the choice of a general type of plan.

41. The objectives emphasis the state of ________ there.

42. The strategy emphasis the process of ________ there.

43. Objectives prescribe ________.

44. To do the ________ and ________ is the major broad objectives of an enterprise.

45. ________ planning reflects the first objective, i.e., to do the right thing.

46. ________ planning underscores the second objectives, i.e., to do things right.

47. The future ________ opportunities point to what a company might do.

48. The distinctive corporate ________ and ________ will point out what a company can do.

49. ________ and ________ will indicate what a company wants to do.

50. ________ responsibility will reflect what a company should do.

51. The objectives must be challenging but ________, ________ and ________ to the executives and their subordinates.

52. Strategy acts as a bridge between our ________ and ________ plans.

53. ________ strategies are simultaneously used.

54. USP stands for ________.

55. Strategy specifies ________ and ________ of business opportunities.

56. Evaluation of opportunities under customer-oriented business planning will be made first by ________ management.

57. The evaluation will be primarily based upon ________, ________ and ________.

58. The ________ management put the final stamp of its decision when the functional specialists have screened and approved the exploitation of business opportunity.

59. SWOT stands for ________.

60. ________ are considered as challenges to be met by strategic planning.

61. Marketing ________ and ________ enables us to scan external environment.

62. Sales audit and cost analysis enable to study ________ environment.

63. ________ answers the question, "what is our business?"

64. ________ answers the question, "what do we want to achieve?"

65. SBU stands for ________.

66. The mission points out the needs to be ________.

67. The objectives indicate ________ standards.

68. Strategic business unit in the corporation has more than ________ divisions.

69. Strategic business unit in reality has ________ divisions.

70. The strategic company planning is done by the _______ management for the whole enterprise.

71. _______ analysis is the starting point in all planning activities.

72. In a new company, segmentation enables the company to identify _______ markets.

73. The marketing plan is built around the four elements of the _______.

74. Annual marketing plan is a short-term marketing plan, covering for _______ year.

75. The main aim strategy is to cope with _______.

76. _______ successfully defines their markets and sub-markets in terms of product functions and benefits.

77. Indian industrialists are concerned about the _______.

78. Marketing mix covers the _______.

79. Promotion covers _______, _______, _______ and _______.

80. _______ includes channels, transport, warehousing and investory control of marketing mix elements.

81. A company can achieve its marketing objectives by _______ and _______ the marketing mix programme.

82. Internal limitations indicate the firm's _______.

83. _______ of the company are the means (inputs).

84. Company objectives are the _______ (output).

85. _______ are determined on the basis of self-analysis of our strengths and weaknesses.

86. External environmental factors are uncontrollable by _______ and _______.

87. The environmental factors reveal _______ and _______.

88. _______ is a marketing mix element which is designed to match customer need.

89. _______ is a marketing mix element which is fixed in terms of customer segments aimed at.

90. Marketing strategy starts with _______ objectives.

91. Channel decisions and physical distribution plan are the components of _______ strategy.

92. Promotion strategy aims at _______, _______ and _______ against rivals.

93. Pricing, strategy involves _______ decisions.

94. Company image will be bright if marketers adopt and practice the _______ responsible marketing policies.

95. _______ consists of two main steps selecting the target market and assembling of marketing mix.

96. JIT stands for _______.

97. Planning for Just-in-time (JIT) management concept is given by _______ country.

98. _______ and _______ must rotate around people-inside customers and outside customers.

99. _______ is a marketing strategy that focuses on spreading information and opinions about a product or service from person to person.

100. CRM approach focuses more on customer retention than customer _______.

Answers for Fill in the Blanks

1.	Marketing	7.	Management
2.	Leadership	8.	Open; adaptive; socio-economic
3.	On going	9.	Non-controllable; changing
4.	Planning	10.	Planning; organizing
5.	Data	11.	Planning; action; control
6.	Planning	12.	Planning

13.	Systems; business	**52.**	Objectives; action
14.	Total integrated	**53.**	Two or three
15.	Needs; wants; desires	**54.**	Unique selling point
16.	Searching; seeking; meeting	**55.**	Selection; ranking
17.	Customer	**56.**	Marketing
18.	Marketing	**57.**	Customer needs; customers; competition
19.	Competition	**58.**	Top level
20.	Strategic	**59.**	Strengths and weaknesses as well as opportunities and threats
21.	Economic; social; cultural; political		
22.	Resources	**60.**	Threats
23.	Planning; control	**61.**	Information; research
24.	Integrated Business Planning	**62.**	Internal
25.	Marketing	**63.**	Mission
26.	Marketing	**64.**	Objectives
27.	Objectives; policies	**65.**	Strategic business unit
28.	Long-term	**66.**	Served
29.	Turnover	**67.**	Performance
30.	Marketing system	**68.**	Six
31.	Marketing	**69.**	Three
32.	Objectives; programmes; strategies	**70.**	Top level
33.	Shorter	**71.**	Situation
34.	Organizational plans	**72.**	Potential target
35.	Responsibilities, timing, costs	**73.**	Marketing mix
36.	Marketing	**74.**	One
37.	Actions	**75.**	Competition
38.	Decisions	**76.**	Marketers
39.	Achieving objectives; coordination; control	**77.**	Future
40.	Strategy	**78.**	4Ps of Marketing Strategy
41.	Being	**79.**	Personal selling; advertising; sales promotion; publicity
42.	Getting		
43.	Ends	**80.**	Place/Distribution
44.	Right thing; things right	**81.**	Selecting; balancing
45.	Strategic	**82.**	Capacity
46.	Tactical	**83.**	Resources
47.	Market	**84.**	Ends
48.	Competence; resources	**85.**	Marketing objectives
49.	Personal values; aspirations	**86.**	Individual firms; marketing management
50.	Social	**87.**	Marketing opportunities; threats
51.	Feasible; motivating; acceptable	**88.**	Product

89.	Price	95.	Marketing strategy
90.	Product	96.	Just-in-time
91.	Distribution	97.	Japan
92.	Communicating; convincing; competing	98.	Marketing; strategy
93.	Hardest	99.	Viral marketing
94.	Socially	100.	Acquisition

TRUE / FALSE

1. In a retail-centered enterprise, marketing management is called upon to assess marketing. (True / False)
2. The leadership has to motivate the personel, evaluate and set goals. (True / False)
3. Planning execution-control is an ongoing process. (True / False)
4. Planning provides the basis for information marketing strategy. (True / False)
5. Questionnaire input provides situation analysis which answers the questions. (True / False)
6. Setting mission and objectives is the first step in organizing. (True / False)
7. Planning is the first management function to be performed in the process management. (True / False)
8. A business enterprise is consumer centered system living in a dynamic environment. (True / False)
9. Situation analysis reveals the non-controllable and changing factors. (True / False)
10. Planning and organizing are the twin management functions acting as the two side of the same coin. (True / False)
11. Planning - action - control is a continuing cycle and these functions are difficult to separate. (True / False)
12. Changing business environment is one of the significant reasons for the growing importance and popularity of business planning. (True / False)
13. Situation approach to marketing management demands synthesis, co-ordinates and integrates. (True / False)
14. The system approach views a business enterprise as a total integrated system of business operating in a dynamic environment. (True / False)
15. Customer-citizen needs, wants and desires are always changing. (True / False)
16. Searching, seeking and meeting customer needs alone can assure profitable growth if any business. (True / False)
17. Customer needs are the probable economic opportunities. (True / False)
18. Marketing executives have to evaluate marketing strategies to overcome competition in the market. (True / False)
19. Consumer is a key element in a company's marketing opportunity. (True / False)
20. Strategic planning is always based on the assessment of competition. (True / False)
21. Customer needs are influenced by economic environment only. (True / False)
22. Research is subject to deterioration. (True / False)
23. Availability resources clearly limit the range of planning and control. (True / False)

24. Expansion of IBP is Integrated Business Planning (True / False)

25. Marketing opportunities are seen in terms of satisfied customer desires. (True / False)

26. Marketing planning of an organization is planning for the organization's revenue earning activities. (True / False)

27. The objectives under marketing planning process must be short-term objectives. (True / False)

28. The first step in the marketing planning process is setting down marketing objectives and policies. (True / False)

29. The objectives of marketing planning process can be fixed in terms of purchase. (True / False)

30. The second step in marketing planning process is designing the marketing system. (True / False)

31. In marketing policies, a company has to design each function with its contribution. (True / False)

32. The third step in the marketing planning process is to develop separate objectives programmes and strategies. (True / False)

33. The fourth step in the marketing planning process is drawing of detailed plans for each function for a longer period. (True / False)

34. The fifth step in marketing planning process is merging the marketing plans into organizational plans. (True / False)

35. The fourth step in marketing planning process is helpful in defining responsibilities, timing and costs. (True / False)

36. Marketing planning is in dispensable in the field of research. (True / False)

37. Without planning, actions become random in nature. (True / False)

38. Without planning, information becomes meaningless. (True / False)

39. The importance of marketing planning is, it helps in coordination, control etc. (True / False)

40. Selection involves the choice of a general type of plan. (True / False)

41. The objectives emphases the state of being there. (True / False)

42. The strategy emphasis the process of getting there. (True / False)

43. Objectives deal with what is to be achieved. (True / False)

44. To do the right thing and things right are the two major broad objectives of an enterprise. (True / False)

45. Tactical planning reflects the first objective, i.e., to do the right thing. (True / False)

46. Strategic planning underscores the second objective, i.e., to do things right. (True / False)

47. The future marked opportunities point to what a company can do. (True / False)

48. The distinctive corporate competence and resources will point out what a company might do. (True / False)

49. Personal values and aspirations will indicate what a company wants to do. (True / False)

50. Social responsibility will reflect what companies try to do. (True / False)

51. The objectives must be challenging but feasible, motivating and acceptable to the executives and their subordinates. (True / False)

52. Strategy acts as a bridge between our planning and objectives. (True / False)

53. In companies, two or three strategies are simultaneously used. (True / False)

54. USP stands for Unique Selling Process. (True / False)

55. Strategy specifies selection and ranking of business opportunities. (True / False)

56. Evaluation of opportunities under customer-oriented business planning will be made first by marketing management. (True / False)

57. The evaluation will be primarily based upon only customer needs. (True / False)

58. The top level management put the final stamp of its decision when the functional specialists have screened and approved the exploitation of business opportunity. (True / False)

59. SWOT stands for strategic wants of opportunities and threats. (True / False)

60. Threats are considered as challenges to be met by strategic planning. (True / False)

61. Marketing information and research enables us to scan internal environment. (True / False)

62. Sales audit and cost analysis enable to study internal environment. (True / False)

63. Objectives answers the question, "what is over business?" (True / False)

64. Mission answers the question, "what we want to achieve?". (True / False)

65. SBU stands for Strategic Business unit. (True / False)

66. The mission points out the needs to be served. (True / False)

67. The objective indicates marketing standards. (True / False)

68. Strategic business unit in the corporation has more than six divisions. (True / False)

69. Strategic business unit in reality has three divisions. (True / False)

70. The strategic company planning is done by middle management for the whole enterprise. (True / False)

71. Situation analysis is the starting point in all planning activities. (True / False)

72. In a new company, segmentation enables the company to identify potential global markets. (True / False)

73. The marketing plan is built around the four elements of the marketing mix. (True / False)

74. Annual marketing plan is a short-term marketing plan, covering for one year. (True / False)

75. The main of strategy is to cope with customer. (True / False)

76. Retailers successfully define their markets and sub-markets in terms of product functions and benefits. (True / False)

77. Indian industrialists are concerned about the future. (True / False)

78. Non-controllable factors represent the marketing mix. (True / False)

79. Product covers personal selling, advertising, sales promotion and publicity. (True / False)

80. Place or distribution includes channels, transport, warehousing and inventory control. (True / False)

81. A company can achieve its marketing objectives by selecting and balance the marketing mix-programme. (True / False)

82. External limitations indicate the firm's capacity or resource position. (True / False)

83. Resources of the company are the means (inputs). (True / False)

84. Company objectives are the ends (output). (True / False)

85. Marketing programme is determined on the basis of self-analysis of our strengths and weakness. (True / False)

86. External environmental factors are uncontrollable by individual firms and marketing management. (True / False)

87. The environmental factors reveal only marketing opportunities. (True / False)

88. Product is designed to match customer need. (True / False)

89. Price is fixed in terms of customer segments aimed at. (True / False)

90. Strategy starts with price objectives. (True / False)

91. Channel decisions and physical distribution plan are the components of distribution strategy. (True / False)

92. Promotion strategy aims at convincing against rivals only. (True / False)

93. Pricing strategy involves hardest decisions. (True / False)

94. Company image will be right if marketers adopt and practice the economic responsible marketing policies. (True / False)

95. Marketing mix consists of two main steps selecting the target market and assembling of marketing mix. (True / False)

96. JIT stands for Just-in-time. (True / False)

97. Planning for Just-in-Time (JIT) management concept is given by Japan. (True / False)

98. Management and strategy must rotate around people - inside and outside customers. (True / False)

99. Word-of-mouth Marketing is the passing of information from person to person by oral communication. (True / False)

100. Strategy provides preferred means to achieve the goals.

Answers for True / False

1.	False	**21.**	False	**41.**	True	**61.**	False	**81.**	True
2.	True	**22.**	False	**42.**	True	**62.**	True	**82.**	False
3.	True	**23.**	True	**43.**	True	**63.**	False	**83.**	True
4.	False	**24.**	True	**44.**	True	**64.**	False	**84.**	True
5.	False	**25.**	False	**45.**	False	**65.**	True	**85.**	False
6.	True	**26.**	True	**46.**	True	**66.**	True	**86.**	True
7.	True	**27.**	False	**47.**	False	**67.**	False	**87.**	False
8.	False	**28.**	True	**48.**	False	**68.**	True	**88.**	True
9.	True	**29.**	False	**49.**	True	**69.**	True	**89.**	True
10.	False	**30.**	True	**50.**	False	**70.**	False	**90.**	False
11.	True	**31.**	False	**51.**	True	**71.**	True	**91.**	True
12.	True	**32.**	True	**52.**	False	**72.**	False	**92.**	False
13.	False	**33.**	False	**53.**	True	**73.**	True	**93.**	True
14.	True	**34.**	True	**54.**	False	**74.**	True	**94.**	True
15.	False	**35.**	True	**55.**	True	**75.**	False	**95.**	False
16.	True	**36.**	False	**56.**	True	**76.**	False	**96.**	True
17.	False	**37.**	True	**57.**	False	**77.**	True	**97.**	True
18.	True	**38.**	False	**58.**	True	**78.**	False	**98.**	False
19.	False	**39.**	True	**59.**	False	**79.**	False	**99.**	True
20.	True	**40.**	False	**60.**	True	**80.**	True	**100.**	True

MULTIPLE CHOICE QUESTIONS

1. In which enterprise, marketing management is called upon to assess marketing opportunity?

(a) Customer-centred
(b) Retail-centred
(c) Wholesale-centred
(d) Manufacture-centred

2. To achieve the set goals, the leadership has to motivate the

(a) Personnel
(b) Evaluate
(c) Adjust marketing effort
(d) All the above

3. Which execution-control is an ongoing process?

(a) Planning
(b) Organizing
(c) Controlling
(d) Staffing

4. Planning provides the basis for _______.

(a) Information marketing strategy
(b) Innovative marketing strategy
(c) Integrated marketing strategy
(d) Independent marketing strategy

5. Situation analysis covers ________.

(a) Market environment
(b) Market demand
(c) Competition
(d) All the above

6. Setting mission and objectives is the first step in ________.

(a) Planning
(b) Organizing
(c) Controlling
(d) Staffing

7. Planning is the ________ management function to be performed in the process of management.

(a) First
(b) Second
(c) Third
(d) Fourth

8. Living in a dynamic environment, a business enterprise is an ________.

(a) Open
(b) Adaptive
(c) Socio-economic system
(d) All the above

9. Which analysis reveals the non-controllable and changing factors?

(a) Business
(b) Situation
(c) Marketing
(d) Information

10. What are the twin management functions acting as the two sides of the same coin?

(a) Planning and organizing
(b) Planning and staffing
(c) Planning and controlling
(d) Planning and directing

11. What are continuing cycles that are difficult to separate?

(a) Planning - organizing - controlling
(b) Planning - staffing - controlling
(c) Planning - action - controlling
(d) Planning - directing - controlling

12. What are the significant reasons accounting for the growing importance and popularity of business planning?

(a) Greater emphasis on ecology
(b) Human resources

(c) Human resources
(d) None of the above

13. Systems approach to business management demands ________.
(a) Synthesis
(b) Coordinates
(c) Integrates
(d) All the above

14. In a dynamic environment, the systems approach views a business enterprise as what system of business operating?
(a) Total integrated
(b) Business integrated
(c) System integrated
(d) Profit integrated

15. The customer - citizens ________ are dynamic and ever changing?
(a) Needs
(b) Wants
(c) Desires
(d) All the above

16. What are the needs of customer alone can assure profitable growth of any business?
(a) Searching
(b) Seeking
(c) Meeting
(d) All the above

17. Customer needs are the probable ______.
(a) Economic opportunities
(b) Market opportunities
(c) Social opportunities
(d) Management opportunities

18. Who have to evaluate marketing strategies to overcome competition in the market?
(a) Marketing executives
(b) Sales executives
(c) Advertising manager
(d) Brand manager

19. What is a key element in a company's marketing opportunity?
(a) Price
(b) Profit
(c) Competition
(d) Consumer

20. Which planning is always based on the assessment of competition?
(a) Product
(b) Strategic
(c) System
(d) Organization

21. Customer needs are also influenced by ________.
(a) Economic environment
(b) Social environment
(c) Cultural environment
(d) All the above

22. Which are subject to deterioration?
(a) Research
(b) Information
(c) Resources
(d) System

23. Availability of resources limits the range of ________.
(a) Planning
(b) Control
(c) Both a and b
(d) None of the above

24. IBP stands for ________.
(a) Integrated business planning
(b) Information business planning
(c) Innovative business planning
(d) Internal business planning

25. Marketing opportunities are seen in terms of ________.
(a) Unsatisfied customer desires
(b) Satisfied customer desires

(c) Unsatisfied customer needs
(d) Satisfied customer needs

26. Which planning of an organization is planning for the organization's revenue earning activities?

(a) Business
(b) Marketing
(c) Management
(d) Information

27. Which is the first step in the marketing planning process?

(a) Marketing business and planning
(b) Marketing objectives and planning
(c) Marketing business and policies
(d) Marketing objectives and policies

28. In marketing planning process, the objectives must be the ________.

(a) Long-term objectives
(b) Short-term objectives
(c) Medium-term objectives
(d) None of the above

29. The marketing planning process objectives can be fixed in terms of ________.

(a) Purchase
(b) Turnover
(c) Supply
(d) Unit

30. Which is the second step in the marketing planning process?

(a) Marketing information
(b) Marketing research
(c) Marketing sources
(d) Marketing system

31. In which a company has to design/define each function with its contribution?

(a) Marketing objectives
(b) Marketing policies
(c) Marketing system
(d) Marketing planning

32. The third step in the marketing planning process is to develop separate ________.

(a) Objectives
(b) Programmes
(c) Strategies
(d) All the above

33. The fourth step in the marketing planning process is drawing of detailed plans for each function for a ________.

(a) Longer period
(b) Shorter period
(c) Medium period
(d) None of the above

34. The fifth step in marketing planning process is merging the ________.

(a) Marketing plans into organization plans
(b) Organizational plans into marketing plans
(c) Marketing plans into effective plans
(d) Effective plans into marketing plans

35. The fourth step in marketing planning process is helpful in defining ________.

(a) Responsibilities
(b) Timing
(c) Costs
(d) All the above

36. Marketing planning is indispensable in the field of ________.

(a) Business
(b) Marketing
(c) Research
(d) Competition

37. Without planning, which become random in nature?

(a) Actions
(b) Decisions

(c) Information
(d) Objectives

38. Without planning, which become meaningless?

(a) Actions
(b) Decisions
(c) Information
(d) Objectives

39. The importance of marketing planning is, it helps in ________.

(a) Achieving objectives
(b) Coordination
(c) Control
(d) All the above

40. Which involves the choice of a general type of plan?

(a) Selection
(b) Sources
(c) Strategy
(d) System

41. The objectives emphasis the state of ________.

(a) Being there
(b) Getting there
(c) Giving there
(d) Doing there

42. The strategy emphasizes the process of ________.

(a) Being there
(b) Getting there
(c) Giving there
(d) Doing there

43. Objectives prescribe ________.

(a) Starts
(b) Stop
(c) Ends
(d) None of the above

44. What are the major broad objectives of an enterprise?

(a) To do the right thing
(b) To do things right
(c) Both a and b
(d) None of the above

45. Which planning reflects the first objective is to do the right thing?

(a) Tactical
(b) Strategic
(c) Dynamic
(d) Project

46. Which planning underscores the second objectives i.e., to do things right?

(a) Tactical
(b) Strategic
(c) Dynamic
(d) Project

47. The future market opportunities point to a company ________.

(a) Wants to do
(b) Should do
(c) Might do
(d) Can do

48. The distinctive corporate competence and resources will point out a company ________.

(a) Wants to do
(b) Should do
(c) Might do
(d) Can do

49. Personal values and aspirations will indicate a company ________.

(a) Wants to do
(b) Should do
(c) Might do
(d) Can do

50. Social responsibility will reflect a company ________.

(a) Wants to do
(b) Should do
(c) Might do
(d) Can do

51. The objectives must be challenging but to the executives and their subordinates it should be ________.

(a) Feasible
(b) Motivating
(c) Acceptable
(d) All the above

52. Strategy acts as a bridge between our ________.

(a) Objectives and action plans
(b) Tactical and action programmes
(c) Planning and objectives
(d) Planning and selling

53. How many strategies are simultaneously used?

(a) One or two
(b) two or three
(c) Three or four
(d) four or five

54. USP stands for ________.

(a) Unique selling process
(b) Unique selling point
(c) Unique selling plan
(d) Unique selling programme

55. What specifies selection and ranking of business opportunities?

(a) Strategy
(b) Resource
(c) Objectives
(d) Survey

56. Evaluation of opportunities under customer-oriented business planning will be made first by ________.

(a) Marketing strategy
(b) Marketing opportunities
(c) Marketing management
(d) Marketing Intelligence

57. The evaluation will be primarily based upon ________.

(a) Customers
(b) Customer needs
(c) Competition
(d) All the above

58. When the functional specialists have screened and approved the exploitation of business opportunity, which management can put the final stamp of its decision?

(a) Top level
(b) Middle level
(c) Low level
(d) None of the above

59. Expansion of SWOT ________.

(a) Strategic and weaknesses as well as opportunities and threats.
(b) Strengths and weaknesses of opportunities and threats.
(c) Strategic wants as well as opportunities and threats
(d) Strategic wants of opportunities and threats.

60. Which are considered as challenges to be met by strategic planning?

(a) Strengths
(b) Opportunities
(c) Threats
(d) Mission

61. Marketing information and research enables us to scan ________.

(a) Internal environment
(b) External environment
(c) Internal resource
(d) External resource

62. What enable to study internal environment?

(a) Sales audit
(b) Cost analysis
(c) Both a and b
(d) None of the above

63. Which answers the question, "what is our business"?

(a) Objectives
(b) Mission
(c) Vision
(d) Firm

64. Which answers the question, what do we want to achieve?

(a) Objectives
(b) Mission
(c) Vision
(d) Firm

65. SBU stands for ________.

(a) System business unit
(b) Strategic business unique
(c) Strategic business unit
(d) None of the above

66. Which points out the needs to be served?

(a) Objectives
(b) Mission
(c) Vision
(d) Firm

67. Which indicate performance standards?

(a) Objectives
(b) Mission
(c) Vision
(d) Firm

68. Strategic business unit in the corporation has more than ________.

(a) Three divisions
(b) Four divisions
(c) Five divisions
(d) Six divisions

69. Strategic business unit in reality has ________.

(a) Three divisions
(b) Four divisions
(c) Five divisions
(d) Six divisions

70. Which level of management is doing the strategic company planning for the whole enterprise?

(a) Top level
(b) Middle level
(c) Low level
(d) None of the above

71. Which analysis is the starting point in all planning activities?

(a) Significant
(b) Segmentation
(c) Situation
(d) Strategic

72. In a new company, segmentation enables the company to identify ________.

(a) Global target markets
(b) Potential target markets
(c) Potential global markets
(d) Global dynamic markets

73. In marketing plan how many elements of the marketing mix are built?

(a) One
(b) two
(c) Three
(d) four

74. Annual marketing plan is a short-term marketing plan, covering for how many years?

(a) Quarter a year
(b) Half a year
(c) One year
(d) None of the above

75. The main of strategy is to cope with ________.

(a) Competition
(b) Market
(c) Product
(d) Customer

76. Who successfully define their markets and sub-markets interms of product functions and benefits?

(a) Retailer
(b) Wholesalers
(c) Marketers
(d) Selling executives

77. Indian industrialists are concerned about the ________.

(a) Past
(b) Present
(c) Future
(d) None of the above

78. Which factors represent the marketing mix?

(a) Controllable
(b) Non-controllable
(c) External
(d) Internal

79. Which one of the following covers personal selling, advertising, sales promotion and publicity?

(a) Product
(b) Price
(c) Place
(d) Promotion

80. Which one of the following includes channels, transport, and warehousing and inventory control?

(a) Product
(b) Price
(c) Place
(d) Promotion

81. A company can achieve its marketing objectives by selecting and balancing the ________.

(a) Marketing mix - policy
(b) Marketing mix - programme
(c) Marketing mix - planning
(d) Marketing mix - position

82. Which limitations indicate the firm's capacity or resource position?

(a) Formal
(b) Informal
(c) Internal
(d) External

83. Resources of the company are ________.

(a) The means
(b) The ends
(c) Both a and b
(d) None of the above

84. Company objectives are ________.

(a) The means
(b) The ends
(c) Both a and b
(d) None of the above

85. Which determined on the basis of self-analysis of our strengths and weakness?

(a) Marketing policy
(b) Marketing programme
(c) Marketing environment
(d) Marketing objectives

86. Which factors are uncontrollable by individual firms and marketing management?

(a) Internal environmental
(b) External environmental
(c) Marketing environmental
(d) All the above

87. The environmental factors reveal ________.

(a) Marketing opportunities
(b) Threats

(c) Both a and b
(d) None of the above

88. Which one of the following of marketing mix element is designed to match customer need?

(a) Product
(b) Price
(c) Promotion
(d) Place

89. Which one of the following of marketing mix element is fixed in terms of customer segments aimed at?

(a) Product
(b) Price
(c) Promotion
(d) Place

90. Strategy starts with ________.

(a) Product objectives
(b) Price objectives
(c) Promotion objectives
(d) Place objectives

91. What are the components of distribution strategy?

(a) Channel decisions plan
(b) Physical distribution plan
(c) Both a and b
(d) None of the above

92. Against rivals promotion strategy aims at ________.

(a) Communicating
(b) Convincing
(c) Competing
(d) All the above

93. Pricing strategy involves ________.

(a) Easiest decisions
(b) Hardest decisions
(c) Longest decisions
(d) Shortest decisions

94. Company image will be bright if marketers adopt and practice which responsible marketing policies?

(a) Social
(b) Economical
(c) Legal
(d) Political

95. Marketing strategy consists of the steps of ________.

(a) Selecting the target market
(b) Assembling of marketing-mix
(c) Both a and b
(d) None of the above

96. JIT stands for ________.

(a) Just-information-target
(b) Just-in-time
(c) Just-in-target
(d) Just-information-time

97. Planning for Just-in-time (JIT) management concept is given by

(a) India
(b) America
(c) Canada
(d) Japan

98. Which must rotate around people-inside customer and outside customer?

(a) Marketing
(b) Strategy
(c) Both a and b
(d) None of the above

99. Relationship marketing is designed to develop strong connections with customers by providing them with ________.

(a) Information directly suited to their needs and interests
(b) By promoting open communication
(c) Both (a) and (b)
(d) None of the above

Answers for MCQ

1.	(a)	18.	(b)	35.	(a)	52.	(d)	69.	(d)	86.	(d)
2.	(d)	19.	(a)	36.	(d)	53.	(a)	70.	(a)	87.	(b)
3.	(a)	20.	(c)	37.	(b)	54.	(b)	71.	(a)	88.	(c)
4.	(c)	21.	(b)	38.	(a)	55.	(b)	72.	(c)	89.	(a)
5.	(d)	22.	(d)	39.	(b)	56.	(a)	73.	(b)	90.	(b)
6.	(b)	23.	(c)	40.	(d)	57.	(c)	74.	(d)	91.	(a)
7.	(a)	24.	(c)	41.	(c)	58.	(d)	75.	(b)	92.	(c)
8.	(a)	25.	(a)	42.	(a)	59.	(a)	76.	(a)	93.	(b)
9.	(d)	26.	(c)	43.	(b)	60.	(a)	77.	(c)	94.	(b)
10.	(b)	27.	(b)	44.	(c)	61.	(c)	78.	(c)	95.	(a)
11.	(c)	28.	(d)	45.	(c)	62.	(b)	79.	(a)	96.	(c)
12.	(c)	29.	(a)	46.	(b)	63.	(c)	80.	(d)	97.	(b)
13.	(c)	30.	(b)	47.	(a)	64.	(b)	81.	(c)	98.	(d)
14.	(d)	31.	(d)	48.	(c)	65.	(a)	82.	(b)	99.	(c)
15.	(a)	32.	(c)	49.	(d)	66.	(c)	83.	(c)		
16.	(d)	33.	(d)	50.	(a)	67.	(b)	84.	(a)		
17.	(d)	34.	(b)	51.	(b)	68.	(a)	85.	(b)		

MATCH THE FOLLOWING

1.	Situation analysis	(a)	Focus on one time sale of the product
2.	Transactional Marketing	(b)	Effective use of marketing mix
3.	Oral Communication	(c)	Advertising
4.	Marketing Strategy	(d)	Marketing environment
5.	Promotion	(e)	Uncontrollable factors
6.	Macro-environmental factors	(f)	Face to face communication

Answers for Match the Following

1.	(d)	2.	(a)	3.	(f)	4.	(b)	5.	(c)	6.	(e)

Chapter 10

Social Responsibility

SUMMARY

The social responsibility of management refers to such decisions and activities of a business firm which provides for the welfare of the society as a whole along with the earning of profit from the firm. It also refers to the ability and willingness of the management to relate plans and policies to the social environment so that it will be mutually beneficial to the organization and the society. In simple terms, a business enterprise must interact with and live in the society as a responsible citizen. Business firms, however, are now interested in performance in terms of profit position along with economic results. The concept of social responsibility of business or management has gained a firm ground at last. Today, it is held by everybody that business or management has social responsibility. As an organ of society, and as an economic institution dependent upon the society for its existence, survival and growth, and using the physical and human resources of the society for its day to day functioning, business has definite responsibility to the society.

According to Koontz and O'Donnell, "Social responsibility is the personal obligation of everyone, as he acts in his own interest, to assure that the rights and legitimate interests of all others are not infringed".

In the words of H. E Bownen, "Social responsibility is the obligation to pursue those policies, to make those decisions or to follow those lines of action which are desirable in terms of objectives and values of our society".

From the above definitions, it is clear that social responsibility of business or management is the responsibility or obligation of the business to act in a way that will not infringe the legitimate rights and interests of others, i.e., the responsibility of business means the obligation of the business to meet the demands and aspirations of the society. In short, it is the responsibility or obligation of the business or management to serve the best interests of the society and to contribute to the welfare of the society.

Every business firm is closely related to the business environment. Therefore, business units must give this back to the society by contributing towards the development of roads, providing drinking water, street lights, building and maintaining hospitals, educational institutions, maintaining public places, parks, etc. Thus business firms must relate to the plans and policies of the social environment in such a way that they are mutually beneficial to the organization and to the society. These actions reflect the attitude of the management, and the firm's involvement in social actions. It is thus believed that any enterprise must interact with and live as a responsible citizen in the society and that the existence, survival and growth of any firm are based on its acceptance by the society and the business environment. Business units must consider the impact of their actions on all that to which the unit is related. The unit and its operations must act as a trustee for the benefit of its employees, investors, consumers, the government and the general public.

Corporate social responsibility is about how companies manage the business processes to produce an overall positive impact on society. Corporate social responsibility (CSR) is also known as corporate responsibility, corporate citizenship, responsible business, sustainable responsible business (SRB) or corporate social performance. It is a form of corporate self-regulation integrated into a business model.

Corporate social responsibility described the body of management systems and tools that help companies minimize their environmental impact, adhere to international labor standards, contribute to their communities and manage toward a more economically sustainable world.

CSR has been defined much more in terms of a philanphropic model. Companies make profits, unhindered except by fulfilling their duty to pay taxes. They then donate a certain share of the profits to charitable causes. It is seen as tainting the act for the company to receive any benefit from the giving. Social responsibility becomes an integral part of the wealth creation process which if managed properly should enhance the competitiveness of business and maximize the value of wealth creation to society.

When times get hard, there is the incentive to practice CSR more and better if it is a philanphropic exercise which is peripheral to the main business, it will always be the first thing to do when push comes to thrust. But as with any process based on the collective activities of communities of human beings there is no 'one size fits all'. In different countries, there will be different priorities, and values that will shape how business act. And even the observations above are changing over time. For instance, the CSR definition used by Business for Social Responsibility is operating a business in a manner that meets or exceeds the ethical, legal, commercial and public expectations that society has of business.

Corporate Social Responsibility (CSR) is the decision making and implementation process that guides all company activities in the protection and promotion of international human rights, labour and environmental standards and compliance with legal requirements within its operations and in its goals. A properly implemented CSR concept can bring along a variety of competitive advantages, such as enhanced access to capital and markets, increased sales and profits, operational cost savings, improved productivity and quality, efficient human resource base, improved brand image and reputation, enhanced customer loyalty, better decision making and risk management processes.

Corporate social responsibility refers to the thought whereby companies make a decision voluntarily to donate to a better society and a cleaner environment. Under corporate social responsibility companies incorporate social and environmental concerns in their business operations and in their interaction with their stakeholders on a charitable basis.

Corporate Social Responsibility (CSR) includes responsibilities in legal sense and in moral or ethical sense. Since the Factory Rule Movement, the specific implementing method of CSR takes mainly multinational enterprises as the implementing principal to place checks on labor standards of a company, the responsibility in moral or ethical sense is more stressed in the society. In fact, the multinational enterprises are passive to a certain extent in implementing the Factory Rules, which takes labor standards as the main content. Their immediate purpose is to maintain their business credit amongst the trade barriers of labor. Specifically, their purpose is to keep their brand name image and avoid negative legal proceedings, avoid consumers' resistance, drop of stock prices, trade sanctions, improve production efficiency, and optimize the management of supply chains.

The legal character of corporate social responsibility must be recognized and stressed. In fact, it is because of the requirement of the legal nature of this movement, transnational enterprises are forced to do so and try all their best to turn the movement commercial for their own interests.

CSR is the factory rules as the basic operation mode of present CSR movement, so far as its nature is concerned, is the legal responsibility of an enterprise or an obligation of an enterprise in the labor relationship. The significance of proposing the obligation of an enterprise in the legal labor relations as its CSR lies in the fact that this legal norm is better combined with social norms to promote the implementation of this legal norm. As a legal norm, the basic requirement to the social responsibility a company takes is to substantiate the obligations undertaken in the legal labor relations. This obligation that an employer undertakes is conditioned upon his enjoyment of his rights at the same time. These rights include recruitment right in individual labor relationship, right of labor instruction, right of work dispatch, right of reward and punishment and right of plant closure in the legal collective labor relations. These rights are regarded as the user's rights in contrast to the rights of the laborers. But at the same time, employers must undertake relevant obligations. This means employers must carry out and implement relevant labor standards to enforce the protection on laborers during the laboring process. Specifically, employers' obligation in an individual legal labor relation should be first of all to make payment, which is also the obligation of an employer in the law of property. Secondly, it is the obligation of labor protection. This obligation is one as prescribed in the law of personality, mainly including the moral rights of protecting laborers' life and health during production process and their personal dignity during production management. In collective legal labor relations, the obligation of an employer is mainly not to hinder the workers to exercise their right of unity. During the process, the workers establish their trade unions, hold collective bargaining and take collective actions, employers should not antagonize by means of resorting to improper labor act. Generally speaking, in individual legal labor relations, the obligation of an employer is mainly an obligation of action, i.e., to take appropriate act to ensure the fulfillment of individual workers' right of labor. In the collective legal labor relations, the obligation of an employer is shown to be one of non-action, i.e., the employer should not take actions to hinder or harm the exercise and fulfillment of laborers. collective rights and interests.

The obligation of an enterprise in the legal labor relation is mainly realized through legal adjustment of the labor relationship. The conventional legal adjustment of labor relations is done by two ways: one is to have the state to stipulate and implement labor standards; the other one is to have workers to organize trade unions and hold collective negotiations and bargaining. Employment rules or factory rules, in conventional legal adjustment of labor relations serves only as a supplement.

In actual practice, people often ignore the form and nature of CSR as legal adjustment of labor relations. One outstanding issue is that the idea and method of human resources management is entirely used to enforce CSR. Though in reality, the management of human resources and that of labor-management relations criss-cross and is inseparable, still, the labor-management relation cannot be dealt with entirely by the method of human resources management. The legal adjustment of human resources management and that of labor relations are two completely different idea and norm systems.

The human resource management is a business management method focusing on the interests of an enterprise and aiming at improving the competitiveness of the enterprise. The power principal of management is the enterprise and workers are merely the passive objects of management. On the other hand, the legal adjustment of labor relation is to coordinate and balance the labor relationship in an enterprise with protecting laborers rights and interests as their basic rationale. The principals of the rights and interests are the two parties of workers and management. The basic method of adjustment involves reciprocal handling and voluntary participation by the two parties of workers and management.

FILL IN THE BLANKS

1. Modern business is large and complex catering to ________ and ________ markets.
2. Modern business exercises a definite and extensive influence on ________ and ________ lifestyles.
3. As a social institution, marketing is responsible to deliver a ________ and ________.
4. Management must consider the ________ and ________ implications of its decisions.
5. Management must consider the impact of company's ________ and ________ on the society and environment.
6. Managers are interested ________ and ________ results.
7. Social needs and goals are compelling the manager to or towards ________ and ________.
8. ________ life satisfies the hunger of mind and spirit.
9. ________ life satisfies the hunger of body.
10. Management has a ________ responsibility to make a profit.
11. A strong ________ and ________ can solve ever growing social problems involving huge expenditure of money.
12. ________ responsibility indicates personal responsibility and obligation of managers and employees.
13. Survival is the basic and ultimate objective of a business under ________, ________ and ________.
14. Survival is the best measure of ________ and ________.
15. ________ responsibility is an essential condition of survival over the long run.
16. ________ is the highway to customer satisfaction.
17. Marketing strategies are developed to achieve the ________ goal.
18. Business needs ________ to justify its existence.
19. Profits are the reward for ________ and ________.
20. ________ is an anti-social activity.
21. Under ________ marketing, serving the ________ of customers is the central marketing function.
22. ________ is the by-product of consumer satisfaction.
23. The concept of service to ________ and to ________ is based on ethical views of marketing practice.
24. Service to consumer-citizen is the master key to both ________ and ________.
25. ________ act as both businessmen and citizens.
26. Self-regulation helps marketers to fulfill ________.
27. CSR stands for ________.
28. Modern business operates in a ________ environment.
29. ________ responsibilities are not merely the talk of the town but also the talk of the world.
30. Marketing involves too much of ________.
31. Shorter channel is more efficient than a ________.
32. Marketing ignores ________ and ________ considerations.
33. Ethical and moral considerations create materialistic and artificial values only to satisfy ________ and ________ needs.
34. ________ and ________ functions are human resources.

35. Planning, organizing, motivation and controlling is a ________ function.
36. ________ is not managerial function.
37. Operating people is a ________ function.
38. ________ is not a managerial function.
39. Money, materials and information is a ________ resource.
40. ________ is not a non-human resource.
41. Business depends on society and environment for ________, ________ and ________.
42. Indian ethics and insights know that subjective is more powerful and effective than ________.
43. Profit in terms of ________, ________ and ________ of society.
44. Customer is much more valuable than ________ merely in terms of money or return on investment.
45. Profit-making money-centered approach is misguiding as it ignores ________ and ________ cost.
46. ________ profit ignores services ideal in business.
47. Profit-making approach is a poor index of health of ________ and ________.
48. Money-oriented balance sheet is ________.
49. ________ oriented balance sheet give a better and more reliable picture of the progress and prosperity of the people and the enterprise.
50. The health of a company depends upon ________ and ________ of the people.
51. Co-operation between ________ and ________ is always fruitful.
52. ________, ________ and ________ form a value chain.
53. Indian insight is not based on ________ and ________.
54. Indian insight is based on ________ and ________.
55. Indian insight solves the correct problems of ________ and ________.
56. An organization must fulfill social responsibility to create ________, ________ and ________ human life.
57. Social responsibility goes with social power as ________ and ________ go hand in hand.
58. Social irresponsible action is also ________ irresponsible action.
59. ________ responsibly is not doing things right but doing what the needs and interests of business as a social institution demands.
60. Corporate strategic response to ________, ________ and ________.
61. ________, ________ and ________ are not contradictory.
62. ________, ________, ________ and ________ are ONE whole jagat (cosmos).
63. The social marketing wants to satisfy ________ demand.
64. ________ is the study of how our decision and actions affects other people.
65. In the annual report, management should disclose ________, ________ and ________ of ecological balance.
66. ________ and ________ development are not inconsistent.
67. Since from the ________ year, the emphasis is on sustainable economic development that meets the needs of ________ and ________ generations.
68. ________ and ________ are complementary aspects; act as two sides of the same coin.
69. The ability of any nation to deal with environmental issues hinges on its ________ capability.

70. The spirit of partnership between the ________, ________ and ________ that has brought successes in assuring sustained economic development and in reducing environmental pollution.

71. Environmental protection must be integrated into ________, ________ and ________.

72. Developed countries have better environmental ________ and ________.

73. ________ are called upon to embark upon rapid economic development in India.

74. In ________ industry at least environmental audits must now become a routine.

75. ________ development is a system of growth that does not limit the options of future generations.

76. Countervailing powers utilized by ________, ________ and ________.

77. EIA stands for ________.

78. Under national environment protection act, ________ and ________ reports must be made mandatory before launching any new project.

79. The ________ should be prepared by a panel of experts approved by the regulatory authority.

80. Comments of ________ should be included in the final Environment Impact Statement.

81. EIS stands for ________.

82. ________ is the only major country which has no mandatory environmental impact assessment.

83. Marketers will have to give top priority to ________ protection in India within a few years.

84. To promote eco-friendly products will become a ________ responsibility.

85. ________ labels on the products can be on effective promotion/marketing tool.

86. The new process has ________, ________ and ________.

87. ________ label on the product is a guarantee that its use will mean less environmental damage.

88. The product must be environment friendly also during ________, ________ and ________.

89. Lead-free petrol in India will remove ________ pollution.

90. In India, ________ is the authority to implement e-commerce scheme on voluntary basis.

91. Western countries ________ labeling has achieved considerable progress.

92. The German Blue Angel Environment labeling scheme by 1997 has ________ products.

93. 'Extracted from nature and cruelty free' means no ________ testing has been carried out.

94. 'Organically grown' means no ________ have been used.

95. India, now exports ________ percent of a specific wheat pesticide production.

96. A criterion may be introduced in future for clean production practices for products to be labeled ________.

97. ISO stands for ________.

98. True work on ecology is healing all the three environments simultaneously that are ________, ________ and ________.

99. Our most important task is to clean the Earth to cleanse ourselves from ________ pollution.

100. ________, ________ and ________ have become integral to the business-society interface in the new world order.

101. ________, ________ and ________ are the bottom-line, the responsible companies present in their annual reports.

102. Financial investors increasingly take a negative view of ________ organizations.

103. ________ and ________ still relate to each other in a confrontational mode.

104. In the field of spirituality, the world ________, ________, ________, ________ do not occur.

105. When the spirit of religion sprouts outward from within, it is called ________.

106. When the spirit of religion sprout inwards from outside it is called ________.

107. ________, ________, ________ values are closely interrelated in all societies in the universe.

108. Ethical, moral, spiritual values constitute the soul of ________, ________ and the ________.

Answers for Fill in the Blanks

1.	National; international	**30.**	Competitive promotion
2.	Economics; social	**31.**	Longer channel
3.	Standard of living; maximize life quality	**32.**	Ethical; moral
4.	Social; ethical	**33.**	Physical; vital
5.	Decisions; actions	**34.**	Managerial; non-managerial
6.	Social; economic	**35.**	Managerial
7.	High quality of life; high economic productivity	**36.**	Information
		37.	Non-managerial
8.	Quality	**38.**	Materials
9.	Quantity	**39.**	Non-human
10.	Social	**40.**	Motivating
11.	Economic base; adequate profits	**41.**	Sustenance; existence; encouragement
12.	Social	**42.**	Gross or objective
13.	Changing environment; demand; competition	**43.**	Goodwill; credibility; trust
		44.	Profit
14.	Economic performance; marketing activity	**45.**	Social; environment
15.	Social	**46.**	Monetary
16.	Service	**47.**	Company; stakeholders
17.	Survival	**48.**	Secondary
18.	Profits	**49.**	People
19.	Risk-bearing; enterprise	**50.**	Service; satisfaction
20.	Profiteering	**51.**	Company; society
21.	Customer-oriented; demand	**52.**	Society; nature; organization.
22.	Profit	**53.**	Money; self-interest
23.	Customers; society	**54.**	Service; satisfaction
24.	Survival; profits	**55.**	Society; environment
25.	Managers	**56.**	Healthy; happy; harmonious
26.	Social responsibilities	**57.**	Responsibility; power
27.	Corporate social responsibility	**58.**	Economically
28.	Socio-economic	**59.**	Acting
29.	Social	**60.**	Societal needs; expectations; aspirations

61.	Business; ethical value; social responsibilities	82.	India
		83.	Environmental
62.	Individuals; organizations; community; ecology	84.	Social
		85.	Ecommerce
63.	Customer	86.	Low cost; product purity; high yield
64.	Ethics	87.	Ecomark
65.	Ethical code; performance; social response	88.	Transport; use; disposal
		89.	Air
66.	Ecology; economic	90.	Central pollution control board.
67.	1986; present; future	91.	Ecomark
68.	Economic development; sound environmental management	92.	5,000
		93.	Animal
69.	Economic	94.	Pesticides or synthetic fertilizers
70.	Industry; community; government	95.	40%
71.	Business planning; business strategies; costing of industries	96.	Eco-friendly
		97.	International standards organization
72.	Awareness; protection	98.	Physical; mental; spiritual
73.	Marketers	99.	Mental
74.	Major; normal	100.	Economic prosperity; environment quality; social equity
75.	Sustainable		
76.	Consumers; commuters; environmentalists	101.	Financial; environmental; social
		102.	Social irresponsible
77.	Environment impact assessment	103.	Business; norms
78.	Environment impact assessment; environment impact statement	104.	Error; merit; demerit; failing
		105.	Ethic- morality
79.	Environment impact assessment	106.	Spiritual
80.	Citizen's organizations	107.	Ethical; moral; spiritual
81.	Environment impact statement	108.	Society; nation; world

TRUE / FALSE

1. Modern business is large and complex catering to national and international markets. (True / False)

2. On social and political lifestyles the modern business exercises a definite and extensive influence. (True / False)

3. As a social institution, marketing is responsible to deliver a standard of living and maximize life quality. (True / False)

4. Management must consider the social and political implications of its decisions. (True / False)

5. Management must consider the impact of company's decision and actions on the market and the environment. (True / False)

6. Managers are interested in social results along with economic results. (True / False)

7. Economic needs and goals are compelling the manager to work toward high quality of life and high economic productivity. (True / False)

8. Quantity life satisfies the hunger of body. (True / False)

9. Quality life satisfies the hunger of mind and spirit. (True / False)

10. Market has a social responsibility to make a profit. (True / False)

11. A strong economic base and adequate profits can solve evergrowing social problems involving huge expenditure of money. (True / False)

12. Social responsibility does not indicate personal responsibility and obligation of managers and employees. (True / False)

13. Survival is the basic and ultimate objective of a business under changing environment, demand and competition. (True / False)

14. Survival is the best measure of economic performance and marketing activity. (True / False)

15. Social responsibility is an essential condition of survival over the short run. (True / False)

16. Service is the highway to customer satisfaction. (True / False)

17. Marketing programmes are developed to achieve the survival goal. (True / False)

18. Business needs profits to justify its existence. (True / False)

19. Profit is the reward for risk-bearing and enterprise. (True / False)

20. Adulterating is an anti-social activity. (True / False)

21. Under customer-oriented marketing, serving the demand of customer is the central marketing function. (True / False)

22. Serving is the by-product of consumer satisfaction. (True / False)

23. The concept of service to customer and to society is based on ethical views of marketing strategy. (True / False)

24. Service to consumer-citizen is the master key to both survival and profits. (True / False)

25. Managers act as both businessmen and citizens. (True / False)

26. Self-regulation helps marketers to fulfill political responsibilities. (True / False)

27. Stakeholders in a firm are four. (True / False)

28. Modern business operates in a socio-economic environment. (True / False)

29. Social responsibilities are not merely the talk of the state but also the talk of the world. (True / False)

30. Marketing involves too much of competitive promotion. (True / False)

31. Wider channel are more efficient than a longer one. (True / False)

32. Marketing ignores ethical and moral considerations. (True / False)

33. Ethical and moral considerations create materialistic and artificial values only to satisfy physical and vital needs. (True / False)

34. Managerial and non-managerial functions are non-human resource. (True / False)

35. Planning, organizing, controlling and motivating is the managerial functions. (True / False)

36. Information is a managerial function. (True / False)

37. Operating people is not a non-managerial function. (True / False)

38. Money is not a non-managerial function. (True / False)

39. Money, materials and information is a non-human resource. (True / False)

40. Motivating is a non-human resource. (True / False)

41. Business depends on society and environment for sustenance, existence and encouragement. (True / False)

42. India ethos and insight knows that subjective is more powerful and effective than gross or objective. (True / False)

43. Profit in terms of goodwill of society only. (True / False)

44. Customer is much more valuable than profit merely in terms of money or return on investment. (True / False)

45. Profit-making or money-centered approach is misguiding as it ignores social and environmental cost. (True / False)

46. Notional profit ignores service ideal in business. (True / False)

47. Profit-making approach is a poor index of health of a company and the stakeholders. (True / False)

48. Money-oriented balance sheet is primary. (True / False)

49. People-oriented balance sheet gives a better and more reliable picture of the progress and prosperity of the people and the enterprise. (True / False)

50. The health of a company depends upon service and satisfaction of the people. (True / False)

51. Co-operation between consumer and cost is always fruitful. (True / False)

52. Society, nature and organization form a value chain. (True / False)

53. Indian insight is based not on money and self-interest. (True / False)

54. Indian insight is based on service and money. (True / False)

55. Indian insight solves the current problems of society and environment. (True / False)

56. An organization must fulfill social responsibility to create awareness in the mind of human life. (True / False)

57. Social responsibility goes with social power as responsibility and power go hand in hand. (True / False)

58. Socially irresponsible action is also politically irresponsible action. (True / False)

59. Marketing responsibly is not doing things right but doing what the needs and interests of business as a social institution demands. (True / False)

60. Corporate strategic response to societal needs, expectations and aspirations. (True / False)

61. Business, ethical value and social responsibilities are contradictory. (True / False)

62. Individuals, organizations, community and ecology are ONE whole jagat (cosmos). (True / False)

63. The economical marketing wants to satisfy customer demand. (True / False)

64. Ethics is the study of how our decisions and actions affects other people. (True / False)

65. In the annual report, management should not disclose ethical code, performance and social response of ecological balance. (True / False)

66. Ecology and economic development are not inconsistent. (True / False)

67. Since from 1956, the emphasis is a sustainable economic development that meets the needs of present and future generations. (True / False)

68. Economic development and sound environmental management are complementary aspects, acts as two sides of the same coin. (True / False)

69. The ability of any nation to deal with environmental issues hinges on its economic capability. (True / False)

70. The spirit of partnership between the industry and the community has the only two which has brought successes in assuring sustained economic development and in reducing environmental pollution. (True / False)

71. Environment protection must be integrated into business planning, strategies and cost of industries. (True / False)

72. Developed countries have better environmental awareness and protection. (True / False)

73. Managers are called upon the embark upon rapid economic development in India. (True / False)

74. In minor industry at least environmental audits must now become a normal routine. (True / False)

75. Sustainable development is a system of growth that does not limit the options of future generations. (True / False)

76. Countervailing powers utilized by consumers, commuters and environmentalists. (True / False)

77. EIA stands for Environment Industry Act. (True / False)

78. Under national environmental protection act, environment impact assessment and environment impact statement reports must be made mandatory before launching any new project. (True / False)

79. The environment industry statement should be prepared by a panel of experts approved by the regulatory authority. (True / False)

80. Comments of citizen's organization should be included in the final environment impact statement. (True / False)

81. EIS stands for Environment Industry Statement. (True / False)

82. India is the only major country which has no mandatory Environmental Impact Assessment (EIA) prior to the initiation of development project. (True / False)

83. Managers will have to give top priority to environmental protection in India within a few years. (True / False)

84. To promote eco-friendly predicts will become a social responsibility. (True / False)

85. Ecomark labels on the products can be an effective promotion / marketing tool. (True / False)

86. The new process has low cost and high yield only. (True / False)

87. Ecomark label on the product is a guarantee that its use will mean less environmental damage. (True / False)

88. The product must be environment friendly only during the use. (True / False)

89. Lead-free petrel in India will remove water pollution. (True / False)

90. The central pollution control Board in India is the authority to implement Ecomark scheme on voluntary basis. (True / False)

91. Western countries ecommerce labeling has achieved considerable progress. (True / False)

92. The German Blue Angel Environmental labeling scheme by 1997 has 15,000 products. (True / False)

93. 'Extracted from nature and cruelty free' means no animal testing has been carried out. (True / False)

94. 'Organically grown' means no pesticides or synthetic fertilizers have been used. (True / False)

95. India, now exports 60% of a specific wheat pesticide production. (True / False)

96. A criterion may be introduced in future for clean production practices for products to be labeled eco-friendly. (True / False)

97. ISO stands for International Standard Organization. (True / False)

98. True work on ecology is healing the environment simultaneously that are physical and metal only. (True / False)

99. Our most important task is to clean the earth to cleanse ourselves from physical pollution. (True / False)

100. Economic prosperity, environmental quality and social equity have become integral to the business-society interface in the new world order. (True / False)

101. The responsible companies present only the financial bottom lines in their annual reports. (True / False)

102. Financial investors increasingly take a negative view of social irresponsible organizations. (True / False)

103. Government and NGOs still relate to each other in a confrontational mode. (True / False)

104. In the field of spirituality, the words error, merit, demerits, failing. (True / False)

105. When the spirit of religion sprouts outward from within, it is called socio-morality. (True / False)

106. When the spirit of religion sprouts inwards from outside it is called spirituality. (True / False)

107. Ethical and moral are the only values that are closely interrelated in all societies in the universe. (True / False)

108. Ethical moral, spiritual values constitute the soul of society, nation and the world. (True / False)

Answers for True / False

1.	True	17.	False	33.	True	49.	True	65.	False
2.	False	18.	True	34.	False	50.	True	66.	True
3.	True	19.	True	35.	True	51.	False	67.	False
4.	False	20.	False	36.	False	52.	True	68.	True
5.	False	21.	True	37.	False	53.	True	69.	True
6.	True	22.	False	38.	True	54.	False	70.	False
7.	False	23.	False	39.	True	55.	True	71.	True
8.	True	24.	True	40.	False	56.	False	72.	True
9.	True	25.	True	41.	True	57.	True	73.	False
10.	False	26.	False	42.	True	58.	False	74.	False
11.	True	27.	False	43.	False	59.	False	75.	True
12.	False	28.	True	44.	True	60.	True	76.	True
13.	True	29.	False	45.	True	61.	False	77.	False
14.	True	30.	True	46.	False	62.	True	78.	True
15.	False	31.	False	47.	True	63.	False	79.	False
16.	True	32.	True	48.	False	64.	True	80.	True

81.	False	**87.**	True	**93.**	True	**99.**	False	**105.**	False
82.	True	**88.**	False	**94.**	True	**100.**	True	**106.**	True
83.	False	**89.**	False	**95.**	False	**101.**	False	**107.**	False
84.	True	**90.**	True	**96.**	True	**102.**	True	**108.**	True
85.	True	**91.**	True	**97.**	True	**103.**	False		
86.	False	**92.**	False	**98.**	False	**104.**	True		

MULTIPLE CHOICE QUESTIONS

1. Modern business is large and complex catering to ________.

(a) National markets
(b) International markets
(c) Both a and b
(d) None of the above

2. On what lifestyle the modern business exercise a definite and extensive influence?

(a) Economic and social
(b) Social and political
(c) Economic and legal
(d) Social and legal

3. As which institution, marketing is responsible to deliver a standard of living and maximize life quantity?

(a) Social
(b) Economical
(c) Political
(d) Legal

4. Which implications of its decisions must be considered by the management?

(a) Economic and social
(b) Social and ethical
(c) Ethical and legal
(d) Social and political

5. Management must consider the impact of company's decisions and actions on ________.

(a) The customer and the environment
(b) The market and the environment
(c) The society and the environment
(d) The demand and the environment

6. Who are interested in social results along with economic results?

(a) Marketers
(b) Managers
(c) Researchers
(d) None of the above

7. What are compelling the managers to work toward high quantity of lift and high economic productivity?

(a) Social needs and goals
(b) Economical needs and goals
(c) Society needs and goals
(d) Political needs and goals

8. What life satisfies the hunger of body?

(a) Internal
(b) External
(c) Quantity
(d) Quality

9. What life satisfies the hunger of mind and spirit?

(a) Internal
(b) External
(c) Quantity
(d) Quality

10. Who has a social responsibility to make a profit?

(a) Organization
(b) Management
(c) Market
(d) Stakeholders

11. Which can only solve ever growing social problems involving huge expenditure?

(a) Strong economic base
(b) Adequate profits
(c) Both a and b
(d) None of the above

12. Which responsibility indicates personal responsibility and obligation of managers and employees?

(a) Social
(b) Economical
(c) Legal
(d) Political

13. Which is the basic ultimate objective of a business under changing environment, demand and competition?

(a) Profitability
(b) Social responsibility
(c) Services
(d) Survival

14. Survival is the best measure of ________.

(a) marketing performance and economic activity
(b) economic performance and marketing activity
(c) marketing performance and social activity
(d) social performance and marketing activity

15. Which responsibility is an essential condition of survival over the long run?

(a) Economic
(b) Social
(c) Legal
(d) Political

16. Which is the highway to customer satisfaction?

(a) Service
(b) Quantity
(c) Quality
(d) survival

17. Which are developed to achieve the survival goal?

(a) Business strategies
(b) Management strategies
(c) Marketing strategies
(d) Social strategies

18. What needs the business to justify its existence?

(a) Finance
(b) Profit
(c) Goals
(d) Planning

19. Profit is the reward for ________.

(a) Risk-bearing
(b) Enterprise
(c) Both a and b
(d) None of the above

20. Which is called as an anti-social activity?

(a) Adulterating
(b) Profiteering
(c) Hoarding
(d) Black marketing

21. Under customer-oriented marketing the central marketing function is ________.

(a) Serving the demand of customers
(b) Serving the quantity of life
(c) Serving the quality of life
(d) None of the above

22. Which is the by-product of consumer satisfaction?

(a) Finance
(b) Profit
(c) Demand
(d) Serving

23. Which concept is based on ethical views of marketing practice?

(a) Service to customers
(b) Service to society
(c) Both a and b
(d) None of the above

24. Service to consumer-citizen is the master key to ________.

(a) Survival
(b) Profits
(c) Both a and b
(d) None of the above

25. Who acts as both businessmen and citizens?

(a) Marketers
(b) Managers
(c) Researchers
(d) Distributors

26. Self-regulation helps marketers to fulfill ________.

(a) Social responsibilities
(b) Economic responsibilities
(c) Legal responsibilities
(d) Political responsibilities

27. Stakeholders in a firm are ________.

(a) Two
(b) Three
(c) Four
(d) Five

28. In which environment the modern business operates?

(a) Socio-economic
(b) Socio-legal
(c) Economic-political
(d) Economic-legal

29. Social responsibilities are not merely ________.

(a) The talk of the world but also the talk of the town
(b) The talk of the town but also the talk of the world
(c) The talk of the state but also the talk of the world
(d) The talk of the world but also the talk of the state.

30. Marketing involves too much of ________.

(a) Competitive product
(b) Competitive price
(c) Competitive promotion
(d) Competitive place

31. Which channel is being more efficient than a longer one?

(a) Wider
(b) Shorter
(c) Big
(d) None of the above

32. Marketing ignores ________.

(a) Ethical considerations
(b) Moral considerations
(c) Both a and b
(d) None of the above

33. Ethical and moral consideration creates materialistic and artificial value only to satisfy ________.

(a) Physical needs
(b) Vital needs
(c) Both a and b
(d) None of the above

34. Managerial and non-managerial functions are ________.

(a) Human resource
(b) Non-human resources

(c) Environment resource
(d) Non-environment resources

35. Which one of the following are managerial functions?

(a) Money
(b) Materials
(c) Information
(d) Organizing

36. Which one of the following are not managerial functions?

(a) Planning
(b) Information
(c) Controlling
(d) Motivating

37. Which one of the following are non-managerial functions?

(a) Motivating people
(b) Operating people
(c) Planning people
(d) Organizing people

38. Which one of the following are not non-managerial functions?

(a) Money
(b) Materials
(c) Information
(d) All the above

39. Which one of the following is non-human resource?

(a) Organizing
(b) Motivating
(c) Information
(d) Controlling

40. Which one of the following is not non-human resource?

(a) Money
(b) Materials
(c) Information
(d) Motivating

41. Business depends on society and environment for ________.

(a) Sustenance
(b) Existence
(c) Encouragement
(d) All the above

42. Indian ethics and insight knows that subjective is more powerful and effective than ________.

(a) Objective
(b) Functions
(c) Responsibility
(d) Planning

43. Profit is in terms of ________.

(a) Goodwill of society
(b) Credibility of society
(c) Trust of society
(d) All the above

44. Who is much more valuable than profit merely in terms of money or return on investment?

(a) Marketers
(b) Customers
(c) Managers
(d) Distributors

45. Profit-making or money-centered approach is misguiding as it ignores ________.

(a) Social cost
(b) Environmental cost
(c) Both a and b
(d) None of the above

46. Which profit ignores service ideal in business?

(a) Monetary
(b) Grass
(c) Net
(d) Notional

47. Which approach is a poor index of health of a company and the stakeholders?

(a) Profit-making
(b) Customer-oriented
(c) Environment
(d) Social responsibility

48. Which balance sheet is secondary?

(a) Customer-oriented
(b) Profit-oriented
(c) Money-oriented
(d) Project-oriented

49. Which balance sheet gives a better and more reliable picture of the progress and prosperity of the people and the enterprise?

(a) Customer-oriented
(b) People-oriented
(c) Money-oriented
(d) Profit-oriented

50. On which does the health of a company depend upon?

(a) Service of the people
(b) Satisfaction of the people
(c) Both a and b
(d) None of the above

51. Co-operation between which is always fruitful?

(a) Company and society
(b) Company and profit
(c) Consumer and needs
(d) Consumer and cost

52. What forms a value chain?

(a) Society
(b) Nature
(c) Organization
(d) All the above

53. Indian insight is not based on ________.

(a) Money and service
(b) Money and self-interest
(c) Self-interest and satisfaction
(d) Self-interest and objectives

54. Indian insight are based on ________.

(a) Satisfaction and profit
(b) satisfaction and self-interest
(c) Service and satisfaction
(d) Service and money

55. Indian insight solves the current problems of ________.

(a) Society and environment
(b) Political and environment
(c) Legal and environment
(d) Ethical and environment

56. An organization must fulfill social responsibility to create ________.

(a) Healthy human life
(b) Happy human life
(c) Harmonious human life
(d) All the above

57. What goes with social power as responsibility and power go hand in hand?

(a) Social action
(b) Social environment
(c) Social responsibility
(d) Social conscience

58. Socially irresponsible action is also ________.

(a) economically irresponsible action
(b) politically irresponsible action
(c) legally irresponsible action
(d) ethically irresponsible action

59. Which responsibly is not doing things right but doing what the needs and interest of business as a social institution demands?

(a) Marketing
(b) Acting

(c) Profiteering
(d) advertising

60. Corporate strategic response to ________.

(a) Societal needs
(b) Expectations
(c) Aspirations
(d) All the above

61. Which of the following are not contradictory?

(a) Business
(b) ethical value
(c) Social responsibilities
(d) All the above

62. Individuals, organizations, community and ecology are one whole ________.

(a) Concept
(b) Enterprise
(c) Cosmos
(d) Spirit

63. Which marketing wants to satisfy customer demand?

(a) Social
(b) Economical
(c) Political
(d) Legal

64. Which is the study of how our decisions and actions affect other people?

(a) Social audit
(b) Ethics
(c) Ecological balance
(d) None of the above

65. In the annual report, management should disclose which of ecological balance?

(a) Ethical code
(b) Performance
(c) Social response
(d) All the above

66. Which development is not inconsistent?

(a) Ecology
(b) Economic
(c) Both a and b
(d) None of the above

67. Since from which year, the emphasis is on sustainable economic development that meets the needs of present and future generations?

(a) 1956
(b) 1966
(c) 1976
(d) 1986

68. Which are complementary aspects that act as two sides of the same coin?

(a) Economics development
(b) Sound environmental management
(c) Both a and b
(d) None of the above

69. The ability of any nation to deal with environmental issues hinges on its ________.

(a) Economic capability
(b) Social capability
(c) Firm's capability
(d) Management capability

70. The spirit of partnership between which has brought successes in assuring sustained economic development in reducing environmental pollution?

(a) The industry
(b) The community
(c) The government
(d) All the above

71. Environmental protection must be integrated into ________.

(a) Business planning
(b) Business strategies
(c) Costing of industries
(d) All the above

72. Which countries have better environmental awareness and environment protection?

(a) Developed
(b) Developing
(c) Underdeveloped
(d) None of the above

73. Who are called upon to embark upon rapid economic development in India?

(a) Managers
(b) Informers
(c) Marketers
(d) Researchers

74. In which industry at least environmental audits must now become a normal routine?

(a) Minor
(b) Medium
(c) Major
(d) All the above

75. Which development is a system of growth that does not limit the options of future generations?

(a) Unsustainable
(b) Sustainable
(c) Non-environmental
(d) Environmental

76. Countervailing powers utilized by ________.

(a) Consumers
(b) Commuters
(c) Environmentalists
(d) All the above

77. EIA stands for ________.

(a) Environment Industry Assessment
(b) Environment Industry Act
(c) Environment Impact Assessment
(d) Environment Impact Act

78. Under National Environmental Protection Act, which reports must be made mandatory before launching any new project?

(a) Environment impact assessment
(b) Environment impact statement
(c) both a and b
(d) None of the above

79. What should be prepared by a panel of experts approved by the regulatory authority?

(a) Environment impact assessment
(b) Environment industry assessment
(c) Environment impact statement
(d) Environment industry statement

80. Comments of what should be included in the final environment Impact statement?

(a) Manager's organizations
(b) Citizen's organizations
(c) Marketer's organizations
(d) Researcher's organizations

81. EIS stands for ________.

(a) Environment Impact Strategy
(b) Environment Industry Strategy
(c) Environment Industry Statement
(d) Environment Impact Statement

82. Which is the only major country which has no mandatory environment impact assessment?

(a) U.S.A
(b) Canada
(c) India
(d) Japan

83. Who will have to give top priority to environment protection in India, within a few years

(a) Marketers
(b) Researchers

(c) Managers
(d) Informers

84. To promote eco-friendly products will become a ________.

(a) Economical responsibility
(b) Social responsibility
(c) Legal responsibility
(d) Political responsibility

85. Which labels on the products can be an effective promotion/marketing tool?

(a) BIS mark
(b) Agmark
(c) Ecomark
(d) None of the above

86. The new process has ________.

(a) Low cost
(b) product purity
(c) High yield
(d) All the above

87. Which label on the product is a guarantee that its use will mean less environmental damage?

(a) BIS mark
(b) Agmark
(c) Ecomark
(d) None of the above

88. The product must be environment friendly also during ________.

(a) Transport
(b) Use
(c) Disposal
(d) All the above

89. Lead-free petrol in India will remove ________.

(a) Air pollution
(b) water pollution
(c) Soil pollution
(d) All the above

90. In India which is the authority to implement ecommerce scheme on voluntary basis?

(a) State pollution control board
(b) Central pollution control board
(c) Environment pollution control board
(d) None of the above

91. In which countries Ecomark labelling has achieved considerable progress?

(a) Eastern
(b) Western
(c) Northern
(d) Southern

92. By 1997, how many products were there in the German Blue Angel Environmental labeling scheme?

(a) 5,000
(b) 15,000
(c) 25,000
(d) 35,000

93. 'Extracted from nature and cruelty free' means ________.

(a) Animal testing has been carried out
(b) No animal testing has been carried out
(c) Pesticides or synthetic fertilizers have been used.
(d) No pesticides or synthetic fertilizers have been used.

94. 'Organically grown' means ________.

(a) Animal testing has been carried out
(b) No animal testing has been carried out
(c) Pesticides or synthetic fertilizers have been used.
(d) No pesticides or synthetic fertilizers have been used.

95. How many per cent of a specific wheat pesticide production is exported by India?

(a) 40%
(b) 50%

(c) 60%
(d) 70%

96. What may be introduced in future for clean production practices for products to be labeled eco-friendly?

(a) Cruelty free
(b) Criterion
(c) Lead-free petrol
(d) Synthetic fertilizers

97. ISO stands for ________.

(a) International standards organization
(b) Internal standards organization
(c) Investment standard organization
(d) Information standards organization

98. True work on ecology is healing the environments simultaneously are ______.

(a) Physical
(b) Mental
(c) Spiritual
(d) All the above

99. Our most important task is to clean the Earth and to cleanse ourselves from ________.

(a) Physical pollution
(b) Mental pollution
(c) Spiritual pollution
(d) None of the above

100. Which have become the integral to the business society interface in the new world order?

(a) Economic prosperity
(b) Environmental quantity
(c) Social equity
(d) All the above

101. What are the bottom lines, the responsible companies?

(a) Financial
(b) Environmental
(c) Social
(d) All the above

102. Financial investors increasingly take a negative view of ________.

(a) Social irresponsible organizations
(b) Economical irresponsible organizations
(c) Physical irresponsible organizations
(d) Legal irresponsible organizations

103. Which are the two that still relate to each other in a confrontational mode?

(a) Business and NGOs
(b) NGOs and Government
(c) Government and market
(d) Market and customer

104. In the field of spirituality, which words do not occur?

(a) Error
(b) Merit
(c) Demerit
(d) All the above

105. When the spirit of religion sprouts outward from within, it is called ________.

(a) Socio-morality
(b) Ethic-morality
(c) Spiritual- morality
(d) Value-morality

106. When the spirit of religion sprouts inwards from outside it is called ________.

(a) Community
(b) Prosperity
(c) Spiritual
(d) None of the above

107. What are the values that are closely interrelated in all societies, in the universe?

(a) Ethical
(b) Moral
(c) Spiritual
(d) All the above

108. Ethical, moral, spiritual values constitute the soul of__________.

(a) Society

(b) Nation

(c) The world

(d) All the above

Answers for MCQ

1.	(c)	19.	(c)	37.	(b)	55.	(a)	73.	(c)	91.	(b)
2.	(a)	20.	(b)	38.	(d)	56.	(d)	74.	(c)	92.	(a)
3.	(a)	21.	(a)	39.	(c)	57.	(c)	75.	(b)	93.	(b)
4.	(b)	22.	(b)	40.	(d)	58.	(a)	76.	(d)	94.	(d)
5.	(c)	23.	(c)	41.	(d)	59.	(b)	77.	(c)	95.	(a)
6.	(b)	24.	(c)	42.	(a)	60.	(d)	78.	(c)	96.	(b)
7.	(a)	25.	(b)	43.	(d)	61.	(d)	79.	(a)	97.	(a)
8.	(c)	26.	(a)	44.	(b)	62.	(c)	80.	(b)	98.	(d)
9.	(d)	27.	(d)	45.	(c)	63.	(a)	81.	(d)	99.	(b)
10.	(b)	28.	(a)	46.	(a)	64.	(b)	82.	(c)	100.	(d)
11.	(c)	29.	(b)	47.	(a)	65.	(d)	83.	(a)	101.	(a)
12.	(a)	30.	(c)	48.	(c)	66.	(c)	84.	(b)	102.	(a)
13.	(d)	31.	(b)	49.	(b)	67.	(d)	85.	(c)	103.	(a)
14.	(b)	32.	(c)	50.	(c)	68.	(c)	86.	(d)	104.	(d)
15.	(b)	33.	(c)	51.	(a)	69.	(a)	87.	(c)	105.	(b)
16.	(a)	34.	(a)	52.	(d)	70.	(d)	88.	(d)	106.	(c)
17.	(c)	35.	(d)	53.	(b)	71.	(d)	89.	(a)	107.	(d)
18.	(b)	36.	(b)	54.	(c)	72.	(a)	90.	(b)	108.	(d)

MATCH THE FOLLOWING

1.	eCommerce	(a)	Planning, organising and directing function
2.	High environmental awareness	(b)	Interests of society
3.	Modern marketing	(c)	Economic performance
4.	Survival of business	(d)	Environment-friendly technology
5.	Social responsibility	(e)	Competitive promotion
6.	Managerial function	(f)	Developed countries

Answers for Match the Following

1.	(d)	2.	(f)	3.	(e)	4.	(c)	5.	(b)	6.	(a)

Chapter 11

Consumerism/Consumer Protection Act and Business Response to Consumerism

SUMMARY

Consumerism is a movement or policies aimed at regulating the products or services, methods or standards of manufacturers, sellers and advertisers in the interest of buyers, such regulation may be institutional, statutory or embodied in a voluntary code occupied by a particular industry or it may result more indirectly from the influence of consumer organizations. The principle of '*caveat emptor*' relieved the seller of the obligation to make disclosure about the quality of the product. In addition, the personal relation between the buyer and seller was one of the major factors in their relations. But with the growth of trade and its globalization the rule no more holds true. It is now impossible for the buyer to examine the goods before hand and most of the transactions are concluded by correspondence. Further on account of complex structure of the modern goods, it is only the producer/seller who can assure the quality of goods. With manufacturing activity becoming more organized, the producers/sellers are becoming stronger and organized whereas the buyers are still weak and unorganized. In the age of revolutionized information technology, Internet and with the emergence of e-commerce and m-commerce related innovations the consumers are further deprived to a great extent. As a result buyer is being misled, duped and deceived day in and day out.

The word consumerism refers to the act of mobilizing consumers so as to ensure they have quality products and services. It involves protecting and informing consumers about their rights concerning goods and services. Consumerism results in honest packaging and improved product standards.

Consumer in India had started its journey with a need to raise his voice against the quality of goods as back as in 1969 through housewives. It took a shape of revolution at later stage and one day the Parliament passed an Act for the welfare of consumers in 1986. This Consumer Protection Act, 1986, had further undergone many challenges, criticisms and even questions on its legal validity was also put before the honorable Supreme Court of India. After hearing all sorts of accusations and constraints from the big business houses, our apex court held this welfare Act very much valid, legal and within the framework of our Constitution.

Since 1986 and after three important amendments to the Act, scenario in the market has drastically changed and consumerism in India is diverted to more of lust than limited to needs. We are now easily confusing the things with what we need and what we want. It's true, if we work hard, we deserve nice things. But stuffing plenty of nice things which we really do not need, deprive the other consumers from the things they require for their survival. Keeping four cars for four persons in the family is ultimately going to affect others and also more consumption of nation's resources like petrol, etc. Our sense of entitlement can muddy the waters when it comes to what you want and what you really need. The sizes of our houses are expanding as per our income and resources, irrespective of the fact of what we had in olden days. People were having more kids but still living in houses far smaller than we're willing to settle for today. Now, we want a room for every child, plus a living room, family room, media room, and kids' playroom. And if we have to share a television, we are very uncomfortable with the idea.

This sense of entitlement is building commercial pressure on our children. Rates of depression, anxiety and other mental illnesses have risen in the past two decades in the children. A report submitted to the inquiry by the National Consumer Council found that children in deprived areas were more obsessed with money and shopping than youngsters from better-off homes. Poorer children wanted a job with a high salary compared with children from affluent areas and they were the main victims of consumerism, as per the report conducted by the charity "The Children's Society"

The consumption patterns are so much a part of our lives that to change them would require a massive cultural overhaul. In consumer society of the day now, people replace their goods with newer ones, use them and throw them away. The question of repair does not arise. People have money to purchase goods in plenty. In case, they do not do so, it leads to recession, massive unemployment. The success of a consumer society is measured with the rate of production, purchase and consumption. The society is considered to be progressing if all above elements are present there. The single most important measure of economic growth is the gross national product (GNP), the sum total of goods.

India is a fast developing country where majority of the people still belong to the rural areas. Such of those people are many times innocent and ignorant of their products. It is due to lack of information or knowledge of the market position.

These are to be given support and protection from the unscrupulous sellers. The marketers are to be socially responsible in protecting the interest of the consumers. Consumers are considered as one of the pillars of the business.

Peter F. Drucker was apt in saying, "it is the consumer who determines what a business is … What the consumer thinks he is buying, what he considers 'value' is decisive – it determines what a business is, what it produces and whether it will prosper."

According to Adam Smith; "Consumption is the sole end and purpose of all production."

The consumer is the king in a free market economy. The consumers must be given priority to enable him to fulfill his wants and desires according to his capacity. He is to be protected from unsafe, harmful, unsuitable alternatives and thus, he will be freed from insecurity and fear of exploitation. Many a times the consumers may not be in a position to approach civil court, as the matter is involved with comparatively small, both in respect of product and price. It will, thus, be seen that only a social movement can ensure such a condition.

Consumerism has been defined again by Philip Kotler as "a social movement seeking to augment the rights and powers of the buyers in relation to sellers". From this it can be known that the consumers are to be treated as kings. But what is the status of consumers, in India? The Indian philosophy of tolerance and perseverance has still been accepted in many parts of India. To create awareness among the consumers, there are many consumer protection organization. To provide awareness towards rights to safety, right to be informed, the right to choose and right to be heard, a special legislation is enacted by the Central Government.

In order to make the consumers more powerful a separate legislation namely, the Consumer Protection Act, 1986 was enacted. To seek speedy/quick, cheap and efficient remedies and to benefit the consumers and consumer groups, the Act was amended, known as The Consumers Protection (Amendment) Act, 1993.

It is also known as COPRA which is not only recognized consumer rights but also established a redressal system, which is unique in nature.

Consumer protection has always been sought to be maintained and enhanced from ancient times in different parts of the world. It is considered as an essential part towards the welfare of the population. People in the society in 320 B.C, Kautilya, have codified the rules of conduct of merchants, artisans, craftsmen and professionals. Manu in his Dharma Shastra, has given a detailed description of unethical trade practices and the punishments to be met by the traders.

Even in Europe, during the middle age period, dishonest traders had their hands cut off and punished in other ways. Sale of adultererated food and drink was subjected to criminal penalties in the 14th century.

Even the American ex-president John F Kennedy made a significant contribution to consumer movement by highlighting four rights of the consumers namely:

(i) The right to safety

(ii) The right to be informed

(iii) The right to choose and

(iv) The right to be heard

According to the principles of the "Consumers International" (formerly IOCU), "The right to satisfaction of basic needs; to have access to basic essential goods and services, adequate food, clothing, shelter, health care, education and sanitation."

Consumer Protection in India

A brief study of the movement towards consumer protection in different countries is given highlighting the salient features of consumerism. It is touching upon the various environments like marketing, advertising, products safety, pricing and so on. The consumerism also enlightened through consumer education and the legislative action as the part of the Government. The Constitution of India, under Article 21, enshrines, "The right to life and liberty" and this has been expanded by the Supreme Court to include the right to live with human dignity, and all that necessarily follows it, such as the basic necessities of life with adequate nutrition, clothing and shelter.

The Consumer Protection Act, 1986

Consumer Protection Act was enacted in the year 1986 to provide a better protection of the interests of consumers and encourage the consumer movements through consumer councils and other authorities for the settlement of consumer's disputes and for matters connected therewith. The Act gives full freedom to consumers in getting legal protection and free from fear, complexities and technicalities involved with the various legal procedure in the regular course of action like complaints and so on. Moreover, there is no court fees or stamp duty to be affixed, no matter whatever may be the amount involved in the complaints. So the Act facilitates the consumers a better, inexpensive and speedy remedy. The Act shall be applicable to all goods and services unless otherwise, expressly provided by the Central Government by notifications. The law shall see to the benefit of the general public, that is the consumers. The act applies in addition to the sale of all goods and services, in the private sector and the public sector as well as Government agencies. It provides for the establishment of Central Consumer Protection Council by the Central Government and likewise State Consumer Protection Councils by the respective State Governments.

The Act is considered as a revolutionary piece of legislative which can grow into an important tool for development. The objects and reasons behind the Act are based on inherent rights. The Act also seeks to provide for better protection of the interests of consumers. In addition to this it also makes provision for the establishment of consumer councils and other authorities for the settlement of consumer disputes.

FILL IN THE BLANKS

1. The term consumerism was first coined by ________.
2. The term consumerism was first coined by businessmen in the mid - ________.
3. ________ is defined as social force designed to protect consumer interests in the market place by organizing consumer pressures or business.
4. Consumer organizations could provide ________ and ________ efforts to fight against unfair marketing practices and to secure consumer protection.
5. Consumerism is society's attempt to redress this imbalance in the exchange transactions between ________ and ________.
6. Consumerism is a protest of consumers against unfair business ________ and ________.
7. Consumerism aims to remove ________ and eliminate unfair ________ practices.
8. ________ and ________ are the main targets of consumerism.
9. The root cause of consumer movement or consumerism is called as ________.
10. ________ means after purchase doubts, dissatisfaction, disillusion and disappointment.
11. Consumers are demanding ________ rights from the company.
12. ________ are demanding rights from the company about the safety, full and accurate information, a choice and a voice about the product and services.
13. Drucker revealed that consumerism is ________ oriented marketing.
14. Consumer choice is influenced by ________.
15. ________ and ________ competition in the market is of definite advantage to the consumer.
16. Competition can reduce ________, ________ and stimulate ________.
17. In ________ and ________ mix the competition can reduce prices, chance quality and stimulate innovation.
18. Innovation means ________.
19. Progress means ________.
20. Competition is the dispenses of justice to ________ and ________.
21. Consumer right constitute ________.
22. The programme for protection of consumer interest as outlined by ________ and in ________ year placed unique importance upon consumerism.
23. Consumers must have assurance regarding ________, ________ and ________.
24. On ________ and ________ the responsibility for safety of finished products is placed.
25. Right to be ________ is a fundamental economic interest of the consumers.
26. Consumers demand positive obligation of full disclosure to be placed on the ________ and ________.
27. Consumer information gap is a cause of ________.
28. The ________ should ensure that his advertisements mean what they say and they say what they really mean.
29. ________ is the keystone of dealer's policy.
30. Right to choose implies that ________ is disliked by consumers.
31. ________ and ________ legislation provide ample protection for the consumers.

32. More efficient information system will enable consumers to make a ______ choice.

33. ______ and ______ provide official information system to make a wide selection of best bargain.

34. ______ implies the existence of a legal framework and government intervention to safeguard consumer interest.

35. Many business firms are utterly indifferent to consumers' ______ and ______.

36. ______ means right to seek redressal against unfair trade practices or unscrupulous exploitation of consumers.

37. If the ______ and ______ be short of expectations, a consumer has a right of redress.

38. ______ will reduce cognitive dissonance or post purchase doubts and grievances.

39. The ______ and ______ authorities often receive complaints from consumer and attempt to resolve them.

40. A business firm should have a ______ department to receive customer complaints and problems and to resolve them amicably.

41. The ______ department should be directly attached to the ______ management.

42. Car is not an example for ______ needs.

43. Drinking water is an example for ______ needs.

44. ______ has been recently added to the consumer bill of rights.

45. Consumerism is defined as an organized expression for an improved ______ of life.

46. Each form of pollution destroys ______ benefits already existing.

47. ______ is directly responsible for many forms of pollution.

48. ______ decisions of industry must ensure quality of community life by preventing the evil efforts of air, water, food and noise pollution.

49. IOCU stands for ______.

50. ______ can lead to more representation on departmental bodies that can take care of various consumer problems.

51. The prime concern of the consumer movement is to prevent ______ exploitation and minimize ______.

52. The purpose of general guidelines for consumer protection was well described by the ______ Nations Secretary General.

53. In the year ______ report, the United Nations Secretary General has described the general guidelines for consumer protection.

54. Over the year the consumers have been exploited by the ______ sector.

55. The problems of the ______ are essentially the problems of ordinary individuals.

56. Certification of goods that are ______ will create environmental consciousness in consumers.

57. The United Nations Conference on the Human Environment was convened in ______ on ______.

58. ______ day is observed as world Environment Day.

59. The ______ island, water, air and the bounties of nature.

60. The ______ is people plants, creatures and animals.

61. The earthly world constitutes the ______.

62. The right implies that consumers by choice can diminish and even avert many threats to the ______ which in turn threaten humanity.

63. The traditional norm of "value for price" must yield to value for ________ and value for the________.

64. ________ trade practices will enable the consumer to get the real value for his money.

65. The backwardness of people is a further obstacle to ________.

66. A majority of the population is ________ and ________.

67. Legislation can protect consumers only when consumers themselves assert their rights and exert necessary pressure on ________, ________ and ________.

68. Marketing is now becoming increasingly ________.

69. ________ is influenced by mass advertising and promotional devices, utilizing highly developed art of persuasion.

70. ________ sources are the core of the existing information system.

71. Consumers find that most ________ and ________ today are false, deceptive or misleading.

72. Consumers wish to meet ________ as equals.

73. Aggressive ________ and ________ make people want the things.

74. The ________ industry in the U.S.A spend $ 700 per person per year to push goods on consumers.

75. In the year ________ the advertising industry in the U.S.A spend 700 $ per person per year to push goods on consumers.

76. The consumer wants protection against ________, ________ and ________ advertisements.

77. ________ need protection under the present circumstances.

78. ________, ________ and ________ are the problem of consumer protection in the market.

79. The ________ interest in the market places is the focus or the heart of enlightened marketing mix.

80. ________ and ________ both aim at the protection of consumer.

81. Business aim at the protection of consumer through ________.

82. The consumerism aim at the protection of consumer through ________.

83. In exchange relationships there are ________ and ________ parties.

84. In the modern market, the ________ is organized and has professional skill.

85. In ________ relationship there are two parties.

86. In the modern market, the buyers is ________ and ________.

87. The problem of consumer protection is ________.

88. ________ is not an example for a problem of consumer protection in the market.

89. Government intervention takes place only to protect the ________ party in the market.

90. Government intervention takes place to prevent the exploitation by the________.

91. Consumer ________ is a rough substitute for self-regulation of business.

92. ________ has fought in many countries for consumer legislation.

93. ________ has the direct responsibility to find out area in which company's products and service fail to fulfill consumer needs and expectations.

94. Marketing management can take immediate and intelligent efforts to improve marketing efficiency and to reduce the________ appreciably.

95. The ________ Act, 1986 provides for better protection of the rights and interests of consumers.

96. The state commission has a judge of the ________ and ________ other members.

97. Any person aggrieved by the order of the state commission can appeal to the ________ commission within one month of the order of the ________ commission.

98. The consumer protection act has given full recognition to the ________ rights.

99. District forum can give compensation to the victimized consumer up to ₹ ________.

100. District forum can give compensation to the state commission up to ₹ ________.

101. The consumer disputes redressal forum is established by the ________ government in each district by notification.

102. ________ consists of a person who is qualified to be the judge of a district court, and two other members one of whom shall be a lady social worker.

103. In district forum every member shall have the tenure of 5 year with age limit of ________.

104. A recent ordinance promulgated on ________.

105. The ________ of India amended the Consumer Protection Act, 1986.

106. Complaints between ₹ 5 lakhs and ₹ 20 lakhs can be filed before the ________.

107. Complaints exceeding ₹ 20 lakhs can be filed before the ________.

108. More ________ forum can be set up at the district level.

109. The consumer forum has have also been empowered to dismiss frivolous or vexatious complaints with costs up to ₹ ________.

110. Marketers in India are gradually showing genuine interest in satisfying today's more ________, ________ and ________ consumers.

111. Indian consumer market of around 300 million is considered to be the largest market in the world ________.

112. Self policy is for more effective and superior than ________ in the field of distribution.

113. Oligopoly means ________.

114. Monopoly means ________.

115. To have an effective consumer protection a practical response on the part of ________, ________ and ________ parties is essential.

116. ________ regulation is the crudest form as well as a last resort to secure a disciplined business conduct.

117. ________ action, to protect the interests of consumers have become quite common everywhere in the world.

118. ________ represents a wonderful opportunity for the forward-looking aggressive business management.

119. Consumerism challenges marketers to be more ________, ________ and ________.

120. The ideal objective before every market is perfect match between the ________ and ________.

121. The basis of marketing concept is adapting the supply to ________.

122. Indian marketing environment in the near future will demonstrate very keen competition among ________ and ________ consumerism.

123. In a matured market all marketers will be obliged to adopt ________ concept.

124. Many aspects of ________ and ________ may involve additional cost to marketers.

125. Consumerism forced the business to build up marketing mix around the ________ and not around the ________.

126. CAC stands for ________.

127. The practice of creating consumer affairs cell is spreading in the ________ countries.

128. Creation of a satisfied consumer - citizen should be the central objective of all _______ and _______.

129. The new marketing concept has _______ dimension covering not only consumer satisfaction but also public welfare.

130. The consumer needs _______ and _______ information.

131. Advertising must be _______.

132. Packaging and labeling must be _______.

133. Marketing communications should not _______.

134. Corporate advertising should not be _______.

135. Marketing is sometimes defined as looking at the world from the _______ end.

136. The appropriate marketing concept is to look at the business from the _______ end.

137. A majority of the consumer problems directly involve marketing _______ and _______.

138. Marketing deserves special study because of its very objectives of _______ and _______ the consumer.

139. "A customer is the most important person on premises, He is not dependent on us we are dependent on him". The best business approach to consumerism is said by _______.

140. Short-run _______ and _______ should be given secondary importance in a consumer relations concept of the public.

141. According to _______ "Consumption is the sole end and purpose of all production."

142. Two-way communications are necessary for better flow of understanding between the _______ and _______.

143. _______ decision must be based on consumer view point which is possible if we have two-way flow of communications in a balanced form.

144. The new avenues to consumer-oriented marketing management are _______, _______ and _______.

145. _______ research will provide grass-root report on consumer problems and complaints.

146. Each company should have a separate _______ cell to handle consumer complaints, supervise advertising claims and conduct tests of consumer product.

147. Growth of consumer movement in the country indicates that business has failed to meet the _______ and _______ of consumers.

148. Marketing _______, _______ and _______ must be in general accord with the consumer interest.

Answers for Fill in the Blanks

1.	Businessmen	11.	Four
2.	1960s	12.	Consumers
3.	Consumerism	13.	Product-
4.	United; organized	14.	Mass advertising
5.	Sellers; buyers	15.	Greater; free
6.	Practices; injustices	16.	Price; enhance quality; innovation
7.	Injustices; marketing	17.	Product; marketing
8.	Marketing practices; marketing policies	18.	Progress
9.	Consumer dissonance	19.	Life
10.	Dissonance	20.	The consumer; the producer

21.	Consumer bill of rights	58.	June 5th
22.	J.F Kennedy; 1962	59.	Earth
23.	Quality; reliability; performance	60.	World
24.	Producers; distributors	61.	Environment
25.	Informed	62.	Environment
26.	Manufacture; dealer	63.	People; environment
27.	Consumerism	64.	Fair
28.	Seller	65.	Consumer organization
29.	Right to choose	66.	Illiterate; ignorant
30.	Monopoly	67.	Producers; dealers; Government
31.	Competition; consumer	68.	Impersonal
32.	Satisfactory	69.	Consumer choice
33.	Consumer legislation; Government regulation	70.	Commercial
34.	Right to be heard	71.	Advertising; promotion
35.	Grievances; protests	72.	Producers
36.	Right to seek redressal	73.	Advertising; salesmanship
37.	Performance; quality	74.	Advertising
38.	Right to redress	75.	1995
39.	Consumer adviser; Government	76.	Deceptive; false; misleading
40.	Consumer affairs	77.	Consumer
41.	New; top	78.	Consumer legislation; consumerism; business
42.	Basic	79.	Consumer
43.	Basic	80.	Business; Consumerism
44.	Right to secure ecological balance	81.	Self-regulation
45.	Quality	82.	Self-help
46.	Social	83.	Seller; buyer
47.	Industry	84.	Seller
48.	Investment	85.	Two
49.	International Organization of Consumer Unions	86.	Unorganized; amateur
50.	Solidarity	87.	Bilateral
51.	Consumer; litigation	88.	Socialism
52.	United	89.	Consumer
53.	1983	90.	Businessmen
54.	Commercial	91.	Legislation
55.	Environment	92.	Consumerism
56.	Environment friendly	93.	Marketing management
57.	Stockholm; June 5, 1972	94.	Cost of distribution

95.	Consumer protection	122.	Sellers; intense
96.	High court; two	123.	Societal marketing
97.	National; state	124.	Consumerism; environmental pollution
98.	Consumer	125.	Consumer; product
99.	5 lakhs	126.	Consumer Affairs cell
100.	20 lakhs	127.	Developed
101.	State	128.	Marketing activities, company actions
102.	District forum	129.	Societal
103.	65 year	130.	Accurate; complete
104.	One 18, 1993	131.	Truthful
105.	President	132.	Honest
106.	State commission	133.	Over promise
107.	National commission	134.	Overemphasized
108.	Consumer	135.	Seller's
109.	10,000	136.	Buyer's
110.	Sophisticated; skeptical; more demanding	137.	Policies; practices
111.	6th	138.	Reaching; selling
112.	State - policing	139.	Mahatma Gandhi
113.	Market with few sellers	140.	Sales; profits
114.	Market with one sellers	141.	Adam Smith
115.	Business; government; consumers	142.	Corporation; consumer
116.	Statutory	143.	Management
117.	Statutory	144.	Consumer research; consumer-interest committees; consumer relation selections
118.	Consumerism	145.	Consumer
119.	Information; effective; truthful	146.	Consumer affairs
120.	Marketing effort; marketing opportunity	147.	Needs; desires
121.	Demand	148.	Strategies; policies; practices

TRUE / FALSE

1. The term consumerism was first coined by a businessman. (True / False)
2. The term consumerism was first coined by businessmen in the mid-1970s. (True / False)
3. Consumerism is defined as social force designed to protect consumer interests in the market place by organizing consumer pressures or business. (True / False)
4. Consumer organization could provide united and organized efforts to fight against unfair marketing practices and to secure consumer protection. (True / False)
5. Socialism is society's attempt to redress this imbalance in the exchange transaction between sellers and buyers. (True / False)

6. Consumerism is a protest of consumers against the unfair business practices only. (True / False)

7. Consumerism aims to remove injustices and eliminate unfair marketing practices. (True / False)

8. Marketing research and information are the main targets of consumerism. (True / False)

9. The root cause of consumer movement or consumerism is called as consumer protection. (True / False)

10. Dissonance means after purchase, doubts, dissatisfaction, disillusion and disappointment. (True / False)

11. Consumers are demanding four rights from the company. (True / False)

12. Sellers are demanding rights from the company about the safety, full and accurate information, a choice and a voice about the product and services. (True / False)

13. Drucker revealed that consumerism is product-oriented marketing. (True / False)

14. Consumer choice is influenced by mass production. (True / False)

15. Greater and free competition in the market is of definite advantage to the consumer. (True / False)

16. Competition can reduce price, enhance quality and stimulated innovation. (True / False)

17. In promotion and price mix the competition can reduce prices, enhance quality and stimulate innovation. (True / False)

18. Innovation means progress. (True / False)

19. Progress means innovation. (True / False)

20. Competition is the dispenser of justice to the consumer and the producer. (True / False)

21. Consumer rights constitute consumer information rights. (True / False)

22. The programme for protection of consumer interest as outlined by J.F. Kennedy in 1962, placed unique importance upon consumerism. (True / False)

23. Consumers must have assurance only regarding the quality. (True / False)

24. On producers and distributors the responsibility for safety of finished products is placed. (True / False)

25. Right to be informed is a fundamental economic interest of the consumers. (True / False)

26. Consumers demand positive obligation of full disclosure to be placed on the marketer and researcher. (True / False)

27. Consumer information gap is a cause of consumerism. (True / False)

28. The producer should ensure that his advertisements mean what they say and they say what they really mean. (True / False)

29. Right to choose is the keystone of dealer's policy. (True / False)

30. Right to choose implies that monopoly is disliked by consumer. (True / False)

31. Market and product legislation provide ample protection for the consumer. (True / False)

32. More efficient information system will enable consumers to make a satisfactory choice. (True / False)

33. Consumer legislation and Government regulation provide official information system to make a wide selection of best bargain. (True / False)

34. Right to be informed implies the existence of a legal framework and government intervention to safeguard consumer interest. (True / False)

35. Many business firms are utterly indifferent to consumer grievances and protests. (True / False)

36. Right to consumer education means right to seek redressal against unfair trade practices or unscrupulous exploitation of consumer. (True / False)

37. If the performance and quality be short of expectations, a consumer has a right to redress. (True / False)

38. Right to redress will increase cognitive dissonance or post-purchase doubts and grievances. (True / False)

39. The consumer adviser and government authorities often receive complaints from consumer and attempt to resolve them. (True / False)

40. A business firm should have a consumer awareness department to receive customer complaints and problems and to resolve them. (True / False)

41. The new department should be directly attached to the middle management. (True / False)

42. Car is not a example for basic needs. (True / False)

43. Drinking water is a example for basic needs. (True / False)

44. Right to seek redressal has been recently added to the consumer bill of rights. (True / False)

45. Consumerism is defined as an organized expression for an improved quality of life. (True / False)

46. Each form of pollution destroys economic benefits already existing. (True / False)

47. Industry is not responsible for any forms of pollution. (True / False)

48. Investment decisions of industry must ensure quality of community life by preventing the evil effects air, water, food and noise pollution. (True / False)

49. IOCU stands for internal organization of consumer unions. (True / False)

50. Solidarity can lead to more representation on departmental bodies that can take care of various consumer problems. (True / False)

51. The prime concern of the consumer movement is to prevent consumer exploitation and maximize litigation. (True / False)

52. The purpose of general guidelines for consumer protection was well described by the United Nations Secretary General. (True / False)

53. In the year 1983 report, the United Nations Secretary General has described the general guidelines for consumer protection. (True / False)

54. Over the years the consumers have been exploited by the production sector. (True / False)

55. The problems of the environment are essentially the problems of ordinary individuals. (True / False)

56. Certification of goods that are "environment friendly" will create environmental consciousness in consumers. (True / False)

57. The United Nations Conference on the Human Environment was convened in stockholm at on June 5, 1962. (True / False)

58. June 5th is observed as world Environment Day. (True / False)

59. The world is land, water, air and bounties of nature. (True / False)

60. The earth is people, plants, creatures and animals. (True / False)

61. The earthly world constitutes the environment. (True / False)

62. The right implies that consumers by choice can diminish and even avert many threats to the environment, which in turn threaten humanity. (True / False)

63. The traditional norm of "value for promotion" must yield to "value for product" and "value for the environment" (True / False)

64. Fair trade practices will enable the consumer to get the real value for his money. (True / False)

65. The backwardness of people is a further obstacle to consumer protection. (True / False)

66. A majority of the population is literate and ignorant. (True / False)

67. Legislation can protect consumers only when consumers themselves assert their rights and exert necessary pressure on the producers, dealers and the government. (True / False)

68. Marketing is now becoming increasingly impersonal. (True / False)

69. Consumer protection is influenced by mass advertising and promotional devices. Utilizing highly developed art of persuasion. (True / False)

70. Commercial sources are the core of the existing information system. (True / False)

71. Market finds that most advertising and promotion today are false, deceptive or misleading. (True / False)

72. Consumer wishes to meet sellers as equals. (True / False)

73. Aggressive advertising and salesmanship make people want the things. (True / False)

74. The advertising industry in the Canada spent $ 700 per person per year to push goods on consumers. (True / False)

75. In the 1995 the advertising industry in the U.S.A spent 700$ per person per year to push goods on consumers. (True / False)

76. The consumer wants protection against only the false advertisement. (True / False)

77. Consumer does need protection under the present circumstances. (True / False)

78. Consumer legislation, consumerism and business are not the problem of consumer protection in the market. (True / False)

79. The consumer interest in the market place is the focus or the heart of enlightened marketing mix. (True / False)

80. Business and consumerism both aim at the protection of consumer. (True / False)

81. Business aim at the protection of consumer through self-help. (True / False)

82. The consumerism aim at the protection of consumer through self-regulation. (True / False)

83. In exchange relationship there is seller and buyer parties. (True / False)

84. In the modern market, the seller is unorganized and has professional skill. (True / False)

85. In exchange relationship there is two parties. (True / False)

86. In the modern market, the buyers is unorganized and amateur. (True / False)

87. The problem of consumer protection is bilateral. (True / False)

88. Capitalism is a problem of consumer protection in the market. (True / False)

89. Government intervention takes places only to protect the consumer in the market. (True / False)

90. Government intervention takes place to prevent the exploitation by the businessmen. (True / False)

91. Consumer protect is a rough substitute for self-regulation of businessmen. (True / False)

92. Consumerism has fought in many countries for consumer legislation. (True / False)

93. Social management has the direct responsibility to find out area in which company's products and service fail to fulfill consumer needs and expectation. (True / False)

94. Marketing management can take immediate and intelligent efforts to improve marketing efficiency and to reduce the cost of distribution appreciably. (True / False)

95. The Consumer Protection Act, 1976 provides for better protection of the rights and interests of consumers. (True / False)

96. The state commission has a judge of the Supreme Court and two other members. (True / False)

97. Any person aggrieved by the order of the state commission can appeal to the national commission within one month of the order of the state commission. (True / False)

98. The Consumer Legislation Act has given full recognition to the consumer rights. (True / False)

99. District forum can give compensation to the victimized consumer up to ₹ 5 lakhs. (True / False)

100. District forum can give compensation to the state commission up to ₹ 20 lakhs. (True / False)

101. The consumer disputes redressal forum is established by the national government in each district but notification. (True / False)

102. District forum consists of a person who is qualified to be the judge of a district court, and two other members one of whom shall be a lady social worker. (True / False)

103. In district forum every member shall have the tenure of 5 year with age limit of 60 years. (True / False)

104. A recent ordinance promulgated on June 18, 1993. (True / False)

105. The prime minister of India amended the Consumer Protection Act, 1986. (True / False)

106. Complaints between ₹ 5 lakhs and ₹ 20 lakhs can be filed before the State commission. (True / False)

107. Complaints exceeding ₹ 20 lakhs can be filed before the National commission. (True / False)

108. More district forum can be set up at the district forum. (True / False)

109. The consumer forum has have also been empowered to dismiss frivolous or vexatious complaints with costs up to ₹ 50,000. (True / False)

110. Marketers in India are gradually showing genuine interest in satisfying today's more sophisticated, skeptical and demanding consumers. (True / False)

111. Our Indian consumer market of around 300 million is considered to be the 6th largest market in the world. (True / False)

112. Self-policy is for more effective and superior than self-regulation in the field of distribution. (True / False)

113. Oligopoly means market with few sellers. (True / False)

114. Monopoly means market with one seller. (True / False)

115. To have an effective consumer protection a practical response on the part of government parties only is essential. (True / False)

116. Statutory regulation is the crudest form as well as a last resort to secure a disciplined business conduct. (True / False)

117. Statutory action, to protect the interests of consumers has become quite common everywhere in the world. (True / False)

118. Capitalism represents a wonderful opportunity for the forward-looking aggressive business management. (True / False)

119. Consumerism challenges marketers to be more informative, effective and truthful. (True / False)

120. The ideal objective before every market is perfect match between the marketing policy and practices. (True / False)

121. The basis of marketing concept is adopting the supply to demand. (True / False)

122. Indian marketing environment in the near future will demonstrate very keen competition among sellers and intense of capitalism. (True / False)

123. In a matured market all marketers will be obliged to adopt societal marketing concept. (True / False)

124. Many aspects of consumerism and environmental pollution may involve minus costs to marketers. (True / False)

125. Consumerism forced the business to build up marketing mix around the product and not around the consumer. (True / False)

126. CAC stands for Consumer Affairs Cells. (True / False)

127. The practice of creating consumer affairs cell is spreading in the under-developed countries. (True / False)

128. Creation of a satisfied consumer - citizen should be the central objective of all marketing activities and company actions. (True / False)

129. The new marketing concept has economical dimension covering only consumer satisfaction. (True / False)

130. The consumer needs accurate and complete information. (True / False)

131. Advertising must be truthful. (True / False)

132. Packaging and labeling must be over-promise. (True / False)

133. Marketing communications should not be Honest. (True / False)

134. Corporate advertising should not be over-emphasized. (True / False)

135. Marketing is sometimes defined as looking at the world from the buyer's end. (True / False)

136. The appropriate marketing concept is to look at the business from the seller's end. (True / False)

137. A majority of the consumer problems directly involve marketing policies and practices. (True / False)

138. Marketing deserves special study because of its very objective of reaching and selling the consumer. (True / False)

139. "A customer is the most important person on our premises, He is not dependent on us we are dependent on him". The best business approach to consumerism is said by Mahatma Gandhi. (True / False)

140. Long run sales and profits should be given secondary importance in a consumer relations concept of the public. (True / False)

141. Management policies and decisions must see that consumer interests are duly protected. (True / False)

142. Two-way communications are necessary for better flow of understanding between the corporation and consumer. (True / False)

143. Planning decisions must be based on consumer viewpoint which is possible if we have two-way flow of communications in a balanced form. (True / False)

144. Consumer research, consumer - interest committees, consumer relation selections are the new avenues to consumer-oriented marketing management. (True / False)

145. Consumer research will provide grass- root report on consumer problems and complaints. (True / False)

146. Each company should have a separate consumer affairs cell to handle consumer complaints. Supervise advertising claims and conduct tests of consumer products. (True / False)

147. Growth of consumer movement in the country indicates that business has failed to meet the total expenditure of consumers. (True / False)

148. Marketing strategies, policies and practices must be in general accord with the consumer interest. (True / False)

Answers for True / False

1.	True	31.	False	61.	True	91.	False	121.	True
2.	False	32.	True	62.	True	92.	True	122.	False
3.	True	33.	True	63.	False	93.	False	123.	True
4.	True	34.	False	64.	True	94.	True	124.	False
5.	False	35.	True	65.	False	95.	False	125.	False
6.	True	36.	False	66.	False	96.	False	126.	True
7.	True	37.	False	67.	True	97.	True	127.	False
8.	False	38.	True	68.	True	98.	False	128.	True
9.	False	39.	False	69.	False	99.	True	129.	False
10.	True	40.	False	70.	True	100.	True	130.	True
11.	True	41.	False	71.	False	101.	False	131.	True
12.	False	42.	True	72.	False	102.	True	132.	False
13.	True	43.	True	73.	True	103.	False	133.	False
14.	False	44.	False	74.	False	104.	True	134.	True
15.	True	45.	True	75.	True	105.	False	135.	False
16.	True	46.	False	76.	False	106.	True	136.	False
17.	False	47.	False	77.	True	107.	True	137.	True
18.	True	48.	True	78.	False	108.	True	138.	True
19.	False	49.	False	79.	True	109.	False	139.	True
20.	True	50.	True	80.	False	110.	True	140.	False
21.	False	51.	False	81.	False	111.	True	141.	True
22.	True	52.	True	82.	False	112.	False	142.	True
23.	False	53.	True	83.	True	113.	True	143.	False
24.	True	54.	False	84.	False	114.	True	144.	True
25.	True	55.	True	85.	True	115.	False	145.	True
26.	False	56.	True	86.	True	116.	True	146.	True
27.	True	57.	False	87.	True	117.	True	147.	False
28.	False	58.	True	88.	False	118.	False	148.	True
29.	True	59.	False	89.	True	119.	True		
30.	True	60.	False	90.	True	120.	False		

MULTIPLE CHOICE QUESTIONS

1. By whom the term consumerism was first coined?

(a) Businessmen
(b) Managers
(c) Marketer
(d) Researcher

2. The term consumerism was first coined by businessmen in the mid -

(a) 1940s
(b) 1950s
(c) 1960s
(d) 1970s

3. Which is defined as social force designed to protect consumer interests in the market place by organizing consumer pressures on business?

(a) Socialism
(b) Consumerism
(c) Communism
(d) None of the above

4. Consumer organizations could provide united and organized efforts ________.

(a) To fight against unfair marketing practices
(b) To secure consumer protection
(c) Both a and b
(d) None of the above

5. Consumerism is society's attempt to redress this imbalance in the exchange transactions between ________.

(a) Sellers
(b) Buyers
(c) Both a and b
(d) None of the above

6. Consumerism is a protest of consumers against unfair ________.

(a) Business practices
(b) Business injustices
(c) Both a and b
(d) None of the above

7. Which aims to remove injustices and eliminate the unfair marketing practices?

(a) Consumerism
(b) Socialism
(c) Communism
(d) All the above

8. What are the main targets of consumerism?

(a) Marketing practices
(b) Marketing policies
(c) Both a and b
(d) None of the above

9. The root of consumer movement or consumerism is ________.

(a) Consumer practice
(b) Consumer dissonance
(c) Consumer protection
(d) Consumer legislation

10. Which means after purchase doubts, dissatisfaction, disillusion, disappointment?

(a) Protection
(b) Dissonance
(c) Legislation
(d) Sovereignty

11. Consumers are demanding how many rights from the company?

(a) Two
(b) Three
(c) Four
(d) Five

12. Consumer are demanding rights from the company about the product and services of ________.

(a) Safety

(b) Full and accurate information

(c) A choice and a voice

(d) All the above

13. Drucker revealed that consumerism is ________.

(a) Product-oriented marketing

(b) Customer-oriented marketing

(c) Price-oriented marketing

(d) Seller-oriented marketing

14. Consumer choice is influenced by ________.

(a) Mass advertising

(b) Mass production

(c) Mass distribution

(d) Mass packaging

15. Which competition in the market is of definite advantage to the consumer?

(a) Greater

(b) Free

(c) Both a and b

(d) None of the above

16. Competition can reduce ________.

(a) Price

(b) Enhance quality

(c) Stimulate innovation

(d) All the above

17. In which mix the competition can reduce prices, enhance quality and stimulate innovation?

(a) Product

(b) Marketing

(c) Both a and b

(d) None of the above

18. Innovation means ________.

(a) Progress

(b) Life

(c) Justice

(d) All the above

19. Progress means ________.

(a) Innovation

(b) Life

(c) Justice

(d) Right

20. Competition is the dispenser of justice to ________.

(a) The consumer

(b) The producer

(c) Both a and b

(d) None of the above

21. Consumer rights constitute ________.

(a) Consumer information rights

(b) Consumer bill of rights

(c) Consumer protection rights

(d) Consumer education rights

22. The programme for protection of consumer interest as outlined by whom and in which year placed unique importance upon consumerism?

(a) J. F. Kennedy in 1962

(b) K. Henry in 1952

(c) N. G. Wagle in 1982

(d) Stockholm in 1972

23. Consumers must have assurance regarding ________.

(a) Quality

(b) Reliability

(c) Performance

(d) All the above

24. On whom the responsibility for safety of finished products is placed?

(a) Producers

(b) Distributors

(c) Both a and b

(d) None of the above

25. Which rights is a fundamental economic interest of the consumers?

(a) Right to protection of health and safety
(b) Right to be informed
(c) Right to choose
(d) Right to be heard

26. On whom the consumers demand positive obligation of full disclosure to be placed _________.

(a) Manufacture
(b) Dealer
(c) Both a and b
(d) None of the above

27. Which gap is a cause of consumerism?

(a) Consumer information
(b) Consumer education
(c) Consumer protection
(d) Consumer dissonance

28. Who should ensure that his advertisements mean what they say and they say what they really mean?

(a) Manufacture
(b) Seller
(c) Dealer
(d) Producers

29. Which right should be the keystone of dealer's policy?

(a) Right to protect
(b) Right to be informed
(c) Right to choose
(d) Right to be heard

30. Right to choose implies that monopoly is _________.

(a) Liked by consumers
(b) Disliked by consumers
(c) Needed to consumers
(d) Not needed to consumers

31. Which legislation provides ample protection for the consumer?

(a) Competition
(b) Consumer
(c) Both a and b
(d) None of the above

32. More efficient information system will enable consumers to make a _________.

(a) Satisfactory choice
(b) Healthy choice
(c) Safety choice
(d) All the above

33. Which provide official information system to make a wide selection of best barging?

(a) Consumer legislation
(b) Government regulation
(c) Government regulation
(d) None of the above

34. Which right implies the existence of a legal framework and Government intervention to safeguard consumer interest?

(a) Right to be informed
(b) Right to choose
(c) Right to be heard
(d) Right to seek redressal

35. Many business firms are utterly indifferent to _________.

(a) Consumer grievances
(b) Consumer protests
(c) Both a and b
(d) None of the above

36. Which right means to seek redressal against unfair trade practices of consumers?

(a) Right to education
(b) Right to choose
(c) Right to be heard
(d) Right to seek redressal

37. If which is to be short of expectations, a consumer has a right of redress?

(a) The performance
(b) The quality
(c) Both a and b
(d) None of the above

38. Which right will reduce cognitive dissonance or post-purchase doubts and grievances?

(a) Right to choose
(b) Right to redressal
(c) Right to be informed
(d) Right to secure ecological balance

39. Who receive complaints from consumer and attempt to resolve them?

(a) The consumer adviser
(b) The Government authorities
(c) Both a and b
(d) None of the above

40. What should a business firm have in to receive customer complaints and problems and to resolve them amicably?

(a) Consumer affairs
(b) Consumer statement
(c) Consumer adviser
(d) All the above

41. From the following which is not a basic needs?

(a) Drinking water
(b) Pure air
(c) Adequate electricity
(d) None of the above

42. From the following which is a basic need?

(a) Education services
(b) Television
(c) Car
(d) All the above

43. Which right has been recently added to the consumer bill of rights?

(a) Right to be heard
(b) Right to seek redressal
(c) Right to consumer's education
(d) Right to secure ecological balance

44. Which is defined more broadly as an organized expression for an improved quality of life?

(a) Socialism
(b) Consumerism
(c) Communism
(d) None of the above

45. Each form of pollution destroys which benefits already existing?

(a) Social
(b) Legal
(c) Economical
(d) Political

46. Which is directly responsible for many forms of pollution?

(a) Consumers
(b) Marketers
(c) Industry
(d) None of the above

47. Which decisions of industry must ensure quality of community life by preventing the evil effects air, water, food and noise pollution?

(a) Product
(b) Investment
(c) Market
(d) Organization

48. IOCU stands for ________.

(a) International organization of consumer unions.
(b) Internal organization of consumer unions.

(c) International organization of community unions.
(d) Internal organization of community unions.

49. Which can lead to more representation on departmental bodies that can take care of various consumer problems?

(a) Criterion
(b) Spirituality
(c) Solidarity
(d) Cruelty free

50. The prime concern of the consumer movement is to prevent ________.

(a) Consumer's exploitation and maximize litigation
(b) Consumer's exploitation and minimize litigation
(c) Seller's exploitation and maximize litigation
(d) Seller's exploitation and minimize litigation

51. The purpose of general guidelines for consumer protection was well described by ________.

(a) The United Nations Secretary General
(b) The United Nations Management General
(c) The United Nations President General
(d) The United Nations Minister General

52. In which year report, the United Nations Secretary General has described the general guidelines for consumer protection?

(a) 1953
(b) 1963
(c) 1973
(d) 1983

53. Over the years the consumers have been exploited by the ________.

(a) Commercial sector
(b) Production sector
(c) Distribution sector
(d) Consumer sector

54. The problems of which are essentially the problems of ordinary individuals ________.

(a) Market
(b) Environment
(c) Resources
(d) Ethics

55. Which certificate of goods will create environmental consciousness in consumers?

(a) Agmark
(b) BIS
(c) ISI
(d) Eco-friendly

56. The United Nations Conference on the Human Environment was convened in ________.

(a) Stockholm
(b) Keem
(c) Skolomowski
(d) Wagle

57. The United Nations Conference on the Human Environment was convened in Stockholm, on ________.

(a) June 5, 1962
(b) May 5, 1962
(c) June 5, 1972
(d) May 5, 1972

58. Which day is observed as world Environment Day?

(a) June 5th
(b) May 5th
(c) January 5th
(d) March 5th

59. The earth is ________.

(a) Land
(b) Water
(c) Air and the bounties of nature
(d) All the above

60. The world is ________.

(a) People plants
(b) Creatures
(c) Animals
(d) All the above

61. The earthly world constitute ________.

(a) The nations
(b) The environment
(c) The creatures
(d) All the above

62. Which right implies that consumers by choice can diminish and even avert many threats to the environment?

(a) Right to protect of health and safety
(b) Right to a healthy environment
(c) Right to secure ecological balance
(d) Right to basic needs

63. The traditional norm of "value for price" must yield to ________.

(a) Values of people
(b) Value for the environment
(c) Both a and b
(d) None of the above

64. Which trade practices will enable the consumer to get the real value for his money?

(a) Market
(b) Fair
(c) Export
(d) Import

65. The backwardness of people is a further obstacle to ________.

(a) Consumer protection
(b) Consumer legislation
(c) Consumer educations
(d) Consumer organization

66. A majority of population is ________.

(a) Illiterate and ignorant
(b) literate and ignorant
(c) Illiterate and not ignorant
(d) literate and not ignorant

67. The legislation can protect consumers only when consumers themselves assert their rights and exert necessary pressure on ________.

(a) The producers
(b) The dealers
(c) The Government
(d) All the above

68. Marketing is now becoming increasingly ________.

(a) Dietician
(b) Impersonal
(c) Sophisticated
(d) Complicated

69. The consumer choice is influenced by ________.

(a) Mass advertising
(b) Promotional devices
(c) Utilizing highly developed art of persuasion
(d) All the above

70. What sources is the core of the existing information system?

(a) Consumer
(b) Market
(c) Commercial
(d) All the market

71. Who find that most advertising and promotion today are false, deceptive or misleading?

(a) Sellers
(b) Consumers
(c) Marketer
(d) Researchers

72. Consumers wish to meet ________.

(a) Producers as equals
(b) Manufactures as equals

(c) Products as equals
(d) Sellers as equals

73. What make people want the things?

(a) Aggressive advertising and salesmanship
(b) Aggressive product and salesmanship
(c) Aggressive advertising and product
(d) Aggressive product and packaging

74. In which country the advertising industry spend $ 700 per person per year to push goods on consumers?

(a) Canada
(b) U.K
(c) U.S.A
(d) Australia

75. In which year the advertising industry in the U.S.A spend $ 700 per person per year to push goods on consumers?

(a) 1965
(b) 1975
(c) 1985
(d) 1995

76. The consumer wants protection against ________.

(a) Deceptive advertisements
(b) False advertisement
(c) Misleading advertisements
(d) All the above

77. Who do need protection under the present circumstances?

(a) Marketer
(b) Producer
(c) Consumer
(d) Manufacture

78. Which one of the following is not the problem of consumer protection in the market?

(a) Consumer legislation
(b) Consumerism
(c) Business
(d) None of the above

79. What is the market place is the focus or the heart of enlightened marketing mix?

(a) Consumer protect
(b) Consumer choice
(c) Consumer interest
(d) Consumer satisfaction

80. Which aim at the protection of consumer?

(a) Business
(b) Consumerism
(c) Both a and b
(d) None of the above

81. The business aim at the protection of consumer through ________.

(a) Self-regulation
(b) Self-help
(c) Self-respect
(d) Self-control

82. The consumerism aim at the protection of consumer through ________.

(a) Self-regulation
(b) Self-help
(c) Self-respect
(d) Self-control

83. Consumerism involves Government assistance when business misbehaves and fails to fulfill ________.

(a) Social responsibilities
(b) Economical responsibilities
(c) Political responsibilities
(d) Legal responsibilities

84. In exchange relationship how many parties are there ________.

(a) One
(b) Two
(c) Three
(d) Four

85. Who are the parties in exchange relationship?

(a) Seller
(b) Buyer
(c) Both a and b
(d) None of the above

86. In the modern market, the seller is ________.

(a) Unorganized and amateur
(b) Organized and has professional skill
(c) Organized and amateur
(d) Unorganized and has professional skill

87. Which one of the following is not a problem of consumer protection in the market?

(a) Consumer legislation
(b) Business
(c) Consumerism
(d) None of the above

88. Which one of the following is a problem of consumer protection in the market?

(a) Market
(b) Business
(c) Socialism
(d) Capitalism

89. In the market the Government intervention takes place only to protect the ________.

(a) Consumer
(b) Buyer
(c) Both a and b
(d) None of the above

90. In the market, the Government intervention takes place to prevent exploitation by the ________.

(a) Consumer
(b) Businessmen
(c) Both a and b
(d) None of the above

91. Which is a rough substitute for self-regulation of business?

(a) Consumer protection
(b) Consumer education
(c) Consumer organization
(d) Consumer legislation

92. Which has fought in many countries for consumer legislation?

(a) Capitalism
(b) Consumerism
(c) Socialism
(d) All the above

93. Which has the direct responsibility of find out areas in which company's products service fail to fulfill consumer needs and expectations?

(a) Marketing management
(b) Business management
(c) Social management
(d) Programme management

94. Marketing management can take immediate and intelligent efforts ________.

(a) To improve marketing efficiency
(b) To reduce the cost of distribution appreciably
(c) Both a and b
(d) None of the above

95. Which Act provides better protection of the rights and interests of consumers?

(a) Consumer Organization Act, 1986
(b) Consumer Protection Act, 1986
(c) Consumer Protection Act, 1976
(d) Consumer Organization Act, 1976

96. The state commission has a judge of ________.

(a) The high court and two other members
(b) The high court and one other member
(c) The supreme court and two other members
(d) The supreme court and one other member

97. Any person aggrieved by the order of the state commission can appeal to ________.

(a) The state commission within one month of the order of the national commission.
(b) The national commission within one month of the order of the state commission.
(c) The central commission within one month of the order of national commission.
(d) The national commission within one month of the order of the central commission.

98. Which Act has given full recognition to the consumer rights?

(a) Consumer protection
(b) Consumer organization
(c) Consumer disputes
(d) Consumer commission

99. District forum can give compensation to the victimized consumer up to ________.

(a) 5 lakhs
(b) 10 lakhs
(c) 15 lakhs
(d) 20 lakhs

100. District forum can give compensation to the state commission up to ________.

(a) 5 lakhs
(b) 10 lakhs
(c) 15 lakhs
(d) 20 lakhs

101. Consumer disputes redressal forum is established by the ________ in each district by notification?

(a) Central Government
(b) State Government
(c) both a and b
(d) None of the above

102. Which consists of a person who is qualified to be the judge of a district court and two other members one of whom shall be a lady social worker?

(a) Central commission
(b) State commission
(c) District forum
(d) Consumer disputes

103. In district forum every member shall have the tenure of 5 years with age limit of ________.

(a) 60 years
(b) 62 years
(c) 64 years
(d) 65 years

104. A recent ordinance promulgated on ________.

(a) June 18, 1993
(b) June 18, 1983
(c) July 18, 1993
(d) July 18, 1983

105. Who amended the Consumer Protection Act, 1986?

(a) The prime minister of India
(b) The president of India
(c) The minister of India
(d) The secretary of India

106. Complaints between ₹ 5 lakhs and ₹ 20 lakhs can be field before the ________.

(a) State commission
(b) Central commission
(c) National commission
(d) All the above

107. Complaints exceeding 20 lakhs can be filed before the ________.

(a) State commission
(b) Central commission
(c) National commission
(d) All the above

108. More consumer forum can be setup at the ________.

(a) District level
(b) State level
(c) National level
(d) International level

109. The consumer forum has have also been empowered to dismiss frivolous or variations complaints with costs up to ________.

(a) ₹ 5,000
(b) ₹ 10,000
(c) ₹ 15,000
(d) ₹ 20,000

110. Marketers in India are gradually showing genuine interest in satisfying today's ________.

(a) More sophisticated consumers
(b) More skeptical consumers
(c) More demanding consumers
(d) All the above

111. Indian consumer market of around 300 million is considered to be the ________ largest market in the world.

(a) 5th
(b) 6th
(c) 7th
(d) 8th

112. In the field of distribution, which is for more effective and superior than state policing?

(a) Self-policing
(b) Statutory-policing
(c) Self-regulation
(d) Self-help

113. Oligopoly means ________.

(a) Market with no sellers
(b) Market with few sellers
(c) Market with one seller
(d) Market with two sellers

114. Monopoly means ________.

(a) Market with no seller
(b) Market with few sellers
(c) Market with one seller
(d) Market with two seller

115. To have an effective consumer protection, a practical response on the part of which parities is essential?

(a) The business
(b) The government
(c) The consumers
(d) All the above

116. Which action, to protect the interests of consumers has become quite common everywhere in the world?

(a) Statutory
(b) Social
(c) Legal
(d) Consumer

117. Which are the crudest form as well as a last resort to secure a disciplined business conduct?

(a) Statutory regulation
(b) Consumer regulation
(c) Social regulation
(d) Voluntary regulation

118. Which represents a wonderful opportunity for the forward-looking aggressive business management?

(a) Consumerism
(b) Socialism
(c) Capitalism
(d) Communism

119. Consumerism challenges marketers to be more ________.

(a) Informative
(b) Effective
(c) Truthful
(d) All the above

120. The ideal objective before every marketer is perfect match between the ________.

(a) Marketing concept and marketing effort
(b) Marketing effort and marketing programme
(c) Marketing effort and marketing opportunity
(d) Marketing concept and marketing opportunity

121. The basis of marketing concept is adapting ________.

(a) The supply to seller
(b) The demand to seller
(c) The supply to demand
(d) The demand to supply

122. Indian marketing environment in the near future will demonstrate very keen competition among ________.

(a) Sellers consumerism
(b) intense consumerism
(c) both a and b
(d) None of the above

123. In a matured market, all marketers will be obliged to adopt ________.

(a) Societal marketing concept
(b) Legal marketing concept
(c) Political marketing concept
(d) Economical marketing concept

124. Which may involve additional costs to marketers?

(a) Consumerism
(b) Environmental pollution
(c) Both a and b
(d) None of the above

125. Consumerism forced the business to build up marketing-mix ________.

(a) Around the consumer and around the product
(b) Around the consumer and not around the product
(c) Not around the consumer and not around the product
(d) Not around the consumer and around the product

126. CAC stands for ________.

(a) Consumer attention cell
(b) Consumer attention centre
(c) Consumer affairs cell
(d) Consumer affairs centre

127. The practice of creating consumer affairs cell is spreading in the ________.

(a) Underdeveloped countries
(b) Developing countries
(c) Developed countries
(d) All the above

128. From the following which one is the central objective of all marketing activities and company actions?

(a) The creation of a satisfied consumer - citizen
(b) Educating consumers about their rights and responsibilities

(c) More responsive to the valid grievances of consumers

(d) Resolving the customer complaints promptly

129. The new marketing concept has societal dimension covering ________.

(a) Consumer satisfaction

(b) Public welfare

(c) Both a and b

(d) None of the above

130. The consumer needs ________.

(a) Accurate information

(b) Complete information

(c) Both a and b

(d) None of the above

131. Advertising must be ________.

(a) Truthful

(b) Honest

(c) Promise

(d) Not over promise

132. Packaging and labeling must be ________.

(a) Truthful

(b) Honest

(c) Promise

(d) Not over promise

133. Marketing communications should ________.

(a) Truthful

(b) Honest

(c) Promise

(d) Not over-promise

134. Corporate advertising should not be ________.

(a) Over truthful

(b) Over honest

(c) Over promise

(d) Overemphasized

135. Marketing is sometimes defined as looking at the world from the ________.

(a) buyer's end

(b) Seller's end

(c) Researcher's end

(d) Informer's end

136. The appropriate marketing concept is to look at the business from the ________.

(a) Buyer's end

(b) Seller's end

(c) Researcher's end

(d) Informer's end

137. A majority of the consumer problems directly involve ________.

(a) Marketing policies

(b) Marketing practices

(c) Both a and b

(d) None of the above

138. Marketing deserves special study because of its very objective of its very objectives of ________.

(a) Reaching the consumer

(b) Selling to the consumer

(c) Both a and b

(d) None of the above

139. "A customer is the most important person on our premises, he is not dependent on us we are dependent on him" The best business approach to consumerism is said by ________.

(a) Mahatma Gandhi

(b) B.R. Ambedkar

(c) Jawaharlal Nehru

(d) Abdul Kamal

140. Which should be given secondary importance in a consumer relations concept of the public?

(a) Long run sales and profits

(b) Medium run sales and profits

(c) Short run sales and profits
(d) None of the above

141. Which must see that consumer interest is duly protected?

(a) Management policies
(b) Management decisions
(c) Both a and b
(d) None of the above

142. Two-way communications are necessary for better flow of understanding between the ________

(a) Corporation and the consumer
(b) Businessmen and the consumer
(c) Informer and the consumer
(d) Distributor and the consumer

143. Which decision must be based on consumer viewpoint which is possible if we have two-way flow of communications in a balanced form?

(a) Marketing
(b) Management
(c) Production
(d) Price

144. Which from the following which is the new a venues to consumer-oriented marketing management?

(a) Consumer research
(b) Consumer relations
(c) Consumer - interest committees
(d) All the above

145. Which will provide grass-root report on consumer problems and complaints?

(a) Consumer research
(b) Shareholder research
(c) Consumer - interest committees
(d) Consumer relations

146. Each company should have a separate consumer affairs cell to ________.

(a) Consumer complaints
(b) Supervise advertising claims
(c) Conduct tests of consumer products
(d) All the above

147. Growth of consumer movement in the country indicates that business has failed to meet the total ________.

(a) Needs of consumers
(b) Desires of consumers
(c) Both a and b
(d) None of the above

148. Which must be in general accord with the consumer interest?

(a) Marketing strategies
(b) Marketing policies
(c) Marketing practices
(d) All the above

Answers for MCQ

1.	(a)	7.	(a)	13.	(a)	19.	(b)	25.	(b)	31.	(c)
2.	(c)	8.	(c)	14.	(a)	20.	(c)	26.	(c)	32.	(a)
3.	(b)	9.	(b)	15.	(c)	21.	(b)	27.	(a)	33.	(c)
4.	(c)	10.	(b)	16.	(d)	22.	(a)	28.	(b)	34.	(c)
5.	(c)	11.	(c)	17.	(c)	23.	(d)	29.	(c)	35.	(c)
6.	(c)	12.	(d)	18.	(a)	24.	(c)	30.	(b)	36.	(d)

37.	(c)	56.	(a)	75.	(d)	94.	(c)	113.	(b)	132.	(b)
38.	(b)	57.	(c)	76.	(d)	95.	(c)	114.	(c)	133.	(d)
39.	(c)	58.	(a)	77.	(c)	96.	(a)	115.	(d)	134.	(d)
40.	(a)	59.	(d)	78.	(d)	97.	(b)	116.	(a)	135.	(b)
41.	(d)	60.	(d)	79.	(c)	98.	(a)	117.	(a)	136.	(a)
42.	(a)	61.	(b)	80.	(c)	99.	(a)	118.	(a)	137.	(c)
43.	(d)	62.	(b)	81.	(a)	100.	(d)	119.	(d)	138.	(c)
44.	(b)	63.	(c)	82.	(b)	101.	(b)	120.	(c)	139.	(a)
45.	(a)	64.	(b)	83.	(b)	102.	(c)	121.	(c)	140.	(c)
46.	(c)	65.	(d)	84.	(b)	103.	(d)	122.	(c)	141.	(c)
47.	(b)	66.	(a)	85.	(c)	104.	(a)	123.	(a)	142.	(a)
48.	(a)	67.	(d)	86.	(b)	105.	(b)	124.	(c)	143.	(b)
49.	(c)	68.	(b)	87.	(d)	106.	(a)	125.	(b)	144.	(d)
50.	(b)	69.	(d)	88.	(b)	107.	(c)	126.	(c)	145.	(a)
51.	(a)	70.	(c)	89.	(a)	108.	(a)	127.	(c)	146.	(d)
52.	(d)	71.	(b)	90.	(b)	109.	(b)	128.	(a)	147.	(c)
53.	(a)	72.	(a)	91.	(d)	110.	(d)	129.	(c)	148.	(d)
54.	(b)	73.	(a)	92.	(b)	111.	(b)	130.	(c)		
55.	(d)	74.	(c)	93.	(a)	112.	(a)	131.	(a)		

MATCH THE FOLLOWING

1.	Consumerism	(a)	Market with four sellers
2.	Consumer movement	(b)	Consumer satisfaction and welfare of society
3.	Environment	(c)	Market with one seller
4.	Oligopoly	(d)	Prevent consumer exploitation and minimize litigation
5.	Monopoly	(e)	Earthly world
6.	Societal marketing concept	(f)	Product consumer interests

Answers for Match the Following

1.	(f)	2.	(d)	3.	(e)	4.	(a)	5.	(c)	6.	(b)

Chapter 12

Product Plan

SUMMARY

A product is anything that can be offered to a market to satisfy a want or need. Products that are marketed include physical goods, services, experiences, events, persons, places, properties, organizations, information and ideas. Product is the most important component of the marketing program. The product policy and strategy is the cornerstone of a marketing mix. If the product fails to satisfy the consumer no other element of the marketing mix can remove the dissatisfaction or improve the product performance in the market place. Good product is a key to market success. Product decisions are taken first by the marketers and these decisions are central to all other marketing decisions such as price, promotion and distribution. Product is the engine that pulls the rest of the marketing program. Products fill the needs of the society. It represents a handle of expectations to consumers and society. In planning its market offering, the marketer needs to think five levels of the product. Each level adds more customer value and the five levels constitute customer value hierarchy. The most fundamental level is the core benefit, i.e., the fundamental service or benefit the customer is really buying. For example, a hotel guest is buying "rest and sleep". Marketers should see themselves as benefit provider. In the second stage, the marketer has to turn the core benefit into a basic product. Thus, a hotel room includes, bed, bathroom, and desk and so on. At the third level, the marketer prepares an unexpected product, a set of attributes and conditions buyers normally expect when they purchased the product.

The product is the most tangible and important single component of the marketing programme. The product policy and strategy is the cornerstone of a marketing mix. Without a product, there is nothing to distribute, nothing to promote, nothing to price. If the product fails to satisfy consumer demand, no additional cost on any of the other ingredients of the marketing mix will improve the product performance in the marketplace.

To the marketer products are the building blocks of a marketing plan. Good products are key to market success. Product decisions are taken first by the marketers and these decisions are central to all other marketing decisions such as price, promotion and distribution. Product is the vehicle by which a company provides consumer satisfactions. It is the engine that pulls the rest of the marketing programme. Products fill in the needs of society. They represent a bundle of expectations to consumers and society.

Good product is more important than ever because customers are demanding greater product variety and are switching more quickly to products with state-of-the-art technology. The impacts of greater product variety and shorter product life cycles have a multiplicative effect on the number of new products and derivative products that need to be designed. For example, just a few years ago, a firm may have produced four different products and each product may have had a product life cycle of ten years. In this case, the firm must design four new products every ten years. Today, in order to be competitive, this firm may produce eight different products with a life cycle of only five years; this firm must introduce eight new products in five years. That represents sixteen new products in ten years or one product every seven and one-half months. In this fast-paced environment, product design ceases to be an ad hoc, intermittent activity and becomes a regular and routine action. For an organization, delays, problems, and confusion in product design shift from being an annoyance to being life threatening.

Product Mix is the list of all products offered for sale by a company. It is defined as "the composite of products offered for sale by a firm or a business unit". For example, if a firm manufactures or deals with different varieties of soap, toothbrush, toothpaste, etc., the group of all these products is called Product Mix.

In product line decision, objectives involved are higher market share for the product line and growth in volume of sales resulting in more profit, price removing more or less stable. Even if prices are decreased a high growth in volume of sales may result in more profit one of the product line and growth in volume of sales resulting in more profit, price, removing more or less stable. Even if prices are decreased a high growth in volume of sales may result in more profit. One of the product line decisions to be made is about deletion of unprofitable or marginal products, multi-product organization can't impart all its products to earn the same profit. Some products may fetch high profit volume while others yield low profit volumes. In such cases the product line decision to be taken is about the development of an optimum product line. Within the framework of the objectives of an organization in terms of availability of production facilities, finance, etc., and the profitability of the items in the product line. Product line decisions are to be made as to how long or short the line should be. Often a line of product is meant to meet various segments of customers.

Position is the outcome of a conscious strategy of marketing. Positioning comes out of marketing management's awareness that a product can't be "everything to everyone." It can be something to someone. Identifying those features imaginatively is the essence of positioning. The product can be positioned, against a competing brand, for an exclusive will to do segment of the market, for men, for children. Positioning theme has to be formulated right from the product ideas stage, positioning is what you do to the minds of the consumers. It means producers and marketing management positioning the product in the minds of the prospects.

The producer is to regularly strive for modifying and improving his products to cater to varying needs and habits of the customers. He needs to go on adding some distinct features and benefits to the existing product. Development and launching of new products are necessary to earn more profits and hence for the company.

Product planning means to decide what type of product is to be produced or what needs or requirements the product is to satisfy and for whom the product is meant. If the existing product lacks in satisfying the needs of the consumers what type of modification it require or if product fails to show the attention of the consumers or becomes unprofitable despite best efforts, it should be eliminated or if there is any other chance should it be improved in terms of the changing needs and preferences of the consumers.

Product Planning is the chief responsibility of the chief executive of the company who coordinates the efforts of all the department executives in taking a decision. It is a team activity and a link in development of a product for management.

Elements of Product Planning

Research before Production: Before taking a decision to produce a new item, market research should be carried out extensively with a view to know the needs, wants, tastes, talents, preferences, attitude, etc., of the consumers. The company must know before hand what should be produced and for whom? It should decide the characteristics of the product, e.g., Size, color, design, brand, packing, price, etc., that can meet the requirements of the people. Such type of research provides the base for product planning.

Possibility of Production: What production method should be followed and is it practicable to develop a product exactly what the consumer wants? This possibility should also be examined before taking a decision of producing a new product.

Modification in Existing Lines: The existing production lines should also be diagnosed whether they can be improved to meet the new requirements of the consumer or a new product is to be developed.

Elimination of the Product: Product planning involves the decision regarding the elimination of the unprofitable product (which has reached final stage of its life cycle) or product lines so that the resources may be used for some other product profitability.

Improvement in the Product: Product planning includes decision regarding the improvement of the existing product in terms of quality, packing, etc., taking in view the competitors strategies in the market.

Importance of Product Planning

Product planning involves decisions regarding the products, at different stages of its life cycle from time to time. Why to produce a particular product; what to be produced; when and why to produce; why not a particular product be improved or abolished from the product line are certain questions which require adequate attention of the management. Any decision regarding the production, modification and elimination of a product may affect the marketing policies, programme, producers and strategies. If decision is taken without proper consideration or planning, it may ruin the firm because other programme, policies, etc., are the outcome of the product plans, so product planning is the starting point of all marketing programme.

This should be the main philosophy of the modern marketing managements. What the customer needs, should be the main consideration in the product planning and it should decide how it must contain those qualities which can satisfy those needs company can sell those product which is required by the customers, otherwise life cycle of the product would be very short and company may lose its existence forever. Thus product planning determines how to satisfy the consumer's needs.

Profit is the main concern of the business. No businessman would be ready to do anything without profit motive. Customer's needs must be satisfied on the one hand and reasonable and sufficient profits must be earned by the firm on the other hand. Product planning is one of the ways to coordinate the customers satisfaction and the profitability.

Product planning is necessary to face the competition in marketing. The success of marketing efforts depends very much upon the extent to which product of the enterprise is able to face the competition. Decisions regarding modification or empowerment in the product are taken with a view to keep the competitive forces out of the market or to have an edge over competitor's products.

New product development is one of the most important components of the most important components of product policy and product management, so far you have learnt in the previous unit about product, it's positioning in the market. A progressive firm will always be considering the introduction of a new product in order to expand its market share in order to have higher profits.

FILL IN THE BLANKS

1. _______ is the heart of marketing mix.
2. _______ is the most tangible and important single component of the marketing programme.
3. The product _______ and _______ is the cornerstone of a marketing mix.
4. Without a product, there is nothing to _______, _______ and _______.
5. To the marketer _______ are the building blocks of a marketing plan.
6. Good products are key to _______.
7. Product decisions are taken first by the _______.
8. Product decisions are central to all other marketing decisions such as _______, _______ and _______.
9. _______ is the engine that pulled the rest of the marketing programme.
10. _______, _______ and _______ dimensions are the product concept.
11. As a basis to planning, product is second only to _______ and _______.
12. The product offering must balance with consumer-citizen _______ and _______.
13. Product _______ and _______ can assure normal rate of return on investment and continuous growth of the enterprise.
14. To the _______ a product is actually a group of symbols or meanings.
15. Product represents _______ and _______ aspects.
16. A product conveys a message indicating a bundle of expectations to a _______.
17. Consumer accepts products as bundle of satisfactions rather than as _______ things.
18. To the society salutary products and desirable products are always welcome as they fulfill the expectations of social _______ and _______.
19. Desirable products offer benefits, _______ and _______ consumer welfare.
20. Salutary products yield _______ advantages but may not have _______ appeal.
21. Eco-marked products are _______.
22. _______ is not an example for product concept.
23. _______ is an example for product concept.
24. The _______ is a bundle of all kinds of satisfaction of both material and non-material kinds, ranging from economic utilities to satisfaction of a social-psychological nature.
25. The product supplies _______ and _______ kinds of utility in the form of social-psychological benefits.
26. A product is the sum total of physical _______, _______ and psychological benefits.
27. _______ must define their market in terms of product functions - what the customer expects from the product.
28. _______ are not interest in the composition of a product.
29. The concept of product as a bundle of _______, _______ and _______ need not be overstressed.
30. A _______ is a company plan for marketing its products.
31. _______ mix of marketing is the entire range of products of a company for sale.
32. The product mix of a company has _______, _______ and _______ characteristics.
33. _______ of the product mix depends upon the number of product groups of product lines found within the company.

34. Depth of the product mix depends upon the number of product items with in each ________.

35. Consistency of the product mix refers to the question whether or not the products have ________ and ________ affinity.

36. General Electric Corporation of the U.S.A has over ________ lakhs of products.

37. There are deficient products which have neither immediate appeal nor ________ benefits.

38. Firms are not interested in deficient products as there is no chance to make any ________.

39. ________ products have a happy combination of high immediate satisfaction and high long-run consumer welfare.

40. Tasty, nutrition, ready-made food products are the examples of ________ products.

41. ________ products are less costly than desirable products.

42. Consumers demand ________ products.

43. The two essentials of successful marketing are ________ and ________.

44. ________ and ________ are expected to be the two sides of the same blade, *viz.*, marketing.

45. A right product is bound to reduce considerably the problems of ________, ________ and ________.

46. PLC stands for ________.

47. Product category exhibits a ________ life cycle.

48. Product forms normally follow the ________ productivity life cycle.

49. In the product life cycle concept, the ________ mean that sales are starting-infant.

50. In the product life cycle concept, ________ mean rising sales an increasing rate.

51. In the product life cycle concept, ________ mean rising sales at decreasing rate.

52. ________ means stable sales, in the production life cycle concept.

53. ________ mean falling sales-decay and exit, in the production life cycle concept.

54. The PLC should be termed as ________ life cycles as it is related to a given particular market.

55. Every product moves through a life cycle having ________ stages.

56. In introduction stage ________ and ________ are considered critical.

57. Growth is the period during which the product is accepted by ________ and ________.

58. The firm gives top priority to ________ volume.

59. The firm gives secondary preference to ________ maintenance.

60. For marketing success, ________ and ________ efficiency are the vital factors.

61. During maturity stage keen competition brings pressure on ________.

62. The ________ stage occurs in the market when all potential buyers are using the product and we have only replacement sales.

63. New products are the real solutions to the problems of ________ and ________ stage of the product life cycle concept.

64. The most essential of the product life cycle is ________ and ________ curve.

65. PLC concept is very useful in the management of life cycle of a product through ________ and ________ strategic planning.

66. The diffusion process is described in the form of the ________ distribution curve.

67. Innovators are the first ________ percent of the market.

68. The thirteen and a half per cent using the product are ________.

69. ________ are educated, rich and more successful than average

70. The 34 per cent are the early majority to adopt the ________.

71. The 34 per cent are the late majority buyers to adopt the ________.

72. In ________ the buyer are older and less educated.

73. Laggards are the last category of ________ per cent of buyers.

74. Marketers develop two distinct marketing programmes one for ________ and ________.

75. Innovate is a current slogan which has rich meaning for business operating in an economy with ________ oriented marketing.

76. An innovation is the act of developing a novel idea into a ________.

77. A successful ________ passes through the idea or invention, the implementation of the idea and the market acceptance.

78. ________ is the most critical to any successful innovation.

79. An adoption process is a process bringing about a change in buyer's ________ and ________.

80. The innovate attitude of marketer is expressed in the watchword ________.

81. The basic function of business enterprise are ________ and ________.

82. ________, ________ and ________ are the methods of obtaining products.

83. ________ is the methods of obtaining products, discovering and developing new products by the firm itself.

84. ________ is the methods of obtaining products, that the securing right to produce the product from a patent holder.

85. ________ is the method of obtaining products, for buying the firm that developed or patented the product by costly means.

86. Acquisition is very ________ but gives ________ rights.

87. Innovation alone assures ________ and ________.

88. Customer-orientation assures ________.

89. ________ is a general term covering the search for new products and new innovations as well as the improvement of existing products.

90. The firm can market its present products to ________ markets.

91. In market development the present is introduced to ________ markets.

92. ________ is the creation of new markets by discovering new applications for existing goods

93. The firm can offer its existing products to ________.

94. ________ occurs when a firm introduces new products to a market.

95. The firm decides to create new products for ________.

96. ________ is the introduction of new products in the present market.

97. ________ occurs when a firm seeks to enter a new market with a completely new product.

98. ________ is introduced for the first time in the new market.

99. Till the year ________, mast marketers had adopted a strategy of differentiating products through branding/packaging.

100. In the year ________ the market segmentation strategy was introduced.

101. ________, ________ and ________ are the expensive stages in new product idea.

102. ________, ________, ________ are the types of new products.

103. ________ and ________ products are new to the company.

104. Social costs of a new product should be incorporated in the ________ analysis.

105. Screening should avoid ________ and ________ errors.

106. Product life cycle requires the product development programme for ________ and ________ opportunities.

107. New product development must be carefully ________ and ________.

108. Business analysis concentrates on ________, ________ and ________ analysis.

109. ________ analysis is a combination of marketing research, cost benefit analysis and assessment of competition.

110. Customer reactions can be tested under ________ market conditions.

111. Mass product will start and all ________ channels will be duly organized.

112. Most of the reasons for failure of new products can be eliminated by the ________.

113. Marketing research is essential to evaluate market ________ and ________.

114. Marketing begins with ________.

115. ________ must fill the needs of the customers.

116. ________ marked product will have a bright future in the 21st century.

117. Japan and Germany have emerged as business leaders today only through quality assurance and ________.

118. TQM stands for ________.

119. Total Quality Management is a ________ planning strategy.

120. Focus on ________ establishes a customer-driven standard.

121. Focus on ________ maintains a customer-driven standard.

122. Freedom from deficiencies reduces customer ________.

123. The focus on product features is ________.

124. Focus on freedom from deficiencies is ________.

125. When the concentration is on ________ features then higher quality costs more.

126. When the concentration is on freedom from ________, higher quality costs less.

127. ISO stands for ________.

128. ISO: A measure of quality launched in ________.

129. ISO certificates are increasingly gaining acceptance around the globe as the ________ mark of quality

130. The ISO comprises ________ technical committees, each responsible for one of the several areas of specialization.

131. The word ISO has been derived from the ________ word.

132. The ISO series consists of ________ standards.

133. A standard terminology on definition and concepts known as ________.

134. The five quality standards is popularly called the ________.

135. ISO certification signifies ________ per cent of the total TQM requirements.

136. Recertification of ISO certification has to be done every ________ years with intermediate evaluations during 4 years.

137. External forces are ________ by the firm.

138. Internal forces are ________ by the firm.

139. Internal forces will very between ________, ________ and stages of ________ life.

140. ________ are expected to adopt a product or product line to the various needs of the market.

141. Unoccupied niche in the market is the best position for a ________.

142. ________ can discover unoccupied niche

143. ________, ________ and ________ are the methods to adopt the product exactly to the market.

144. Market aggregation is equivalent to standardization of ________.

145. The product policy is supported by powerful ________ and ________.

146. Marketers can adopt only one or a few market segments for their products is known as ________.

147. Excessive market segmentation amounts to market fragmentation and it leads to ______.

148. Marketer has ________ and ________ routes available to meet competition.

149. ________ route makes the marketer to totally dependent on the product to face competition.

150. ________ and ________ helps the firm to fight on a non-price plank.

151. Product differentiation is done through ________ and ________.

152. ________ implies that supply is prepared to adjust itself to meet customer preferences or demand.

Answers for Fill in the Blanks

1.	Product plan	27.	Marketers
2.	Product	28.	Buyers
3.	Policy; strategy	29.	Utilities; satisfaction; benefits
4.	Distribute; promote; price	30.	Product strategy
5.	Products	31.	Product
6.	Market success	32.	Width; depth; consistency
7.	Marketers	33.	Width
8.	Price; promotion; distribution	34.	Product line
9.	Product	35.	Production; marketing
10.	Managerial; consumer; societal	36.	Two and a half
11.	Market; marketing research	37.	Long run
12.	Needs, desires	38.	Profit
13.	Planning; development	39.	Desirable
14.	Consumer	40.	Desirable
15.	Utility; non-utility	41.	Pleasing
16.	Buyer	42.	Pleasing
17.	Physical	43.	Products; markets
18.	Welfare; interests	44.	Products; markets
19.	Immediate satisfaction; long run	45.	Pricing; promotion; distribution
20.	Long run; immediate	46.	Product life cycle
21.	Environment friendly	47.	Longest
22.	Product	48.	Standard
23.	Managerial	49.	Introduction
24.	Product	50.	Growth
25.	Economic; supplementary	51.	Maturity
26.	Economic; social	52.	Saturation

53.	Decline	92.	Market development
54.	Product market	93.	New markets
55.	Five	94.	Product development
56.	Product development; product design	95.	Existing markets
57.	Consumer; traders	96.	Product development
58.	Sales	97.	Diversification
59.	Quality	98.	Innovation
60.	Manufacturing; distribution	99.	1950
61.	Prices	100.	1956
62.	Saturation	101.	Development; testing; launching
63.	Maturity; decline	102.	Innovative; Emulative; Adoptive
64.	Sales; profit	103.	Innovative; Emulative
65.	Corporate; marketing	104.	Cost-benefits
66.	Normal	105.	Rejecting an idea; accepting an idea
67.	Two and a half	106.	New products; new profit
68.	Early adopters	107.	Planned; managed
69.	Early adopters	108.	Demand; cost ; profitability
70.	New product	109.	Business
71.	Innovation	110.	Normal
72.	Late majority	111.	Distribution
73.	16	112.	Company
74.	Innovators; early adopters	113.	Needs ; prospects
75.	Customer	114.	Consumers
76.	Product	115.	Product
77.	Innovation	116.	Eco
78.	Market acceptance	117.	Total quality management
79.	Attitudes; perception	118.	Total Quality Management
80.	Innovate or die	119.	Corporate
81.	Marketing; innovation	120.	Quality planning
82.	Internal development; licensing; acquisition	121.	Quality control
		122.	Dissatisfaction
83.	Internal development	123.	Sales
84.	Licensing	124.	Costs
85.	Acquisition	125.	Product
86.	Costly; exclusive	126.	Deficiencies
87.	Growth; survival	127.	International organization for standardization
88.	Survival		
89.	Product development	128.	1987
90.	Cresting	129.	Hall
91.	New	130.	180

131.	Greek	143.	Market aggregation; market segmentation; product differentiation
132.	Six		
133.	ISO 8402	144.	Marketing policy
134.	ISO series	145.	Advertising, promotion
135.	30	146.	Market concentration
136.	4	147.	Losses
137.	Uncontrollable	148.	Price; non-price
138.	Controllable	149.	Non-price
139.	Firms; product; product	150.	Product differentiation ; product positioning
140.	Marketers		
141.	Product	151.	Branding; packaging
142.	Market research	152.	Market segmentation

TRUE / FALSE

1. The pricing plan is the heart of the marketing mix. (True / False)
2. The product is the most tangible and important single component of the marketing programme. (True / False)
3. The product policy and strategy is the cornerstone of a marketing management. (True / False)
4. Without a product, there is nothing to distributes promote and price. (True / False)
5. To the marketer product are the building blocks of a marketing plan. (True / False)
6. Very good products are key to market research. (True / False)
7. Product decisions are taken first by the marketers. (True / False)
8. Product decision are central to marketing decision of distribution. (True / False)
9. Product is the engine that pulls the rest of the marketing programme. (True / False)
10. Managerials, consumers and societal dimensions are the product concept. (True / False)
11. As a basis to planning, promotion is second only to market and marketing research. (True / False)
12. The product offering must balance with consumer-citizen needs and desires. (True / False)
13. Product planning and development can assure normal rate of return on borrowing and continues growth of the enterprise. (True / False)
14. To consumer a product is actually a group of symbols or meanings. (True / False)
15. A product represents both utility and non-utility aspects. (True / False)
16. A product conveys a message indicating a bundle of expectations to a seller. (True / False)
17. Consumer accepts products as bundle of satisfactions rather than as physical things. (True / False)
18. To the society salutary products and desirable products are always welcome as they fulfill the expectations of social welfare and interests. (True / False)

19. Desirable products offer long run consumer interests. (True / False)

20. Salutary products offer short run advantages and immediate satisfaction. (True / False)

21. Eco-marked products would be environment friendly. (True / False)

22. Consumer is not a product concept. (True / False)

23. Managerial is a product concept. (True / False)

24. Promotion is a bundle of all kinds of satisfaction of both material and non-material kinds. (True / False)

25. In the product supplies economic and supplementary kinds of utility, in the form of social psychological benefits. (True / False)

26. A product is the sum total of physical benefits. (True / False)

27. Marketers must define their market in terms of product functions - what the customer expects from the product. (True / False)

28. Consumer is not interested in the composition of a product. (True / False)

29. The concept of product as a bundle of utilities, satisfaction and benefits need not be over stressed. (True / False)

30. Pricing strategy is a company plan for marketing is products. (True / False)

31. Product mix of marketing is the entire range of products of a company for sale. (True / False)

32. The main characteristics of product mix of a company are width, depth and consistency. (True / False)

33. Depth of the product mix depends upon the number of product groups of product lines found within the company. (True / False)

34. Width of the product mix depends upon the number of items within each product line. (True / False)

35. Consistency of the product mix refers to the questions whether or not the products have production and marketing affinity. (True / False)

36. General Electric corporation of the U.S.A has over 2 1/2 lakhs of products. (True / False)

37. There are salutary products which have neither immediate appeal nor long-run benefits. (True / False)

38. Firms are interested in deficient products as there is a chance to make profit. (True / False)

39. Desirable products have a happy combination of high immediate satisfaction and high long run consumer welfare. (True / False)

40. Tasty, nutritious, ready-made food products are the examples of deficient products. (True / False)

41. Pleasing product are less costly than desirable products. (True / False)

42. Consumers demand desirable products. (True / False)

43. The two essentials of successful marketing are products and markets. (True / False)

44. Products and price are expected to be the two sides of the same blade, *viz.*, marketing. (True / False)

45. A right product is bound to reduce considerably the problems of pricing, promotion and distribution. (True / False)

46. PLC stands for product life centre. (True / False)

47. Product category exhibits a longest life cycle. (True / False)

48. Product forms normally follow the standard productivity life cycle. (True / False)

49. In the product life cycle concept, the introduction means that stable sales. (True / False)

50. Growth means that rising sales at increasing rate in the product life cycle concept. (True / False)

51. In product life cycle concept, the maturity means that rising sales at decreasing rate. (True / False)

52. Decline means stable sales, in the product life cycle concept. (True / False)

53. Saturation means falling sales-decay and exit, in the production life cycle concept. (True / False)

54. The PLC should be termed as product market life cycle as it is related to a given particular market. (True / False)

55. Every product moves through a life cycle having four stages. (True / False)

56. In introduction stage product development and design are considered critical. (True / False)

57. Saturation is the period during which the product is accepted by consumer and the traders. (True / False)

58. The firm gives top priority to sales volume. (True / False)

59. The firm gives secondary preference to quality maintenance. (True / False)

60. For marketing success, distribution efficiency is the only vital factors. (True / False)

61. During maturity stage keen competition brings pressure on prices. (True / False)

62. The decline stage occurs in the market when all potential buyers are using the product and we have only replacement sales. (True / False)

63. New products are the real solutions to the problems of maturity and decline. (True / False)

64. The most essential feature of the product life cycle is the difference between sales revenue. (True / False)

65. PLC concept is very useful in the management of life cycle of a product through corporate and marketing strategic planning. (True / False)

66. The diffusion process is described in the form of the normal production curve. (True / False)

67. Innovators are the first two and a half percent of the market. (True / False)

68. The $14\frac{1}{2}$ per cent using the products are early adopters. (True / False)

69. Early adopters are educated rich and more successful than average. (True / False)

70. The 34 per cent are early majority to adopt the new product. (True / False)

71. To adopt the innovation, 34 per cent are the innovators. (True / False)

72. Late majority they are older and less educated buyers. (True / False)

73. In laggards there are 14 per cent of buyers. (True / False)

74. Marketers develop one distinct marketing programmes for innovators. (True / False)

75. Innovate is a current slogan which has rich meaning for business operating in an economy with customer-oriented marketing. (True / False)

76. An innovation is the act of developing a novel idea into a price. (True / False)

77. A successful innovation passes through the idea, implementation of the idea and market acceptance. (True / False)

78. Market acceptance is the most critical to any successful innovation. (True / False)

79. An adoption process is a process bringing about a change in seller's attitudes and perception. (True / False)

80. The innovate attitude of marketer is expressed in the watchword. "Innovate or die." (True / False)

81. The two basic function of business enterprise is one marketing and innovate. (True / False)

82. Licensing is the only method of obtaining products. (True / False)

83. Internal development are discovering and developing new products. (True / False)

84. Acquisition is the methods of obtaining products that are securing right to produce the product from a patent holders. (True / False)

85. Licensing is the method of obtaining products for buying the firm that developed or patented the product by costly means. (True / False)

86. Acquisition is very cheap and gives inclusive rights. (True / False)

87. Innovation alone assures growth and survival. (True / False)

88. Customer-orientation assures growth. (True / False)

89. Product development is a general term covering the search for new products and new innovations as well as the improvement of existing products. (True / False)

90. The firm can market its present products to new markets. (True / False)

91. In market development the present is introduced to new markets. (True / False)

92. Market penetration is the creation of new markets by discovering new application for existing goods. (True / False)

93. The firm can offer its existing products to new markets. (True / False)

94. Product penetration occurs when a firm introduces new products to a market. (True / False)

95. The firm decides to create new products for existing markets. (True / False)

96. Product development is the introduction of new products in the present market. (True / False)

97. Penetration occurs when a firm seeks to enter a new market with a completely new product. (True / False)

98. Innovation is introduced for the first time in the new market. (True / False)

99. Till 1942, most marketers had adopted a strategy, of differentiating products through branding/packaging. (True / False)

100. In 1946 the market segmentation strategy was introduced. (True / False)

101. Development, testing and launching are the expensive stages in new product idea. (True / False)

102. Innovative, emulative and adaptive are the types of new products. (True / False)

103. Emulative and adaptive products are new to the company. (True / False)

104. Social costs of a new product should be incorporated in the cost-benefits analysis. (True / False)

105. Screening should avoid the errors of rejecting an idea that could later fails. (True / False)

106. Product life cycle requires the product development programme for new products and new profit opportunities. (True / False)

107. Existing product development must be carefully planned and managed. (True / False)

108. Business analysis concentrates on demand analysis only. (True / False)

109. Business analysis is a combination of marketing research, cost benefit analysis and assessment of competition. (True / False)

100. Most of the reasons for failure of new products can be eliminated by the consumers. (True / False)

111. Mass production will start and all distribution channels will be duly organized. (True / False)

112. Buyers resections can be tested under normal market conditions. (True / False)

113. Marketing information is essential to evaluate market needs and prospects. (True / False)

114. Marketing begins with consumers. (True / False)

115. Product must fill the needs of the consumers. (True / False)

116. BIS-marked product will have a bright future in the 21st century. (True / False)

117. German and Japan have emerged as business leaders today only through quality assurance. (True / False)

118. TQM stands for Total Quality Management. (True / False)

119. Total Quality Management is a pricing planning strategy. (True / False)

120. Focus quality planning establishes a customer driven standard. (True / False)

121. Focus on quality control maintains a customer driven standard. (True / False)

122. Freedom from deficiencies reduces customer satisfaction. (True / False)

123. The focus on product feature is profits. (True / False)

124. Focus on freedom from deficiencies is costs. (True / False)

125. When the concentration is on product features then higher quality costs less. (True / False)

126. When the concentration is on freedom from deficiencies, higher quality costs more. (True / False)

127. IOS stands for International Organization for Standardization. (True / False)

128. ISO: A measure of quality launched in 1967. (True / False)

129. ISO certificates are increasingly gaining acceptance around the glade as the Hallmark of quality. (True / False)

130. ISO comprises 180 technical committees, each responsible for one of the several areas of specialization. (True / False)

131. The word ISO has been derived from the Latin word. (True / False)

132. The ISO series consists of six standards. (True / False)

133. A standards terminology definition and concepts known as ISO 8402. (True / False)

134. The five quality standards is popularly called the ISI series. (True / False)

135. ISO certification signifies 30 per cent of the total TQM requirements. (True / False)

136. Recertification of ISO certification has to be done every 5 years with intermediate evaluations during 4 years. (True / False)

137. External forces are uncontrollable by the firm. (True / False)

138. Internal forces are controllable by the firm. (True / False)

139. External forces will very between firms, products and stages of product life. (True / False)

140. Marketers are expected to adopt a product or product line to the various needs of the market. (True / False)

141. Occupied niche in the market is the best position for a product. (True / False)

142. Market research can discover unoccupied niche. (True / False)

143. Market segmentation, aggregation and product differentiation are the methods to adopt the product exactly to the market. (True / False)

144. Market segmentation is equivalent to standardization of marketing policy. (True / False)

145. The product policy is supported by powerful advertising and promotion. (True / False)

146. Marketers can adopt only one or a few market segments for their products are know as market segmentation. (True / False)

147. Excessive market segmentation amounts to market fermentation and it leads to losses. (True / False)

148. Marketer has price and non-route to meet competition. (True / False)

149. Price-route makes the marketer to totally dependent on the product to face competition. (True / False)

150. Product differentiation and positioning helps the firm to fight on a non-price plank. (True / False)

Answers for True / False

1.	False	31.	True	61.	True	91.	True	121.	True
2.	True	32.	True	62.	False	92.	False	122.	False
3.	False	33.	False	63.	True	93.	True	123.	False
4.	True	34.	False	64.	False	94.	False	124.	True
5.	True	35.	True	65.	True	95.	True	125.	False
6.	False	36.	True	66.	False	96.	True	126.	False
7.	True	37.	False	67.	True	97.	False	127.	True
8.	False	38.	False	68.	False	98.	True	128.	False
9.	True	39.	True	69.	True	99.	False	129.	True
10.	True	40.	False	70.	True	100.	False	130.	True
11.	False	41.	True	71.	False	101.	True	131.	False
12.	True	42.	False	72.	True	102.	True	132.	True
13.	False	43.	True	73.	False	103.	False	133.	True
14.	True	44.	False	74.	False	104.	True	134.	False
15.	True	45.	True	75.	True	105.	False	135.	True
16.	False	46.	False	76.	False	106.	True	136.	False
17.	True	47.	True	77.	True	107.	False	137.	True
18.	True	48.	True	78.	True	108.	False	138.	True
19.	False	49.	False	79.	False	109.	True	139.	False
20.	False	50.	True	80.	True	110.	False	140.	True
21.	True	51.	True	81.	True	111.	True	141.	False
22.	False	52.	False	82.	False	112.	True	142.	True
23.	True	53.	False	83.	True	113.	False	143.	True
24.	False	54.	True	84.	False	114.	True	144.	False
25.	True	55.	False	85.	True	115.	True	145.	True
26.	False	56.	True	86.	False	116.	False	146.	False
27.	True	57.	False	87.	True	117.	False	147.	True
28.	False	58.	True	88.	False	118.	True	148.	True
29.	True	59.	True	89.	True	119.	False	149.	False
30.	False	60.	False	90.	False	120.	True	150.	True

MULTIPLE CHOICE QUESTIONS

1. Which is the heart of the marketing mix?

(a) Product plan
(b) Price plan
(c) Promotion plan
(d) Place plan

2. Which is the most tangible and important single component of the marketing programme?

(a) Product
(b) Price
(c) Promotion
(d) Place

3. Which is the cornerstone of a marketing mix?

(a) Product policy
(b) Product strategy
(c) Both a and b
(d) None of the above

4. Without a product, there is nothing ________.

(a) To distribute
(b) To promote
(c) To price
(d) All the above

5. Which are the building blocks of a marketing plan?

(a) Product
(b) Price
(c) Promotion
(d) Place

6. Which of the following is (are) the key to market success?

(a) Products
(b) Good products
(c) Very good products
(d) Excellent products

7. Which decisions are taken first by the marketers?

(a) Product
(b) Price
(c) Promotion
(d) Place

8. Product decisions are central to all other marketing decisions are ________.

(a) Price
(b) Promotion
(c) Distribution
(d) All the above

9. Which is the engine that pulls the rest of the marketing programme?

(a) Product
(b) Price
(c) Promotion
(d) Place

10. What are the dimensions of product concept?

(a) Managerial dimensions
(b) Consumer dimensions
(c) Societal dimensions
(d) All the above

11. As a basis to planning, which is second only to market and marketing research?

(a) Product
(b) Price
(c) Promotion
(d) Place

12. The product offering must balance with consumer-citizen ________.

(a) Needs
(b) Desires
(c) Both a and b
(d) None of the above

13. What can assure normal rate of return on investment and continuous growth of the enterprise?

(a) Product planning
(b) Product development
(c) Both a and b
(d) None of the above

14. To the consumer a product is actually a group of _________.

(a) Thing
(b) symbols
(c) Number
(d) template

15. Products represents _________.

(a) Utility aspects
(b) non-utility aspects
(c) Both a and b
(d) None of the above

16. A product conveys a message indicating a bundle of expectations to a _________.

(a) Buyer
(b) Seller
(c) Manufacturer
(d) Dealer

17. Who accepts products as bundle of satisfactions rather than as physical things?

(a) Consumer
(b) Marketer
(c) Manufacturer
(d) Dealer

18. To the society which products are always welcome as they fulfil the expectations of social welfare and social interests?

(a) Salutary
(b) Desirable
(c) Both a and b
(d) None of the above

19. What benefits the desirable products offer?

(a) Immediate satisfaction
(b) Long run consumer welfare
(c) Both a and b
(d) None of the above

20. Salutary products yield _________.

(a) Short run advantages and immediate appeal
(b) Short run advantages and not immediate appeal
(c) Long run advantages and immediate appeal
(d) Long run advantages and not immediate appeal

21. Which products would be environment friendly?

(a) Agmarked
(b) Ecomarked
(c) BIS-marked
(d) ISI-marked

22. Which one of the following is not a product concept?

(a) Product
(b) Managerial
(c) Consumer
(d) Societal

23. Which one of the following is a product concept?

(a) Product
(b) Service offered
(c) Managerial
(d) Brand

24. Product is bundle of all kinds of satisfaction of both material and non-material kinds, ranging from economic utilities to satisfaction of a _________.

(a) Economical-psychological nature
(b) Social-psychological nature

(c) Political-psychological nature

(d) Legal-psychological nature

25. In the form of social-psychological benefits, a product supplies what kinds of utility?

(a) Economic utility

(b) Supplementary utility

(c) Both a and b

(d) None of the above

26. A product is the sum total of ________.

(a) Physical benefits

(b) Economic benefits

(c) Social and psychological benefits

(d) All the above

27. Who must define their market in terms of product functions-what the customer expects from the product?

(a) Marketers

(b) Informers

(c) Researchers

(d) Producers

28. Who are not interested in the composition of a product?

(a) Consumer

(b) Buyers

(c) Manufacturers

(d) Dealers

29. What bundle need not be overstressed in the concept of product?

(a) Utilities

(b) Satisfaction

(c) Benefits

(d) All the above

30. What is a company plan for marketing its products?

(a) Product strategy

(b) Pricing strategy

(c) Promotion strategy

(d) Distribution strategy

31. Which mix of marketing is the entire range of products of a company for sale?

(a) Product

(b) Price

(c) Promotion

(d) Place

32. The main characteristics of product mix of a company is ________.

(a) Width

(b) Depth

(c) Consistency

(d) All the above

33. Which of the product mix depends upon the number of product groups of product lines found within the company?

(a) Width

(b) Depth

(c) Consistency

(d) None of the above

34. Which of the product mix depends upon the number of product items within each product line?

(a) Width

(b) Depth

(c) Consistency

(d) All the above

35. Which of the product mix refers to the questions whether or not the products have production affinity, marketing affinity?

(a) Width

(b) Depth

(c) Consistency

(d) None of the above

36. How many products are their in general electric corporations of the U.S.A.?

(a) Over 1 lakhs

(b) Over 1 1/2 lakhs

(c) Over 2 lakhs

(d) Over 2 1/2 lakhs

37. There are deficient products which have neither ________.

(a) Immediate appeal nor long-run benefits

(b) Immediate appeal nor short-run benefits

(c) Immediate appeal nor medium-run benefits

(d) None of the above.

38. In which products the firms are not interested as there is no chance to make any profit at all?

(a) Salutary

(b) Deficient

(c) Material

(d) Pleasing

39. Which products have a happy combination of high immediate satisfaction and high long-run consumer welfare?

(a) Salutary

(b) Deficient

(c) Material

(d) Pleasing

40. Tasty, nutrition, ready-made food products are the example of ________.

(a) Salutary products

(b) Deficient products

(c) Desirable products

(d) Pleasing products

41. Which products are less costly?

(a) Salutary products

(b) Deficient products

(c) Desirable products

(d) Pleasing products

42. What are the essentials of successful marketing?

(a) Salutary products

(b) Deficient products

(c) Desirable products

(d) Pleasing products

43. What are the essentials of successful marketing?

(a) Products

(b) Markets

(c) Both a and b

(d) None of the above

44. What are expected to be the two sides of the same blade, i.e., marketing?

(a) Products

(b) Markets

(c) Both a and b

(d) None of the above

45. A right product is bound to reduce considerably the problems of ________.

(a) Pricing

(b) Promotion

(c) Distribution

(d) All the above

46. PLC stands for ________.

(a) Product life cycle

(b) Product life centre

(c) Pricing life cycle

(d) Pricing life centre

47. Product category exhibits a ________.

(a) Short life cycle

(b) Medium life cycle

(c) Longest life cycle

(d) All the above

48. Product forms normally follows the ____.

(a) Sales productivity life cycle

(b) Standard productivity life cycle

(c) Demand productivity life cycle

(d) Shapes of productivity life cycle

49. In the product life cycle concept, what does the introduction mean?

(a) Sales are starting-infant

(b) Stable sales

(c) Rising sales at increasing rate

(d) Rising sales at decreasing rate

50. What does growth mean, in the product life cycle concept?

(a) Sales are starting-infant
(b) stable sales
(c) Rising sales at increasing rate
(d) Rising sales at decreasing rate

51. What does maturity mean, in the product life cycle concept?

(a) Stable sales
(b) Falling sales-decay and exit
(c) Rising sales at increasing rate
(d) Rising sales at decreasing rate

52. In production life cycle concept, what does saturation means?

(a) Stable sales
(b) Falling sales-decay and exit
(c) Rising sales at increasing rate
(d) Rising sales at decreasing rate

53. What does decline means, in the production life cycle concept?

(a) Stable sales
(b) Falling sales-decay and exit
(c) Rising sales at increasing rate
(d) Rising sales at decreasing rate

54. As the PLC is related to a given particular market, the PLC should be termed as ________.

(a) Product information life cycle
(b) Product market life cycle
(c) Product management life cycle
(d) Product margin life cycle

55. Every product moves through a life cycle having ________.

(a) Three stages
(b) Four stages
(c) Five stages
(d) Six stages

56. In introduction stage which are considered critical?

(a) Product development
(b) Product design
(c) Both a and b
(d) None of the above

57. Which is the period during which the product is accepted by consumers and the traders?

(a) Introduction
(b) Growth
(c) Maturity
(d) Saturation

58. The firm gives top priority to ________.

(a) Sales volume
(b) Quality maintenance
(c) Rate of return
(d) All the above

59. The firm gives secondary preference to ________.

(a) Sales volume
(b) Quality maintenance
(c) Rate of return
(d) None of the above

60. For marketing success, which are the vital factors?

(a) Manufacturing efficiency
(b) Distribution efficiency
(c) Both a and b
(d) None of the above

61. During which stage been competition brings pressure on prices?

(a) Growth
(b) Maturity
(c) Saturation
(d) Decline

62. Which stage occurs in the market when all potential buyers are using the product and we have only replacement sales?

(a) Growth
(b) Maturity
(c) Saturation
(d) Decline

63. New products are the real solution to the problems of ________.

(a) Growth and maturity
(b) Maturity and decline
(c) Saturation and maturity
(d) Saturation and decline

64. The most essential feature of the product life cycle is ________.

(a) Sales curve
(b) Profit curve
(c) Both a and b
(d) None of the above

65. PLC concept is very useful in the management of life cycle of a product through ________.

(a) Corporate strategic planning
(b) Marketing strategic planning
(c) Both a and b
(d) None of the above

66. The diffusion process is described in the form of the ________.

(a) Normal distribution curve
(b) Normal sales curve
(c) Normal profit curve
(d) Normal production curve

67. Who are the first two and a half per cent of the market?

(a) Innovators
(b) Early majority
(c) Early adopters
(d) Late majority

68. The next thirteen and a half per cent using the products are ________.

(a) Innovators
(b) Early majority
(c) Early adopters
(d) Late majority

69. Who are educated, rich and more successful than averages?

(a) Innovators
(b) Early majority
(c) Early adopters
(d) Late majority

70. To adopt the new product the 34 per cent are the ________.

(a) Innovators
(b) Early majority
(c) Early adopters
(d) Late majority

71. To adopt the innovation the 34 per cent are the ________.

(a) Innovators
(b) Early majority
(c) Early adopters
(d) Late majority

72. In late majority they are ________.

(a) Older and less educated buyers
(b) Older and more educated buyers
(c) Younger and less educated buyers
(d) Younger and more educated buyers

73. In which of the following they are 16 per cent of lost category of buyers?

(a) Early adopter
(b) Early majority
(c) Late majority
(d) Laggards

74. Marketers develop two distinct marketing programmes: one for ________.

(a) Innovators
(b) Early adopters

(c) Both a and b
(d) None of the above

75. Which is a current slogan which has rich meaning for business operating in an economy with customer-oriented marketing?

(a) Innovate
(b) Implicate
(c) Adopted
(d) Laggard

76. An innovation is the act of developing a novel idea into a ________.

(a) Distribution
(b) Product
(c) Price
(d) Promotion

77. A successful innovation passes through ________.

(a) The idea or invention
(b) The implementation of the idea
(c) The market acceptance
(d) All the above

78. Which is the most critical to any successful innovation?

(a) The idea or invention
(b) The implementation of the idea
(c) The market acceptance
(d) All the above

79. An adoption process is a process bringing about a change in ________.

(a) Buyer's attitudes
(b) Buyer's perception
(c) Both a and b
(d) None of the above

80. The innovate attitude of marketer is expressed in the watch word ________.

(a) Innovate or die
(b) Do or die
(c) Create or die
(d) None of the above

81. The basic function of business enterprise are ________.

(a) Marketing
(b) Innovation
(c) Both a and b
(d) None of the above

82. What are the method of obtaining products?

(a) Internal development
(b) Licensing
(c) Acquisition
(d) All the above

83. Which is the method of obtaining products are discovering and developing new products by the firm itself?

(a) Internal development
(b) Licensing
(c) Acquisition
(d) None of the above

84. Which is the method of obtaining products are securing right to produce the product from a patent holder?

(a) Internal development
(b) Licensing
(c) Acquisition
(d) None of the above

85. Which is the method of obtaining products are buying the firm that developed or patented the product by costly means?

(a) Internal development
(b) Licensing
(c) Acquisition
(d) Market development

86. Which methods of obtaining products is very costly but gives exclusive rights?

(a) Licensing
(b) Internal development
(c) Acquisition
(d) Market development

87. Innovation alone assures ________.

(a) Growth and survival
(b) Only growth
(c) Only survival
(d) None of the above

88. Customer-orientation assures ________.

(a) Growth and survival
(b) Only growth
(c) Only survival
(d) None of the above

89. Which is a general term covering the search for new products and new innovations as well as the improvement of existing products?

(a) Product planning
(b) Product development
(c) Product Information
(d) Product research

90. The firm can market its present products to existing markets ________.

(a) Existing markets
(b) New market
(c) Potential
(d) Dynamic markets

91. In market development the present is introduced to ________.

(a) Existing markets
(b) New market
(c) Potential
(d) Dynamic markets

92. Which is to creation of new markets by discovering new applications for existing goods?

(a) Market penetration
(b) Marketing strategy
(c) Market development
(d) Marketing programme

93. The firm can offer its existing products to ________.

(a) New markets
(b) Potential markets
(c) Dynamic markets
(d) Existing markets

94. What occurs when a firm introduces new product to a market?

(a) Market development
(b) Product development
(c) Market penetration
(d) Product penetration

95. The firm decides to create new product for ________.

(a) New markets
(b) Potential markets
(c) dynamic markets
(d) Existing markets

96. Which is the introduction of new products in the present market?

(a) Market development
(b) Product development
(c) Market penetration
(d) Product penetration

97. What occurs when a firm seeks to enter a new market with a completely new product?

(a) Market development
(b) Product development
(c) Market penetration
(d) Product penetration

98. What is introduced for the first time in the new market?

(a) Innovation
(b) Information
(c) Market expertise
(d) Product knowledge

99. Most marketers had adopted a strategy of differentiating products through branding/packing till the year ________.

(a) 1940
(b) 1942

(c) 1950
(d) 1952

100. In which year the market segmentation strategy was introduced?

(a) 1946
(b) 1956
(c) 1966
(d) 1976

101. What are the expensive stages in new product idea?

(a) Development
(b) Testing
(c) Launching
(d) All the above

102. From the following which are the types of new products?

(a) Innovative new products
(b) Emulative new products
(c) Adaptive new products
(d) All the above

103. Which products are new to the company?

(a) Innovative new products
(b) Emulative new products
(c) Adaptive new products
(d) All the above

104. Which costs of a new product should be incorporated in the cost benefit analysis?

(a) Social
(b) Economical
(c) Political
(d) Legal

105. Screening should avoid the errors of ________.

(a) Rejecting an idea
(b) Accepting an idea
(c) Both a and b
(d) None of the above

106. Product life cycle requires the product development programme for ________.

(a) New products
(b) New profit opportunities
(c) Both a and b
(d) None of the above

107. Which product development must be carefully planned and managed?

(a) New
(b) Existing
(c) Deficient
(d) Salutary

108. Business analysis concentrates on ________.

(a) Demand analysis
(b) Cost analysis
(c) Profitability
(d) All the above

109. Which analysis is a combination of marketing research, cost benefit analysis and assessment of competition?

(a) Business analysis
(b) Demand analysis
(c) Profitability analysis
(d) Cost analysis

110. Whose reactions can be tested under normal market conditions?

(a) Sellers
(b) Buyers
(c) Manufactures
(d) Dealers

111. Which production will start and all distribution channels will be duly organized?

(a) Mass
(b) Marketing
(c) Innovative
(d) Planning

112. Most of the reasons for failure of new products can be eliminated by the ________.

(a) Consumer
(b) Company
(c) Markets
(d) None of the above

113. Which is essential to evaluate market needs and prospects?

(a) Marketing information
(b) Marketing strategy
(c) Marketing research
(d) Marketing management

114. Who must fill the needs of the consumers?

(a) Consumers
(b) Producers
(c) Manufacturers
(d) Dealers

115. Who must fill the needs of the consumers?

(a) Packaging
(b) Branding
(c) Labeling
(d) Product

116. Which product will have a bright future in the 21st century?

(a) Ecomarked
(b) Hallmarked
(c) BIS marked
(d) Agmarked

117. Today, only through quality assurance and total quality management which countries have emerged as business leaders?

(a) Germany and Canada
(b) U.K and U.S.A
(c) Japan and Germany
(d) Japan and Asia

118. TQM stands for ________.

(a) Terminal quality management
(b) Total quantity management
(c) Total quantity market
(d) Terminal quantity market

119. Total quantity management is a ______.

(a) Corporate planning strategy
(b) Product planning strategy
(c) Market planning strategy
(d) Pricing planning strategy

120. Focus on what establishes a customer-driven standard?

(a) Quality improvement
(b) Quality control
(c) Quality planning
(d) Quality satisfaction

121. Focus on what maintains a customer-driven standard?

(a) Quality improvement
(b) Quality control
(c) Quality planning
(d) Quality satisfaction

122. Freedom from deficiencies reduces customer ________.

(a) Dissatisfaction
(b) Satisfaction
(c) legislation
(d) Non-legislation

123. The focus on product features is ________.

(a) Profit
(b) Costs
(c) Sales
(d) Expenses

124. Focus on freedom from deficiencies is ________.

(a) Profit
(b) Costs

(c) Sales

(d) Expenses

125. When the concentration is on product features then ________.

(a) Lower quality costs more

(b) Lower quality costs less

(c) Higher quality costs more

(d) Higher quality costs less

126. When the concentration is on freedom from deficiencies then ________.

(a) Lower quality costs more

(b) Lower quality costs less

(c) Higher quality costs more

(d) Higher quality costs less

127. IOS stands for ________.

(a) International organization for standardization

(b) International organization for standardization

(c) International organization for specialization

(d) Internal organization for specialization

128. ISO ________ A measure of quality launched in which year?

(a) 1957

(b) 1967

(c) 1977

(d) 1987

129. Which certificates are increasingly goining acceptances around the globe as the hallmark of quality?

(a) ISI

(b) ISO

(c) BIS

(d) Ecomarked

130. How many technical committees are comprised by IOS, who are each responsible for one of the several areas of specialization?

(a) 160

(b) 170

(c) 180

(d) 190

131. The word ISO has been derived from the ________.

(a) Greek word

(b) Latin word

(c) Both a and b

(d) None of the above

132. How many standards the ISO series consists?

(a) Four

(b) Five

(c) Six

(d) Seven

133. A standard terminology on definition and concepts known as ________.

(a) ISO 8402

(b) ISO 7804

(c) ISO 8901

(d) ISO 9401

134. The Five quality standards is popularly called the ________.

(a) ISO series

(b) ISI series

(c) ISO certificates

(d) ISI certificates

135. ISO certification signifies how many percent of the total TQM requirements?

(a) 20

(b) 25

(c) 30

(d) 35

136. Recertification of ISO certification has to be done in how many years with intermediate evaluation during 4 years?

(a) Three

(b) Four

(c) Five
(d) Six

137. External forces are ________.

(a) Uncontrollable
(b) Controllable
(c) Formal
(d) Informal

138. Internal forces are ________.

(a) Uncontrollable
(b) Controllable
(c) Formal
(d) Informal

139. Internal forces will vary between ________.

(a) Firms
(b) Products
(c) Stages of product life
(d) All the above

140. Who are expected to adopt a product or product line to the various needs of the market?

(a) Managers
(b) Marketers
(c) Informers
(d) Dealers

141. Unoccupied niche in the market is the best position for a ________.

(a) Product
(b) Package
(c) Brand
(d) Advertisement

142. Who can discover unoccupied niche?

(a) Market research
(b) Management research
(c) Market Aggregation
(d) Management Aggregation

143. What are the methods to adopt the product exactly to the market?

(a) Market aggregation
(b) Market segmentation
(c) Product differentiation
(d) All the above

144. Which is equivalent to standardization of marketing policy?

(a) Market aggregation
(b) Market segmentation
(c) Product differentiation
(d) All the above

145. The product policy is supported by powerful ________.

(a) Advertising
(b) Promotion
(c) Both a and b
(d) None of the above

146. Marketers can adopt only one or a few market segments for their products is known as ________.

(a) Market aggregation
(b) Market concentration
(c) Market segmentation
(d) Market differentiation

147. Excessive market segmentation amounts to market fragmentation and it leads to ________.

(a) Sales
(b) Costs
(c) Profits
(d) Losses

148. To meet competition the marketer has ________.

(a) Price-route
(b) Non-price route
(c) Both a and b
(d) None of the above

149. Which route makes the marketer totally dependent on the product to face competition?

(a) Price-route
(b) Non-price route
(c) Product-route
(d) Non-product route

150. What helps the firm to fight on a non-price plank?

(a) Product differentiation
(b) Product positioning
(c) Both a and b
(d) None of the above

151. Product differentiation is done through ________.

(a) Branding and packaging
(b) Labeling and branding
(c) Advertising and packaging
(d) Packaging and labeling

152. What implies that supply is prepared to adjust itself to meet customer preferences or demand?

(a) Market aggregation
(b) Market segmentation
(c) Market concentration
(d) Market differentiation

Answers for MCQ

1.	(a)	27.	(a)	53.	(b)	79.	(c)	105.	(a)	131.	(a)
2.	(a)	28.	(b)	54.	(b)	80.	(a)	106.	(c)	132.	(c)
3.	(c)	29.	(d)	55.	(c)	81.	(c)	107.	(a)	133.	(a)
4.	(d)	30.	(a)	56.	(c)	82.	(d)	108.	(d)	134.	(a)
5.	(a)	31.	(a)	57.	(b)	83.	(a)	109.	(a)	135.	(c)
6.	(b)	32.	(d)	58.	(a)	84.	(b)	110.	(b)	136.	(b)
7.	(a)	33.	(a)	59.	(b)	85.	(c)	111.	(a)	137.	(a)
8.	(d)	34.	(b)	60.	(c)	86.	(c)	112.	(b)	138.	(b)
9.	(a)	35.	(c)	61.	(b)	87.	(a)	113.	(c)	139.	(d)
10.	(d)	36.	(d)	62.	(c)	88.	(c)	114.	(d)	140.	(b)
11.	(a)	37.	(a)	63.	(b)	89.	(b)	115.	(d)	141.	(a)
12.	(c)	38.	(b)	64.	(c)	90.	(a)	116.	(a)	142.	(a)
13.	(c)	39.	(c)	65.	(c)	91.	(b)	117.	(c)	143.	(d)
14.	(b)	40.	(c)	66.	(a)	92.	(c)	118.	(b)	144.	(a)
15.	(c)	41.	(d)	67.	(a)	93.	(a)	119.	(a)	145.	(c)
16.	(a)	42.	(d)	68.	(c)	94.	(b)	120.	(c)	146.	(b)
17.	(a)	43.	(c)	69.	(c)	95.	(d)	121.	(b)	147.	(d)
18.	(c)	44.	(c)	70.	(b)	96.	(b)	122.	(a)	148.	(c)
19.	(c)	45.	(d)	71.	(d)	97.	(b)	123.	(c)	149.	(b)
20.	(d)	46.	(a)	72.	(a)	98.	(a)	124.	(b)	150.	(c)
21.	(b)	47.	(c)	73.	(d)	99.	(c)	125.	(c)	151.	(a)
22.	(a)	48.	(b)	74.	(c)	100.	(b)	126.	(d)	152.	(b)
23.	(c)	49.	(a)	75.	(a)	101.	(d)	127.	(a)		
24.	(b)	50.	(c)	76.	(b)	102.	(d)	128.	(d)		
25.	(c)	51.	(d)	77.	(d)	103.	(a)	129.	(b)		
26.	(d)	52.	(a)	78.	(c)	104.	(a)	130.	(c)		

MATCH THE FOLLOWING

1.	Product	**(a)**	Product and sales volume/value
2.	Laggards	**(b)**	Sales and profits decline
3.	Internal factor	**(c)**	New markets
4.	Market development	**(d)**	Heart of marketing-mix
5.	Product obsolescence	**(e)**	Controllable by the form
6.	Product life cycle	**(f)**	Traditional outlook

Answers for Match the Following

1.	(d)	**2.**	(f)	**3.**	(e)	**4.**	(c)	**5.**	(b)	**6.**	(a)

Chapter 13

Product-related Strategies

SUMMARY

Product strategy is a plan for marketing a good that is founded upon an analysis of the nature of the intended market, how much market share is to be achieved, how the good is to be marketed and how much profit is anticipated. Most business marketing directors will develop a clear and realistic product strategy prior to the launch of a new product into its intended market.

A product strategy draws from the ultimate vision of the product. It states where the product will end up. By setting a product strategy, you can determine the direction of your product efforts. Similar to making effective use of a map, you first need a destination, and then you can plan your route. Just as a business has a strategic vision of what it wants to be when it grows up, the product has its own strategy and destination.

Market Penetration: It involves expansion of sales of existing products in existing markets by selling more to present customers or gaining new customers in existing markets. The firm can market its present products to existing markets (Cell-A). This is done through a more aggressive marketing mix. Customers from rivals or potential buyers can also be attracted. Existing buyers may be induced to increase their rate of use.

Market Development: In market development a present product is introduced to a new market or segment. Market development is the creation of new markets by discovering new applications for existing goods, e.g., Mini-bus may be made available for goods or passengers. The firm can offer its existing products to new markets. This is another alternative to expand market opportunity, prolong product life cycles, profitability and survival.

Product Development: Product development occurs when a firm introduces new products to a market in which it is well established. Product development is the introduction of new products in the present market, e.g., new synthetic fibers for new textile products. The firm may decide to create new products for existing market. (Cell C). Established firms with high customer patronage may have new product additions upon existing market successes. The firm by offering new or improved products to present markets can satisfy better the present customers.

Product Diversification: Product diversification occurs when a firm seeks to enter a new market with a completely new product. Such a firm has neither market expertise nor product knowledge. The firm may adopt a daring strategy by creating new products for entirely new markets. The innovations are introduced for the first time in the new markets. Only innovating marketers venture to go the diversification of products. The strategy is risky but the innovator can have spectacular results. In 1960, Polaroid cameras and television were in this category in many countries. We have entirely unfamiliar market. Factors rating for a new product introduction are:

1. Marketability
2. Durability,
3. Productive ability and
4. Growth potential.

Philips is an example of diversification or lateral integration: light, bulbs, radio lamp, television tube, radio sets, tape recorder and wide range of luminaries or lamp shades.

New Product Development Strategy

Exploration of New Ideas: The development of new product starts with the exploration of new ideas. There may be number of sources of exploring these new ideas.

Screening of Ideas: At this stage, ideas collected are scrutinized. All the ideas collected may not be acceptable. Ideas which are quite inconsistent with the product policies and objectives of the firm may be dropped out rightly. There may be some other ideas which are good and consistent with company's product policies and objectives but these cannot be developed due to certain limitation, e.g., non- availability of raw materials or technology required or short of financial resources, or limited plant capacity or managerial ability. Thus due to these constraints, such ideas are also dropped.

Business Analysis: This is a continuation of the above stage. When an idea is finally selected, a further analysis is necessary. A rough idea is studied in detailed manner, determining its desirable market feasibility and features of the product and developing specifications and establishing a definite programme for the product.

Product Development: At this stage, the management goes ahead to produce the goods in its physical form. The idea, thus, is converted into a product that is worth producing. Under this stage, all decisions to bring the idea to final physical form are taken. The final decision whether a product should be accepted for production on commercial scale is taken in this stage.

Testing the Product: After designing, the next step is testing the product in the market. The product, under this stage, is introduced in the whole market or in a segment of the market. If it is an industrial product, cost of testing will be much less because the users of such products are less and can be approached easily. In case it is consumer product, it will take more time for testing the product and the cost of testing will be much higher. The result of testing is then analyzed and if the product proves successful, the decision to produce it on commercial basis is taken. If unfortunately, it proves unsatisfactory it may be withdrawn or it may be modified in the light of the opinions and suggestions of the consumers or dealers.

Commercialization of Product: If the product is proved successfully in testing, a decision to produce it on commercial basis may be taken. Thus, the last in the product development is the introduction or launching or marketing the product. This is also expensive. From top to bottom everyone is busy in calculating for the vast investments as the product may not prove profitable for three or four years in future.

Branding is the management process by which a product is branded. It is a general term covering various activities such as Giving a brand name to a product, designing a brand mark and establishing and popularizing it.

According to the American Management Association, "Brand name is a part of a brand consisting of a word, letter, group of words or letters comprising of a name which is intended to identify the products or services of a seller or group of seller and to differentiate them from those of companies".

Types of Branding

Manufacturer's/Producer's Brands: A brand which is owned by a manufacturer and registered as a trademark under the producers name is called 'manufacturer's/producer's brand'. When a manufacturer's sells a variety of products, he has, to decide whether to sell each product under a separate brand or use family brand for its entire product.

(i) **Individual Brands:** In case the manufacturer decides to sell each product under a separate brand, it is called individual brand. The manufacturer has to promote each individual brand in the market separately. The foremost advantage of individual brand name is that the promotion if each product can be undertaken with superior aggressiveness. However, the overall cost of advertising and sales promotion is liable to increase.

(ii) **Family or Umbrella Brand:** The term family or umbrella brand refers to the one brand which a company adopts for a variety of its products, i.e., all the different products are sold under one brand name only. Large sized multinational and national companies usually adopt family brands. Many such family brands have achieved national and international reputation. Some of the family brands have become household names and are recognized all over the world. For example, Tata, Birla, Godrej, Gwalior, Videocon, etc., The foremost goodwill and image of the company as well as of the product in the eyes of the customer, however if the quality of a particular product has gone down along with decrease in its sales, it is liable to affect the sales of their other products also.

(iii) **Combination Brands:** The term combination brand refers to the use of individual brand for some products and family brand for other products. Thus it is the combination of both the brands, i.e., individual and family brands. This is made in order to take advantage of popularity of both the types of brands. This policy enables the company to avoid the disadvantages of both types of brands for, e.g., Tata house is using this combination brand device. Each product has an individual name but it also has the family brand to indicate the business house producing the product, such as Tata Tea under this type of brand.

Distributors/ Private Brands: Branding can be done by distributors such as wholesalers and large sized retailers. Wholesalers and large sized retailers may get their own brand registered under the trademark act. In India, this practice is popular in the woolen and sports products. The manufacturer merely provides products as per specifications and requirement of distributors. The distributor may himself offer his own brand. Distributors enjoy full freedom in pricing products sold under their own control and have full control over distribution.

Mixed Brands: Under this type of branding the manufacturer uses both his own brand as well as distributors brand in respect of his products. The manufacturer sells some products in the own brands and the rest may be sold under their own brand names.

The product life cycle stages explain the growth and decline of revenues and profits associated with a product or service. Many companies in addition to marketing and sales managers have product managers who are responsible for specific products or services. The company has to develop appropriate strategies and tactics in each of these product life cycle stages in order to improve its market position and profitability which is called product life cycle management. Product life cycle management deals with different challenges at each stage and approaches the market with different strategies and tactics in each of these stages.

FILL IN THE BLANKS

1. ________ one of the example of generic thing.

2. The long-term brand management starts with ________ and ________.

3. ________ is one of the examples for brand name.

4. The word 'Brand' has its origin in the Norwegian word *'Brand'* which means to ____.

5. ________ is a symbol or a design used for the purpose of identification.

6. The legal version of a brand mark is ________.

7. ________ is an example for trademark.

8. ________ is an example for brand name.

9. David Ogilvy defined a brand as ________.

10. ________ is one of the examples which are easy to pronounce and remember.

11. ________ makes shopping easier.

12. Brand is a means of ________.

13. Brand loyalty can developed through successful ________.

14. ________ is recognized as moisturizing soap.

15. ________ is one of the top ten brands of Indian companies.

16. Each product having a special and unique brand name called as________.

17. ________ is an example for individual brand name.

18. One line of products which complete the sales cycle is called as ________.

19. ________ is an example for family brand name.

20. Family brand name helps combined ________ and ________.

21. The name of the company or the manufacturer such type of branding is known as________.

22. ________ is the best example for umbrella brand.

23. The product having individual name but has umbrella brand to indicate the business house producing the product is known as ________.

24. ________ is an example of combination device.

25. Branding done by distributors is known as ________.

26. ________ rarely known who is the manufacturer of the dealer's brand.

27. ________ can create initially brand awareness and recognition.

28. ________ indicates that a customer regards the brand favorably.

29. By brand ________ enables manufacturers to establish his own price competition.

30. A brand image is built up through the years by ________

31. Increasing competition leads to branding of product by a manufacturer to ________.

32. Branding helps in ________.

33. ________ can act as a medium of advertisement.

34. ________ makes word-of-mouth advertisement very effectively.

35. ________ has a very great pulling power in our market.

36. All products in their product mix are sold under ________.

37. ________ is based on some unique selling preposition.

38. Launching a brand name in India, today involves ________.

39. In 1980, the brands of bathing soaps were hardly ________.

40. ________ is an example for non- branded products.

41. The important legs of our brand ________, ________ and ________.

42. Brand franchise is important to the aspects of the brand ________.

43. In 1995 brands of bathing soaps were ______.

44. In U.S.A there is a special act, Fair packing and labeling Act to ensure truth in their packing in ________.

45. ________ is merely a physical action and provides a handling consumer.

46. Packing is necessary to prevent flowing out of liquids like ________.

47. ________ is an example of danger of adulteration.

48. Increase in price exceeds the ________ of packing.

49. ________ is the utility function fulfilled by packing design.

50. ________ has been considered as the century of environment awareness in all countries.

51. ________ has issued guidelines on environmental effects throughout the product life cycle.

52. ________ is an example for the product with intricate and elaborate mechanism.

53. Labels on contain factual information on which consumers can rely________.

54. The law has now altered the famous maxim "Let the Buyer Beware" to give due recognition to its substitute________.

55. Fuel disclosure of warranty information will ensure the consumer's ________.

56. ________ Act has given legal protection in the form of implied conditions and warranties.

57. ________ is an assurance of the quality, service and performance.

58. Competitive advantage = ________.

59. ________ is the promise of the makes that the product its of average saleable quality.

60. ________ is a specific promise in writing made by the manufacturer or trader relating to quality.

61. The core product that a markets offer may be matched by his competita, where he can score is that ________.

62. ________ is an important aspect of marketing transaction.

63. ________ is an example for costly and durable goods.

64. After-sales service prevents ________ of customers.

65. After-sales service is much more important than ________, ________ and ________.

Answers for Fill in the Blanks

1.	Soap	16.	Individual brand name
2.	Brand concept, name selection	17.	Surf
3.	Lux	18.	Family brand name
4.	Burn	19.	Amul
5.	Brand mark	20.	Advertising, sales promotion
6.	Trademark	21.	Umbrella Brand
7.	Ashok masala	22.	Tata's
8.	Good night	23.	Combination device
9.	Customer's idea of a product	24.	Tata's Tej
10.	ONIDA	25.	Middleman's brands
11.	Brand name	26.	Consumer
12.	Product identification	27.	Sales promotion
13.	Promotion	28.	Brand recognition
14.	Dove	29.	Product differentiation
15.	HMT	30.	Quality of product

31.	Face competition	**49.**	Protection
32.	Advertising	**50.**	21st century
33.	Packing	**51.**	European community
34.	Brand name	**52.**	Radio
35.	Vim	**53.**	Drugs
36.	Family	**54.**	Let the seller beware
37.	Positioning	**55.**	Right to know
38.	₹ 6 to ₹ 12 crores	**56.**	Sale of goods
39.	10 to 12	**57.**	Warranty
40.	Rice	**58.**	Product + service
41.	Franchise; equity; images	**59.**	Implied warranties
42.	Development	**60.**	Express warranties
43.	50 brands	**61.**	Key supplementary services
44.	1967	**62.**	After sales service
45.	Packing	**63.**	Typewriter
46.	Drinks	**64.**	Dissatisfaction
47.	Butter	**65.**	Price; style; beauty
48.	Additional cost		

TRUE / FALSE

1. Soap is one of the examples of generic thing. (True / False)

2. The long-term brand management starts with brand concept and name selection. (True / False)

3. Lux is one of the examples for brand name. (True / False)

4. The word 'Brand' has its origin in the Latin word brand which means to buy. (True / False)

5. Brand mark is a symbol or a design used for the purpose of identification. (True / False)

6. The legal version of a brand mark is ISI. (True / False)

7. Ashok masala is not an example for trademark (True / False)

8. GoodKnight is not an example for brand name. (True / False)

9. David Ogilvy defined a brand as profit. (True / False)

10. ONIDA is not an example for brand. (True / False)

11. Brand name makes shopping easier. (True / False)

12. Branding is a means of product identification. (True / False)

13. Brand loyalty can be developed through successful marketing. (True / False)

14. Dove is recognized as moisturizing soap. (True / False)

15. HMT is one of the top ten brands of Indian companies. (True / False)

16. Each product having a special and unique brand name called as umbrella brand name. (True / False)

17. Surf is not an example for individual brand name. (True / False)

18. One line of products which complete the sales cycle is called as family brand name. (True / False)
19. Amul is an example for family brand name. (True / False)
20. Family brand name helps combined advertising. (True / False)
21. We may have for all products the name of the company such type of branding is called as individual brand. (True / False)
22. Tata's is not an example for umbrella brand. (True / False)
23. The product having individual name but has umbrella brand to indicate the business house producing the product is known as combination device. (True / False)
24. Tata's Tej is an example combination device. (True / False)
25. Branding done by distributors is known as middleman's brand. (True / False)
26. Consumer rarely known the dealer's brand. (True / False)
27. Sales promotion cannot create initial brand awareness. (True / False)
28. Brand recognition indicates that a customer regards the favourable brand. (True / False)
29. By branding product differentiation enable manufactures to fix price. (True / False)
30. A brand image is built up through the year of quality of service. (True / False)
31. Increasing competition leads to branding of product by a manufacturer to face losses. (True / False)
32. Branding helps in advertising.(True / False)
33. Packing acts as a medium of advertisement. (True / False)
34. Brand name makes word-of-mouth advertisement very effectively. (True / False)
35. VIM has a very great pulling power in our market. (True / False)
36. All products in their product mix are sold under individual brand. (True / False)
37. Positioning is based on some unique selling preposition. (True / False)
38. Launching a brand name in India today involves only ₹ 1 crore. (True / False)
39. In 1980, the brands of bathing soaps were hardly two. (True / False)
40. Rice is not an example for non-branded product. (True / False)
41. The important legs of brand are price profit and advertising. (True / False)
42. Brand franchise is not important for band development. (True / False)
43. In 1995 brands of bathing soaps were 50. (True / False)
44. In U.S.A there is a special Act, Fair Packing and Labeling Act to ensure truth in their packing in 1967. (True / False)
45. Packing is merely a physical action (True / False)
46. Packing is necessary to prevent flowing out of liquids. (True / False)
47. Butter is not an example of danger of adulteration. (True / False)
48. Increase in price exceeds the additional cost of selling. (True / False)
49. Protection is the utility function fulfilled by packing design. (True / False)
50. 21st century has been considered as the century of environmental awareness in all countries. (True / False)
51. European community has issued guidelines on environmental effects throughout the product life cycle. (True / False)
52. Radio is not an example for intricate and elaborate mechanism product. (True / False)

53. Labels on drugs do not contain anything. (True / False)

54. The law now altered the famous maxim "let the buyer beware" to its substitute " let the company beware". (True / False)

55. Fuel disclosure of warranty information will ensure the consumer's right to know. (True / False)

56. Sales of Goods Act has given legal protection in the form of implied conditions and warranties. (True / False)

57. Warranty is an assurance of the quality, service and performance. (True / False)

58. Competitive advantage = product – service. (True / False)

59. Implied warranties are the promise of the makes that the product is of average saleable quality. (True / False)

60. Express warranties are a specific promise in writing made by the manufacturer or trader relating to quality. (True / False)

61. The core product that a marketer offers may be matched by his competitor, where he can score in the key supplementary service. (True / False)

62. After-sales service is an important aspect of the consumers. (True / False)

63. Typewriter is not an example for costly and durable goods. (True / False)

64. After-sales service prevents dissatisfaction of customers. (True / False)

65. After-sale service is much more important than style, price and beauty. (True / False)

Answers for True / False

1.	True	**14.**	True	**27.**	False	**40.**	False	**53.**	False
2.	True	**15.**	True	**28.**	True	**41.**	False	**54.**	False
3.	True	**16.**	False	**29.**	True	**42.**	False	**55.**	True
4.	False	**17.**	False	**30.**	False	**43.**	True	**56.**	True
5.	True	**18.**	True	**31.**	False	**44.**	True	**57.**	True
6.	False	**19.**	True	**32.**	True	**45.**	True	**58.**	False
7.	False	**20.**	True	**33.**	True	**46.**	True	**59.**	True
8.	False	**21.**	False	**34.**	True	**47.**	False	**60.**	True
9.	False	**22.**	False	**35.**	True	**48.**	False	**61.**	True
10.	False	**23.**	True	**36.**	False	**49.**	True	**62.**	False
11.	True	**24.**	True	**37.**	True	**50.**	True	**63.**	False
12.	True	**25.**	True	**38.**	False	**51.**	True	**64.**	True
13.	False	**26.**	True	**39.**	False	**52.**	False	**65.**	True

MULTIPLE CHOICE QUESTIONS

1. Which of the following is the example of core or generic thing?

(a) Soap
(b) Tea
(c) Toothpaste
(d) All the above

2. The long-term brand management starts with the ________.

(a) Brand concept
(b) Name selection
(c) Both a & b
(d) Quality of product

3. Which of the following is an example for brand name?

(a) Lux

(b) Hamam

(c) Liril

(d) All the above

4. The word "Brand" has its origin in the Norwegian word *"Brand"* which means to ________.

(a) Attract

(b) Burn

(c) Sell

(d) Quality

5. Which of the following is a symbol or a design used for the purpose of identification?

(a) Brand

(b) Brand mark

(c) Labeling

(d) Packing

6. The legal version of a brand mark is ________.

(a) Legal mark

(b) Trademark

(c) ISI

(d) Both b & c

7. Which of the following is a example for trademark?

(a) Ashok masala

(b) Good health atta

(c) Both a & b

(d) Pillsbury atta

8. Which of the following is an example for a brand name which reflect directly or indirectly some aspects for the product?

(a) Ezee

(b) GoodKnight

(c) Puma

(d) All the above

9. David Ogilvy defined a brand as the ________.

(a) Customer's idea of a product

(b) Customer's demand

(c) Customer's standard of living

(d) Manufacturers ability

10. Give an example which is easy to pronounce and remember ________.

(a) Onida

(b) Thums Up

(c) Bajaj

(d) All the above

11. Which of the following is makes shopping easier?

(a) Packing

(b) Brand name

(c) Seller name

(d) Quality

12. Branding is a means of ________.

(a) Product identification

(b) Product storing

(c) Product selling

(d) Product alteration

13. Brand loyalty can be developed through successful ________.

(a) Sales

(b) Promotion

(c) Marketing

(d) Advertising

14. Which of the following is decolonized as moisturizing soap?

(a) Dove

(b) Hamam

(c) Liril

(d) Lifebuoy

15. Doordarshan, Nirma, VIP luggage, Dalda, Tata, HMT,Usha, SBI, Godrej and Dabur are the ________.

(a) Top ten brands of Indian companies

(b) Top ten brands by A & B magazine

(c) Top ten branded quality products
(d) Top ten highly purchased products

16. Each product having a special and unique brand name is called as ________.

(a) Individual brand name
(b) Multiple brand name
(c) Unique brand name
(d) Brand name of a product

17. Which of the following is an example for individual brand name?

(a) Ranipal
(b) Surf
(c) Ovaltine
(d) All the above

18. One line of products which complete the sales cycle is called as ________.

(a) Branding
(b) Family brand name
(c) Product brand name
(d) All the above

19. Which of the following is an example for family brand name?

(a) Soaps
(b) Amul
(c) Surf
(d) Papad

20. Family brand name helps combined ________.

(a) Advertising
(b) Sales promotion
(c) Both a & b
(d) Marketing

21. We may have for all products the name of the company or the manufacture, such type of branding is known as ________.

(a) Umbrella brand
(b) Family brand
(c) Individual brand
(d) Common brand

22. The best example for umbrella brand is ________.

(a) Bru
(b) Tata's
(c) Usha
(d) LIRIL

23. The product having individual name but has umbrella brand to indicate the business house producing the product know as ________.

(a) Combination device
(b) Marketing device
(c) Manufacturing device
(d) Marketing objective

24. Which of the following is an example of combination device?

(a) Tata's Tej
(b) Tata's
(c) Surf
(d) Cosmetics

25. Branding done by manufactures or distributors is known as ________.

(a) Middleman's brand
(b) Wholesaler's brand
(c) Retailers brand
(d) None of the above

26. Which of the following is rarely knows who is the manufactures of the private or dealer's brand?

(a) Consumer
(b) Manufactures
(c) Wholesaler
(d) Retailer

27. Which of the following is the initially brand awareness and recognition?

(a) Advertising
(b) Sales promotion

(c) Both a & b
(d) Brand franchise

28. Which of the following indicates that a customer regards the brand favorably but will accept a substitute the shop?

(a) Brand franchise
(b) Brand image
(c) Brand recognition
(d) Brand preference

29. By branding it enables manufacturers to establish his own price and eliminate price competition ________.

(a) Quality of product
(b) Price of the product
(c) Product differentiation
(d) Monopoly selling

30. A brand image is built up through the years by________.

(a) Quality of product
(b) Services offered
(c) Company's reputation
(d) All the above

31. Increasing competition leads to branding of product by a manufacturer to________.

(a) Face competition
(b) Market
(c) Both a & b
(d) All the above

32. Branding helps in ________.

(a) Advertising
(b) Display
(c) Sales promotion
(d) All the above

33. Which of the following is the act as a medium of advertisement?

(a) Packing
(b) Grading
(c) Labeling
(d) Branding

34. Which of the following makes words - of - mouth advertisement very effective?

(a) Brand loyalty
(b) Brand name
(c) Customers
(d) Brand preference

35. Which of the following is a very great pulling power in our market?

(a) Vim
(b) Colgate
(c) Lux
(d) All the above

36. All products in their product mix are sold under ________.

(a) Family brand
(b) Individual brand
(c) Umbrella brand
(d) Private brand

37. Which of the following is based on some unique selling proposition?

(a) Brand
(b) Positioning
(c) Customers
(d) Preference

38. Launching a brand name in India today involves ________.

(a) ₹ 6 to ₹ 2 crores
(b) ₹ 1 to ₹ 5 crores
(c) ₹ 5 to ₹ 10 crores
(d) ₹ 2 to ₹ 8 crores

39. In 1980, the brand of bathing soaps were hardly ________.

(a) 10 to 15
(b) 10 to 12
(c) 8 to 10
(d) 9 to 12

40. Which of the following is an example for non - branded products?

(a) Salt
(b) Pulses

(c) Rice
(d) All the above

41. The important legs of brand are ________.

(a) Brand equity
(b) Brand image
(c) Brand franchise
(d) All the above

42. Which of the following is important to these aspects of the brand?

(a) Strategy
(b) Develop
(c) Strengthen
(d) All the above

43. In 1995 brand of bathing soaps were ________.

(a) 20 brands
(b) 25 brands
(c) 12 brands
(d) 50 brands

44. In U.S.A there is a special Act, Fair Packaging and Labeling Act to ensure truth in packing in ________.

(a) 1967
(b) 1961
(c) 1960
(d) 1962

45. Which of the following is a physical action and provides a handling consumer?

(a) Labeling
(b) Packing
(c) Branding
(d) Grading

46. Packing is necessary to prevent flowing out of such liquids like ________.

(a) Milk
(b) Drinks
(c) Both a & b
(d) All the above

47. Give an example of danger of adulteration ________.

(a) Butter
(b) Cheese
(c) Spices
(d) All the above

48. Increase in price exceeds the ________ of packing.

(a) Additional cost
(b) Production cost
(c) Fixed cost
(d) Variable cost

49. Which of the following is the utility function fulfilled by packing design?

(a) Protection
(b) Identification
(c) Convenience
(d) All the above

50. Which of the following is considered as the century of environmental awareness in all countries?

(a) 18th century
(b) 19th century
(c) 21st century
(d) 20th century

51. Which of the following is issued guidelines on all important environmental effects throughout the product life cycle?

(a) European community
(b) Asian community
(c) Australian community
(d) Indian community

52. Which of the following is an example for the product with intricate and elaborate mechanism?

(a) Radio
(b) Television
(c) Motorcar
(d) All the above

53. Labels on these contain factual information on which consumers can rely ________.

(a) Drugs
(b) Food
(c) Dangerous products
(d) All the above

54. The law has now altered the famous ________ "Let the Buyer Beware" to give due recognition to its substitute.

(a) Let the seller beware
(b) Let the manufacturer beware
(c) Let the advertises beware
(d) Let the retailer beware

55. Full disclosure of warranty information will ensure the consumer's ________.

(a) Willingness
(b) Right to know
(c) Right to information
(d) Right to feedback

56. Which of the following Act has given legal protection on the form of implied conditions and warranties?

(a) Manufacture of goods
(b) Advertising of goods
(c) Sales of goods
(d) Packaging of goods

57. Which of the following is an assurance of the quality service and performance?

(a) Guarantee
(b) Warranty
(c) Surety
(d) All the above

58. Competitive advantage =

(a) Product + service
(b) Packaging + labeling
(c) Packaging + advertising
(d) Storing + selling

59. Which of the following is the promise of the maker that the product is of average saleable quality?

(a) Implied guarantees
(b) Implied warranties
(c) Implied Quality
(d) Implied packing

60. Which of the following is a specific promise in writing made by the manufacturer or trader relating to quality?

(a) Implied warranties
(b) Express warranties
(c) Express guarantees
(d) Implied guarantees

61. The core product that a marketing offers may be matched by his competitor, where he can score is the ________.

(a) Key supplementary services
(b) Key implementer service
(c) Supplementary services
(d) Quality services

62. Which of the following is an important aspect of a marketing transaction?

(a) Free - home delivery
(b) Discounts
(c) After - sales service
(d) Repairs on damages

63. Which of the following is example for costly and durable goods?

(a) Typewriters
(b) Duplicators
(c) T.V
(d) All the above

64. After-sales service prevents ________.

(a) Dissatisfaction
(b) Frustration
(c) Ill - will among customers
(d) All the above

65. After-sales service is much more important than ________.

(a) Price
(b) Style
(c) Beauty
(d) All the above

Answers for MCQ

1.	(d)	12.	(a)	23.	(a)	34.	(b)	45.	(b)	56.	(c)
2.	(c)	13.	(b)	24.	(a)	35.	(d)	46.	(c)	57.	(b)
3.	(d)	14.	(a)	25.	(a)	36.	(a)	47.	(d)	58.	(a)
4.	(b)	15.	(a)	26.	(a)	37.	(b)	48.	(a)	59.	(b)
5.	(c)	16.	(a)	27.	(c)	38.	(a)	49.	(d)	60.	(b)
6.	(b)	17.	(b)	28.	(c)	39.	(b)	50.	(c)	61.	(a)
7.	(c)	18.	(b)	29.	(b)	40.	(d)	51.	(a)	62.	(b)
8.	(d)	19.	(b)	30.	(d)	41.	(d)	52.	(d)	63.	(d)
9.	(a)	20.	(c)	31.	(c)	42.	(d)	53.	(d)	64.	(d)
10.	(d)	21.	(a)	32.	(d)	43.	(c)	54.	(a)	65.	(d)
11.	(b)	22.	(b)	33.	(a)	44.	(a)	55.	(b)		

MATCH THE FOLLOWING

1.	Durable good	(a)	Product identification
2.	Lux	(b)	Umbrella brand
3.	Branding	(c)	Brand name.
4.	Dove	(d)	Family brand
5.	Amul	(e)	Moisturizing soap
6.	Tata chemicals	(f)	Typewriter

Answers for Match the Following

1.	(f)	2.	(c)	3.	(a)	4.	(e)	5.	(d)	6.	(b)

Chapter 14

Price (Unique Element in Marketing Mix)

SUMMARY

The pricing decision is a critical one for most marketers, yet the amount of attention given to this key area is often much less than is given to other marketing decisions. One reason for the lack of attention is that many believe price setting is a mechanical process requiring the marketer to utilize financial tools, such as spreadsheets, to build their case for setting price levels. While financial tools are widely used to assist in setting price, marketers must consider many other factors when arriving at the price for which their product will sell.

Pricing decisions and policies have a direct influence on sales volume and profits of a business. This is an important element in marketing mix. Right pricing can be determined through pricing research and testing marketing demand, cost, competition, government regulations etc, are the vital factors that must be taken into consideration in the determination of price. Price is a source of revenue and a main determinant of profit. Price is matter of vital importance to both the seller and buyer in the market place. In money economy, without prices there cannot be marketing. Only when the buyer and seller agree on price, there can be exchange of goods and services leading to transfer of ownership. In a competitive market, price is determined by free play of demand and supply. With changing demand and supply conditions the price increases or decreases. It influences consumer purchase decisions. It reflects purchasing power of currency; it can determine the general living standards. Pricing governs the very feasibility of any marketing program because it is the only element in a marketing mix accounting for demand and sales revenue. Other elements are cost factors. Pricing decisions interconnect marketing actions with the financial objectives of the enterprise. Among the most important marketing variables influenced by pricing decisions are: sales volume, profit margins, rate of return on investment, trade margins, advertising and sales promotion, product image, new product development. Therefore, pricing decisions play a very important role in the design of marketing mix. Price is a powerful marketing factor with the financial objectives of the enterprise. Among the most important marketing variables influenced by pricing decisions are: sales volume, profit margins, rate of return on investment, trade margins, advertising and sales promotion, product image, new product development.

Importance of Price

When marketers talk about what they do as part of their responsibilities for marketing products, the tasks associated with setting price are often not at the top of the list. Marketers are much more likely to discuss their activities related to promotion, product development, market research and other tasks that are viewed as the more interesting and exciting parts of the job.

Some reasons pricing is important include:

1. **Most Flexible Marketing Mix Variable:** For marketers price is the most adjustable of all marketing decisions. Unlike product and distribution decisions, which can take months or years to change, or some forms of promotion which can be time consuming to alter (e.g., television

advertisement), price can change very rapidly. The flexibility of pricing decisions is particularly important in times when the marketer seeks to quickly stimulate demand or respond to competitor price actions. For instance, a marketer can agree to a field salesperson's request to lower price for a potential prospect during a phone conversation. Likewise a marketer in charge of online operations can raise prices on hot selling products with the click of a few website buttons.

2. **Setting the Right Price:** Pricing decisions made hastily without sufficient research, analysis, and strategic evaluation can lead to the marketing organization losing revenue. Prices set too low may mean the company is missing out on additional profits that could be earned if the target market is willing to spend more to acquire the product. Additionally, attempts to raise an initially low priced product to a higher price may be met by customer resistance as they may feel the marketer is attempting to take advantage of their customers. Prices set too high can also impact revenue as it prevents interested customers from purchasing the product. Setting the right price level often takes considerable market knowledge and, especially with new products, testing of different pricing options.
3. **Trigger of First Impressions:** Often times customers' perception of a product is formed as soon as they learn the price, such as when a product is first seen when walking down the aisle of a store. While the final decision to make a purchase may be based on the value offered by the entire marketing offering (i.e., entire product), it is possible the customer will not evaluate a marketer's product at all based on price alone. It is important for marketers to know if customers are more likely to dismiss a product when all they know is its price. If so, pricing may become the most important of all marketing decisions if it can be shown that customers are avoiding learning more about the product because of the price.
4. **Important Part of Sales Promotion:** Many times price adjustments are part of sales promotions that lower price for a short-term to stimulate interest in the product. However, as we noted in our discussion of promotional pricing in the Sales Promotion tutorial, marketers must guard against the temptation to adjust prices too frequently since continually increasing and decreasing price can lead customers to be conditioned to anticipate price reductions and, consequently, withhold purchase until the price reduction occurs again.

Price Decisions

Pricing the product is one of the important elements in marketing mix. Until recently, it has been one of the most neglected areas. Even today, pricing in some firms is simply based on the concepts of cost, market position, competition and necessary profits.

Price is the exchange value of the goods or services in terms of money the exchange value of product is called price. The value and utility of a product have to be set against its price. When barter economy changed into money economy the importance of price and money grew and they became the soul of exchange of the economy. Pricing decision means decision of determining price of a product. A concern has to take a number of factors like cost of production, cost of distribution, cost of transportation, cost of advertisement and personal selling, competitive forces, purchasing power of the consumer etc., other than the demand and supply position of the product in the market. Decision concerning price to be followed for a period of time may be called as "Price Decision". The price of a product must be determined in such a manner as to offer a reasonable amount of profit to the manufacturer, a reasonable remuneration to middleman and the maximum satisfaction to consumers.

Factors Influencing of Pricing Decision

Two categories of factors – internal and external factors influence the pricing decisions of any enterprise. In each of these categories some may be economic factors and some psychological factors, again some factors may be quantitative and yet qualitative.

Internal Forces: The firm has certain objectives long-term and immediate in pricing. For example, it has certain costs of manufacturing and marketing and it seeks to recover these costs through the price. The firm is also seeking a particular public image through its pricing policies. It may have a basic philosophy on pricing. The pricing decisions of the firm have to be consistent with this philosophy. Pricing also has to be consistent with the overall objectives of the firm. All these constitute the internal factors that influence pricing. Moreover, pricing strategy has to fit into the overall marketing strategy. It cannot exist independently. In this sense, overall marketing strategy is another internal factor that influences pricing.

External Forces: In addition to all the internal forces mentioned above, any business firm has to encounter a set of external factors while formulating its pricing strategy. In the first place, the nature of the economy and the nature of competition have to be reckoned with. The purchasing power of the consumer as well as consumer behaviour, in the larger sense of the term, also has to be reckoned with. In countries, like India, the State exercises a lot of influence on price decisions in respect of a large variety of products. It includes direct price controls through statutorily fixed maximum selling prices as well as indirect pressures to hold the price line at certain levels. Such external dimensions also have to be reckoned with while formulating the pricing decision.

FILL IN THE BLANKS

1. ________ is the exchange value of a product or service always expressed in money.
2. Price is the mechanism or device for translating in to ________.
3. Price is the amount charged for the ________.
4. Price must be equal to the total amount of benefits like ________, ________ and ________ benefit.
5. Any change in the price will also bring about alteration in ________.
6. Money or price is equal to ________.
7. The bundle of expectation is included with ________ and ________.
8. Pricing is equivalent to the total ________.
9. Price influences consumer's________.
10. Pricing decision a very important role on the design of the ________.
11. Low price increases ________.
12. Pricing factor regulates________.
13. A right price can stimulate the desired ________.
14. ________ and ________ are objective co-ordinate to produce the desired increase in sales.
15. Investment in ________ process should pay back within a specified period.
16. Capital expenditure on any project must be recovered within ________.
17. ________ is the price determined by the free play of demand and supply.
18. In consumer point of view satisfaction is equal to ________.

19. ________ is another psychological dimension of pricing.

20. In penetration pricing, the price of the product is kept ________.

21. Markup pricing is common in ________ and ________ trade.

22. ________ is another psychological dimension of pricing accounting for a common marketing price.

23. Price quality relationship applies to product whose quality is difficult to ________.

24. ________ is an example for premium pricing.

25. In the customer's view TV set costing less than ₹ 3,000 would generate ________ and ________.

26. Marketing must take in to account all ________ and ________.

27. The price structure will define the product's ________.

28. ________ is a plan of action to adjust with changing condition of the market place

29. Basic price is a realistic ________.

30. Internal variables are involved under the multi-stage process of ________.

31. The marketer can identify basic price alternative after pinpointing the ________.

32. ________ is a managerial tool that emphasizes the relationship among decision variables.

33. ________ are the costs which are fixed in the business.

34. ________ costs vary with the output or member of units produced.

35. ________ is an important concept in break-even analysis.

36. When sales Revenue is equal to total cost then it is ________.

37. Sales volume is a function of ________

38. ________ is a financial ratio of profit to equity.

39. ________, ________ and ________ is important to capture the market.

40. Consumer goods are branded in foreign countries like ________ and ________.

41. Prices of national brand are higher because of heavy expenditure of ________.

42. Non-price competition tends to increase due to ________, ________ and ________.

43. ________ is used to build up the image of quality and prestige for a new product.

44. The best pricing method in competitive market is ________.

45. Premium pricing is based on ________.

46. ________ is a kind of functional discount.

47. ________ and ________ is a price concession offered to traders in the form of deduction.

48. Trade discount is given to the buyers for ________.

49. ________ is a rebate or a concession given to the trader to encourage him to pay in full by cash.

50. Brokerage allowance is given for linking ________ and ________.

51. In order to encourage a customer to make bulk purchase at a time the seller offers ________.

52. ________ is an example for sales promotion.

53. ________ and ________ always superior than compulsory rule.

54. ________ is used to create an illusion of bargain.

55. ________ buyers constitute the target market for premium pricing.

56. ________ mark is now adopting premium pricing in India.

57. ________ is an aggressive pricing strategy.

58. _______ company has different rates for domestic and industrial customers.

59. Pricing helps in creating expected _______.

60. The principle of pricing is _______ and _______.

61. _______ can give rich dividend when buyers are not price conscious.

62. Premium pricing assures _______ and _______.

Answers for Fill in the Blanks

1.	Price	33.	Fixed cost
2.	Quantitative terms	34.	Variable cost
3.	Product or service	35.	Contribution
4.	Physical; economic; social ecological	36.	Break-even point
5.	Satisfaction side	37.	Prices charged
6.	Bundle of expectations	38.	Return on investment
7.	Attributes; physical product	39.	Branding; packaging, advertising
8.	Product offering	40.	U.S.A; U.K.
9.	Purchase decision	41.	Advertising
10.	Marketing mix	42.	Fashion; quality; service
11.	Sales turnover	43.	Skim the cream price
12.	Return on investment	44.	Market price
13.	Sales increase	45.	What the customer will bear
14.	Price, non-price	46.	Trade discount
15.	Research and development	47.	Discount; allowances
16.	5 to 10 years	48.	Buying for resale
17.	Market price	49.	Cash discount
18.	Benefit - cost	50.	Buyer, seller
19.	Charm pricing	51.	Quantity discount
20.	Low	52.	Free samples
21.	Retail, wholesale	53.	Self regulation; self discipline
22.	Price lining	54.	Psychological pricing
23.	Judge	55.	Upper-middle class
24.	Cosmetics	56.	Cosmetic
25.	Doubts ; suspicion	57.	Premium pricing
26.	Relevant costs; elasticity of demand	58.	Electricity
27.	Selling prices	59.	Motivation
28.	Strategy	60.	Cost of service principle; value of service principle
29.	Market price		
30.	Price determination	61.	Premium pricing
31.	Estimating demand	62.	Growth, profit
32.	Break-even analysis		

TRUE / FALSE

1. Price is the exchange value of a product or service always expressed in money. (True / False)
2. Price is the mechanism or device for translating it into quantitative terms. (True / False)
3. Price is the amount charged for the product. (True / False)
4. Price must be equal to the total amount of benefits. (True / False)
5. Any change in the price will also bring about alteration in satisfaction side. (True / False)
6. Money or price is not equal to bundle of expectations. (True / False)
7. The bundle of expectation is included with attributes and physical product. (True / False)
8. Pricing is equivalent to the total product offering. (True / False)
9. Price influences consumer's purchasing power. (True / False)
10. Pricing decision play a very important role in the design of the promotion mix. (True / False)
11. Low price increases loss. (True / False)
12. Pricing factor does not regulate return on investment. (True / False)
13. A right price can stimulate the desired profit. (True / False)
14. Price is not an objective coordinate to produce the desired increase in sales. (True / False)
15. Investment in research and development process should pay back within a specified period. (True / False)
16. Capital expenditure on any project must be recovered within 2 years. (True / False)
17. Market price is the price determined by the free play of demand and supply. (True / False)
18. In consumer point of view satisfaction is equal to benefit + service. (True / False)
19. Charm pricing is another psychological dimension of pricing. (True / False)
20. In penetrative pricing, the price of the product is kept low. (True / False)
21. Only handful of buyers would seriously consider purchasing TV set costing only ₹ 1000. (True / False)
22. Price lining is another psychological dimension of pricing accounting for a common marketing price. (True / False)
23. Price quality relationship applies to product whose quality is difficult to judge. (True / False)
24. Cosmetics are not an example for premium pricing. (True / False)
25. In the customer's view TV set costing less than ₹ 3,000 would generate doubts. (True / False)
26. Marketing must take into account all relevant costs. (True / False)
27. The price structure will define the products market price. (True / False)
28. Strategy is a plan of action to adjust with changing conditions of the market place. (True / False)
29. Basic price is a realistic product price. (True / False)
30. Internal variable are involved under the multi-stage process of price determination. (True / False)
31. The marketer can identify basic price alternative after pinpointing the estimating supply. (True / False)

32. Break-even analysis is a managerial tool that emphasizes the relationship among decision variables. (True / False)

33. Fixed costs are the costs which vary in business. (True / False)

34. Variable costs are those which are fixed in business. (True / False)

35. Contribution is an important concept in break-even analysis. (True / False)

36. When sales revenue is equal to total cost then it is profit point. (True / False)

37. Sales volume is a function of price changed. (True / False)

38. Return on investment is a financial ratio of profit to equity. (True / False)

39. Branding is not important to capture the market. (True / False)

40. Consumer goods are not branded in U.K. (True / False)

41. Price of national brand is higher because of advertising expenditure. (True / False)

42. Non-price competition tends to increase due to fashion. (True / False)

43. Skim the cream price is used to build up the image of quality for a new product. (True / False)

44. The best pricing method in competitive market is cost price. (True / False)

45. Seasonal discount is given during slack season (True / False)

46. Trade discount is a kind of functional discount. (True / False)

47. Discount is a price concessions offered to traders. (True / False)

48. Trade discount is give to the buyers for buying for resale. (True / False)

49. Cash discount is a concession for traders to encourage pay in full by cash. (True / False)

50. The period to avail the cash discount is usually one week. (True / False)

51. In order to encourage a customer to make bulk purchase at a time the seller offers quantity discount. (True / False)

52. Free sample is an example for allowance. (True / False)

53. Self regulation is always superior to compulsory rule. (True / False)

54. Psychological pricing is used to create an illusion of bargain. (True / False)

55. Upper-middle class buyers do not constitute the target market for premium pricing. (True / False)

56. Cosmetic mark is not adopting premium pricing in India. (True / False)

57. Premium pricing is an aggressive pricing strategy. (True / False)

58. Electricity company has different rates for domestic and industrial customers. (True / False)

59. Pricing helps in creating profit. (True / False)

60. One of the principles of pricing is cost of service principle. (True / False)

61. Premium pricing can give rich dividend when buyers are not price conscious. (True / False)

62. Premium pricing assumes growth. (True / False)

Answers for True / False

1.	True	**5.**	True	**9.**	False	**13.**	False	**17.**	True
2.	True	**6.**	False	**10.**	False	**14.**	False	**18.**	False
3.	True	**7.**	True	**11.**	False	**15.**	True	**19.**	True
4.	True	**8.**	True	**12.**	False	**16.**	False	**20.**	True

21.	False	**30.**	True	**39.**	False	**48.**	True	**57.**	True
22.	True	**31.**	False	**40.**	False	**49.**	False	**58.**	True
23.	True	**32.**	True	**41.**	True	**50.**	False	**59.**	False
24.	False	**33.**	False	**42.**	True	**51.**	True	**60.**	True
25.	True	**34.**	False	**43.**	True	**52.**	True	**61.**	True
26.	True	**35.**	True	**44.**	False	**53.**	True	**62.**	True
27.	False	**36.**	False	**45.**	True	**54.**	True		
28.	True	**37.**	True	**46.**	True	**55.**	False		
29.	False	**38.**	True	**47.**	True	**56.**	False		

MULTIPLE CHOICE QUESTIONS

1. Which of the following is the exchange value of a product or service always expressed in money?

(a) Price
(b) Cost
(c) Profit
(d) None of the above

2. Price is the mechanism or device for translating in to________.

(a) Qualitative terms
(b) Mechanic terms
(c) Quantitative terms
(d) Both b and c

3. Price as the amount charged for the product or service including any ________.

(a) Delivery
(b) Discounts
(c) Services
(d) All the above

4. Price must be equal to the total amount of benefits like________.

(a) Physical benefit
(b) Economic benefit
(c) Social ecological benefit
(d) All the above

5. Any change in the price will also bring about alteration in the________.

(a) Satisfaction
(b) Selling side
(c) Consumer side
(d) Advertiser's side

6. Money or price is equal to ________.

(a) Bundle of expectations
(b) Bundle of quantity
(c) Bundle of quality
(d) Bundle of manufacturing cost

7. The bundle of expectation is included with ________.

(a) Physical product
(b) Attributes
(c) Both a & b
(d) Sale services

8. Pricing is equivalent to the ________.

(a) Total product offering
(b) Total market offering
(c) Total manufacturing goods
(d) Raw materials used

9. Price influence consumer's ________.

(a) Purchase decision
(b) Budget decision
(c) Standard of living
(d) Purchasing capacity

10. Pricing decision play a very important role in the design of the ________.

(a) Marketing - mix
(b) Promotion - mix
(c) Purchasing - mix
(d) Advertising - mix

11. Low price increases ________.

(a) Total production
(b) Sales turnover
(c) Mass production
(d) All the above

12. Pricing factor regulates ________.

(a) Return on investment
(b) Cost + profit
(c) Cost + profit + service
(d) Both a & b

13. A right price can stimulate the desired________.

(a) Production increase
(b) Sales increase
(c) Marketing increase
(d) Product purchase

14. Which of the following objectives are coordinated to produce the desired increase in sales?

(a) Price objectives
(b) Non-price objectives
(c) Both a & b
(d) Pricing policy

15. Investment in this process should pay back within a specified period ________.

(a) Research and development
(b) Promotion
(c) Market development
(d) All the above

16. Capital expenditure on any project must be recovered within ________.

(a) 2 to 4 year
(b) 5 to 10 year
(c) 6 to 8 year
(d) 10 to 12 year

17. Which of the following is the price determined by the free play of demand and supply?

(a) Market price
(b) Cost price
(c) Manufactured price
(d) None of the above

18. In consumer point of view satisfaction is equal to ________.

(a) Benefit + cost
(b) Cost + price
(c) Benefit - cost
(d) Cost + profit

19. Which of the following is the psychological dimension of pricing?

(a) Casual pricing
(b) Profit pricing
(c) Charm pricing
(d) Market pricing

20. The reasonable price range for a new television set for most customers is between ________.

(a) ₹ 8,000 - 14,000
(b) ₹ 10,000 - 15,000
(c) ₹ 20,000 - 30,000
(d) ₹ 50,000 - 70,000

21. Only handful of buyers would seriously consider purchasing TV set costing ________.

(a) ₹ 10,000
(b) ₹ 15,000
(c) ₹ 16,000
(d) ₹ 4,000

22. Which of the following is another psychological dimension of pricing accounting for a common marketing price?

(a) Price
(b) Pricing strategy
(c) Price lining
(d) Pricing policy

23. Price Quality relationship applies to product whose quality is difficult to ________.

(a) Not judge
(b) Judge
(c) Quantity
(d) All the above

24. Which of the following is an example for high quality products?

(a) Cosmetics
(b) Jewellery
(c) Clothing
(d) All the above

25. In the customer's view TV set costing less than ₹ 3000 would generate ________.

(a) Doubts
(b) Suspicion
(c) Attraction
(d) Both a & b

26. Marketing must take in to account all ________.

(a) Relevant costs
(b) Elasticity of demand
(c) Both a & b
(d) Cost of advertising

27. The price structure will define the products ________.

(a) Selling price
(b) Permissible discounts
(c) Allowances
(d) All the above

28. Which of the following is a plan of action to adjust with changing conditions of the marketplace?

(a) Policy
(b) Strategy
(c) Process
(d) Pricing

29. Basic price is a realistic ________.

(a) Market price
(b) Competitor's price
(c) Monopoly price
(d) Cost price

30. Internal variables are involved under the multi-stage process of ________.

(a) Price termination
(b) Price determination
(c) Pricing process
(d) Market price

31. The marketer can identify basic price alternative after pinpointing the ________.

(a) Market
(b) Estimating demand
(c) Discovering rival's prices
(d) All the above

32. Which of the following is a managerial tool that emphasizes the relationship among decision variables?

(a) Break-even analysis
(b) Profit analysis
(c) Cost analysis
(d) Market analysis

33. These are the cost which is fixed in the business ________.

(a) Fixed cost
(b) Market cost
(c) Variable cost
(d) Profit cost

34. These costs vary with the output or member of units produced ________.

(a) Semi-variable cost
(b) Fixed cost
(c) Variable cost
(d) Both a & b

35. Which of the following is an important concept in break-even analysis?

(a) Sales
(b) Contribution
(c) Variable cost
(d) Fixed cost

36. When sales revenue is equal to total cost then it is ________.

(a) Profit point
(b) Break-even point
(c) Recession point
(d) Loss point

37. Sales volume is a function of ________.

(a) Prices changed
(b) Amount of products sold
(c) Both a & b
(d) None of the above

38. Which of the following is a financial ratio of profit to equity?

(a) Rate of investment
(b) Return on investment
(c) Cost + profit
(d) None of the above

39. Which of the following is important to capture the market?

(a) Branding
(b) Packing
(c) Advertising
(d) All the above

40. Consumer goods are branded in foreign countries like ________.

(a) U.S.A
(b) U.K
(c) Both a & b
(d) All the above

41. Prices of national brands are higher because of heavy expenditure of ________.

(a) Advertising
(b) Sales promotion
(c) Both a & b
(d) None of the above

42. None-price competition tends to increase due to ________.

(a) Fashion
(b) Quality
(c) Service
(d) All the above

43. Which of the following is used to build up the image of quality and prestige for a new product?

(a) Skim the cream price
(b) Price
(c) Quality
(d) Quantity

44. The best pricing method in competitive market is ________.

(a) Purchase price
(b) Market price
(c) Manufacturing cost
(d) Whichever is less in a & b

45. Premium pricing is based on ________.

(a) What the customer will bear
(b) Ability to buy
(c) a & b
(d) None of the above

46. Which of the following is a kind of function discount?

(a) Cash discount
(b) Credit discount
(c) Trade discount
(d) Discount

47. Which of the following is a price concessions offered to trades in the form of deduction?

(a) Discounts
(b) Allowances
(c) Perquisites
(d) Both a & b

48. Trade discount is given to the buyers for________.

(a) Buying at discount
(b) Buying for resale
(c) Both a & b
(d) None of the above

49. Which of the following is a rebate or a concession given to the trader to encourage him to pay in full

(a) Discount
(b) Commission
(c) Brokerage
(d) Cash discount

50. Brokerage allowance is given for ________.

(a) Bulk purchase
(b) Display of product
(c) Linking buyer and seller

51. In order to encourage a customer to make but or large purchase at a time, with seller this is made________.

(a) Quantity
(b) Cash discount
(c) Concession
(d) All the above

52. Which of the following is an example for allowance?

(a) Advertising allowance
(b) Free samples
(c) Free display material
(d) All the above

53. Which of the following is always superior to compulsory rule?

(a) Self-regulation
(b) Self-discipline
(c) Both a & b
(d) Self-respect

54. Which of the following is used to create an illusion of bargain?

(a) Psychological pricing
(b) Market pricing
(c) Competitor pricing
(d) None of the above

55. Which of the following is buyer constitute the target market for premium pricing?

(a) Middle class
(b) Upper middle-class
(c) Lower class
(d) Higher class

56. This market is now adopting premium pricing in India________.

(a) Cosmetic
(b) Food products
(c) Toileties
(d) Both a and c

57. Which of the following is an aggressive pricing strategy?

(a) Pricing
(b) Premium pricing
(c) Pricing strategy
(d) Pricing policy

58. These company have different rates for domestic and industrial customers _____.

(a) Electricity
(b) Food products
(c) Water
(d) None of the above

59. It adopted this pricing strategy for ________ fabrics.

(a) Reliance
(b) Raymond
(c) Both a & b
(d) None of the above

60. Pricing helps in creating expected ______.

(a) Motivation
(b) Demand
(c) Profit
(d) Sales

61. The pricing of pricing is ________.

(a) Cost of service principle
(b) Value of service pricing
(c) Both a & b
(d) Cost of product

62. Which of the following gives rich dividend when buyers are not price conscious?

(a) Premium pricing
(b) Premium policy
(c) Pricing objectives
(d) All the above

63. Premium pricing assures ________.

(a) Growth
(b) Higher profit
(c) Both a & b
(d) None of the above

Answers for MCQ

1.	(a)	**12.**	(a)	**23.**	(b)	**34.**	(c)	**45.**	(c)	**56.**	(d)
2.	(c)	**13.**	(b)	**24.**	(d)	**35.**	(b)	**46.**	(c)	**57.**	(b)
3.	(d)	**14.**	(c)	**25.**	(d)	**36.**	(b)	**47.**	(d)	**58.**	(a)
4.	(d)	**15.**	(d)	**26.**	(b)	**37.**	(c)	**48.**	(b)	**59.**	(c)
5.	(a)	**16.**	(b)	**27.**	(d)	**38.**	(b)	**49.**	(d)	**60.**	(a)
6.	(a)	**17.**	(a)	**28.**	(b)	**39.**	(d)	**50.**	(c)	**61.**	(c)
7.	(c)	**18.**	(b)	**29.**	(a)	**40.**	(c)	**51.**	(a)	**62.**	(a)
8.	(a)	**19.**	(c)	**30.**	(b)	**41.**	(c)	**52.**	(d)	**63.**	(c)
9.	(a)	**20.**	(a)	**31.**	(d)	**42.**	(d)	**53.**	(c)		
10.	(a)	**21.**	(c)	**32.**	(a)	**43.**	(a)	**54.**	(a)		
11.	(d)	**22.**	(c)	**33.**	(a)	**44.**	(b)	**55.**	(b)		

MATCH THE FOLLOWING

1.	Free sample	**(a)**	Kind of functional discount
2.	Trade discount	**(b)**	Sales promotion
3.	Fixed cost	**(c)**	Window display
4.	Low price	**(d)**	Speed up payment
5.	Cash discount	**(e)**	Costs are fixed.
6.	Promotional allowance	**(f)**	Penetration pricing

Answers for Match the Following

1.	(b)	**2.**	(a)	**3.**	(e)	**4.**	(f)	**5.**	(d)	**6.**	(c)

Chapter 15

Promotion

SUMMARY

Promotion consists of those attributes that are designed to bring a company's goods and services to the favourable attention of the customers.

Significance of Promotion

The significance of Promotion can be summarized as follows:

(i) Promotion tends to focus on how to go about attracting the attention of consumers and providing enough information to hold their interest long enough to motivate a purchase.

(ii) The marketers will look closely at the many ways of advertising the product line and decide which methods are most likely to reach the desired consumer demographic.

(iii) This is taking into consideration factors such as age, gender, location and economic class for effective promotion.

(iv) The marketer can decide whether investing time and resources in television and print advertising is likely to be effective, or not.

(v) The activity of promotion has become important because of the widening of the market. The physical distance between producer and consumer and also the increase in the number of prospective buyers, promotion has gained importance.

(vi) In order to meet the competition, the producer has to make the consumer aware of his products and the outstanding features along with a comparative view of the competitor's products. This helps the consumers to select the right type of product.

Promotion Mix

Promotion mix is the marketing strategies used by a company to market and promote its products and services. These strategies include advertising, sales promotion, personal selling, publicity and direct marketing.

Advertising is a form of communication used to persuade an audience like viewers, readers or listeners to take some action with respect to products, ideas, or services. Most commonly, the desired result is to drive consumer behavior with respect to a commercial offering, although political and ideological advertising is also common. Advertising messages are usually paid for by sponsors and viewed via various traditional media; including mass media such as newspaper, magazines, television commercial, radio advertisement, outdoor advertising or direct mail; or new media such as websites and text messages.

Commercial advertisers often seek to generate increased consumption of their products or services through "Branding," which involves the repetition of an image or product name in an effort to associate certain qualities with the brand in the minds of consumers. Non-commercial advertisers who spend money to advertise items other than a consumer product or service include political parties, interest groups, religious organizations and governmental agencies. Non-profit organizations may rely on free modes of persuasion, such as a public service announcement

Sales promotions are another way to advertise. Sales promotions are double purposed because they are used to gather information about what type of customers you draw in and where they are, and to jumpstart sales. Sales promotions include things like contests and games, sweepstakes, product giveaways, samples coupons, loyalty programs and discounts. The ultimate goal of sales promotions is to stimulate potential customers to action.

Internet Marketing or Online Marketing

Internet marketing, online marketing or e-marketing are terms used for marketing your products or services over the Internet. Internet marketing is a great way to reach a wide, international audience at a relatively low cost. The nature of the medium allows consumers to find what they are looking for when they want, at their own convenience. It provides instant response and is very interactive. Internet marketing methods include search engine marketing, display advertising, email marketing, and interactive advertising, all completed through your website. Internet marketing can be very creative, cost effective and interactive.

Television

Television provides a means for reaching a great number of people in a short period of time. Small businesses will typically use either spot television or cable television. A spot television ad is placed on one station in one market. The number of target audience who see your ad depends upon how many viewers are tuned into the television station at a specific time. Cable advertising is placed either on a local cable television channel or on a cable network. The number of people reached by cable advertising depends upon the cable penetration and cable/channel programme viewership in a given market.

Beyond television's reach, an additional advantage is its ability to convey your message with sight, sound, and motion. The disadvantages of television advertising are: relatively higher cost - both in terms of airtime and production, limited length of exposure, short airtime (making it difficult to present a complex or detailed message) and the clutter of many other ads.

Television ads may require multiple exposures to achieve message retention and consumer action. Also, many commercials are considered intrusive, prompting viewers to switch channels to avoid them.

Radio

Radio, like television, has the ability to quickly reach a large number of consumers. The major advantage of radio lies in its ability to efficiently target narrowly defined segments of consumers. The vast array of radio programme formats lets an advertiser gear ads to almost any target audience.

Beyond this advantage, radio is commonly used by small businesses because it is relatively inexpensive (both in terms of airtime and production costs) and because deadlines for placing radio advertising are relatively short, providing an advertiser with increased flexibility. The disadvantages of radio are: an advertiser is limited to an audio message so there is no visual product or service identification, ad clutter can be high and exposure to the message is short and fleeting. Finally, similar to television, multiple exposures may be required for message retention and consumer reaction. Also, listeners may change stations to avoid commercials.

Newspapers

Newspapers permit an advertiser to reach a large number of people within a specified geographic area. Newspaper advertising has several advantages for the small business. An advertiser has flexibility in terms of size and placement within the newspaper. Exposure to the ad is not limited, so readers can take their time with your message. Short deadlines permit quick response to changing market conditions.

Sales promotion is a part of promotional mix. Sales promotion refers to the activities which supplement and coordinate personal selling and advertising to attract customers buy a product. Sales promotion methods include displays, demonstrations, expositions, exhibitions and other non-recurrent selling efforts which aim at impelling spot buying action by prospective customers. Sale promotion techniques are indirect and non-personal. Sales promotion activities are more common for consumer's goods marketing than for industrial goods. Consumers are attracted by displays, packaging and publicity. Sales promotion devices are also a source of information to the customers.

Sales Promotion consist of those cultivates that are designed to bring a company's goals or services to the favorable attention of customers.

Objectives of Sales Promotion

1. **To provide information:** The producer generally provides the information regarding the quality, uses, different uses of the products and the price, etc., to the consumers while introducing the product.
2. **To increase in sales:** The main purpose of all promotional activities is to increase the sales of the products of the company. Promotional activities increase the sales by changing the elasticity of demand of the product through various techniques, i.e., by distributing samples, free gifts, purchase premiums, discounts, etc. Such activities make the product popular.
3. **To reduce seasonal decline:** During off-season, the promotional activities help in maintaining the sales of the product. Customers and middlemen are offered attractive discounts and free gifts along with the products to induce them to purchase their products.
4. **To keep memory alive:** One of the objectives of the sales promotion is to keep the memory of the product alive in the minds of the present customers.
5. **To induce middlemen to purchase more:** The middlemen-wholesalers and retailers are induced to purchase mere stock by offering more facilities such as credit facilities, higher trade and cash discount and free gifts etc.

Features of Sales Promotion

(i) Sales promotion does not include advertisement, personal selling and publicity.

(ii) Sales promotion activities are not regular activities. These are purely temporary and are performed at certain times such as display, free samples, exhibitions, demonstration, etc.

(iii) It makes advertisement and personal selling more effective.

(iv) Sales promotion encourages dealers, distributors and consumers.

Types of Sales Promotions

(i) Sales Promotional Letters: Several large companies utilize the medium of letters for sales promotion. These letters serve different purposes. Sometimes, they are used to give information about the company's products, sometimes; they are reminders to continue to buy a particular brand.

(ii) Catalogues: Catalogues carry essential information on the products offered by the company. Well designed catalogues give complete information relating to the products, their pictures, size specifications, colors, packing, uses and prices.

(iii) PoP: Point of purchase (PoP) promotion is one of the most widely used sales promotions. It is also sometimes referred to as point of sales promotion. Various kinds of display materials like posters, dangers, strickers, mobile wobblers and streamers are used at the retail shop level to induce purchase.

(iv) Demonstrations: Companies resort to product demonstrations for sales promotion especially, when they are coming up with a product new to the market. In India, recently, several low unit price products like light beverages and washing powders and high unit price products like washing machines and personal computers utilized product demonstration for sales promotion.

(v) **Trade Fair and Exhibitions:** Trade fairs and exhibitions are extensively used sales promotion. They also form one of the oldest practices in sales promotion. Trade fairs and exhibitions provide companies with the opportunity of introducing and displaying their products.

Personal Selling

Personal selling refers to the face-to-face selling in which a seller attempts to persuade a buyer to make a purchase. It is when an individual salesperson sells a product, service or solution to a client.

Publicity

Publicity is the deliberate attempt to manage the public's perception of a subject. The subjects of publicity include people, goods and services, organizations of all kinds and works of art or entertainment.

Direct Marketing

Direct Marketing is a form of advertising in which physical marketing materials are provided to consumers in order to communicate information about a product or service. Direct marketing does not involve advertisements placed on the internet, on television or over the radio. Types of direct marketing materials include catalogues, mailers and fliers.

FILL IN THE BLANKS

1. ________ is a form of communication activity whose main objective is making profit.
2. Promotion is the ________ element of marketing mix.
3. Promotion is important in _______ market.
4. Promotion is the process of marketing communication involving ______, ______ and ______.
5. _______ is the spark plug of our marketing mix.
6. ______ is an important marketing strategy.
7. Purposes of promotion are providing marketing information to ________.
8. Promotion persuades and convinces the ________ and influences his/her behaviour to take the desired action.
9. In competitive market nothing can be sold without ________.
10. Promotion message has two basic purposes namely ________ and ________.
11. Promotion is responsible for ________ for your product.
12. ________ helps you to maintain the demand for your product.
13. Promotion mix includes ______, _______ and ________.
14. ________ is non- personal presentations and impersonal salesmanship for mass selling.
15. ________ is a best means of oral and face to face communication for making sales.
16. Promotional element of marketing mix are ________, ________ and ________.
17. The overall objective of promotion is influencing the buyer's ________ and ________.
18. ________ is more effective in the awareness stages.
19. Components of marketing mix are ______, ________, ________ and ________.
20. ______ is essential part of communication.

21. Communication takes place between ________ and ________.
22. Marketing communication is undertaken by marketers through the device of ______.
23. Devices of promotion are ________, ________ and ________.
24. Word-of-mouth communication helps to accelerate the spreading over ______.
25. Effective communication takes place only when ________ and ________.
26. Effective communication is equal to ________.
27. In marketing action means decision to ________.
28. ________ desires to promote his product.
29. Forms of promotion are ________, ________ and ________.
30. ________ is the target market segment.
31. Message is received and interpreted by consumers and they decide to ________.
32. ________ is important to receive feedback from the receiver.
33. The salesman can balance the message on the basis of feedback from ________.
34. ________ is the most effective form of communication.
35. Mass communication is essentially ________ communication.
36. ________ is difficult and usually delayed.
37. Marketing research is used to get feedback from ________ and ________.
38. ________ in promotion channel arises due to transmission or interference in sales.
39. ________ communication constitutes the most serious noise.
40. The message transmitted through all forms of promotion must describe the product features in terms of ________.
41. ________ approach is better while transmitting the message.
42. ________ message develops better understanding of customer needs.
43. ________ are the buyers of bundle of benefits.
44. Promotion message must achieve ________ basic object.
45. For effective communication, sender and receiver must have a common background of experience like common ________ and ________.
46. The promotion message is arranged to facilitate the consumer decision making process like ________, ________ and ________.
47. Promotion message is one source of information at the disposal of a ________.
48. If promotion message is useful, the buyer will be influenced and persuaded to take action as desired by the ________.
49. Communication involves ______ of ideas.
50. ________ communicates message very effectively.
51. ________ and ________ can attract the attention of consumers quickly
52. ________ is stronger and longer than a word contact.
53. ________ permits easier association for the viewer.
54. ________ is a perfect medium of advertising.
55. Promotion influences buyer behaviour and alter the location and shape the demand curve in factor of ________.
56. Promotional strategies may adversely influence ______ and ______ environment.
57. The marketing activities may aggravate the social problems such as ________, ________ and ________.
58. ________ are forced to pay for all promotion expenses at the end.
59. Promotion means ________.

60. Consumerism has given importance for more ________.

61. The best example of misleading promotion is ________.

62. Promotion devices should not mislead the ________.

63. It must be ________ in making comparisons with products of rivals.

64. Buyer can be induced by ________ to attract towards products.

65. The ________ formula proposed awareness or attention, interest and desire stages

66. The adoption process proposed the stages of ________.

67. Marketing communications try to influence predispositions of buyers toward the firm like ________ and ________.

68. Marketing communications try to influence predisposition. of buyers towards the firm like ________ and ________.

69. Buyer's pre-dispositions and behaviour are governed by the ________, ________and ________ characteristics.

70. ________ groups influence the buyer behaviour.

71. The receiver is an active participant in the ________ process.

72. ________ will determine the receivers behaviour and action towards a company.

73. The response to promotion is subjective and entirely depends upon ________.

74. Each receiver finds his own meaning to the messages sent by ________.

75. The consumer will accept communication which ________ him.

76. Promotion strategy lays down the broad principles to secure an advantage over ________.

77. Promotion has ________ sides of equal importance.

78. Advertising medium for promotion are ________ and ________.

79. The promotion strategy deals with the blend of ________ activities.

80. ________ and ________ determines the form of promotions.

81. Toys, toilet soaps and cosmetic are ________ which are effectively shown on television.

82. ________ advertisement is unsuitable for children.

83. Mass selling consumer goods can be easily promoted through ________ and ________ advertisement.

84. Industrial and specialty goods should be promoted through ________.

85. The solution to the problem of buyer, the marketer must known customer ________ and ________.

86. Marketers must have ________ information about consumer demand and behaviour.

87. Corporate advertisements usually emphasize more on ________ of marketing firm.

88. Effectiveness of communication depends upon firm's ________ in the market.

89. Retailers demand the highly advertised product from ________.

90. A pull strategy is also called as ________.

91. ________ and ________ promotion is necessary to generate consumer demand.

92. ________ has less emphasis at all stages of the marketing channel.

93. Push strategy is also called as ________.

94. ________ strategy places heavy emphasis on personal selling.

95. ________ are mostly the push type strategy relying primarily on personal selling.

96. In push type promotion marketers rely on ________.

97. Push strategy can be successful used for ________.

98. Consumer goods manufactures adopt and ________ strategy to sell their product.

99. The ratio of pull to push may differ according to the requirements of ________.

100. Salesmen are used to push the goods through ________ to accelerate sales.

101. ________ and ________ will support personal selling to accelerate sales.

102. When the marketing plan is ready, we can develop a total promotion programme to approach ________.

103. Promotion objectives must be set before we decide on message contents and ________.

104. ________ are based on strengths and weakness of the various media vehicles.

105. ________ is based on the needs of carry particular types of messages.

106. The constituents of promotion programme is ________.

107. Promotion budget is fixed by the top management regarding the decision on ________.

108. The promotion budget, to implement marketing plan will be approved by ______.

109. ________ is an important instrument in marketing to lubricate the marketing efforts.

110. Sales promotion is a ________.

111. Sales promotion is not an ________.

112. Sales promotion is an investment which can pay ________.

113. ______ is an integral part of the marketing effort.

114. Sales promotion is referred to the promotional activities other than ________, ________ and ________.

115. Sales promotion helps to stimulate consumer purchasing and dealer effectiveness like ________, ________ and ________.

116. Sales promotion is a plus ingredient of ________.

117. ________ and ________ are the essential and basic ingredients in the marketing mix.

118. The two wings of promotion are ________ and ________.

119. Use a large picture or headline to insure quick________.

120. The manufacturer can get orders from ________.

121. Sales promotion is a vital link between ________ and ________.

122. In sales promotion all prospective buyers must be ________ and ________ to buy your product.

123. ________ is a highly competitive field.

124. Sales promotion can ________ of customers.

125. Many sales promotion campaigns involve the use of ________.

126. Sales promotion is often thought as to accelerate________.

127. The company's marketing objective and strategies influence the development of sales promotion ________ and ________.

128. There can be a member of sales promotion objectives depending upon________.

129. Additional market share, develop brand franchise and expand the target market are objectives of ________.

130. The main objectives of reactive sales promotion are ________.

131. According to Schultz and Robinson, sales promotion management, Chicago: Crain books, 1982, objectives of sales promotion should be ________, ________ and ________.

132. ________ and ________ are the target audiences.

133. When objectives are expressed in numerical terms, they are called as ________.

134. ________ are broad action plans to achieve the stated goals.

135. Marketing objectives and strategies are related to the ________ of a company.

136. Promotion objectives and strategies are related to ________.

137. Promotion mix depends directly upon marketing ________ and ________.

138. Promotion objectives have ________ and ________.

139. Sales promotion strategies focus on different ________ and ________.

140. The main objective of sales promotion is ________.

141. The sales volume of any product depends on basic factors of marketing line ________, ________ and ________.

142. Sales promotion cannot be a substitute for weaknesses in ________.

143. The reason companies to go for short term increase in sales volume is to reduce inventories before ________.

144. ________ contribute more towards increasing sales volume.

145. Demographic, economic and technological are ________.

146. Brand switchers sometimes get exposed to ________ and ________ of products.

147. Sales promotion may contribute to increasing ________.

148. The companies cannot match the substantial advertising budgets who have ________.

149. ________ is more effective in indusing trial of a new product to consumers.

150. Personal care products are ________, ________ and ________.

151. Repeat purchase by customer leads to ________.

152. Advertising is a ________ communication.

153. Sales promotions are communicated to encourage existing consumers to buy like ________.

154. New product launches by competing companies are backed up by aggressive advertising and ________.

155. A firm that feels threatened would like to protect its loyal customers from switching to ________.

156. The interval between two successive purchases should be ________.

157. The main objective of sales promotion is to encourage re-seller participation in ________.

158. ________ is a powerful tool to enhance sales.

159. Display attracts consumer attentions who are ________ and ________.

160. The space available for displays in retail store and display materials are ________.

161. In an average store there may not be more than ________ items to display

162. ________ creates a negative effect on sales.

163. Publicity is also called as ________.

164. The firm having a poor public image will have lower ________ and ________.

165. Feedback helps to modify ________.

Answers for Fill in the Blanks

1.	Promotion	5.	Promotion
2.	Third	6.	Promotion
3.	Competitive	7.	Consumers
4.	Information; persuasion and influence	8.	Buyer

9.	Promotion	**48.**	Marketer
10.	Persuasive communication and tool of competition	**49.**	Transmission
		50.	Picture
11.	Stimulating consumer demand	**51.**	Non- verbal media and visual
12.	Promotion	**52.**	Visual contact
13.	Advertising; publicity; personal selling	**53.**	Picture
14.	Advertising	**54.**	Television
15.	Personal selling	**55.**	Products
16.	Information, persuasion and reminding	**56.**	Social and political
17.	Behaviour and predispositions	**57.**	Waste disposal; media control and deceptive advertising practices
18.	Publicity		
19.	Product; price; promotion and place	**58.**	Consumers
20.	Message	**59.**	Right information and persuasion
21.	Sender of message and its receiver	**60.**	Information
22.	Promotion	**61.**	Superlative advertisements
23.	Advertising; publicity and sales promotion	**62.**	Average consumers
		63.	Accurate
24.	Marketing communication	**64.**	Advertising
25.	Sender sends message and receiver responds to it	**65.**	AIDA formula
		66.	Awareness and interest
26.	Acceptance and action for the message	**67.**	Attitudes and values
27.	Purchase	**68.**	Attitudes and values
28.	Marketing	**69.**	Socio-economic; demographic; personality
29.	Media; channels and sending the message		
30.	Receiver	**70.**	Social
31.	Purchase	**71.**	Promotion
32.	Personal salesmanship	**72.**	Perception of receiver
33.	Buyer	**73.**	Message and the receiver
34.	Personal interaction	**74.**	Marketers
35.	One- way	**75.**	Interests
36.	Feedback	**76.**	Competitors
37.	Consumer surveys and electronic devices	**77.**	Four
38.	Noise	**78.**	Radio and television
39.	Competitive	**79.**	Promotional
40.	Customer wants and desires	**80.**	Product and buyer
41.	Problem solving	**81.**	Products
42.	Promotion	**82.**	Press
43.	Customers	**83.**	Radio and television
44.	Communication of message	**84.**	Technical journals
45.	Culture and language	**85.**	Needs and desires
46.	Awareness; knowledge and preference	**86.**	Up to date
47.	Buyer	**87.**	Reputation

88.	Image	127.	Objectives and strategies
89.	Wholesales	128.	Firm's policies
90.	Suction strategy	129.	Sales promotion
91.	Advertising and sales	130.	Generate short-term cash
92.	Personal selling	131.	Specific; clear and affordable
93.	Pressure strategy	132.	Consumers and resellers
94.	Push	133.	Quantitative objectives
95.	Industrial marketing strategies	134.	Strategies
96.	Selective distribution	135.	Marketing-mix
97.	Highly priced product	136.	Promotion mix
98.	Push pull strategy	137.	Strategies and objectives
99.	Market situation	138.	Consumer promotion and trade deals
100.	Marketing channel	139.	Consumer promotion and trade deals
101.	Advertising and sales promotion	140.	Increase sales volume
102.	Target audience	141.	Product quality; price and distribution
103.	Delivery of message	142.	Marketing strategy
104.	Layout decisions	143.	Financial - closing
105.	Delivery decisions	144.	Marginal buyers
106.	Promotion objectives	145.	Macro-environmental factors
107.	Promotion programme	146.	Better product and repeat purchase
108.	Top management	147.	Sales volume
109.	Sales promotion	148.	Small market share
110.	Necessity	149.	Free sample
111.	Expenditure	150.	Shampoos; cosmetic; laundry products
112.	Rich dividends	151.	Increased sales volume
113.	Sales promotion	152.	One way
114.	Personal salesmanship; advertising, publicity	153.	Buy one get one free
		154.	Sales promotion campaigns
115.	Exhibitions; demonstrations, free samples	155.	New competing brand
116.	Marketing mix	156.	Long
117.	Advertising and personal salesmanship	157.	Contests
118.	Advertising and personal salesmanship	158.	Display
119.	Visibility	159.	Passerby and window shopper
120.	Dealers	160.	Limited
121.	Advertising and field- selling	161.	10 to 15
122.	Attracted and persuaded	162.	High price
123.	Retailing	163.	Marketing public relations
124.	Arouse enthusiasm	164.	Sales and profits
125.	Incentives	165.	Product offering
126.	Sales		

TRUE / FALSE

1. Promotion is a form of communication activity whose main objective is making profit. (True / False)
2. Promotion is the third element of marketing mix. (True / False)
3. Promotion is not important in competitive market. (True / False)
4. Promotion is the process marketing communication involving information, persuasion and influence. (True / False)
5. Promotion is the spark plug of our marketing mix. (True / False)
6. Promotion is not an important marketing strategy. (True / False)
7. Purposes of promotion are providing marketing information to consumers. (True / False)
8. Promotion persuades and convinces the buyer and influences his/her behaviour to take the desired action. (True / False)
9. In competitive market nothing can be sold without promotion. (True / False)
10. Promotion message has two basic purposes namely persuasive communication and tool of competition. (True / False)
11. Promotion is not responsible for stimulating consumer demand for your product. (True / False)
12. Promotion helps you to maintain profitability for your product. (True / False)
13. Promotion mix includes advertising, publicity and personal selling. (True / False)
14. Advertising is non-personal presentation and impersonal salesmanship for mass selling. (True / False)
15. Personal selling is a best means of telephone communication for making sales. (True / False)
16. Promotion element of marketing mix are information, persuasion and reminding. (True / False)
17. The overall objective of promotion is influencing the buyer's behaviour predispositions. (True / False)
18. Publicity is more effective in the awareness stage. (True / False)
19. Components of marketing mix are product, price, place and promotion. (True / False)
20. Message is not essential part of communication. (True / False)
21. Marketing communication is not undertaken by marketers through the device of personal selling. (True / False)
22. Advertising, publicity and sales promotion are devices promotion. (True / False)
23. Word-of- mouth communication helps to accelerate the spreading over of advertising. (True / False)
24. Effective communication takes place only when sender sends message and receiver responds to it. (True / False)
25. Effective communication is not equal to acceptance and action for the message. (True / False)
26. In marketing action means decision to purchase. (True / False)
27. Marketer desires to drive his product. (True / False)
28. Media, channels and the message are important aspects of promotion. (True / False)
29. Receiver is the target market segment. (True / False)
30. Message is received and interpreted by consumers and they decide to sell. (True / False)

31. Personal salesmanship is not important to receive feedback from the manufacturer. (True / False)

32. The salesman can balance the message on the basis of feedback from buyer. (True / False)

33. Mass communication is essentially two-way communication. (True / False)

34. Personal interaction is the most effective form of communication. (True / False)

35. Feedback is difficult and very easy to obtain. (True / False)

36. Marketing research is used to get feedback from consumer surveys and electronic devices. (True / False)

37. Noise in promotion channel arises due to transmission or intervenience in sales. (True / False)

38. Competitive communication constitutes the most serious noise. (True / False)

39. The message transmitted through all forms of promotion must the product features in terms of customer wants and desires. (True / False)

40. Problem-solving approach is better while receiving the message. (True / False)

41. Promotion message develops better understanding of manufacturers needs. (True / False)

42. Customers are the buyers of bundle of benefits. (True / False)

43. Promotion message must achieve communication of message basic object. (True / False)

44. For effective communication, sender and receiver must have a common background of experience like common culture and language. (True / False)

45. The promotion message is arranged to facilitate the consumer decision making process. (True / False)

46. Promotion message is one source of information at the disposal of a manufacture. (True / False)

47. If promotion message is useful, the buyers will be influenced and personal to take action as desired by the marketer. (True / False)

48. Communication involves transmission of ideas. (True / False)

49. Picture communicates message very effectively. (True / False)

50. Non-verbal media and visual can attract the attention of consumers quickly. (True / False)

51. Visual contact is stronger and longer than a word contact. (True / False)

52. Picture permits easier association for the viewer. (True / False)

53. Television is not a perfect medium of advertising. (True / False)

54. Promotion influences buyer behaviour and alters the location and shape the demand cure in favour of products. (True / False)

55. Promotion strategies may adversely influence social and political environment. (True / False)

56. The marketing activities may aggravate the political problems. (True / False)

57. Consumers are forced to pay for all promotion expenses at the end. (True / False)

58. Promotion means right information and persuasion. (True / False)

59. Consumerism has give less importance for information. (True / False)

60. The best example of misleading promotion is superlative advertisements. (True / False)

61. Promotion devices should mislead the total consumers. (True / False)

62. It must be accurate in making comparisons with products of rivals. (True / False)

63. Buyer can be induced to personal salesman to attract towards products. (True / False)

64. The AIDA formula proposed awareness or attention, interest and desire stages. (True / False)

65. The adoption process proposed the stages of awareness and interest. (True / False)

66. Marketing communications try to influence predispositions of buyers toward the firm like attitudes and values. (True / False)

67. Television provides a means for reaching a great number of people in a short period of time. (True / False)

68. Social groups influence the seller behaviour. (True / False)

69. The receiver is an active participant in the promotion process. (True / False)

70. Perception of receiver will determine the receiver's behaviour and action towards a company. (True / False)

71. The response to promotion is subjective and entirely depends upon message and receiver. (True / False)

72. The consumer will accept communication which does not attracts him. (True / False)

73. Each receiver finds his own meanings to the message sent by marketers. (True / False)

74. Promotion strategy lays down the broad principles to secure an advantage over consumers. (True / False)

75. Promotion has sides of equal importance. (True / False)

76. Advertising medium for promotion are radio and advertisement. (True / False)

77. The promotion strategy deals with the blend of promotion activities. (True / False)

78. Product and buyer determines the forms of promotions. (True / False)

79. Toys, toilet soaps and cosmetic are products which are effectively shown on television. (True / False)

80. Television advertisement is unsuitable for children. (True / False)

81. Industrial and speciality goods should be promotion through window display. (True / False)

82. Mass selling consumer goods can be easily promoted through radio and television advertisement. (True / False)

83. The solution to the problem of buyer, the marketer must know customer needs and desires. (True / False)

84. Marketers must have up to date information about consumer demand and behaviour. (True / False)

85. Corporate advertisement usually emphasizes more on sales of marketing firm. (True / False)

86. Effectiveness of communication depends upon firm's profit in the market. (True / False)

87. Retailers demand the highly advertised product from manufacturers. (True / False)

88. A pull strategy is also called as suction strategy. (True / False)

89. Advertising and sales promotion is necessary to generate consumer demand. (True / False)

90. Personal selling has less emphasis at all stages the marketing channel. (True / False)

91. Push strategy is also called as pressure strategy. (True / False)

92. Push strategy places heavy emphasis on personal selling. (True / False)

93. Industrial marketing strategies are mostly the push type strategies, relying primarily on advertising. (True / False)

94. In push promotion marketers rely on wholesale distribution. (True / False)

95. Push strategy can be successfully used when highly priced product to their sales man. (True / False)

96. Consumer goods manufacturer adopt only push strategy to sell their product. (True / False)

97. The ratio of pull to push may differ according to the requirements of seller. (True / False)

98. Salesmen are used to push the goods through marketing mix to accelerate sales. (True / False)

99. Advertising and sales promotion will support personal selling to accelerate sales. (True / False)

100. When the marketing plan is ready, we can develop a total promotion programme to approach target audience. (True / False)

101. Promotion objectives must be set before we decide on message contents and delivery of message. (True / False)

102. Layout decisions are based on strengths and weakness of the various media vehicles. (True / False)

103. Delivery decision is not based on needs of carry particular types of messages. (True / False)

104. The constituents of promotion programme is promotion mix. (True / False)

105. Promotion budget is fixed by the top management regarding advertising mix. (True / False)

106. The promotion budget, to implement marketing plan will be approved by low-level management. (True / False)

107. Sales promotion is an important instrument in marketing to lubricate the marketing efforts. (True / False)

108. Sales promotion is not a necessity. (True / False)

109. Sales promotion is expenditure. (True / False)

110. Sales promotion is an investment which can pay interests. (True / False)

111. Sales promotion is an integral part of the marketing effort. (True / False)

112. Sales promotion is refered to the promotional activities others than personal salesmanship. (True / False)

113. Sales promotion helps to stimulate consumer purchasing and dealers effectiveness like demonstration and free samples. (True / False)

114. Sales promotion is a plus ingredient of advertising mix. (True / False)

115. Advertising and personal salesmanship are the essential and basic ingredients in the promotional mix. (True / False)

116. The two wings of promotion are buyer and sellers. (True / False)

117. The manufacturer can get orders from wholesalers. (True / False)

118. The manufacturer or wholesaler may have a attractive packages at reasonable price. (True / False)

119. Sales promotion is a vital link between advertising and field selling. (True / False)

120. In sales promotion all prospective buyers must be attracted and persuaded to buy your product. (True / False)

121. Retailing is a highly competitive field. (True / False)

122. Sales promotion can arouse enthusiasm of customers. (True / False)

123. Many sales promotion campaigns involve the use of incentives. (True / False)

124. Sales promotion is often thought as special buying effort to accelerate sales. (True / False)

125. The company's marketing objective and strategies influence the development of sales promotion policies. (True / False)

126. There can be a number of sales promotion objectives depending upon goodwill of firm. (True / False)

127. Additional market share, develop brand franchise and expand the target market are objectives of marketing mix. (True / False)

128. The main objectives of reaction sales promotion is to create wealth.(True / False)

199. According to Schultz and Robinson, sales promotion management, Chicago: Crain books, generate short - term cash. (True / False)

130. Consumers and resellers are the target audiences. (True / False)

131. When objectives are expressed in numerical terms, they are called as profit. (True / False)

132. Strategies are broad action plans to achieve the stated goals. (True / False)

133. Marketing objectives and strategies are related to the promotion-mix of a company. (True / False)

134. Promotion objectives and strategies are related to promotion mix. (True / False)

135. Promotion mix depends directly upon marketing strategies and objectives. (True / False)

136. Promotion objective have consumer and trade orientation. (True / False)

137. Sales promotion strategies forces on different consumer promotions and trade deals. (True / False)

138. The main objective of sales promotion is to increase goodwill. (True / False)

139. The sales volume of any product depends on basic factors of marketing line. (True / False)

140. Sales promotion can be a substitute for weaknesses in marketing strategy. (True / False)

141. The reason for companies to go for short-term increase in sales volume is to reduce inventories. (True / False)

142. Marginal buyers contribute more towards increasing profit. (True / False)

143. Demographic, economic and technological are micro-environmental factors. (True / False)

144. Brand switchers sometimes get exposed to better products. (True / False)

145. Sales promotion may contribute to increasing dividends. (True / False)

146. The companies cannot match the substantial advertising budgets who have larger market share. (True / False)

147. Free samples is more effective in inducing trial of a new product to consumers. (True / False)

148. Personal care products are shampoos, cosmetic and laundry products. (True / False)

149. Repeat purchase by customer leads to increased sales volume. (True / False)

150. Sales promotion are communicated to encourage existing consumers to buy like buy one get one free. (True / False)

151. New product launches by competing companies are backed up by aggressive advertising and sales promotion campaigns. (True / False)

152. A firm that feels threatened would like to protect its loyal customers from switching to new competing brand. (True / False)

153. The interval between two successive purchases should be long for consumers. (True / False)

154. The main objective of sales promotion is to encourage re-seller participation in contests. (True / False)

155. Display is not a powerful tool to enhance sales. (True / False)

156. Display attracts consumer attentions who are not passerby and window shoppers. (True / False)

157. The space available for displays in retail store and display materials is unlimited. (True / False)

158. In an average store there may not be more than 20 to 25 items to display. (True / False)

159. High price creates a negative effect on sales. (True / False)

160. Publicity is also called as marketing public relations. (True / False)

161. The firm having a poor public image will have lower profit and sales. (True / False)

162. Feedback helps to modify product offering. (True / False)

Answers for True / False

1.	False	34.	True	67.	True	100.	True	133.	False
2.	True	35.	False	68.	False	101.	True	134.	True
3.	False	36.	True	69.	True	102.	True	135.	True
4.	True	37.	True	70.	True	103.	False	136.	True
5.	True	38.	True	71.	True	104.	False	137.	True
6.	False	39.	True	72.	False	105.	False	138.	False
7.	True	40.	False	73.	True	106.	False	139.	True
8.	True	41.	False	74.	False	107.	True	140.	False
9.	True	42.	True	75.	False	108.	False	141.	True
10.	True	43.	True	76.	True	109.	True	142.	False
11.	False	44.	True	77.	True	110.	False	143.	False
12.	False	45.	True	78.	True	111.	True	144.	True
13.	True	46.	False	79.	True	112.	True	145.	False
14.	True	47.	True	80.	False	113.	True	146.	False
15.	False	48.	True	81.	False	114.	False	147.	True
16.	True	49.	True	82.	True	115.	False	148.	True
17.	True	50.	False	83.	True	116.	False	149.	True
18.	True	51.	True	84.	True	117.	False	150.	True
19.	True	52.	True	85.	False	118.	True	151.	True
20.	False	53.	False	86.	False	119.	True	152.	True
21.	False	54.	True	87.	False	120.	True	153.	True
22.	True	55.	True	88.	True	121.	True	154.	True
23.	False	56.	False	89.	True	122.	True	155.	False
24.	True	57.	True	90.	True	123.	True	156.	False
25.	False	58.	True	91.	True	124.	False	157.	False
26.	True	59.	False	92.	True	125.	False	158.	False
27.	True	60.	True	93.	False	126.	False	159.	True
28.	True	61.	False	94.	False	127.	False	160.	True
29.	True	62.	True	95.	True	128.	False	161.	True
30.	False	63.	False	96.	False	129.	False	162.	True
31.	False	64.	True	97.	False	130.	True		
32.	True	65.	True	98.	False	131.	False		
33.	False	66.	True	99.	True	132.	True		

MULTIPLE CHOICE QUESTIONS

1. Promotion is a form of communication activity whose main focus is on ________.
   (a) Product
   (b) Service or idea industries
   (c) Channel of distribution
   (d) All the above

2. Promotion is the ________ element of marketing mix.
   (a) Second
   (b) Third
   (c) First
   (d) Fifth

3. Promotion is important in ________.
   (a) Competitive market
   (b) Global
   (c) Wider market
   (d) Local market

4. Promotion is the process of marketing communication involving ________.
   (a) Information
   (b) Persuasion
   (c) Influence
   (d) All the above

5. Which of the following is the spark plug of our marketing mix?
   (a) Promotion
   (b) Price
   (c) Product
   (d) Place

6. Which of the following is an important marketing strategy?
   (a) Advertisement
   (b) Marketing
   (c) Promotion
   (d) Channel of distribution

7. Purposes of promotion are ________.
   (a) Providing marketing information to consumers
   (b) Providing marketing information to users
   (c) Providing marketing information to resellers
   (d) All the above

8. Promotion persuades and convinces the and influences his/her behaviour to take the desired action ________.
   (a) Buyer
   (b) Seller
   (c) Wholesalers
   (d) Retailers

9. In competitive market nothing can be sold without ________.
   (a) Price
   (b) Product
   (c) Promotion
   (d) None of the above

10. Promotion message has two basic purposes ________.
    (a) Persuasive communication
    (b) Tool of competition
    (c) Both a and b
    (d) None of the above

11. Promotion is responsible for ________.
    (a) Stimulating consumer demand for product
    (b) Advertising the product
    (c) Pricing the product
    (d) None of the above

12. Which of the following helps you to maintain the demand for your product?
    (a) Publicity
    (b) Marketing

(c) Personal selling
(d) Promotion

13. Promotion mix includes ________.

(a) Advertising, publicity
(b) Personal selling
(c) All forms of sales promotion
(d) All the above

14. Which of the following is non-personal presentation and impersonal salesmanship for mass selling ________.

(a) Advertising
(b) Publicity
(c) Personal selling
(d) Sales promotion

15. Which of the following is a best means of oral and face to face communication for making sales ________.

(a) Personal selling
(b) Sales promotion
(c) Advertising
(d) Marketing

16. Promotional element of marketing mix is information ________.

(a) Information
(b) Persuasion
(c) Reminding
(d) Combination of a b and c

17. The overall objective of promotion is ________.

(a) Influencing the buyers behaviour
(b) Influencing the buyer predispositions
(c) Both a and b
(d) None of the above

18. Which of the following is more effective in the awareness stage?

(a) Publicity
(b) Both a and b
(c) Personal selling
(d) All the above

19. Components of marketing mix are ______.

(a) Product
(b) Price
(c) Promotion and place of distribution
(d) All the above

20. Essential parts of communication ______.

(a) Source
(b) Message
(c) Receiver
(d) All the above

21. True communication takes place between ________.

(a) Sender of message and its receiver
(b) Only between the sender
(c) Both a and b
(d) None of the above

22. Marketing communication is undertaken by marketing through the device of ________.

(a) Price
(b) Promotion
(c) Place
(d) Product

23. Device of promotion are ________.

(a) Advertising
(b) Salesmanship and sales promotion
(c) Publicity
(d) All the above

24. Word-of-mouth communication helps to accelerate the spreading over of ______.

(a) Face- to- face communication
(b) Marketing communication
(c) Both a and b
(d) None of the above

25. Effective communication takes place only when ________.

(a) Sender sends the message
(b) Receiver responds to the received massage

(c) Only through face - to - face
(d) Combination of a and b

26. Effective communication is equal to ________.

(a) Receipt of the message
(b) Understanding
(c) Acceptance and action
(d) Combination of a and b

27. In marketing action means ________.

(a) Decision to purchase
(b) Decision to advertise
(c) Decision to produce
(d) None of the above

28. Who derives to promote his product?

(a) Manufacturer
(b) Marketing
(c) Salesman
(d) Personal selling

29. Forms of promotion are ________.

(a) Media
(b) Channels of communicating
(c) Sending the message
(d) All the above

30. Who is the target market segment?

(a) Receiver or audience
(b) Buyer or seller
(c) None of the above
(d) Wholesaler or retailer

31. Message is received and interpreted by consumers and they decide to ________.

(a) Purchase
(b) Not to purchase
(c) Sell
(d) Resell

32. When it takes place the seller may have ________ feedback from the receiver?

(a) Advertising
(b) Marketing
(c) Personal salesmanship
(d) None of the above

33. The salesman can balance the message on the basis of feedback from ________.

(a) Producer
(b) Retailer
(c) Wholesaler
(d) Buyer

34. Which of the following is the most effective form of communication?

(a) Telephone conversation
(b) Personal interaction
(c) Advertising
(d) All the above

35. Mass communication is essentially ________.

(a) Two-way communication
(b) Five-way communication
(c) One-way communication
(d) Three-way communication

36. Which of the following is difficult and usually delayed?

(a) Production
(b) Selling
(c) Distribution
(d) Feedback

37. Marketing research is used to get feedback ________.

(a) Consumer
(b) Electronic devices
(c) Both a and b
(d) All the above

38. Which of the following helps to arise due to transmission, faulty reception or interference in sales?

(a) Noise in the promotion channel
(b) Marketing strategy
(c) Advertising
(d) None of the above

39. It constitute the most serious noise ________.

(a) Comparative communication
(b) Competitive communication
(c) Face- to- face communication
(d) Telephone conversation

40. The message transmitted through all form of promotion must describe the product features in terms of ________.

(a) Customer wants and desires
(b) Wholesaler wants
(c) Manufacturer wants
(d) Retailer wants

41. Which of the following is better while transmitting the message?

(a) Problem solving approach
(b) Need satisfaction approach
(c) Both a and b
(d) Basically approach

42. Which of the following develops better understanding of customer needs?

(a) Promotion message
(b) Wholesaler and retailer relationship
(c) Producer and consumer relationship
(d) None of the above

43. Who are the buyers of bundle of benefits?

(a) Manufacturer
(b) Wholesaler
(c) Customers
(d) Retailer

44. Promotion message must achieve these basic objects ________.

(a) Communication
(b) Persuasion
(c) Satisfaction
(d) Both a and b

45. For effective communication, sender and receiver must have a common background of experience like ________.

(a) Common culture
(b) Common language
(c) Concepts and events in an under stable manner
(d) All the above

46. The promotion message is arranged to facilitate the consumer decision-making process like ________.

(a) Awareness
(b) Knowledge
(c) Preference
(d) All the above

47. Promotion message is one source of information at the disposal of a ________.

(a) Seller
(b) Manufacturer
(c) Retailer
(d) Buyer

48. If promotion message is useful, the buyer will be influenced and persuaded to take action as desired by the ________.

(a) Marketer
(b) Consumer
(c) Seller
(d) None of the above

49. Communication involves ________.

(a) Transmission of ideas
(b) Seller
(c) Both a and b
(d) None of the above

50. It communicates message very effectively ________.

(a) Written words
(b) Music
(c) Spoken words
(d) Picture

51. It can attract the attention of consumers quickly ________.

(a) Non-verbal media
(b) Visual
(c) Printed message
(d) Both a and b

52. Which of the following is stronger and longer than a word contact?

(a) Written contact
(b) Visual contact
(c) Music
(d) All the above

53. Which of the following permits easier association for the viewer?

(a) Written
(b) Spoken
(c) Picture
(d) Music

54. Which of the following is a perfect advertising medium?

(a) Radio
(b) Television
(c) Newspaper
(d) None of the above

55. Promotion influences buyer behaviour and alter the location and shape the demand curve in favour of ________.

(a) Advertisement
(b) Products
(c) Consumer
(d) Market

56. Promotion strategies may adversely influence ________.

(a) Social environment
(b) Political environment
(c) Both a and b
(d) All the above

57. The marketing activities may aggravate the social problems such as ________.

(a) Media control
(b) Waste disposal
(c) Deceptive advertising practice
(d) All the above

58. Who are forced to pay for all promotion expenses at the end?

(a) Manufacturer
(b) Retailer
(c) Wholesaler
(d) Consumer

59. Promotion means ________.

(a) Right information and persuasion
(b) Tolerable
(c) Justifiable
(d) All the above

60. Consumerism has given importance for ________.

(a) More information
(b) Less persuasive marketing communications
(c) Both a and b
(d) None of the above

61. The best example of misleading promotion is ________.

(a) Superlative advertisements
(b) Puffery in advertising
(c) Culture based advertisements
(d) Both a and b

62. Promotion devices should not ________.

(a) Mislead the average consumers
(b) Abuse the findings of research
(c) Manipulate consumer behaviour and market conditions
(d) All the above

63. It must be________ in making comparisons with products of rivals.

(a) Accurate
(b) Credulous
(c) Fair
(d) All the above

64. Buyer can be induced to ________.

(a) Visit a store
(b) Listen to radio commercials
(c) Watch television jingles
(d) All the above

65. The AIDA formula proposed these stages ________.

(a) Awareness or attention
(b) Interest and desire
(c) Action
(d) All the above

66. The adoption process proposed the stages ________.

(a) Awareness and interest
(b) Evaluation and trial
(c) Adoption
(d) All the above

67. Distinct kinds of consumer response to promotion are ________.

(a) Awareness and knowledge emphasizing cognitive response
(b) Changed attitudes, emphasizing effective response
(c) New behavior indication motivational response
(d) Combination of a , b and c

68. Marketing communications try to influence predispositions of buyers towards the firm like ________.

(a) Attitudes, values
(b) Beliefs, goals
(c) Both a and b
(d) None of the above

69. Buyer's predispositions and behaviour are governed by the ________.

(a) Socio- economic characteristics
(b) Demographic characteristics
(c) Personality characteristics
(d) All the above

70. Which of the following influence the buyer behavior?

(a) Social groups
(b) Culture groups
(c) Economic groups
(d) Both a and b

71. The receiver is an active participant in the ________.

(a) Promotion process
(b) Manufacturing process
(c) Marketing process
(d) Selling process

72. Which of the following determine the receiver's behaviour and action toward a company and its product?

(a) Perceptions of receiver
(b) Attitudes of receiver
(c) Needs of receiver
(d) Both a and b

73. The response to promotion is subjective and entirely depends upon ________.

(a) Mental frame of the message
(b) Satisfaction of the receiver of the message
(c) Both a and b
(d) None of the above

74. Each receiver finds his own meanings to the messages sent by ________.

(a) Manufacture
(b) Marketers
(c) Buyer
(d) Seller

75. The consumer will accept communication which ________.

(a) Demotivates him
(b) Discourages him
(c) Interests him
(d) All the above

76. Promotion strategy lays down the broad principles by which a company hopes to secure an advantage over ________.

(a) Competitors
(b) Attractiveness to buyers
(c) Leads to full exploitation of company resources
(d) All the above

77. Promotion strategy has four sides of equal importance namely ________.

(a) Product in the marketing communication
(b) Prospect to be converted into a customer
(c) Sponsor who under takes promotion and the channel of distribution
(d) All the above

78. Advertising medium for promotion ____.

(a) Radio
(b) Television
(c) Both a and b
(d) Window display

79. The promotion strategy deals with the blend of promotional activities like ________.

(a) Publicity
(b) Advertising
(c) Personal selling and sales promotion
(d) Combination of a, b and c

80. Factors determining the form of promotions ________.

(a) Product
(b) Company and channel choice
(c) Buyer
(d) All the above

81. Examples of product which are effectively shown on television ______.

(a) Toys
(b) Toilet soaps
(c) Cosmetic
(d) All the above

82. This advertisements are unsuitable for children ________.

(a) Press advertisement
(b) Radio advertisement
(c) Television advertisement
(d) Pamphlets

83. Mass selling consumer goods can be easily promoted through ________.

(a) Radio advertisement
(b) Television advertisement
(c) News paper advertisement
(d) Both a and b

84. Industrial and specialty goods should be promoted through ________.

(a) Technical journals
(b) Advertisement
(c) Sales engineers
(d) Both a and b

85. To provide realistic solution to the problem of buyer, the marketer must know ________.

(a) Their customers
(b) Needs and desires
(c) Attitudes and values
(d) All the above

86. Marketers must have ________ information about consumer demand and consumer behaviour.

(a) Up to date
(b) Past
(c) Future
(d) Combination of a and b

87. Corporate advertisements usually emphasize more on ________.

(a) Reliability
(b) Innovation
(c) Responsibility of marketing firm
(d) All the above

88. Effectiveness of communication depends upon ________.

(a) Firm's images in the market
(b) Production process
(c) Marketing strategy
(d) All the above

89. Retailers demand the highly advertised product from ________.

(a) Consumer
(b) Wholesalers
(c) Manufacturer
(d) Both a and b

90. A pull strategy is also called as ________.

(a) Promotion strategy
(b) Suction strategy
(c) Mrketing strategy
(d) Production strategy

91. It is necessary to generate consumer demand ________.

(a) Advertising promotion
(b) Sales promotion
(c) Both a and b
(d) None of the above

92. Which of the following has less emphasis at all stages of the marketing channel?

(a) Advertising
(b) Publicity
(c) Personal selling
(d) Sales promotion

93. Push strategy is also called as ________.

(a) Pressure strategy
(b) Pull strategy
(c) Both a and b
(d) None of the above

94. Which of the following places heavy emphasis is on personal selling?

(a) Push strategy
(b) Pull strategy
(c) Both a and b
(d) None of the above

95. They are mostly the push type strategies relying primarily on personal selling ____.

(a) Marketing strategies
(b) Industrial strategies
(c) Industrial marketing strategies
(d) All the above

96. In push type promotion marketers rely on ________.

(a) Marketing distribution
(b) Selective distribution
(c) Both a and b
(d) All the above

97. Push strategy can be successfully used when ________.

(a) High quality product with unique selling points
(b) High- priced product
(c) Offer adequate incentives to middlemen and their salesman
(d) All the above

98. Most consumer goods manufacturer generally employs this strategy to sell their product ________.

(a) Push strategy
(b) Pull strategy
(c) Push pull strategy
(d) Both a and b

99. The ratio of pull to push may differ according to the requirements of ______.

(a) Production process
(b) Market situation
(c) Advertisement
(d) All the above

100. Salesmen are used to push the goods through which to accelerate sales ________.

(a) Advertising
(b) Sales promotion

(c) Marketing channel
(d) None of the above

101. It will support personal selling to accelerate sales ________.

(a) Advertising
(b) Push strategy
(c) Sales promotion
(d) Both a and b

102. When the marketing plan is ready, we can develop a total promotion programme to approach ________.

(a) Target audience
(b) Population
(c) Both a and b
(d) None of the above

103. Promotion objectives must be set before we decide on ________.

(a) Message contents
(b) Layout and delivery of message
(c) Only (a)
(d) Both a and b

104. They are based on strengths and weakness of the various media vehicles ________.

(a) Contents
(b) Layout decisions
(c) Both a and b
(d) All the above

105. Which of the following is based on the needs of carrying particular types of messages?

(a) Delivery decisions
(b) Marketing decisions
(c) Marketing strategy
(d) None of the above

106. The constituents of promotion programme are ________.

(a) Promotion objectives
(b) Message design
(c) Message delivery and promotion budget
(d) All the above

107. Promotion budget is fixed by the top management regarding the decisions on ________.

(a) Promotion programme
(b) Marketing programme
(c) Production programme
(d) None of the above

108. The promotion budget, to implement marketing plan will be approved by ____.

(a) Top level management
(b) Middle level management
(c) Low level management
(d) All the above

109. Which of the following is an important instrument in marketing to lubricate the marketing efforts?

(a) Sales promotion
(b) Marketing promotion
(c) Advertising promotion
(d) Personal selling

110. Sales promotion is a ________.

(a) Necessity
(b) Not merely a luxury
(c) Not a fashion
(d) All the above

111. Sales promotion is not an ________.

(a) Income
(b) Expenditure
(c) Both a and b
(d) None of the above

112. Sales promotion is an investment which can pay ________.

(a) Interest
(b) Rich dividends
(c) Both a and b
(d) None of the above

113. It is an integral part of the marketing effort ________.

(a) Personal selling
(b) Market
(c) Marketing mix
(d) Sales promotion

114. Sales promotion is referred to the promotional activities other than ________.

(a) Personal salesmanship
(b) Advertising
(c) Publicity
(d) All the above

115. Sales promotion helps to stimulate consumer purchasing and dealer effectiveness like ________.

(a) Exhibitions and showrooms
(b) Demonstrations
(c) Free samples
(d) All the above

116. Sales promotion is a plus ingredient of ________.

(a) Promotion mix
(b) Marketing mix
(c) Advertising mix
(d) None of the above

117. These are the essential and basic ingredients in the marketing mix ________.

(a) Advertising
(b) Personal salesmanship
(c) Both a and b
(d) All the above

118. The two wings of promotion are ________.

(a) Advertising and personal salesmanship
(b) Exhibitions and showrooms
(c) Demonstrations and free samples
(d) None of the above

119. The manufacturer or wholesaler may have a ________.

(a) Good product
(b) Reasonable price
(c) Attractive packages
(d) All the above

120. The manufacturer can get orders from ________.

(a) Dealers or retailers
(b) Through questionnaire
(c) Salesman
(d) Combination of b and c

121. Sales promotion is a vital link between ________.

(a) Advertising and personal salesmanship
(b) Advertising and window display
(c) Advertising and field - selling
(d) All the above

122. In sales promotion all prospective buyers must be ________.

(a) Attracted
(b) Urged
(c) Persuaded to buy your product
(d) All the above

123. Which of the following is a highly competitive field?

(a) Selling
(b) Retailing
(c) Manufacturing
(d) Marketing

124. Sales promotion can ________.

(a) Arouse enthusiasm
(b) Create mood
(c) Spark an immediate reaction from consumers
(d) All the above

125. Many sales promotion campaigns involve the use of ________.

(a) Salary
(b) Interest
(c) Commission
(d) Incentives

126. Sales promotion is often thought as ________.

(a) Special selling effort to accelerate sales
(b) To increase production
(c) To create demand for the product
(d) Combination of b and c

127. The company's marketing objectives and strategies influence the development of ________.

(a) Increasing profit
(b) Sales promotion objectives and strategies
(c) Wealth maximization
(d) All the above

128. There can be a number of sales ________.

(a) Firm's policies
(b) Marketing objectives
(c) Nature of the product and its stage in product life cycle
(d) All the above

129. Objective of sales promotion ________.

(a) Additional market share
(b) Expand the target market
(c) Develop brand franchise
(d) All the above

130. The objective of reactive sales promotion are ________.

(a) Response to competitive moves
(b) Excessive inventory piles up
(c) Generate short - term cash
(d) All the above

131. According to Schultz and Robinson, sales promotion, management, Chicago: Gain Books, 1982, objectives of sales promotion are ________.

(a) Specific, measurable, practical
(b) Clear and concise
(c) Affordable and attainable
(d) Combination of a, b and c

132. Who are the target audiences?

(a) Consumers
(b) Resellers
(c) Manufacturers
(d) Both a and b

133. When objectives are expressed in numerical terms, they are called as ________.

(a) Aims
(b) Features
(c) Quantitative objectives
(d) None of the above

134. They are broad action plans to achieve the stated goals ________.

(a) Policies
(b) Achievements
(c) Strategies
(d) All the above

135. Marketing objectives and strategy are related to the ________.

(a) Promotion - mix of a company
(b) Advertising - mix of a company
(c) Marketing - mix of a company
(d) Goals of a company

136. Promotion objectives and strategies are related to ________.

(a) Promotion mix only
(b) Advertising mix only
(c) Marketing mix only
(d) None of the above

137. Promotion mix depends directly upon________.

(a) Marketing strategy
(b) Marketing objectives
(c) Marketing mix
(d) Both a and b

138. Promotion objectives are aimed at ________.

(a) Consumers
(b) Trade
(c) Both a and b
(d) None of the above

139. Sales promotion strategies focus on ________.

(a) Different consumer promotions
(b) Consumers
(c) Trade deals
(d) Both a and c

140. The main objective of sales promotion is ________.

(a) Attract new product and increase trial
(b) To block competitor's moves
(c) To increase store traffic
(d) Increase sales volume

141. The sales volume of any product depends on basic factors of marketing like ________.

(a) Product quality
(b) Its price, distribution
(c) Effectiveness of marketing communications
(d) All the above

142. Sales promotion cannot be a substitute for weaknesses in ________.

(a) Marketing strategy
(b) Marketing objective
(c) Marketing communication
(d) Marketing mix

143. The reason for companies to go for short- term increase in sales volume like ________.

(a) Reduce inventories before financial year- costing
(b) Increase the stock-holding of retailers
(c) Push stocks of old brand before the introduction of new model
(d) All the above

144. Who contribute more towards increasing sales volume?

(a) Brand switchers or marginal buyers
(b) Brand switchers or marginal buyers
(c) Both a and b
(d) None of the above

145. Which are macros-environment factors?

(a) Demographic
(b) Economic
(c) Technological
(d) All the above

146. Brand switchers sometimes get exposed to ________.

(a) Better products
(b) Some times repeat purchase of product
(c) Both a and c
(d) All the above

147. Sales promotion may contribute to increasing ________.

(a) Wealth maximization
(b) Wealth of stake holders
(c) Sales- volume
(d) Profit

148. Who find sales promotion?

(a) Small companies which cannot afford sustained advertising expenditures to introduce a new product
(b) Match the competitive advertising blitz

(c) Both a and b
(d) None of the above

149. The companies cannot match the substantial advertising budgets that have ________.

(a) Large market share
(b) Medium market share
(c) Small market share
(d) None of the above

150. Which of the following is more effective in inducing trial of a new product to consumers?

(a) Free sample
(b) Coupon of some value
(c) Providing discount
(d) All the above

151. Personal care products are ________.

(a) Shampoos, cosmetics
(b) Toilets soaps or laundry products
(c) Detergent powders and cakes
(d) All the above

152. Colgate Palmolive launched ________.

(a) Toilets
(b) Detergents
(c) Palmolive toilet soaps
(d) None of the above

153. Colgate Palmolive launched 'Palmolive' toilet soap in ________.

(a) 1969
(b) 1989
(c) 1979
(d) 1999

154. Repeat purchase by customer leads to ________.

(a) Increased profit
(b) Increased wealth
(c) Increased sales volume
(d) Increased production

155. Sales promotion are communicate to encourage existing consumers to forward buy like ________.

(a) Get on free on purchase of four
(b) Buy one get one free
(c) Buy four get an offer of ₹ 5
(d) Both a and b

156. New product launches by competing companies are backed up by ________.

(a) Aggressive advertising
(b) Sales promotion campaigns
(c) Marketing mix
(d) Both a and b

157. A firm that feels threatened would like to protect its loyal customers from switching to ________.

(a) New competing brand
(b) Old competing brand
(c) Quality branded product
(d) All the above

158. The interval between two successive purchases should be ________.

(a) Long for consumers
(b) One- by- one for consumers
(c) Small for consumers
(d) Medium for consumers

159. The main objective of sales promotion is to encourage re- seller participation in ________.

(a) Displays and contests
(b) More sales
(c) Competition
(d) Competition

160. Which of the following is a powerful tool to enhance sales?

(a) Marketing
(b) Advertising
(c) Display
(d) Personal selling

161. Display attract consumer attention who are________.

(a) Passer- by
(b) Window shopper
(c) Both a and b
(d) Addicted

162. The space available for displays in retail store and display materials are ________.

(a) Large
(b) Small
(c) Limited
(d) According to requirement

163. Which of the following is correct? In an average store there may not be more than ________.

(a) 5 to 10 items to display
(b) 10 to 15 items to display
(c) 15 to 20 items to display
(d) 20 to 25 items to display

164. It creates a negative effect on sales ______.

(a) Cost
(b) Profit
(c) Price
(d) None of the above

165. Publicity is also called as ________.

(a) Marketing public relations
(b) Marketing buyers relations
(c) Marketing
(d) None of the above

166. The firm having a poor public image will have ________.

(a) Lower sales
(b) Lower profits
(c) Both a and b
(d) All the above

167. Feedback helps to modify ________.

(a) Product offering
(b) Product service
(c) Essentials of product
(d) None of the above

Answers for MCQ

1.	(d)	**17.**	(c)	**33.**	(d)	**49.**	(a)	**65.**	(d)	**81.**	(d)
2.	(b)	**18.**	(a)	**34.**	(b)	**50.**	(d)	**66.**	(d)	**82.**	(a)
3.	(a)	**19.**	(d)	**35.**	(c)	**51.**	(d)	**67.**	(d)	**83.**	(d)
4.	(d)	**20.**	(d)	**36.**	(d)	**52.**	(b)	**68.**	(c)	**84.**	(d)
5.	(a)	**21.**	(a)	**37.**	(c)	**53.**	(c)	**69.**	(d)	**85.**	(d)
6.	(c)	**22.**	(b)	**38.**	(a)	**54.**	(c)	**70.**	(d)	**86.**	(a)
7.	(d)	**23.**	(d)	**39.**	(b)	**55.**	(b)	**71.**	(a)	**87.**	(d)
8.	(a)	**24.**	(b)	**40.**	(a)	**56.**	(c)	**72.**	(d)	**88.**	(a)
9.	(c)	**25.**	(d)	**41.**	(c)	**57.**	(d)	**73.**	(c)	**89.**	(b)
10.	(c)	**26.**	(d)	**42.**	(a)	**58.**	(d)	**74.**	(b)	**90.**	(b)
11.	(a)	**27.**	(a)	**43.**	(c)	**59.**	(d)	**75.**	(c)	**91.**	(c)
12.	(d)	**28.**	(b)	**44.**	(d)	**60.**	(c)	**76.**	(d)	**92.**	(c)
13.	(d)	**29.**	(d)	**45.**	(d)	**61.**	(a)	**77.**	(d)	**93.**	(a)
14.	(a)	**30.**	(a)	**46.**	(d)	**62.**	(d)	**78.**	(c)	**94.**	(a)
15.	(a)	**31.**	(a)	**47.**	(d)	**63.**	(d)	**79.**	(d)	**95.**	(c)
16.	(d)	**32.**	(c)	**48.**	(a)	**64.**	(d)	**80.**	(d)	**96.**	(b)

97.	(d)	**109.**	(a)	**121.**	(c)	**133.**	(c)	**145.**	(d)	**157.**	(a)
98.	(b)	**110.**	(d)	**122.**	(d)	**134.**	(b)	**146.**	(c)	**158.**	(a)
99.	(c)	**111.**	(b)	**123.**	(b)	**135.**	(c)	**147.**	(c)	**159.**	(a)
100.	(d)	**112.**	(b)	**124.**	(d)	**136.**	(a)	**148.**	(c)	**160.**	(c)
101.	(d)	**113.**	(d)	**125.**	(d)	**137.**	(d)	**149.**	(c)	**161.**	(c)
102.	(a)	**114.**	(d)	**126.**	(a)	**138.**	(c)	**150.**	(a)	**162.**	(c)
103.	(d)	**115.**	(d)	**127.**	(b)	**139.**	(d)	**151.**	(d)	**163.**	(b)
104.	(c)	**116.**	(b)	**128.**	(d)	**140.**	(d)	**152.**	(c)	**164.**	(c)
105.	(a)	**117.**	(c)	**129.**	(d)	**141.**	(d)	**153.**	(b)	**165.**	(a)
106.	(d)	**118.**	(a)	**130.**	(d)	**142.**	(a)	**154.**	(c)	**166.**	(c)
107.	(a)	**119.**	(d)	**131.**	(d)	**143.**	(d)	**155.**	(d)	**167.**	(a)
108.	(a)	**120.**	(a)	**132.**	(d)	**144.**	(a)	**156.**	(d)		

MATCH THE FOLLOWING

1.	e-Marketing	**(a)**	Non-personal presentation
2.	Advertising	**(b)**	Commercially significant news
3.	Marketing mix	**(c)**	Business to Customer
4.	Consumer	**(d)**	Medium of advertisement
5.	Television	**(e)**	Ultimate user of the product
6.	Publicity	**(f)**	4 Ps

Answers for Match the Following

1.	(c)	**2.**	(a)	**3.**	(f)	**4.**	(e)	**5.**	(d)	**6.**	(b)

Chapter 16

Personal Selling

SUMMARY

Personal selling is the delivery of a specially designed message to a prospect by a seller, usually in the form of face-to-face communication, personal correspondence, or a personal telephone conversation. Unlike advertising, a personal sales message can be more specifically targeted to individual prospects and easily altered if the desired behavior does not occur. Personal selling, however, is far more costly than advertising and is generally used only when its high expenditure can be justified. For example, the marketing of a sophisticated computer system may require the use of personal selling, while the introduction of a new product to millions of consumers would not. Two other forms of personal selling that are not used with high-end products are door-to-door selling and home demonstration parties. These two personal selling methods are primarily used for personal care products, cosmetics, cookware, encyclopedias, books, toys, food, and other items of special interest to homemakers. Ideally, personal selling should be supported by advertising to strengthen its impact.

Personal Selling is a two way communication between the seller and the buyer usually face-to-face, via the Internet, the phone. A seller attempts to persuade a buyer to make a purchase under personal selling.

Challenges in Personal Selling

(i) At first, personal selling is dyadic in nature. Dyadic simply means of or relating to two people. Thus, personal selling revolves around a marketing relationship developed between two people. Frequently, personal salespeople enlist the help of others in their organizations to sell to and service customers. And just as frequently, personal salespeople find themselves making presentations to small groups of people or working with multiple individuals within customers' firms. However, ultimately a successful marketing relationship is built by two people one person selling and person buying. Successful salespeople identify that person early on and work to win their trust and confidence.

(ii) Secondly, personal selling is a process, not a single activity. And done correctly, the process continues indefinitely. Salespeople, sales managers, and others inside the seller's organization frequently see the selling process as culminating or ending with a signed order. However, in these days of so-called "relationship marketing" and "customer relationship management" successful organizations recognize that signed orders simply represent one point of positive feedback in an ongoing and continuous process.

(iii) Third, personal selling is highly interactive. In advertising, information flow occurs initially in a one-way direction. What feedback the advertiser receives arrives late well after an advertisement has aired. Moreover, without costly research, the attitudinal effects of advertising may never be known. In personal selling, feedback is largely instantaneous and continuous.

The two-way flow of information that characterizes personal selling creates a communication channel rich with information, much of it nonverbal. Effective personal salespeople become adept at interpreting this information quickly and adapting their responses to it.

(iv) Personal selling is about problem solving. As the marketing concept is adopted by more and more firms, the emphasis of personal salespeople will be more on identifying customers with a true need for the firm's products and applying those products to solve customer problems. Less emphasis will be placed on simply making a sale. The focus on problem solving in personal selling reflects a larger trend toward building relationships between customers and clients. Marketers know that to develop these relationships, they must be willing to forego short term gains, particularly when the salesperson realizes that at that moment a purchase might not be in the customer's best interests.

Nature of Personal Selling

1. The greatest freedom to adjust a message to satisfy customers informational needs, dynamic.
2. Most precision, enabling marketers to focus on most promising leads vs. advertising, publicity and sales promotion.
3. Give more information.
4. Two way flow of information, interactivity.
5. Discover the strengths and weaknesses of new products and pass this information on to the marketing department.
6. Highest cost. Businesses spend more on personal selling than on any other form of promotional mix.
7. Goals range from finding prospects, convincing prospects to buy, keeping customers satisfied and help them pass the word along.

Essentials of Personnel Selling

There are six prerequisites of effective selling or essentials of personnel selling-

Knowledge of the company: Most products especially costly and complicated products are not judged on their merits. They are judged by the name of the company that manufactures them. Hence, salesmen must be company-oriented.

Knowledge of about the product: A salesman should know about his product:

(a) Materials from which it is made
(b) How it is used and how it is maintained
(c) Product features
(d) Customer benefits
(e) Selling point of the product in relation to its rivals and so on.

1. Knowledge about the competition: It is required to study the product effort by his competitors and determine their strengths and weaknesses in comparison to his own products.

2. Knowledge of the customers: A sales man must have adequate knowledge about both the customer's wants and desire. And the products offered by the firm to satisfy customers.

3. Knowledge of about the selling process: To move the customer through the stages in the buying process the salesman undertakes the stages in the selling process, *viz*., protecting, preparation presentation and post sales activities.

4. Knowledge about himself: Know yourself is one of the most essentials of personnel selling.

Trends in Selling

While the basic premise of personal selling, building relationships, has not changed much in the last 50 years, there are a number of developments that are impacting this method of promotion including:

1. **Selling Trends: Controlled Word-of-Mouth**

One of the most influential forms of promotion occurs when one person speaks highly of a product to someone else, particularly if the message sender is considered an unbiased source of information. Until recently, marketers have had little control over person-to-person promotion that did not involve salespeople (i.e., biased source). However, marketers are beginning to experiment with new methods of promotion that strategically takes advantage of the benefits offered by word-of-mouth promotion. Unlike salespeople who attempt to obtain an order from customers, controlled word-of-mouth promotion uses real people to help spread information about a product but do not directly elicit customer orders.

With controlled word-of-mouth promotion a marketer hires individuals to spread positive information about a product but in a way that does not make it obvious to others that they are being paid to do so. The technique is especially useful when building awareness of new products and this approach has been dubbed "buzz" marketing as a way to describe its objective of building a high level of awareness for a product. For example, a brewer may form a team of word-of-mouth marketers who visit local taverns and night spots. As part of their job these marketers may "talk up" a new beer sold by the brewer and even purchase the product for some customers. But in the course of doing so they do not directly disclose that they are being compensated by the brewer for their efforts.

Controlled word-of-mouth has received a great deal of publicity though much of it has focused on potential ethical concerns. Some have expressed concern that paying people to "act" as if they are interested in a product without any indication of their relationship with the product breaches ethical standards. As more companies explore controlled word-of-mouth marketing it is expect to become an even more scrutinized form of personal selling.

2. **Selling Trends: Customer Information Sharing**

The most dramatic change is to occur in how salespeople function on a day to day basis involves the integration of customer relationship management (CRM) systems into the selling arena. CRM is the name given to both the technology and the philosophy that drives companies to gain a better understanding of their customers with the goal of building stronger long-term relationships. The essential requirement for an effective CRM system is the need for all customer contact points to gather information so that this can be shared with others in the company.

But CRM has faced some rough times within the sales force for the exact reason it is important: salespeople must share their information. Salespeople have historically been very good at developing relationships and learning about customers, but often loath sharing this since, in effect, information is what makes them important. In the minds of some salespeople, letting go of the information reduces their importance to the company. For example, some salespeople feel that sharing all they know about a customer will make them expendable as a salesperson since a company can simply insert someone new into their spot at anytime. While the attitude toward CRM has made its implementation difficult in many companies, salespeople should understand that it is not going away. CRM and information sharing has proven to be critical for maintaining strong customer relations and salespeople must learn to adapt to it.

3. **Selling Trends: Mobile and Web Computing**

The move to an information sharing approach is most effective when salespeople have access to information sharing features when they need it most. Mobile technologies, such as wireless internet and cellular Internet access, allow salespeople to retrieve needed information at any time. For example, if a salesperson takes a customer to lunch, the salesperson can quickly access company material to respond to questions such as how long it may take to receive product if an order is placed.

Additionally, there is a growing trend to make key business applications available through a browser rather than having programs loaded on a salesperson's computer. This allows for the application to be accessed from anywhere at any time. For example, many companies have moved to web-based CRM systems where simply having Internet access allows salespeople to enter and retrieve information. Also, many new office productivity applications, such as word processing and spreadsheets, are now becoming web-accessible.

New generation cell phones or smart phones along with other handheld devices, such as personal digital assistants (PDA), lighten the burden of carrying laptop computers. But because these handheld devices are web-enabled they provide access to much of the same information as a standard computer. While the computing power of handheld devices is still underpowered compared to conventional computers, the move to web-based computing may someday make the handheld the main instrument for inputting and outputting information.

4. **Selling Trends: Electronic Sales Training**

Developing the skills and techniques needed to be successful at selling requires an extensive commitment by the individual seller and the seller's company to sales training. Sales training is the hallmark of professional selling. If there is one thing that separates the truly successful salesperson from those who are not, it is the amount of training and preparation they engage in.

Most organizations that employ a sales force offer new salespeople an extensive formal training program often held at dedicated training facilities. These training programs can range from a few days to many months depending on the industry. But once a salesperson has made the move to the field, training does not stop. Those involved in selling must continue to stay abreast of their products, customers, markets and competitors. While many companies may continue to employ the same methods used when they first trained their salespeople, a large number of firms are finding that ongoing training can be just as effective using electronic options such as delivering training over the Internet, through downloadable computer programs or through interactive CDs or DVDs.

While feedback using electronic means is not as personal as it might be with in-person training, sophisticated electronic training programs are effective in educating and testing trainee's knowledge. Also, a live trainer can be contacted very quickly via e-mail, online chat or by a phone call if a question does arise.

Using electronic delivery, the cost to the company for adding or updating training material is inexpensive and quick compared to the cost and time needed to produce and ship paper-based materials. Additionally, the use of RSS feeds or email enables salespeople to be quickly notified when new training material is available. This is useful when the sales force must be made aware of a recent change that will impact how products are promoted such as a price change, new information to be used as comparison to competitor's products, a potential problem that has arisen when installing or using a product or some other adjustment.

5. **Selling Trends: Use of Customer Teams**

   As we noted in our discussion of technical specialists, salespeople may require the assistance of others in their organization to effectively deal with prospects. In fact, many companies are moving away from the traditional sale force arrangement, where a single salesperson handles nearly all communication with an account, in favor of a team approach where multiple people are involved.

   Teams consist of individuals from several functional areas such as marketing, manufacturing, distribution, and customer service. In some configurations all members share bonuses if the team meets sales goals. Clearly to be effective a team approach requires the implementation of customer relationship management systems that we discussed earlier.

Types of Salespersons

1. **Professional Visitor:** This person doesn't have any problem making appointments. In fact, they thrive on it. They enjoy visiting and talking to people, getting to know them, and may even engage in a casual discussion of their customers' problems. Their conversation with a customer or prospect may or may not eventually involve the subject of how their products or services can benefit the buyers, and if it does, it usually has to be instigated by the customer or prospect. A typical sales presentation will be oral, with very little use of visual materials, product brochures, or printed proposals.
2. **Order Taker:** These people don't mind talking to customers, clients or prospects, if they don't have to initiate the call. They are uncomfortable making appointments, and would rather have the customer or prospect come to them. The telephone presents just as much a problem for these people. If the phone rings, they'll take the call and even discuss the customer's needs. But it's tough for them to pick up the receiver and dial a customer's number. They operate best from a base of "low price," and have difficulty handling objections. They would rather wait until someone asks for something specific, then they have no trouble filling the order.
3. **Peddler:** These are "sales-oriented" people. They have good product knowledge, but severely lack in "people skills." They operate from a sort of "hit-and-run" approach. This person will assume a certain level of product knowledge on the part of the customer, and spend very little, if any, time establishing rapport with them. These people are either "product-oriented," or "price-oriented." Their entire presentation is based on product features or price, with little regard to how the product or service will benefit the customer. The peddler is the most prevalent type of salesperson you will find. Telemarketers who work the consumer market fit nicely into this category. Even with do not call laws in place, it seems like it never fails. You just get home from a tough day at work and are relaxing with the kids, working in the yard, or perhaps even eating dinner. Then the phone rings. It's for you. The person on the other end dives right into their presentation with no regard for the person they're calling, whose privacy they are interrupting, or what laws they may be breaking. For most people, especially professional

salespeople, this inconvenience and the salesperson's level of incompetence is most aggravating. In these types of calls, the salesperson shows no concern for the prospect's time, inconvenience, present level of product knowledge, or whether or not there's any level of need, want or desire to know more about what they're selling. The assumption is made by the caller that what he or she is offering the prospect in terms of a product, service or convenience is the same or better than what the prospect currently has, and that the entire prospect is interested in is price. This type of approach is an insult to the prospect or customer, and is one of the biggest mistakes a salesperson can make.

4. **Problem Solver:** These are salespeople who enjoy getting in front of people, ferreting out problems, needs and wants, and discussing workable solutions. They have empathy for the customer, can see the customer's needs from the customer's point of view, and enjoy helping the customer solve their problems. The problem solving person is good at establishing rapport with the prospect or customer, identifying what their needs, wants and desires are, developing creative, and needs and wants satisfying proposals, and making effective presentations.

5. **Counselor:** In the business world, it's not uncommon for companies and corporations to have a staff of lawyers, or "legal counsel," on retainer to give advice in matters pertaining to the law, taxes, investments, mergers, or other difficult or legal situations. The Counselor knows that when it comes to important buying decisions, his or her customers, be they companies, corporations, or individuals, should be no different. To them, buying any type of product or service is a serious matter, not to be taken lightly, and can be an important tool for solving a need, satisfying a problem or adding to their profits, convenience or lifestyle. They know that their customers need professional and qualified representation and advice, and the Counselor will do whatever it takes to provide it for them.

FILL IN THE BLANKS

1. An organization can derive maximum benefit by giving importance to ______.
2. Personal selling enhances customer's confidence in the ______.
3. Personal selling promotes long-term business relation through ______.
4. Personal selling facilitates the seller to understand each customer's ______.
5. Personal selling provides a human touch to ______ transactions.
6. Personal selling helps to build long term relations between ______ and ______.
7. Personal selling is an effective tool in convincing the customer about the ______.
8. Personal selling provides a package of inputs of experts from difficult areas such as ______, ______ and ______.
9. ______ are the focal strategies that a company uses to achieve its marketing objectives.
10. Personal selling is useful in formulating ______.
11. ______, ______ and ______ helps to frame prudent price policy for the product.

12. ________ has a significant role to play in personal selling and distribution.

13. The end result of any distribution effort is the ready availability of ________.

14. If product is not available when actually needed then the whole of ________ becomes useless.

15. Sales force plays an important role in ________ the product's utility.

16. Duty of a sales person is to provide ________ about the product.

17. It actually support the efforts of the sales force through ________ and ________.

18. Personal selling means ________ conversation.

19. No other tool of promotion or communication is as strong as ________.

20. Personal selling is more effective in the trial stage of the ________ process.

21. Personal selling takes place between ________ and ________.

22. Personal selling is a ________ communication.

23. Due to seller-buyer interaction, personal selling provides immediate ________.

24. In olden days, primary emphasis was on ________ at any cost.

25. In year________ high-pressure salesman were employed to pressurise innocent customers.

26. ________ salesmanship was popular in the case of door-to-door salesman.

27. An example for high pressure salesmanship is________.

28. Modern salesmanship depends on ________ approach.

29. Growth of consumerism and emergence of buyer's market indicates that high pressure salesmanship has ________ its utility.

30. ________ involves the ability to influence or persuade people.

31. Modern salesmanship does not rely on ________.

32. ________, ________ and ________ does not have place in modern salesmanship.

33. Modern salesmanship has the power of ________ and ________.

34. The main aim of modern salesmanship is at winning the ________ of buyers.

35. Modern salesmanship is based on Idea of ________.

36. Salesmanship aims at discovering the problem and providing a solution to the ________.

37. ________ is not the art of making a profit at the cost of the buyer.

38. Salesmanship should benefit both the ________ and ________.

39. Salesmanship helps him to obtain maximum return for________ by him.

40. Salesmanship is an ________ process.

41. Salesmanship is ________.

42. Salesmanship is winning the ________.

43. Salesmanship aims at ________.

44. Salesmanship is also a ________.

45. There are ___ types of salesmen.

46. Salesmanship is responsible for creation of demand through a ________ approach.

47. ________, ________ and ________ are the first step in creative process.

48. Creative process is salesmanship requires ________ and ________.

49. Traditional concept of salesmanship is a________.

50. Types of Salesmanship are ________, ________ and ________.

51. The unique aspects of industrial marketing is ________ and ________ organization.

52. ________ and ________ organizations are professionals and experts in their own line.

53. Industrial sellers interaction takes place between ________.

54. ________ salesman needs a technical background in engineering to understand the problem.

55. The sophisticated and expert purchasing agent looks for results in form of ________ and ________.

56. Showing the goods, waiting for an order and receiving the payment is ________ job.

57. Modern salesmanship is based on the ________.

58. Industrial buyers are appealed mainly through ________ motives.

59. Direct sales refer to passing goods directly to ________.

60. Components spare parts, office supplies are the example of ________.

61. Personal selling enjoys the lion's show in the industrial marketing as the tool of ________ and ________.

62. Advertising plays a secondary role in industrial marketing facilitating the job of ________.

63. Industrial salesman is the company to an ________.

64. The reputation of the company is represented by ________.

65. The duty of salesman is to know thoroughly his ________, ________ and ________.

66. Industrial marketing is also known as ________.

67. Industrial salesman may represent ________.

68. Sales engineers have employed highly technical products to study customer problems such as ________, ________ and ________ training.

69. Consumer goods are ________ and ________ goods.

70. ________ involves quantity selling of all types of consumer goods to retailers.

71. Merchant salesmanship operates in the ________ and ________ goods market.

72. The Wholesalers, Distributors, Retailers are the customers of ________ salesman.

73. They operate mainly in ________.

74. Example of service market is ________.

75. Merchant salesman also operate in the service markets for ________.

76. Speciality salesman, missionary salesman, creative salesman and detail salesman are varieties of ________.

77. Vacuum cleaner, refrigerators and cosmetics are ________.

78. ________ is called upon to sell consumer specialities and business goods.

79. Industrial products, material supplies are the examples of ________.

80. Speciality salesman specializes in introducing ________ in the market.

81. Speciality salesman adopts the techniques of ________.

82. Missionary salesman is responsible for ________ and ________.

83. Missionary salesmanship helps in ________.

84. Missionary salesman assists dealers in all types of sales promotion activities at the ________.

85. They act as store demonstrators to distribute samples for customers who come into the ________.

86. He is a ________ salesman who seeks to introduce a new brand into the market and create a demand for such a novelty

87. Creative salesman is also called as ________.

88. Creative salesman cultivates and develops ________

89. He is diametrically opposite to a mere counter salesman in a ________.

90. Detailing is a form of ________.

91. The detail salesmen visit those types of customers to sell their products ________.

92. Medical representative of drug manufacturing companies are ________.

93. Retail salesmanship is necessary for selling high ________.

94. Door-to-door canvassing and selling is done through ________.

95. Indoor consumer selling takes place in ________.

96. Outdoor selling to consumers take place in their ________ or ________.

97. Route salesman, independent consumer salesman and controlled consumer salesman are types of ________.

98. The route salesman follows a regular route serving consumers like ________ and ________.

99. The independent consumer salesman sells on his own account like ________, ________ and ________.

100. The controlled consumer salesman is the employee of ________.

101. Kitchen-ware, magazines and cosmetics are the examples of ________.

102. Insurance agents or salesman sell the services of ________ to people.

103. Computer printers, software are the examples of ________.

104. Sales people spend much time for selling and less time doing paper work which increases their ________.

105. Expansion of AIDAS is ________.

Answers for Fill in the Blanks

1.	Personal selling	20.	Production
2.	Sellers	21.	Sales person; prospective customer
3.	Personal intimacy	22.	Two-way
4.	Preference	23.	Feed back
5.	Business	24.	Sales volume
6.	Business; consumer	25.	1960
7.	Product	26.	High pressure
8.	Installation; trouble shooting; sales	27.	Eskimo family forced to purchase refrigerator
9.	Marketing mix		
10.	Pricing strategies	28.	Problem-solving
11.	Competitor's price; sentiment; market reaction	29.	Outlived
		30.	Salesmanship
12.	Sales policy	31.	Pressure tactics
13.	Product	32.	Misrepresentation; cheating; dishonesty
14.	Business	33.	Suggestion; imaginative handling
15.	Advocating	34.	Confidence
16.	Confidence	35.	Services
17.	Advertising; public relations	36.	Problem
18.	Face-to-face	37.	Salesmanship
19.	Personal selling	38.	Buyer; seller

39.	Money spent	**73.**	Resale market
40.	Educational	**74.**	Hoteling
41.	Persuasion	**75.**	Selling services
42.	Buyer's Confidence	**76.**	Merchant salesman
43.	Mutual benefit	**77.**	Consumer specialities
44.	Creative process	**78.**	Speciality salesman
45.	Three	**79.**	Business goods
46.	Problem-solving	**80.**	New products
47.	Learn buyer's problem; buyer's motive; habits	**81.**	Aggressive salesmanship
		82.	Promoting sales; creating demand
48.	Creativity, initiative; empathy	**83.**	Arranging store displays
49.	Mechanical job	**84.**	Point of purchase
50.	Industrial; Merchant; consumers	**85.**	Retail stores
51.	Buyer-seller interdependence; product copy	**86.**	Creative
		87.	Pioneering salesman
52.	Selling; buying	**88.**	Sales territories
53.	Two professionals	**89.**	Retail shop
54.	Industrial	**90.**	Speciality selling
55.	Increased sales; lower cost	**91.**	Architects; engineers
56.	Mechanical	**92.**	Detail salesman
57.	Ideas of service	**93.**	Cost articles
58.	Rational buying	**94.**	Travelling salesman
59.	Consumers	**95.**	Retail stores
60.	Industrial goods	**96.**	Homes; offices
61.	Promotion; distribution	**97.**	Outdoor consumer salesmen
62.	Industrial salesman	**98.**	Baked goods; laundry
63.	Industrial Consumer	**99.**	Street vendors; peddlers; mobile retailers
64.	Salesman		
65.	Product; Company; Consumer	**100.**	Company
66.	Business marketing	**101.**	Tangible goods
67.	Manufacturers	**102.**	Insurances
68.	Mechanical; electrical; chemical	**103.**	Modern gadget
69.	Shopping; speciality	**104.**	Productivity
70.	Wholesale selling	**105.**	Attention, interest, desire, action and satisfaction
71.	Consumer; Industrial		
72.	Merchant		

TRUE / FALSE

1. An organization can derive maximum benefit by giving importance to personal selling. (True / False)
2. Personal selling enhances customer's confidence in the manufacturers. (True / False)
3. Personal selling promotes long-term business relation through personal intimacy. (True / False)
4. Personal selling facilitates the seller to understand each customer's budget. (True / False)
5. Personal selling provides a human touch to business transactions. (True / False)
6. It helps to build long term relations between business and consumers. (True / False)
7. It is an effective tool in convincing the customer about the product. (True / False)
8. Personal selling does not provide a package of inputs of experts from different areas. (True / False)
9. Marketing mix are the focal strategies that a company uses to achieve its marketing objectives. (True / False)
10. Personal selling is useful in formulating pricing strategies. (True / False)
11. Competitor's price does not help to frame prudent price policy for the product. (True / False)
12. Sales policy does not play any role in personal selling and distribution. (True / False)
13. The end result of any distribution effort is the ready availability of product. (True / False)
14. If product is not available when actually needed then whole of business becomes useless. (True / False)
15. Sales force plays an important role in advocating the price utility. (True / False)
16. Duty of a sales person is to provide information about the product. (True / False)
17. It actually supports the efforts of the sales force through advertising. (True / False)
18. Personal selling means telephone conversation. (True / False)
19. Personal selling is a stronger tool of promotion or communication.(True / False)
20. Personal selling is more effective in the trial stage of the production process. (True / False)
21. Personal selling takes place between sales person and prospective customer. (True / False)
22. Personal selling is a two-way communication. (True / False)
23. There is a delay in feedback from customers due to personal selling. (True / False)
24. In olden days, primary emphasis was on profit volume at any cost. (True / False)
25. In olden days, the job of a salesman was to simply book orders as demand were more than supply. (True / False)
26. High pressure salesmanship is popular in the case of door-to-door salesman. (True / False)
27. Eskimo family forced to purchase refrigerator is an example of high pressure salesmanship. (True / False)
28. Modern salesmanship depends on problem solving approach. (True / False)
29. Growth of Consumerism and emergence of buyer's market indicates that high pressure salesmanship has outlived its utility. (True / False)

30. Salesmanship does not involve the ability to influence or persuade people. (True / False)

31. Modern salesmanship does not rely on pressure tactics. (True / False)

32. Cheating and dishonesty have place in modern salesmanship. (True / False)

33. Modern salesmanship has the power of suggestion and imaginative handling. (True / False)

34. The main aim of modern salesmanship is at winning the confidence of buyers. (True / False)

35. Modern salesmanship is based on idea of service. (True / False)

36. Salesmanship aims at discovering the problem and providing a solution to the problem. (True / False)

37. Salesmanship is the art of making a profit at the cost of the buyer. (True / False)

38. Salesmanship does not help him to obtain maximum return for money spent by him. (True / False)

39. Salesmanship should benefit both the buyer and seller. (True / False)

40. Salesmanship is a profit making process. (True / False)

41. Salesmanship is high-pressure process. (True / False)

42. Salesmanship is winning the buyer's confidence. (True / False)

43. Salesmanship aim at mutual benefit. (True / False)

44. Salesmanship is not a creative process. (True / False)

45. There are five types of salesman. (True / False)

46. Salesmanship is responsible for creation of demand through a problem solving approach. (True / False)

47. Learn buyer's problem, motive and habits these are the first step in creative process. (True / False)

48. Creative process is salesmanship requires creativity, initiative and empathy. (True / False)

49. Modern concept of salesmanship is a technical job. (True / False)

50. Industrial salesmanship, merchant salesmanship and consumer salesmanship are types of salesmanship. (True / False)

51. The unique aspect of industrial marketing is buyer-seller interdependence. (True / False)

52. Selling and buying organizations are professionals and experts in their own line. (True / False)

53. These interaction takes place between three of professionals. (True / False)

54. Industrial salesman needs a technical background in engineering to understand the problem. (True / False)

55. The sophisticated and expert purchasing agent looks for results in form of increased sales and lower cost. (True / False)

56. Showing the goods, waiting for an order and receiving the payment are mechanical job. (True / False)

57. Modern salesmanship is based on the ideas of selling. (True / False)

58. Industrial buyers are appealed mainly through rational buying motives. (True / False)

59. Direct sales refer to passing goods directly through manufacturer and wholesales. (True / False)

60. Components spare parts, office supplies are examples of cosmetic goods. (True / False)

61. Personal selling enjoys the lion's share in the industrial marketing as the tool of promotion and distribution. (True / False)

62. Advertising plays a secondary role in industrial marketing facilitating the job of industrial salesman. (True / False)

63. Industrial salesman is the company to an Industrial consumer. (True / False)

64. The reputation of the company is represented by producer. (True / False)

65. The duty of salesman is to know thoroughly his product, company and consumers. (True / False)

66. Industrial marketing is also known as business marketing. (True / False)

67. Industrial salesman also represents sellers. (True / False)

68. Sales engineers have employed highly technical products to study consumer problems. (True / False)

69. Consumer goods are shopping and speciality goods. (True / False)

70. Wholesale selling involves quantity selling of all types of consumer goods to sellers. (True / False)

71. Merchant salesmanship does not operate in the consumer and industrial goods market. (True / False)

72. The wholesalers, distributors, retailers are the customers of merchant salesman. (True / False)

73. Merchant salesman mainly operates in wholesale market. (True / False)

74. Hoteling is not an example of service market. (True / False)

75. Merchant salesman also operates in the service markets for selling services. (True / False)

76. Speciality salesman is a kind of merchant salesman. (True / False)

77. Vacuum cleaner, refrigerator and cosmetics are consumer specialities. (True / False)

78. Speciality salesman is called upon to sell consumer specialities and business goods. (True / False)

79. Industrial products, material supplies are the example of business goods. (True / False)

80. Speciality salesman specializes in introducing already existing product in the market. (True / False)

81. Speciality salesman adopts the techniques of aggressive salesmanship. (True / False)

82. Missionary salesman are responsible for advertising goods in market. (True / False)

83. Missionary salesman is a type of salesmanship help in arranging store displays. (True / False)

84. Missionary salesmen assist dealers in all types of sales promotion activities at the point of purchase. (True / False)

85. They act as store demonstrators to distribute samples for customers. (True / False)

86. Creative salesman is responsible to introduce a new brand into the market. (True / False)

87. Creative salesman is also called as pioneering salesman. (True / False)

88. Creative salesman cultivates and develops sales territories. (True / False)

89. He is diametrically opposite to a mere counter salesman in a wholesale shop. (True / False)

90. Detailing is a form of creative selling. (True / False)

91. The detail salesmen visit architects to sell their product. (True / False)

92. Medical representative of drug manufacturing companies are detail salesman. (True / False)

93. Retail salesmanship is necessary for selling low cost articles. (True / False)

94. Door-to-door canvassing and selling is done through travelling salesman. (True / False)

95. Indoor consumer selling takes places in retail stores. (True / False)

96. Outdoor selling to consumer takes place in their homes. (True / False)

97. Route salesmanship is a type of controlled consumer salesman. (True / False)

98. The route salesman follows a regular route serving consumer like baked goods and laundry. (True / False)

99. The independent consumer salesman sells on his own account like street vendors, pedlars, etc. (True / False)

100. The controlled consumer salesman is the employee of private company. (True / False)

101. Kitchenware is a tangible good. (True / False)

102. Insurance agents or salesman sell the services of insurance to people. (True / False)

103. Computer printer is an example of modern gadget. (True / False)

104. Sales people spend much time for selling and less time doing paper work which increases productivity. (True / False)

105. AIDAS stands for Attention, Interest, Desire, Action and Satisfaction. (True / False)

Answers for True / False

1.	True	22.	True	43.	True	64.	False	85.	True
2.	False	23.	False	44.	False	65.	True	86.	True
3.	True	24.	False	45.	False	66.	True	87.	True
4.	False	25.	True	46.	True	67.	False	88.	True
5.	True	26.	True	47.	True	68.	True	89.	False
6.	True	27.	True	48.	True	69.	True	90.	False
7.	True	28.	True	49.	False	70.	True	91.	True
8.	False	29.	True	50.	True	71.	False	92.	True
9.	True	30.	False	51.	True	72.	True	93.	False
10.	True	31.	True	52.	True	73.	False	94.	True
11.	False	32.	True	53.	False	74.	False	95.	True
12.	False	33.	True	54.	True	75.	True	96.	True
13.	True	34.	True	55.	True	76.	True	97.	False
14.	True	35.	True	56.	True	77.	True	98.	True
15.	True	36.	True	57.	False	78.	True	99.	True
16.	True	37.	False	58.	True	79.	True	100.	False
17.	True	38.	False	59.	False	80.	False	101.	True
18.	False	39.	True	60.	False	81.	True	102.	True
19.	True	40.	False	61.	True	82.	False	103.	True
20.	True	41.	True	62.	True	83.	True	104.	True
21.	True	42.	True	63.	True	84.	True	105.	True

MULTIPLE CHOICE QUESTIONS

1. An organization can drive maximum benefit by giving importance to ______.

(a) Sales Promotion
(b) Marketing
(c) Personal Selling
(d) Production

2. Personal selling enhances customer's confidence in the ______.

(a) Marketer
(b) Sellers
(c) Advertiser
(d) Consumer

3. Personal selling promotes long-term business relation through ______.

(a) Personal selling
(b) Personal intimacy
(c) Both a and b
(d) None of the above

4. Personal selling facilitates the seller to understand each customer's ______.

(a) Preferences
(b) Attitudes
(c) Demand
(d) All the above

5. Personal selling provides a human touch to ______.

(a) Business transactions
(b) Marketing transactions
(c) Cash transactions
(d) Production transactions

6. Which of the following helps to build long-term relations?

(a) Wholesalers and retailers
(b) Retailers and consumers
(c) Business and consumer
(d) None of the above

7. Which of the following is an effective tool in convincing the customer?

(a) Market
(b) Goods
(c) Products
(d) All the above

8. Personal selling provides a package of inputs of experts from different areas such as ______.

(a) Installation
(b) Trouble shooting
(c) Sales
(d) All the above

9. They are the focal strategies that a company uses to achieve its marketing objectives ______.

(a) Product
(b) Price
(c) Promotion and distribution
(d) All the above

10. It is useful in formulating ______.

(a) Pricing policies
(b) Pricing decision
(c) Pricing strategies
(d) Both a and b

11. If helps to frame prudent price policy to the management for the product ______.

(a) Competitor's price
(b) Market reaction.
(c) Customer's sentiments
(d) All the above

12. Which of the following has a significant role to play in personal selling and Distribution?

(a) Sales price
(b) Sales force

(c) Sales policy

(d) None of the above

13. The end result of any distribution effort is the ready availability of ________.

(a) Price

(b) Place

(c) Product

(d) Promotion.

14. When does the whole of business becomes useless?

(a) Product is not available when actually needed.

(b) Production is less.

(c) Customers dislike the product

(d) All the above

15. Sales force plays an important role in ________.

(a) Coordinating

(b) Lessoning

(c) Advocating the product's utility

(d) All the above

16. Duty of a sales person is ________.

(a) Motivation

(b) Generate interest

(c) Confidence about the product

(d) All the above

17. It actually supports the efforts of the sales force ________.

(a) Advertising

(b) Public relations

(c) Both (a) and (b)

(d) All the above

18. Personal selling refers to ________.

(a) Telephone conversation

(b) Oral face-to-face interaction

(c) Both (a) and (b)

(d) None of the above

19. No other tool of promotion or communication is as strong as ________.

(a) Personal selling

(b) Sales promotion

(c) Radio advertising

(d) All the above

20. Personal selling is more effective in the trial stage of the ________.

(a) Production process

(b) Purchase process

(c) Communication process

(d) Marketing process

21. Personal selling takes place between ________.

(a) Manufactures to retailer

(b) Sales person and prospective customer

(c) both a and b

(d) None of the above

22. Personal selling is a ________.

(a) Two-way communication

(b) One-way communication

(c) Three-way communication

(d) Four-way communication

23. Due to seller-buyer interaction, personal selling provides immediate ________.

(a) Reaction

(b) Feedback

(c) Written note

(d) None of the above

24. In olden days, primary emphasis was on ________.

(a) Production volume at any cost

(b) Sales volume at any cost

(c) Profit volume

(d) All the above

25. In which year high-pressure salesman were employed to pressurize innocent customers ________.

(a) 1996
(b) 1960
(c) 1970
(d) 1990

26. It was popular in the case of door-to-door salesman ________.

(a) High pressure salesmanship
(b) Low pressure salesmanship
(c) Medium pressure salesmanship
(d) None of the above

27. Which of the following is an example for high pressure salesmanship?

(a) Eskimo family forced to purchase refrigerator.
(b) Eskimo family not forced to purchase refrigerator.
(c) Both a and b
(d) None of the above

28. Modern salesmanship depends on ________.

(a) Talking approach
(b) Problem solving approach
(c) Interacting approach
(d) Presenting approach

29. Growth of Consumerism and emergence of buyers market indicates that high pressure salesmanship has ________.

(a) Outlined its utility
(b) Updated its utility
(c) Both a and b
(d) None of the above

30. It involves the ability to influence or persuade people ________.

(a) Salesmanship
(b) Marketing
(c) Publicity
(d) All the above

31. Modern salesmanship does not reply on ________.

(a) Pressure tactics
(b) Increase in sales
(c) Increase in profit
(d) Increase in wealth

32. It does not have place in modern salesmanship ________.

(a) Misrepresentation
(b) Cheating
(c) Dishonesty
(d) All of the above

33. Modern salesmanship has the power of ________.

(a) Suggestion
(b) Imaginative handling
(c) Both a and b
(d) All the above

34. The main aim of modern salesmanship is at winning the ________.

(a) Confidence of buyer
(b) Producing more goods
(c) Selling more goods
(d) All the above

35. Modern salesmanship is based on _____.

(a) Idea of service
(b) Idea of production
(c) Idea of selection
(d) Idea of execution

36. Salesmanship aims at discovering the problem and providing a solution to the ________.

(a) Production
(b) Problem
(c) Selling
(d) Distribution

37. Which of the following is not the art of making a profit at the cost of the buyer?

(a) Salesmanship
(b) Personal selling
(c) Advertising
(d) None of the above

38. Salesmanship should benefit both the ________.

(a) Buyer and seller
(b) Manufacturer and retailer
(c) Manufacture and wholesaler
(d) both a and b

39. Salesmanship helps him to obtain maximum return for ________.

(a) Money spent by him
(b) Cost incurred
(c) Expenses made
(d) Advertising

40. Salesmanship is an ________.

(a) Entertainment process
(b) Education process
(c) Selling process
(d) None of the above

41. Salesmanship is ________.

(a) High Pressure process
(b) Low pressure process
(c) Medium Pressure process
(d) Both a and c

42. Salesmanship is winning the ________.

(a) Buyer's Confidence
(b) Seller's Confidence
(c) Advertiser's Confidence
(d) Company's Confidence

43. Salesmanship aims at ________.

(a) Buyer's Benefit
(b) Mutual Benefit
(c) Sellers Benefit
(d) Wholesalers Benefit

44. Salesmanship is also a ________.

(a) Destroying process
(b) Demonstration process
(c) Creative process
(d) Selection process

45. How many types of salesman are there?

(a) Two
(b) Three
(c) Four
(d) Five

46. Salesmanship is responsible for creation of demand through a ________.

(a) Problem-solving approach
(b) Educational approach
(c) Creative approach
(d) Sales approach

47. What is the first step in creative process?

(a) Learn buyer's problem
(b) Buyer's motives
(c) Habits
(d) All the above

48. Creative process in salesmanship requires ________.

(a) Creativity
(b) Initiative
(c) Empathy
(d) All the above

49. Modern Concept of Salesmanship is a

(a) Mechanical job
(b) Non-mechanical job
(c) Practical job
(d) Difficult job

50. Industrial salesmanship, Merchant salesmanship and consumer salesmanship are ________.

(a) Types of salesman
(b) Not types of salesmanship
(c) Both a and b
(d) None of the above

51. The unique aspects of industrial marketing is ________.

(a) Buyer-seller interdependence
(b) Product complexity
(c) Both a and b
(d) All the above

52. They are professionals and experts in their own line ________.

(a) Selling organization
(b) Buying organization
(c) Both a and b
(d) All the above

53. The interaction takes place between the ________.

(a) Two professionals
(b) None of them
(c) Both a and b
(d) only sellers

54. Who needs a technical background in engineering to understand the problem?

(a) Industrial salesman
(b) Agricultural salesman
(c) Merchant salesman
(d) All the above

55. The sophisticated and expert purchasing agent looks for results in form of ________.

(a) Increased sales
(b) Lower cost
(c) Increased profit
(d) Both a and b

56. Showing the goods, waiting for an order and receiving the payment is ________.

(a) Mechanical job
(b) Cytological job
(c) Physical job
(d) None of the above

57. Modern salesmanship is based on the ________.

(a) Ideas of motive
(b) Ideas of production
(c) Ideas of service
(d) Ideas of marketing

58. Industrial buyers are appealed mainly through ________.

(a) Rational buying motives
(b) Lump sum buying motives
(c) Demand-basis motives
(d) All the above

59. Direct sales refers to passing goods directly through ________.

(a) Wholesales and retailer
(b) Wholesaler and semi-wholesaler
(c) Wholesales and semi-retailer
(d) None of the above

60. Examples of Industrial goods are ________.

(a) Components
(b) Spare parts
(c) Office supplies and Consumable goods
(d) All the above

61. Personal selling enjoys the lion's share in industrial marketing as the tool of ________.

(a) Promotion and Marketing
(b) Promotion and distribution
(c) Production and distribution
(d) Manufacturing and selling

62. Advertising plays a secondary role in industrial marketing facilitating the job of ________.

(a) Industrial salesman
(b) Marketing salesman
(c) Distribution
(d) None of the above

63. Industrial salesman is the company to an ________.

(a) Industrial producer
(b) Industrial seller
(c) Industrial customer
(d) both a and b

64. The reputation of the company is represented by ________.

(a) Marketer
(b) Producer
(c) Advertiser
(d) Salesman

65. The duty of salesman is to know thoroughly ________.

(a) His product
(b) His customer
(c) His company
(d) All the above

66. Industrial marketing is also known as ________.

(a) Marketing process
(b) Business marketing
(c) Business process
(d) Marketing process

67. Industrial salesman may also represent ________.

(a) Manufacturers
(b) Industrial distributors or wholesalers
(c) Manufacturer's agents or will supply house
(d) All the above

68. Sales engineers have employed highly technical products to study customer problems such as ________.

(a) Mechanical
(b) Electrical
(c) Electronic and chemical
(d) All the above

69. Consumer goods are ________.

(a) Convenience
(b) Shopping and specialty goods
(c) Both a and b
(d) None of the above

70. Which of the following involves quantity selling of all types of consumer goods to sellers?

(a) Industrial salesmanship
(b) Wholesale selling
(c) Consumer salesmanship
(d) None of the above

71. Merchant salesmanship operate in the consumer goods market and ________.

(a) Industrial goods market
(b) Marketing goods market
(c) Advertising goods market
(d) All the above

72. The wholesalers, distribution, retailers, co-operatives, institutions and industrial buyer are the customers of ________.

(a) Merchant salesman
(b) Consumer salesman
(c) Retail salesman
(d) Industrial salesman

73. They operate mainly in ________.

(a) Resale market
(b) Wholesale market
(c) Retail market
(d) All the above

74. Which of the following is an example of service markets?

(a) Advertising communication
(b) Hoteling
(c) Travelling and tourism
(d) All the above

75. Merchant salesman also operate in the service markets for ________.

(a) Selling goods
(b) Selling services.

(c) Selling both goods and services
(d) All the above

76. Speciality salesman, Missionary salesman, creative salesman and Detail salesman are ________.

(a) Examples of salesman
(b) Varieties of salesman
(c) Varieties of merchant salesman
(d) All the above

77. The consumer specialities are ________.

(a) Vacuum cleaner
(b) Refrigerators
(c) Cosmetics or books
(d) All the above

78. He is called upon to sell consumer specialities and business goods ______.

(a) Speciality salesman
(b) Missionary salesman
(c) Creative salesman
(d) Detail salesman

79. Example of business goods are ______.

(a) Industrial products
(b) Material supplies
(c) both a and b
(d) None of the above

80. Speciality salesman specialize in introducing ________.

(a) New products or innovations in the market
(b) Specially advertised products
(c) Costly products
(d) None of the above

81. Speciality salesman adopt the techniques of ________.

(a) Aggressive salesmanship
(b) Creative salesmanship
(c) Skilled salesmanship
(d) All the above

82. Missionary salesman is responsible for ________.

(a) Promoting sales
(b) Creating demand
(c) Both a and b
(d) None of the above

83. This type of salesmanship help in _____.

(a) Arranging store displays
(b) Planning store sales
(c) Training salesman of retailers
(d) All the above

84. Missionary salesman assist dealers in all types of sales promotion activities at the ________.

(a) Point of selling
(b) Point of purchase
(c) Point of production
(d) Point of marketing

85. They act as store demonstrators to distribute samples for customers who come into the ________.

(a) Retail stores
(b) Production place
(c) Wholesale stores
(d) None of the above

86. He is a salesman who seeks to introduce a new brand into the market and create a demand for such a novelty ________.

(a) Speciality salesman
(b) Missionary salesman
(c) Creative salesman
(d) Detail salesman

87. Creative salesman is also called as ________.

(a) Pioneering salesman
(b) Aggressive salesman
(c) Both a and b
(d) None of the above

88. Creative salesman cultivates and develops ________.

(a) Sales territories
(b) Sales marketing
(c) Introducing new product
(d) Retail sales

89. He is diametrically opposite to a mere counter salesman in a ________.

(a) Retail shop
(b) Wholesaler shop
(c) Both a and b
(d) None of the above

90. Detailing is a form of ________.

(a) Speciality selling
(b) Personal selling
(c) Wholesale selling
(d) Creative selling

91. The detail salesman visit these type of customers to sell their products ______.

(a) Doctors
(b) Engineers
(c) Architects
(d) All the above

92. Medical representative of drug manufacturing companies are ________.

(a) Speciality salesman
(b) Detail salesman
(c) Missionary salesman
(d) Creative salesman

93. Retail salesmanship is necessary for selling high ________.

(a) Cost articles
(b) Consumer goods
(c) Electronic items
(d) None of the above

94. Door-to-door canvassing and selling is done through ________.

(a) Travelling salesman
(b) Consumer salesman
(c) Prospective buyers
(d) Salesman

95. Indoor consumer selling takes place in ________.

(a) Wholesale stores
(b) Retail stores
(c) Provision stores
(d) Homes

96. Outdoor selling to consumers take place in their ________.

(a) Homes
(b) Office
(c) Streets
(d) Both a and b

97. The types of outdoor consumer salesman are ________.

(a) Route salesman
(b) Independent consumer salesman
(c) Controlled consumer salesman
(d) All the above

98. The route salesman follows a regular route serving consumers like ________.

(a) Baked goods
(b) Laundry
(c) Both a and b
(d) None of the above

99. The independent consumer salesman sells on his own account like ________.

(a) Street vendors
(b) Pedalers
(c) Mobile retailers
(d) All the above

100. The controlled consumer salesman is the employee of ________.

(a) Manufacturer
(b) Retailer
(c) Insurance company
(d) All the above

101. Example of tangible goods ________.

(a) Kitchen-ware
(b) Magazines or books
(c) Cosmetic
(d) All the above

102. Insurance agents or salesman sell the service of ________.

(a) Insurance to people
(b) Service to people
(c) Obtaining premium
(d) None of the above

103. Which of the following is an example of modern gadget?

(a) Computer printers
(b) Software
(c) Cosmetics
(d) Both a and b

104. Sales people spend much time for selling and less time doing paper work which increases their ________.

(a) Productivity
(b) Profitability
(c) Sales
(d) None of the above

105. Expand AIDAS ________.

(a) Attention, Interest, Desire, Action and Satisfaction
(b) Attract, Inspire, Desire, Activity and Satisfaction
(c) Assure, Interest, During, Activity and Service
(d) None of the above

Answers for MCQ

1.	(c)	**19.**	(a)	**37.**	(a)	**55.**	(d)	**73.**	(a)	**91.**	(d)
2.	(b)	**20.**	(b)	**38.**	(a)	**56.**	(a)	**74.**	(d)	**92.**	(b)
3.	(b)	**21.**	(a)	**39.**	(a)	**57.**	(c)	**75.**	(b)	**93.**	(a)
4.	(a)	**22.**	(a)	**40.**	(b)	**58.**	(a)	**76.**	(c)	**94.**	(a)
5.	(a)	**23.**	(b)	**41.**	(a)	**59.**	(a)	**77.**	(d)	**95.**	(b)
6.	(c)	**24.**	(b)	**42.**	(a)	**60.**	(d)	**78.**	(a)	**96.**	(d)
7.	(c)	**25.**	(b)	**43.**	(b)	**61.**	(b)	**79.**	(c)	**97.**	(d)
8.	(d)	**26.**	(a)	**44.**	(c)	**62.**	(a)	**80.**	(a)	**98.**	(c)
9.	(d)	**27.**	(a)	**45.**	(b)	**63.**	(c)	**81.**	(a)	**99.**	(d)
10.	(c)	**28.**	(b)	**46.**	(a)	**64.**	(d)	**82.**	(c)	**100.**	(d)
11.	(d)	**29.**	(a)	**47.**	(d)	**65.**	(d)	**83.**	(d)	**101.**	(d)
12.	(c)	**30.**	(a)	**48.**	(d)	**66.**	(b)	**84.**	(b)	**102.**	(a)
13.	(c)	**31.**	(a)	**49.**	(a)	**67.**	(d)	**85.**	(a)	**103.**	(d)
14.	(a)	**32.**	(d)	**50.**	(a)	**68.**	(d)	**86.**	(c)	**104.**	(a)
15.	(d)	**33.**	(c)	**51.**	(c)	**69.**	(b)	**87.**	(a)	**105.**	(a)
16.	(d)	**34.**	(a)	**52.**	(c)	**70.**	(b)	**88.**	(a)		
17.	(c)	**35.**	(a)	**53.**	(a)	**71.**	(a)	**89.**	(a)		
18.	(b)	**36.**	(b)	**54.**	(a)	**72.**	(a)	**90.**	(a)		

MATCH THE FOLLOWING

1.	Personal selling	**(a)**	Medical representatives
2.	2 way communication	**(b)**	Problem solving approach
3.	Modern salesmanship	**(c)**	long-term relationship
4.	Detailing	**(d)**	Professionals
5.	Industrial buying	**(e)**	Store display
6.	Missionary salesman	**(f)**	Personal selling

Answers for Match the Following

1.	(c)	**2.**	(f)	**3.**	(b)	**4.**	(a)	**5.**	(d)	**6.**	(e)

Chapter 17

Sales Management

SUMMARY

Sales management is attainment of an organization's sales goals in an effective and efficient manner through planning, staffing, training, leading and controlling organizational resources. Revenue, sales, and sources of funds fuel organizations and the management of that process is the most important function.

Sales management is a business discipline which is focused on the practical application of sales techniques and the management of a firm's sales operations. It is an important business function as net sales through the sale of products and services and resulting profit drive most commercial business. These are also typically the goals and performance indicators of sales management.

Sales Responsibilities

The duties and responsibilities of the sales persons can vary depending upon the nature of the business.

1. A salesperson should have all the knowledge about the product so that he may communicate with the customers.
2. He should sell the products with persuasion and it is the responsibility of sales person to satisfy the customers while they are looking for the products.
3. Salesperson should also handle and maintain the cash.
4. Salesperson is also responsible to greet the customers, to help the customers in identifying their requirements, to promote products, to answer the customers' questions regarding the products, to negotiate the price on the spot, to arrange the merchandise properly and to supervise the ordering the supplies.

Sales Planning

Sales planning are the process of determining the number of sales persons or sales force required the sales targets to be achieved, the expenditures to be incurred and everything required for an effective sales organization in the firm.

Types of Sales Manager

There are four types of sales managers. Here is an in-depth discussion of the different types of sales manager in any kind of company.

1. **The Dictator Manager:** There are managers that are called as dictators. These managers love to dictate and usually want their opinions to be done all the time. Their listening skills are only limited and they do not regard the opinions of their subordinates. Although the dictator managers are regarded as evil managers, there is still an advantage of being one. In fact, your subordinates exactly know where they stand and therefore do not cross the line. Since being a dictator means that you follow the guidelines strictly, then you can be ensured that your subordinates will also learn the rules themselves. However, the major drawback about being one is that you tend to monopolize the entire work place. Moreover, your subordinates will follow you not because they respect you but because they are afraid.

2. **The Disappearing Managers:** These managers have a lot of things to do and are often out from the office most of the time. This type of manager is always on the go. If you are this kind of manager, then you need to make sure that you change yourself. As found out, this type of manager can be very frustrating since they are nowhere around when their representatives need them.
3. **The Demonstrator Manager:** This particular manager loves to work most of them time on their own without the need to work with others. Although this is good, sometimes the manager does not give his or her subordinates a chance to work for themselves. The downside to this manager is that he or she does not elicit the value of teamwork among the subordinates.
4. **The Developer Manager:** This manager takes time with his or her subordinates and develops ways to improve them. In all types of managers, this particular manager is the best type of all. This makes the subordinates feel comfortable with the manager thus they perform well with their jobs.

Salesmanship is the process of including and assisting a prospective buyer to buy a commodity or service or to act to favorable upon an idea that has commercial significance to the seller.

Features of Salesmanship

The fundamental features of salesmanship can be enumerated as follows:

1. **Persuasion character:** Salesmanship involves the ability to influence people. It is the skill in handling people which makes for a successful salesman.
2. **Winning the buyer's confidence:** Modern salesmanship does not use doubtful methods of influencing buyer.
3. **High pressure:** High-pressure salesmanship under which innocent buyers were pressurized and hypnotized by their sales talk and dramatic sale presentation.
4. **Aims at mutual benefit:** Salesmanship is not the art of making a profit at the cost of the buyer on the contrary, salesmanship should benefit both the buyer and the seller.
5. **Education process:** Salesmanship educated people about their needs very offer people are not aware of their needs. Salesmen perform the function of the educating the customers about their needs and their satisfaction.

Qualities of a Successful Salesman

(i) Personality is a composition of various characteristics of a man, personal appearance, habits, manners, way of dressing and addressing, posture, carriage, voice, etc.

(ii) He should possess good stamina to work hard and continuously, i.e., he should not get exhausted quickly and easily.

(iii) Presence of mind, i.e., he should be quite to grasp the situation and handle it according to the needs of the time.

(iv) Imaginative to appreciate, understand and satisfy the requirements of the customers by putting oneself mentally in the position.

(v) Sharp memory, i.e., a capacity to recognize his customer, recall his interviews and results their specific requirements and suggestions.

(vi) Likable disposition, i.e., politeness, courteous, good manners cheerfulness, good humour, refinement in taste; pleasant habits make a man likeable.

All commercial enterprises in the same sector that is engaged in sales management and precisely this management activity is carried out by the sales of such business entity. The role of sales management is carried on planning, execution and control activities related to sales. Because during the implementation of the respective schemes usually applied in the administration of sales, surprises happen, because usually the sales management department shall monitor and constant control of all activities that revolve about sales management. Despite this logical necessity, many companies often use some types of control procedures are inadequate.

Even found some determinants with respect to these control procedures for managing sales of which we can say that, for example, small firms mostly have less control than large companies and conducting a work is much more efficient which allows them to clearly define all objectives, as well as establish systems by which to measure the efficiency of sales management. On the other hand, we must point out that less than half the commercial companies know the utilities of all individual products.

FILL IN THE BLANKS

1. Sales management is generally known as ________.
2. A sales force serves as a company's personal link to ________.
3. Marketing stresses the importance of satisfying consumer needs and wants through a process of ________.
4. ________ and ________ are directly related to each other.
5. The advertising and marketing magazine defines business is ________.
6. ________ is the primary sales tool of salespeople.
7. ________ is the most frequently used promotional technique in business markets.
8. Management of the sales force is an important quality component of any ______.
9. Modern sales management is a ________ process.
10. Sales management generally refers to ____.
11. Sales force strength and qualification affect both the ability to provide competitive service levels and increase in sales of the ________.
12. ________ and ________ has an impact on the morale of the sales force and help in retaining successful salespeople.
13. _____ allow above-average compensation for the most successful salespeople.
14. ________ and ________ are intricately linked, particularly in India's highly volatile market.
15. Demand for medium and heavy commercial vehicles grew by over 100% between ________ and ________.
16. ________ and ________ are the training provided by sales force.
17. The main responsibilities of sales manager are achieving ________ and ________.
18. There must be control over the various activities of he sales force by the ________.
19. Beyond control, sometimes it leads to intractable problem in a ________.
20. Sales force requires delegation of authority in preparing ________.
21. Sales force provide assurance regarding ________.
22. Target-setting is necessary for achieving ________.
23. Sales targets are fixed on the basis of ________, ________ and ________.
24. ________ depends on meticulous planning and dynamic strategies.
25. Sales management is a vital subsystem of ________.
26. Marketing plans, strategies and policies are implemented through ________.

27. Sales management acts behind the marketing management as ________.

28. Modern sales mangers is not only profit-oriented but also ________.

29. Sales management is a ________ profession.

30. Sales management is responsible for ________, ________ and ________.

31. Sales execution must assure the delivery of products with ________.

32. Modern sales manager is a marketing executive and not merely a sales executive for ________.

33. Planning refers to choosing from the ________.

34. Sales planning is a part of ________.

35. Sales planning includes sales ________, ________ and ________.

36. ________ refers to deciding in advance a future course of action regarding the marketing or selling of product.

37. ______ is the primary managerial function and it proceeds all other managerial functions.

38. Sales programme is based on ________, ________ and ________.

39. Sales controls assure realization of ________.

40. ________ is the guiding principles set by the company to govern actions.

41. The backbone of successful sales policies is ________ and ________.

42. High reputation takes place through ______.

43. The pillars of firm's credibility and goodwill is ________.

44. The p's of marketing mix are ________, ________, ________ and ________.

45. ____ is a foundation for effective execution of sales policy and sales programme.

46. The duty of sales manager is to recognize ________ and ________.

47. Sales organization is the medium to execute ________.

48. Sales organization is the counter part of ________.

49. Sales department produces mass market with the help of ________, ________ and ________.

50. ________ is necessary among all the departments to achieve target.

51. ________ and ________ helps to create a sound sales organization.

52. ________ and ________ are of the sales organization in of planning, organizing, directing and controlling all the activity relating to selling function.

53. ________ is responsible for co-ordinating and controlling all the activities of the department.

54. A sales organization is like a power station sending out energy which is devoted to the ________.

55. Sales efforts are necessary through which sound sales organization can prevent ______.

56. Sales manager must assure he optimum contribution of personals selling efforts to the overall ________ of the company.

57. ________ is responsible for management and development of sales personnel.

58. The duty of the sales manager is recruitment, selection, training, supervision, evaluation and control of ________.

59. The sales manager looks after both administrative and operating duties and responsibilities in a ________.

60. Administrative sales manager of a sales organization are suitable for ________.

61. Administrative work is done by ________.

62. Administrative work refers to ________, ________, ________ and ________.

63. Operating work is the work involved in ________.

64. The part played by a modern sales manager is similar to that of a ________.

65. Sales manager is responsible for all activities relating to ________.

66. Sales manager has to formulate sales ________, ________ and ________.

67. The sales manager has to ensure ________ and ________.

68. The sales manager has to execute the ________ and ________.

69. ________ helps to take decision at the right time.

70. Sales cost analysis can help sales manager to control selling ________ and ________.

71. Without sales budget and sales cost analysis sales manager cannot have ________.

72. ________ is the primary responsibility of the sales manager.

73. The sales manager is responsible for providing and managing ________.

74. ________ must be financed in anticipation of seasonal demand.

75. ________ and ________ are essential in selling and distribution of goods.

76. Sales manager is in charge of management of sales to assure ________.

77. Long-term success of a firm depends on ________ and ________.

78. ________ are the invaluable of the firm.

79. ________ and ________ provides a sound foundation for a good vibrant sales organization and sales management.

80. ________ can provide job specifications of the required sales positions.

81. ________ deals with securing as many qualified people to fill the vacancies.

82. ________ is the information gathering, evaluation and decision-making required to seen and choose applicants.

83. ________ is an indispensable device in selecting salespeople.

84. ________ is the heart of the selection technique.

85. Intelligence test, aptitude test and personality test are the types of ________.

86. ________ are able to secure sales orders more quickly sell and manage.

87. Salespeople must have ________ to be effective in their selling field.

88. Sales skill training is given on the job by a ________.

89. Sales attitude training tries to strengthen salesman's ________.

90. ________ is essential on the job training.

91. Ready-made programmed instructional courses can be prepared by ________ and ________ trainers.

92. At present these gadgets are used for training salesman ________ and ________.

93. Most salespeople are earning ________ apart from ________.

94. A good salesperson earns over ________ of salary as increment.

95. All sales persons are given many other perks like ________, ________ and ________.

96. The main objective of sales supervisor is to motivate salesman and ________.

97. Sales analysis refers to analysis by ________.

98. Effective direction is done through two-way communication and ________.

99. Sound selection facilitates training and training facilitates ________.

100. ________ and ________ incentives is necessary to accomplish best performance.

Answers for Fill in the Blanks

1.	Backbone of marketing	38.	Objective; policies; procedures
2.	Customers	39.	Sales target
3.	Exchange	40.	Policies
4.	Marketing; selling	41.	Consumer satisfaction; consumer goodwill
5.	Marketing	42.	Fair trading
6.	Computer	43.	Sound sales policies
7.	Personal selling	44.	Product; price; place; promotion
8.	Selling effort	45.	Sales organization
9.	Customer oriented	46.	Human values; human relations
10.	Management of sales force	47.	Marketing plan
11.	Organisation	48.	Factory
12.	Compensation; Incentives	49.	Salesmanship; advertising; sales Promotion
13.	Incentive		
14.	Budget plans; incentive system	50.	Coordination
15.	1993; 1996	51.	Division of labour; proper delegation of authority
16.	In-house training; on-the job training		
17.	Sales target; profit	52.	General sales manager; chief executive
18.	Sales manager's	53.	Sales manager
19.	Sales organization	54.	Selling
20.	Tour programme	55.	Wastage in distribution
21.	Quality	56.	Marketing objectives
22.	Organizational goals	57.	Field sales manager
23.	Past experience; time period; brand position	58.	Sales force
24.	Accuracy	59.	Small firm
25.	Marketing management	60.	Larger company
26.	Sales management	61.	Top-management
27.	Dynamic force	62.	Planning; organizing; coordinating; controlling
28.	Customer oriented		
29.	Challenging	63.	Sales executing plan
30.	Sales volume; handling sales operation; contribution to profit	64.	Marketing manager
		65.	Merchandising
31.	Satisfying experience	66.	Budget; policies; programmes
32.	Maximum sales volume	67.	Growth; profit
33.	Alternative courses of action	68.	Plans; programmes
34.	Marketing planning	69.	Marketing research
35.	Forecasting; programmes; goals	70.	Cost; expenses
36.	Sales planning	71.	Profit planning
37.	Planning	72.	Administration of sales department

73.	Funds of marketing	87.	Product related training
74.	Inventories	88.	Skilled trainer
75.	Cash; credit	89.	Positive attitude
76.	Market share profit	90.	Field training
77.	Sales volume; salesman power	91.	Skilled; expert
78.	Sales people	92.	Videotape; close-circuit TV
79.	Recruitment; selection	93.	Incentive, salary
80.	Job analysis	94.	20 %
81.	Recruitment	95.	Medical aid; pension; gratuity
82.	Selection process	96.	Good working condition
83.	Personal Interview	97.	Sales results
84.	Interview	98.	Coordination
85.	Psychological test	99.	Managerial control
86.	Trained salesman	100.	Financial; non-financial

TRUE / FALSE

1. Sales management is generally known as backbone of marketing. (True / False)
2. A sales force serves as a company's personal link to manufacturer. (True / False)
3. Marketing stresses the importance of satisfying consumer needs and wants through a process of exchange. (True / False)
4. Marketing and selling are directly related to each other. (True / False)
5. The advertising and marketing magazine defines business is advertising. (True / False)
6. Computer printer is the primary sales tool of sales people. (True / False)
7. Personal selling is the most frequently used promotional technique in business markets. (True / False)
8. Management of the sales force is an important quality component of any selling effort. (True / False)
9. When a company has specialized products, it may create product based sales organisation. (True / False)
10. Sales force management is neither 100% centralized nor 100 % decentralized. (True / False)
11. Sales force strength and qualification affect both the ability to provide competitive service levels and economics of the sales force. (True / False)
12. Compensation and incentives has an impact on the morale of the sales force and help in retaining successful salespeople. (True / False)
13. Incentive allows above-average compensation for the cost successful salespeople. (True / False)
14. Budget plans and incentive system are intricately linked, particularly in India's highly relative market. (True / False)
15. Demand for medium and heavy commercial vehicles grew by over 100% between 1980 and 1990. (True / False)
16. In-house training and on the job training are not provided by sales force. (True / False)

17. The duty of sales manager is organizing sales research and product research. (True / False)

18. There must be control over the various activities of the sales force by supervisors. (True / False)

19. Beyond control, sometimes it leads to intractable problems in a sales organization. (True / False)

20. Sales force requires delegation of authority in fixing prices. (True / False)

21. Target setting is not necessary for achieving organizational goals. (True / False)

22. Sales targets are fixed on the basis of past experience, time period and brand position. (True / False)

23. Accuracy depends on meticulous planning and dynamic strategies. (True / False)

24. Sales management is a vital sub-system of marketing management. (True / False)

25. Marketing plans, strategies and policies are implemented through sales marketing. (True / False)

26. Sales management acts behind the marketing management as dynamic as dynamic force. (True / False)

27. Modern sales manager is not only profit oriented but also wealth-oriented. (True / False)

28. Sales management is a challenging process. (True / False)

29. Sales management is responsible for sales volume and contribution to profit. (True / False)

30. Modern sales manager is a marketing executive and not merely a sales executive for maximum sales volume. (True / False)

31. Sales executives must assure the delivery of products with satisfying experience. (True / False)

32. Planning refers to choosing from the alternative courses of action. (True / False)

33. Sales planning is a part of marketing process. (True / False)

34. Sales planning includes sales forecasting, programmes and goals. (True / False)

35. Sales planning refers to deciding in advance a future course of action regarding the marketing or selling of products. (True / False)

36. Planning is the primary managerial function and it preceed all other managerial function. (True / False)

37. Sales controls assure realization of profit. (True / False)

38. Sales programme is based on wealth of the company. (True / False)

39. Strategies is the guiding principles set by the company to govern actions. (True / False)

40. The backbone of successful sales policies is consumer satisfaction and consumer goodwill. (True / False)

41. High reputation does not take place through fair trading. (True / False)

42. The pillars of firm's credibility and goodwill are marketing process. (True / False)

43. Product, price, place, and promotion are the four p's of marketing mix. (True / False)

44. Sales organization is a foundation for effective execution of sales policy and sales programme. (True / False)

45. The duty of sales manager is to recognize human values and relations. (True / False)

46. Sales organization is the medium to execute advertising plan. (True / False)

47. Sales organization is the counter part of factory. (True / False)

48. Sales department producers mass market with the help of salesmanship.(True / False)

49. Coordination is necessary among all the departments to achieve target. (True / False)
50. Division of labour helps to create a sound sales organization. (True / False)
51. General sales manager and chief executive are not of the sales organization in controlling all the activities relating to selling function. (True / False)
52. Sales manager is not responsible for coordinating and controlling all the activities of the department. (True / False)
53. A sales organization is not devoted to advertising and selling. (True / False)
54. Sales efforts are necessary through which sound sales organization can prevent wastage in distribution. (True / False)
55. Sales manager must assure the optimum contribution of personal selling efforts to the overall marketing objective. (True / False)
56. Field sales manager is not responsible for management and development of sales personnel. (True / False)
57. The duty of the salesman is recruitment, selection and control of sales force. (True / False)
58. The sales manager should look after administrative and operating duties and responsibilities in large firm. (True / False)
59. Administrative sales manager of a sales organization are suitable for larger company. (True / False)
60. Administrative work is done by low-level management. (True / False)
61. Administrative work refers to estimation of cost of production. (True / False)
62. Operating work is the work involved in executing and operating plan. (True / False)
63. The part played by a modern sales manager is equal to marketing manager. (True / False)
64. Sales manager is responsible for all activities relating to liquid assets. (True / False)
65. Sales manager has to formulate sales budget and policies. (True / False)
66. The sales manager is responsible to ensure growth and manage changes. (True / False)
67. The sales manager has no right to execute the plans and programmes. (True / False)
68. Marketing research helps to take decision at the right time. (True / False)
69. Sales cost analysis can help sales manager to control selling cost and expenses. (True / False)
70. Without sales budget and sales cost analysis sales manager cannot have profit planning. (True / False)
71. Administration of sales department is the secondary responsibility of sales manager. (True / False)
72. The sales manager is responsible for providing and managing funds of marketing. (True / False)
73. Furniture must be financed in anticipation of seasonal demand. (True / False)
74. Cash and credit are essential in selling and distribution of good. (True / False)
75. Sales manager is in charge of management of sales to assure market share and profit. (True / False)
76. Long-term success of a firm does not depend on sales volume. (True / False)
77. Salespeople are the invaluable resource of the firm. (True / False)
78. Recruitment does not provide a sound foundation for a good sales organization and sales management. (True / False)
79. Job analysis cannot provide job specifications of the required sales positions. (True / False)

80. Recruitment deals with securing as many qualified people to fill the vacancies. (True / False)

81. Selection-process is the information gathering, evaluation and decision making required to screen and choose applicants. (True / False)

82. Personal interview is an indispensable device in selecting salespeople. (True / False)

83. Interview is the heart of the selection technique. (True / False)

84. Intelligence test is not a type of psychological test. (True / False)

85. Trained salesman is not able to secure sales orders more quickly. (True / False)

86. Salespeople must have attitude training quality to be effective in their selling field. (True / False)

87. Sales skill training as given on the job by a skilled trainer. (True / False)

88. Sales attitude training tries to strengthen sales man's negative attitude. (True / False)

89. Field training is essential on the job training. (True / False)

90. Ready-made programmed instructional courses. (True / False)

91. Market is a place, area and demand concept. (True / False)

92. At present these broad casts are used for training salesman videotape and close - circuit TV. (True / False)

93. Most salespeople are earning less than ₹ 10,000 per month. (True / False)

94. A good salesperson earns over ₹ 8,000 per month. (True / False)

95. All sales persons are given many other perks like medical aid, pension and gratuity. (True / False)

96. The main objective of sales supervisor is not to provide good working condition. (True / False)

97. Contest awards refer to cash prizes. (True / False)

98. Effective direction is done through two-way communication and co-ordination. (True / False)

99. Sound selection facilitates training and training facilities does not facilitate managerial control. (True / False)

100. Financial and non-financial incentives is necessary to accomplish best performance. (True / False)

Answers for True / False

1.	True	12.	True	23.	False	34.	True	45.	True
2.	False	13.	True	24.	True	35.	True	46.	False
3.	True	14.	True	25.	False	36.	True	47.	True
4.	True	15.	False	26.	True	37.	False	48.	True
5.	False	16.	False	27.	False	38.	False	49.	True
6.	False	17.	True	28.	False	39.	False	50.	True
7.	True	18.	False	29.	True	40.	True	51.	False
8.	True	19.	True	30.	True	41.	False	52.	False
9.	True	20.	True	31.	True	42.	False	53.	False
10.	True	21.	False	32.	True	43.	True	54.	True
11.	True	22.	True	33.	False	44.	True	55.	True

56.	False	**65.**	True	**74.**	True	**83.**	True	**92.**	True
57.	True	**66.**	True	**75.**	True	**84.**	False	**93.**	False
58.	False	**67.**	False	**76.**	True	**85.**	False	**94.**	True
59.	True	**68.**	True	**77.**	True	**86.**	True	**95.**	True
60.	False	**69.**	True	**78.**	False	**87.**	True	**96.**	False
61.	False	**70.**	True	**79.**	False	**88.**	False	**97.**	True
62.	True	**71.**	False	**80.**	True	**89.**	True	**98.**	True
63.	True	**72.**	True	**81.**	True	**90.**	True	**99.**	False
64.	False	**73.**	False	**82.**	True	**91.**	True	**100.**	True

MULTIPLE CHOICE QUESTIONS

1. Sales management is generally known as ________.

(a) Backbone of marketing
(b) Process of marketing
(c) Type of marketing
(d) process marketing

2. A sales force serves as a company's personal link to ________.

(a) Wholesaler
(b) Retailer
(c) Customers
(d) Sellers

3. Marketing stresses the importance of satisfying consumer needs and wants throug' a process of ________.

(a) Exchange
(b) Marketing
(c) Selling
(d) Buying

4. Which of the following are directly related to each other?

(a) Marketing
(b) Selling
(c) Buying
(d) Both a & b

5. The advertising and marketing magazine defines business is ________.

(a) Marketing
(b) Selling
(c) Distribution
(d) None of the above

6. Which of the following is the primary sales tool of sales people?

(a) Computer
(b) e-banking
(c) Tele-marketing
(d) e-commerce

7. Which of the following is the most frequently used promotional technique in business markets?

(a) Personal selling
(b) Salesmanship
(c) Advertising
(d) Publicity

8. Management of the sales force is an important quality component of any ________.

(a) Buying effort
(b) Selling effort
(c) Manufacturing effort
(d) Advertising effort

9. Which of the following has separated sales forces for its audio and colour television business?

(a) Philips
(b) BPL
(c) Aiwa
(d) Whirlpool

10. Which of the following sold its consumer electronics and refrigerator lines through the same sales force?

(a) BPL
(b) Onida
(c) Philips
(d) USHA

11. Sales force strength and qualification affect both the ability to provide competitive service level and ________.

(a) Economics of the profit force
(b) Economics of the sales force
(c) Economics of marketing force
(d) Economics of advertising force

12. Which of the following has an impact on the morale of the sales force and help in retaining salespeople?

(a) Compensation
(b) Incentives
(c) Both a & b
(d) Sales force

13. Which of the following allows above-average compensation for the most successful salespeople?

(a) Incentives
(b) Allowances
(c) Bonus
(d) Increment

14. These both are intricately linked, particularly in India's highly volatile market ________.

(a) Budget plans and incentive system
(b) Working and incentive system
(c) Manufacturing and selling system
(d) Marketing and distribution system

15. Demand for medium and heavy commercial vehicles grew by over 100% between ________.

(a) 1993 and 1996
(b) 1992 and 1994
(c) 1991 and 1991
(d) 1996 and 1999

16. These are the training provided by sales force ________.

(a) In-house training
(b) On-the-Job training
(c) Off-the-Job training
(d) Both a & b

17. The duty of marketing manager includes ________.

(a) Sales research
(b) Product research
(c) Marketing research
(d) Both a and b

18. There must be control over the various activities of the sales force by the ______.

(a) Sales manager's
(b) Supervisor's
(c) Top level management
(d) None of the above

19. Beyond control, sometimes it leads to intractable problem in a ________.

(a) Sales proceeds
(b) Sales organization
(c) Sales marketing
(d) Sales force

20. Sales force requires delegation of authority in ________.

(a) Preparing tour programme
(b) Fixing policies
(c) Fixing strategies
(d) Fixing claims

21. Sales force provides assurance regarding ________.

(a) Quality
(b) Quantity
(c) Both a & b
(d) None of the above

22. Target-setting is necessary for achieving ________.

(a) Organizational goals
(b) Organizational strategies
(c) Organizational objectives
(d) Organizational policies

23. Sales targets are fixed on the basis of ________.

(a) Past experience
(b) Time period
(c) Brand positioning in market
(d) All the above

24. It depends on meticulous planning and dynamic strategies ________.

(a) Accuracy
(b) Period
(c) Demand
(d) Product

25. Sales management is a vital sub-system of ________.

(a) Marketing management
(b) Marketing strategy
(c) Marketing process
(d) Marketing policy

26. Marketing plans, strategies and policies are implemented through ________.

(a) Sales marketing
(b) Sales management
(c) Sales proceeds
(d) None of the above

27. Sales management acts behind the marketing management as ________.

(a) Sales force
(b) Dynamic force
(c) Both a & b
(d) None of the above

28. Modern sales manager is not only profit oriented but also ________.

(a) Wealth-oriented
(b) Quality-oriented
(c) Customer-oriented
(d) Sales-oriented

29. Sales management is a ________.

(a) Challenging profession
(b) Education profession
(c) Marketing profession
(d) Profiting profession

30. Sales management is responsible for ________.

(a) Sales volume
(b) Handling sales operations
(c) Contribution to profit
(d) All the above

31. Sales executives must assure the delivery of product with ________.

(a) High sales
(b) Satisfying experiences
(c) Increasing profit
(d) Large market

32. Modern sales manager is a marketing executive and not merely a sales executive for ________.

(a) Maximum sales volume
(b) Maximum profit volume
(c) Minimum sales volume
(d) Minimum profit volume

33. Planning refers to choosing from the ________.

(a) Alternative courses of action
(b) Past experience
(c) Future estimation process
(d) All the above

34. Sales planning is a part of ________.

(a) Marketing strategy
(b) marketing planning
(c) marketing
(d) All the above

35. Sales planning includes ________.

(a) Sales forecasting
(b) Sales programmes
(c) Sales goals and budget
(d) All the above

36. Which of the following refers to deciding in advance a future course of action regarding the marketing or selling of product?

(a) Sales goals
(b) Sales planning
(c) Sales programme
(d) None of the above

37. Which of the following is the primary managerial function and it precedes all other managerial functions?

(a) Planning
(b) Organizing
(c) Controlling
(d) Coordinating

38. Sales programmes is based on ________.

(a) Objectives
(b) Policies
(c) Procedures
(d) All of the above

39. Sales controls assure realization of ________.

(a) Profit
(b) Sales target
(c) Sales marketing
(d) None of the above

40. Which of the following are the guiding principles set by the company to govern actions?

(a) Strategies
(b) Policies
(c) Procedures
(d) Both a & b

41. The backbone of successful sales policies is ________.

(a) Consumer satisfaction
(b) Consumer goodwill
(c) Both a & b
(d) Consumer budget

42. High reputation takes place through ________.

(a) Fair trading
(b) Foreign trading
(c) Maximum trading
(d) Quality trading

43. The pillars of firm's credibility and goodwill are ________.

(a) Sound sales policies
(b) Reliable quality of goods
(c) Fair trade practices
(d) All the above

44. The p's of marketing mix are ________.

(a) product
(b) price
(c) place
(d) All the above

45. Which of the following is a foundation for effective execution of sales policy and sales programme?

(a) Sales organization
(b) Sales policies
(c) Sales strategy
(d) Sales marketing

46. The duty of sales manager is to recognizes ________.

(a) Human values
(b) Human relations
(c) Both a and b
(d) None of the above

47. Sales organization is the medium to execute ________.

(a) Sales press
(b) Sales plan
(c) Marketing plan
(d) Marketing

48. Sales organization is the counter part of ________.

(a) Factory
(b) Industry
(c) Business
(d) Organization

49. Sales department produces mass market with the help of ________.

(a) Salesmanship
(b) Advertising
(c) Sales promotion
(d) All the above

50. It is necessary among all the departments to achieve target ________.

(a) Organizing
(b) Coordination
(c) Planning
(d) implementing

51. Which of the following helps to create a sound sales organization?

(a) Division of labour
(b) Proper delegation of authority
(c) Both a & b
(d) None of the above

52. They are of the sales organization in charge of planning, organizing, directing and controlling all the activities relating to selling function ________.

(a) General sales manager
(b) Chief executive
(c) Manager
(d) both a & b

53. Who is responsible for coordinating and controlling all the activities of the department?

(a) Sales person
(b) Sales coordination
(c) Sales manager
(d) Sales executive

54. A sales organization is like a power station sending out energy which is devoted to the ________.

(a) Advertising
(b) Selling
(c) Both a & b
(d) Marketing

55. Sales efforts are necessary through which sound sales organization can prevent ________.

(a) Wastage in sales
(b) Wastage in distribution
(c) Wastage in production
(d) Wastage in marketing

56. Sales manager must assure the optimum contribution of personal selling efforts to the overall ________.

(a) Marketing objectives of company
(b) Planning
(c) Controlling all sales efforts
(d) Coordination of employees

57. Who is responsible for management and development of sales personnel?

(a) Administrative sales personnel.
(b) Operating of field sales manager
(c) Sales manager
(d) Personnel manager

58. The duty of the sales-man is recruitment, selection, training, supervision, evaluation and ________.

(a) Control of sales force
(b) Control of raw material
(c) Control over employees
(d) Control over organisation

59. The sales manager should look after both administrative and operating duties and responsibilities in a ________.

(a) Small firm
(b) Large firm
(c) Medium firm
(d) Organization

60. Administrative sales manager's of a sales organization are suitable for ________.

(a) Smaller company
(b) Larger company
(c) Charitable trust
(d) Public company

61. Administrative work is done by ________.

(a) Top management
(b) Middle management
(c) Low-level management
(d) All the above

62. Administrative work refers to ________.

(a) Planning
(b) Organizing
(c) Coordinating and controlling
(d) All the above

63. Operating work is he work involved in ________.

(a) Operating and executing plans
(b) Operating the machine
(c) Controlling the work of an employee
(d) Converting input into output

64. The part played by a modern sales manager is similar to that of a ________.

(a) Marketing manager
(b) Supervisor
(c) General Supervisor
(d) Chief executive

65. Sales manager is responsible for all activities relating to ________.

(a) Product development or merchandising
(b) Increase sales
(c) Increase profit at low cost
(d) Marketing

66. Sales manager has to formulate ________.

(a) Sales plans and budgets
(b) Sales policies
(c) Sales programmes
(d) All the above

67. The sales manager is also called upon for ensuring ________.

(a) Growth
(b) Managing change
(c) Both a & b
(d) None of the above

68. The sales manager has to execute the ________.

(a) Plans and programmes
(b) Pricing policies
(c) Marketing strategies
(d) Customer

69. Which of the following helps to take decision at the right time?

(a) Marketing research
(b) Research and Development
(c) Questionnaire
(d) Survey

70. Sales cost analysis can help sales manager to ________.

(a) Control selling costs
(b) Control selling expenses
(c) Both a & b
(d) Fix price for the product

71. Without sales budget and sales cost analysis sales manager cannot have ____.

(a) Profit planning
(b) Sales control
(c) Production budget
(d) Fixation of price

72. Which of the following is the primary responsibility of the sales managers?

(a) Administration of sales department
(b) Marketing the goods
(c) Good transportation
(d) Earn profit

73. The sales manager is responsible for providing and managing ________.

(a) Funds of marketing
(b) Funds of Advertising
(c) Both a & b
(d) None of the above

74. Which of the following must be financed in anticipation of seasonal demand?

(a) Funds
(b) Raw materials
(c) Inventories
(d) Good will

75. They are essential in selling and distribution of goods ________.

(a) Cash
(b) Credit
(c) Discount
(d) Both a & b

76. Sales manager is in charge of management of sales to assume ________.

(a) Market share and profit
(b) Shares and debentures
(c) Promissory
(d) Exchange of currencies

77. Long-term success of a firm depends on ________.

(a) Sales volume
(b) Sales manpower
(c) Both a & b
(d) Profit margin

78. They are the invaluable resources of the firm ________.

(a) Sales manager
(b) Sales people
(c) Assets
(d) None of the above

79. Which of the following provides a sound foundation for a good vibrant sales organization and sales management?

(a) Recruitment and selection
(b) Planning
(c) Coordination
(d) Controlling

80. Which of the following can provide job specification of the required sales positions?

(a) Recruitment
(b) Job analysis
(c) Job rotation
(d) None of the above

81. Which of the following deals with securing as many qualified people to fill the vacancies?

(a) Selection
(b) Recruitment
(c) Interview
(d) None of the above

82. Which of the following is the information gathering evaluation and decision making required to screen and choose applicants?

(a) Decision making process
(b) Selection process
(c) Recruitment
(d) All the above

83. Which of the following is an indispensable device in selecting sales people?

(a) Personal interview
(b) Group discussion
(c) Voice test
(d) Performance test

84. Which of the following is the heart of the selection technique?

(a) Interview
(b) Written test
(c) Physical test
(d) IQ-test

85. Which of the following is a type of psychological test?

(a) Intelligence tests
(b) Aptitude tests
(c) Interest and personality test
(d) All the above

86. They are able to secure sales orders more quickly, sell and manage ________.

(a) Skilled salesman
(b) Unskilled salesman
(c) Ordinary salesman
(d) Trained salesman

87. Salespeople must have these qualities to be effective in their selling field ________.

(a) Knowledge
(b) Skill
(c) Attitude training
(d) All the above

88. Sales skill training is given on the job by a ________.

(a) Manager
(b) Supervisor
(c) Skilled trainer
(d) None of the above

89. Sales attitudes training try to strengthen salesman's ________.

(a) Positive attitudes
(b) Working ability
(c) IQ power
(d) Hidden skills

90. Which of the following is essential on the job training?

(a) Field training
(b) Mechanical training
(c) Both a and b
(d) None of the above

91. Ready-made programmed instructional courses can be prepared by ________.

(a) Skilled and expert trainers
(b) Top-level management
(c) Middle-level management
(d) Supervisors

92. At present these broadcasts are used for training salesman ________.

(a) Videotape
(b) Close-circuit TV
(c) Both a and b
(d) None of the above

93. Most sales people earning ________.

(a) Salary
(b) Incentives
(c) Both a and b
(d) Promotion

94. A good salesperson can earn incentives ________.

(a) 10 % of salary
(b) 15 % of salary
(c) 20 % of salary
(d) 30 % of salary

95. All sales persons are given many other perks like ________.

(a) Medical aid
(b) Pension
(c) Gratuity
(d) All the above

96. The main objective of sales supervision is to ________.

(a) Motivate salesman
(b) Good conditions of work
(c) Strict training
(d) Both a and b

97. Contest awards refers to ________.

(a) Cash prizes or merchandise prizes
(b) Their combinations

(c) Both a and b
(d) Awards

98. Effective direction is done through ______.

(a) Two-way communication
(b) Co-ordination
(c) Recruiting
(d) Both a and b

99. Sound selection facilitates training and training facilitates ________.

(a) Employees control
(b) Managerial control
(c) Increase in profit
(d) None of the above

100. Which of the following is necessary to accomplish best performance?

(a) Financial incentives
(b) Non-financial incentive
(c) Both a & b
(d) None of the above

Answers for MCQ

1.	(a)	18.	(a)	35.	(d)	52.	(d)	69.	(a)	86.	(d)
2.	(c)	19.	(b)	36.	(b)	53.	(c)	70.	(c)	87.	(d)
3.	(a)	20.	(a)	37.	(a)	54.	(b)	71.	(a)	88.	(c)
4.	(d)	21.	(a)	38.	(d)	55.	(b)	72.	(a)	89.	(a)
5.	(a)	22.	(a)	39.	(b)	56.	(a)	73.	(a)	90.	(a)
6.	(a)	23.	(d)	40.	(b)	57.	(b)	74.	(c)	91.	(a)
7.	(a)	24.	(a)	41.	(c)	58.	(a)	75.	(d)	92.	(c)
8.	(b)	25.	(a)	42.	(a)	59.	(a)	76.	(a)	93.	(a)
9.	(a)	26.	(b)	43.	(a)	60.	(b)	77.	(c)	94.	(c)
10.	(a)	27.	(b)	44.	(d)	61.	(a)	78.	(b)	95.	(d)
11.	(b)	28.	(c)	45.	(a)	62.	(d)	79.	(a)	96.	(d)
12.	(c)	29.	(a)	46.	(c)	63.	(a)	80.	(b)	97.	(a)
13.	(a)	30.	(d)	47.	(b)	64.	(a)	81.	(b)	98.	(d)
14.	(a)	31.	(b)	48.	(a)	65.	(a)	82.	(b)	99.	(b)
15.	(a)	32.	(a)	49.	(d)	66.	(d)	83.	(a)	100.	(c)
16.	(d)	33.	(a)	50.	(b)	67.	(c)	84.	(a)		
17.	(d)	34.	(b)	51.	(c)	68.	(a)	85.	(d)		

MATCH THE FOLLOWING

1.	Sales management	(a)	Organizational goal
2.	Target setting	(b)	Primary sales tool
3.	Computer	(c)	Heart of selection technique
4.	Interview	(d)	Backbone of marketing
5.	Sales manager	(e)	Knowledge and skills
6.	Sales training	(f)	Motivation of salesman

Answers for Match the Following

1.	(d)	2.	(a)	3.	(b)	4.	(c)	5.	(f)	6.	(e)

Chapter 18

Advertising

SUMMARY

Advertising is a form of communication used to persuade an audience like viewers, readers or listeners to take some action with respect to products, ideas, or services. Most commonly, the desired result is to drive consumer behavior with respect to a commercial offering, although political and ideological advertising is also common. Advertising messages are usually paid for by sponsors and viewed via various traditional media; including mass media such as newspaper, magazines, television commercial, radio advertisement, outdoor advertising or direct mail; or new media such as websites and text messages.

Advertising is a type of commercial communication. It is for giving information to consumers. It aims at encouraging consumers to purchase a specific product. It is used as a sales promotion technique by manufacturers and traders. Advertising is for giving information about products in an attractive manner. It facilitates sales promotion.

Advertising plays a significant role in awareness creation and attitude formation. It can even generate a trial and purchase as long as all other elements of the marketing mix play a contributory role. Thus, it has to be appreciated that advertising has a limited role in marketing strategy. A marketing plan and strategy takes into account several marketing tools to achieve marketing objectives. These are product, packaging, customer service, pricing, sales promotion and channel relationships.

Although advertising is a potent instrument of communication that serves the dual purpose of making product awareness and an increased profit margin yet it suffers for a number of limitations as well. Advertising is a deferred revenue expenditure, the result of which we can't get immediately rather after a considerable period of time. And, after all advertising occupies a substantial portion of the total budget of the organization. So, investing a large sum in it does not necessary yield immediate results thus limiting its utility. So, advertising is economically beneficial but not socially justifiable.

History of Advertising

Egyptians used papyrus to make sales messages and wall posters. Commercial messages and political campaign displays have been found in the ruins of Pompeii and ancient Arabia. Lost and found advertising on papyrus was common in Ancient Greece and Ancient Rome. Wall or rock painting for commercial advertising is another manifestation of an ancient advertising form, which is present to this day in many parts of Asia, Africa, and South America. The tradition of wall painting can be traced back to Indian rock art paintings that date back to 4000 BC. History tells us that out-of-home advertising and billboards are the oldest forms of advertising.

As the towns and cities of the Middle Ages began to grow, and the general populace was unable to read, signs that today would say cobbler, miller, tailor or blacksmith would use an image associated with their trade such as a boot, a suit, a hat, a clock, a diamond, a horse shoe, a candle or even a bag of flour. Fruits and vegetables were sold in the city square from the backs of carts and wagons and their proprietors used street callers to announce their whereabouts for the convenience of the customers.

There has been a long tradition of advertising in India, since the first newspapers published in India in the 19th century carried advertising. The first advertising agency was established in 1905, B. Datram and Company, followed by The India-Advertising Company in 1907, the Calcutta Advertising Agency in 1909, S.H. Bensen in 1928, J. Walter Thompson Associates through its Indian associate, Hindustan Thompson Associates in 1929, Lintas (Lever International Advertising Services) in 1939 and McCann Erikson in 1956. Advertising expenditure in the 1950s was estimated at $US 300,000. Under the more socialist political environment of the 1960s and 1970s there was little incentive for companies to advertise because advertising was not tax deductible. In the 1970s there was a 58% growth in the number of registered agencies from 106 in 1969 to 168 in 1979, and this included a growth in Indian agencies. The first advertising appeared on state television in 1976.

Essentials for Good Advertising

1. **Use a Dominant Element:** Use a large picture or headline to insure quick visibility. Photographs and realistic drawings have about equal attention-getting value, but photographs of real people win more readership. So do action pictures. Photographs of local people or places also have high value. Use good art work. It will pay-off in extra readership.
2. **Make the Ad Copy Complete:** Sizes and colors available are important, pertinent information. The copy should be enthusiastic, sincere. A block of copy written in complete sentences is easier to read than one composed of phrases and random words. In designing the layout of a copy block, use a boldface lead-in. Small pictures in sequence will often help readership. Don't be too clever, or use unusual or difficult words.
3. **Make your Ads Easily Recognizable:** Advertisements which are distinctive in their use of art, layout techniques and typefaces usually enjoy higher readership than run-of-the-mill advertising. Make your account's ads distinctively different in appearance from the advertising of competitors. Then keep the ad's appearance consistent. This way, readers will recognize your account's ads even before they read them
4. **Use a Prominent Benefit Headline:** The first question a reader asks of an ad is: "What's in it for me?" Select the main benefit which the merchandise offers and feature it in a compelling headline. "How to" headlines encourage full copy readership, as do headlines which include specific information or helpful suggestions. The headline will be easier to read if it is black-on-white and not printed over part of an illustration.
5. **Specify Branded Merchandise:** If the item is a known brand, say so in the ad. Manufacturers spend large sums to sell their goods, and the retailer can capitalize on their advertising while enhancing the reputation of the retailer's store by featuring branded items.
6. **Use a Simple Layout:** The layout should catch the reader's eye through the message easily and in proper sequence: from headline to illustration to explanatory copy to the store's name. Avoid the use of too many different type faces, overly decorative borders and reverses. These devices are distracting and reduce the number of readers who receive the entire message.
7. **Let White Space Work for You:** Don't overcrowd the ad, White space is an important layout element in newspaper advertising. White space focuses the reader's attention on the ad and will make the headline and

illustration stand out. When a "crowded" ad is necessary such as for a sale, departmentalize the items so that the reader can find his way through them easily.

8. **Urge your Readers to Buy now:** The ad should ask for the sale. Prompt action can be stimulated by using such phrases as "limited supply" or "this week only". If mail-order coupons are included in ads, provide spaces large enough for customers to fill them in easily. Don't generalize; be specific at all times.

Features of Advertising

Advertising as any paid form of non-personal presentation and promotion of ideas, goods or services by an identified sponsor. The main features of Advertising are as follows:

(i) It is a paid communication where paid is made by the advertiser to the media owner.

(ii) It is non-personal salesmanship performing similar functions like personal salesmanship.

(iii) It has the ability to expose large groups of prospects at a low cost per prospect.

(iv) It can help to introduce a new product quickly.

Importance of Advertising

(i) It increases sales volume by creating attraction towards the products and also the profits of the concern.

(ii) It helps easy introduction of new products into the markets by the same manufacturer.

(iii) It increases the rate of return over the stock because demand is already created by advertisement.

(iv) It ensures more economical selling because selling overheads are reduced.

(v) It helps in eliminating the middlemen by establishing direct contracts between producers and consumers. It results in cheaper goods.

(vi) It helps them to know where and when the products are available. This reduces their shopping time.

Media of Advertising

(i) **Mural Advertising:** Mural advertising which has a general and wide appeal. It can attract attention of numerous people. It is good to remind prospects. An advertiser has simple scope to use his skill and art in advertising. However, mural advertising has certain limitations. It cannot have a long message. It is not useful in selective advertising or for specialized products. It has a low retention value. Its effectiveness cannot be accurately measured and it may lead to considerable wastage also.

(ii) **Radio Advertisement:** Radio uses only an audio signal. The copy can be submitted up to air time. It has a very wide appeal. Spoken word has greater impact than written word. However, radio cannot permit selective advertising. It cannot give detailed information. People remember for more of what they see than of what they hear. Its cost is high.

(iii) **Television Advertisement:** Television can appeal through ear as well as eye. Product can be demonstrated with explanation. Television reaches the audiences almost like personal face-to-face contact. To that extent it is just like personal salesmanship. Full opportunity exists for product demonstration and the amplification of selling points with audio presentation; it is really a wonder full means of mass communication for creating market.

(iv) **Transit Advertising:** It refers to the car-card advertising, which is located within buses, subways, railways and outside displays, which appear on the front and backs sides of buses or other public transport and at transportation terminals. Transit advertising is the lowest-cost media. It gives geographic selectivity and seasonal selectivity. However, non-riders are now exposed to car-cards located inside the vehicle.

(v) Direct Mail: Direct mail is the most personal and selective media. It reaches only the desired prospects. It has minimum waste in circulation. The advertising copy can be very flexible. It has maximum possible personal features even without personal contact. Its effectiveness is measurable. It can be timed as per advertiser's will. It has maximum personal appeal. It is not in direct competition with the rivals matter. The results of direct mail advertising can be checked by means of an offer incorporated in the mailing. However, direct mail is costly.

Advertising Layout

Advertising layout deals with proper and attractive physical arrangement for the best presentation of the message or sales communication.

Advertising Budget

Advertisement budget refers to the financial plan of the expected expenditure on the advertising activities of a firm. It includes budgeting for media costs, advertising expenses, development costs etc.

Advertising Theme

Advertising theme is the central idea around which the advertisement is created. It is called the unique sales proposition. It represents a specific point of view or idea to be stressed in the advertisement. It is the heart and soul of advertising copy or message.

Scientific Advertisement

Scientific advertising refers to the planned advertising based upon a serious deliberation of all factors that have a bearing upon its success. It involves the use of the logical method or reasoning method. Scientific advertising implies the development and use of fact-finding approach to the formulation.

Advertising Copy

Advertising copy is the written or spoken part of the advertisement; it consists of headlines, sub heads, and the text which carries the theme of the message.

The importance of a good advertisement copy can hardly be overemphasized. All the planning, research and expense would go waste if proper care is not taken in drafting an advertisement copy that will achieve the purpose of advertising.

FILL IN THE BLANKS

1. Promotion means communicating about the company's offering with the present and potential ________ and ________.
2. ________ is a branch of marketing management.
3. The short-term objective of advertising is ________.
4. The long-term objective of advertising is to bring behavioural changes in ________.
5. Promotion mix consists of ______, ______, ________, ________ and ________.
6. Advertising management is mainly focused on ________, ________ and ______.
7. ________ is also called as mass means of communication.
8. Advertising offers wide choice of channels for transmission of messages such as ________, ________ and ________.
9. Mission, Money, Message, Media and Measurement are 5Ms of________.
10. Advertising media's are ______, ______ and ________.

11. Advertising lacks in ______ and ______.
12. Advertising is necessary for sale of goods on services by unique means of ______.
13. Advertising is very helpful for quickly introducing a ______.
14. Advertising helps to identify the product's ______.
15. Advertising message can be addressed to numerous persons at a time collectively called ______.
16. Advertising is a ______ and ______ of communication.
17. Advertising takes place through various ______.
18. Salesmanship is individual communication through personal interview between ______ and ______.
19. Mass production and mass distribution totally depends on all form of ______ and ______.
20. Advertising by facilitating mass production and mass distribution has provided immence ______.
21. Advertising is responsible for creating and rising the ______.
22. Advertising must be carried on by a ______.
23. Advertising is a paid form of ______.
24. In a sense, paid publicity is ______.
25. ______ can make money without advertising.
26. Mass production and mass distribution totally depends on all forms of ______ and ______.
27. Advertising has made ______ in many country.
28. Refrigerators, cameras, transistors are ______.
29. Advertising is an indispensable tool supplemented by ______ and ______.
30. The wheels of industry of commerce cannot move without power of ______.
31. The real purpose of advertising is to ______.
32. Advertising helps in promotion of ______.
33. Advertising helps for actual closing is ______.
34. Advertising reduces ______.
35. Advertising create and retain a brand ______ and ______.
36. We can have advertising relevant to each stage in the ______.
37. Advertising creates immediate ______.
38. Advertising is the usual medium for ______ and ______.
39. Well advertised brands are ______.
40. Advertising assures accelerating ______.
41. The transmitted idea is the ______.
42. Channels are the advertising media to transmit the messages such as ______, ______ and ______.
43. ______ are the target market for advertising.
44. Advertising objectives in terms of communication may be to secure higher ______ and ______.
45. The ultimate result will naturally be increase in the number of buyers and ______.
46. Present predispositions and habits change ______.
47. The total objective of marketing programme is increasing ______.
48. The main objective of advertising is to ______.
49. Advertising is an element of marketing mix and ______.
50. Russell Colley in 1961 pioneered ______.
51. The ultimate purpose of most advertising is to help the profitability of ______.

52. The base minimum goal of advertising is ________.

53. ________ Shows brand preference intention to buy the product in near future.

54. ________ moves a prospect through the entire cycle of communication spectrum.

55. In industrial goods ________ is a complementary force of communication.

56. In industrial goods ________ is the dominating force of communication.

57. The advertising has no role of promotion in ________.

58. Personal selling can sell the products to consumers in a few minutes of ________.

59. Advertising is used to develop ________.

60. An advertising campaign is a series to ________.

61. All promotional efforts are directed towards ________.

62. Planning and execution of our advertising and sales promotion campaign can be entrusted to ________.

63. ________ has a general and wide appeal.

64. ________ has long life.

65. ________ and ________ are not welcome today on the highways due to adverse public opinion.

66. ________ is the advertising suitable for only literate people.

67. The expiry of Newspapers are ________.

68. Mural advertising is also known as ________.

69. Professional advertising is undertaken by ________ and ________.

70. ________ is the most expensive medium of advertising.

Answers for Fill in the Blanks

1.	Stakeholders; general public	20.	Employment opportunity
2.	Advertising management	21.	Standard of living
3.	Increasing sales of product	22.	Identified sponsor
4.	Attitude of customers	23.	Communication
5.	Personal selling; sales promotion; advertising; publicity; public relations	24.	Advertising
		25.	Mint
6.	Analysis; planning; controlling	26.	Advertising; publicity
7.	Advertising	27.	Economic development
8.	Visual; auditory; actual	28.	Consumer durables
9.	Advertising	29.	Salesmanship; sales promotion
10.	Newspaper; Radio; television	30.	Promotion mix
11.	Credibility; trustworthiness	31.	Sell something
12.	Mass customers	32.	New product
13.	New product	33.	Sales
14.	Sponsor	34.	Selling cost
15.	Audience of advertisement	35.	Loyalty, preference
16.	Non-personal; Indirect means	36.	Buying process
17.	Media of advertisement	37.	Buying action
18.	Salesperson; prospect	38.	Coupons; samples
19.	Advertising; publicity	39.	Pre-sold goods

40.	Distribution	56.	Personal selling
41.	Advertising message	57.	Door-to-door selling
42.	Radio; television; press	58.	Persuasive selling
43.	Audience	59.	Corporate goals
44.	Higher brand preference	60.	Achieve goals
45.	Higher market share	61.	Maximum sales and service
46.	Very slowly	62.	Advertising agency
47.	Sales of market share	63.	Newspaper
48.	Produce sales	64.	Outdoor advertising
49.	Communication tool	65.	Bill boards; hoardings
50.	Dagmar	66.	Newspaper
51.	Sales of a product or service	67.	24 hours
52.	Awareness	68.	Outdoor advertising
53.	Conviction level	69.	Lawyers; accountants
54.	Mail order advertising	70.	TV
55.	Advertising		

TRUE / FALSE

1. Promotion means communicating about the company's offering with the present and potential stockholders and general public. (True / False)
2. Advertising management is a branch of marketing management. (True / False)
3. The short-term objective of advertising is to increase profit. (True / False)
4. The long-term advertising is to bring behavioural changes in attitude of manufacturers. (True / False)
5. Promotion mix is of 6 types. (True / False)
6. Advertising management is mainly focused on estimation of cost. (True / False)
7. Advertising is also called as mass means of communication. (True / False)
8. Advertising offers wide choice of channels for transmission of messages such as visual, aural and aural and visual. (True / False)
9. Mission, money, message, media and measurement are 5Ms of marketing mix. (True / False)
10. Advertising media's are newspaper, Radio and Television. (True / False)
11. Advertising lacks in credibility and trustworthiness. (True / False)
12. Advertising is necessary for sale of goods or services by unique means of mass customers. (True / False)
13. Advertising is very helpful for quickly introducing an already exciting product. (True / False)
14. Advertising helps to identify the product's seller. (True / False)
15. Advertising message can be addressed to numerous persons at a time collectively called audience of advertisement. (True / False)
16. Advertising is a non-personal and indirect means of communication. (True / False)

17. Advertising takes place through personal selling only. (True / False)
18. Salesmanship is individual communication through personal interview between manufacturer and wholesaler. (True / False)
19. Mass production and mass distribution totally depends on all form of advertising and publicity. (True / False)
20. Advertising by facilitating mass production and mass distribution has provided immense profit opportunity. (True / False)
21. Advertising is responsible for creating and rising the standard of living. (True / False)
22. Advertising can be carried on by any sponsor. (True / False)
23. In a sense, paid publicity is promotion. (True / False)
24. Advertising is a paid form of communication. (True / False)
25. Mint can make money without advertising. (True / False)
26. Mass production and mass distribution does not depend on publicity. (True / False)
27. Advertising has made economic development in many countries. (True / False)
28. Refrigerators, motor cars, cameras, radio are some of modern amenities. (True / False)
29. Advertising is an indispensable tool supplemented by salesmanship and sales promotion. (True / False)
30. The wheels of industry and commerce cannot move without power of advertising mix. (True / False)
31. The real purpose of advertising is to buy something. (True / False)
32. Advertising helps in promotion of old product. (True / False)
33. Advertising helps for actual closing of production. (True / False)
34. Advertising reduces profit. (True / False)
35. Advertising creates and retains a brand loyalty and preference. (True / False)
36. We can have advertising relevant to each stage in the buying process. (True / False)
37. Advertising creates immediate buying action. (True / False)
38. Advertising is the usual medium for coupons and samples. (True / False)
39. Well advertised brands are pre-sold goods. (True / False)
40. Advertising does not accelerate distribution. (True / False)
41. The transmitted idea is the promotion message. (True / False)
42. Channels are the advertising media to transmit the message such as radio, television and press. (True / False)
43. Manufacturers are the target market for advertising. (True / False)
44. Advertising objectives in terms of communication may be to secure higher and higher brand preference. (True / False)
45. The ultimate result will naturally be increase in the member of buyers and higher market share. (True / False)
46. Present predispositions and habits change very quickly. (True / False)
47. The total objective of marketing programme is increasing sales of market segment. (True / False)
48. The main objective of advertising is to increase goodwill of the organization. (True / False)
49. Advertising is an element of marketing mix and communication tool. (True / False)
50. Russell colley in 1930 pioneered DAG. (True / False)

51. The ultimate purpose of most advertising is to help the profitability of sales of a product or service. (True / False)

52. The bare minimum good of advertising is awareness. (True / False)

53. Conviction level shows brand preference and intention to buy the product in near future. (True / False)

54. Main order advertising moves a prospect through the entire cycle of communication spectrum. (True / False)

55. In industrial goods advertising is not a complimentary force of communication. (True / False)

56. In industrial goods personal selling is the dominating force of communication. (True / False)

57. The advertising has a role of promotion in door-to-door selling. (True / False)

58. Personal selling can sell the products to consumers in a few minutes of persuasive selling. (True / False)

59. Advertising is used to develop corporate goals. (True / False)

60. An advertising campaign is a series to achieve profit. (True / False)

61. All promotional efforts are directed towards maximum sales and service. (True / False)

62. Planning and execution of our advertising and sales promotion campaign can be entrusted to advertising agency. (True / False)

63. Newspaper has a general and wide appeal. (True / False)

64. Outdoor advertising does not have long life. (True / False)

65. Bill boards and hoardings are not welcome today on the highways due to adverse public opinion. (True / False)

66. Newspaper is the advertising suitable for only illiterate people. (True / False)

67. The expiry of newspapers are 24 hours. (True / False)

68. Mural advertising is also known as transit advertising. (True / False)

69. Commercial advertising includes industrial advertising. (True / False)

70. TV is the most expensive medium advertising. (True / False)

Answers for True / False

1.	True	15.	True	29.	True	43.	False	57.	False
2.	True	16.	True	30.	False	44.	True	58.	True
3.	False	17.	False	31.	False	45.	True	59.	True
4.	False	18.	False	32.	False	46.	False	60.	False
5.	False	19.	True	33.	False	47.	False	61.	True
6.	False	20.	False	34.	False	48.	False	62.	True
7.	True	21.	True	35.	True	49.	True	63.	True
8.	True	22.	False	36.	True	50.	False	64.	False
9.	False	23.	False	37.	True	51.	True	65.	True
10.	True	24.	True	38.	True	52.	True	66.	False
11.	True	25.	True	39.	True	53.	True	67.	True
12.	True	26.	False	40.	False	54.	True	68.	False
13.	False	27.	True	41.	False	55.	False	69.	True
14.	False	28.	True	42.	True	56.	True	70.	True

MULTIPLE CHOICE QUESTIONS

1. Promotion means communicating about the company's offering with the present and potential ________.

(a) Stakeholders
(b) General public
(c) Creditors
(d) Both a & b

2. Which of the following is a branch of marketing management?

(a) Advertising management
(b) Sales promotion
(c) Direct marketing
(d) Marketing mix

3. The Short-term objective of advertising is ________.

(a) Increasing sales of product
(b) Increasing profit on sales
(c) Decrease of cost
(d) Increasing wealth

4. The long-term objectives of advertising is to bring behavioural changes in ________.

(a) Attitude of customers
(b) Attitude of creditors
(c) Attitude investors
(d) Attitude of marketer

5. Promotion mix is of ________..

(a) 2 types
(b) 3 types
(c) 5 types
(d) 8 types

6. Advertising management is mainly focused on ________.

(a) Analysis
(b) Planning
(c) Control and decision making activities
(d) All the above

7. Which of the following is also called as mass mean of communication?

(a) Marketing
(b) Selling
(c) Advertising
(d) Promotion

8. Advertising offers wide choice of channels for transmission of messages such as ________.

(a) Visual
(b) Aural
(c) Aural and visual
(d) All the above

9. Mission, Money, Message, Media and Measurement are 5Ms of ________.

(a) Marketing mix
(b) Marketing
(c) Advertising
(d) Channels of distribution

10. Advertising Medias ________.

(a) Newspapers and magazines
(b) Radio
(c) Television
(d) All the above

11. Advertising lacks in ________.

(a) Credibility
(b) Trustworthiness
(c) Creditworthiness
(d) Both (a) and (b)

12. Advertising is necessary for sale of goods or services by unique means of ________.

(a) Mass population
(b) Mass communication
(c) Mass customers
(d) Large producer

13. Advertising is very helpful for quickly introducing a ________.

(a) Pricing policy
(b) New product
(c) New brand
(d) Credibility

14. It helps to identify the product's ________.

(a) Manufacturer
(b) Sponsor
(c) Wholesaler
(d) Marketer

15. Advertising message can be addressed to numerous persons at a time collectively called ________.

(a) Audience of advertisement
(b) Listeners of advertisement
(c) Viewers of advertisement
(d) Readers of advertisement

16. Advertising is a ________.

(a) Non-personal
(b) Indirect means of communication
(c) Both a & b
(d) None of the above

17. Advertising takes place through various ________.

(a) Marketing mix
(b) Media of advertisement
(c) Promotion mix
(d) Pricing strategy

18. Salesmanship is individual communication through personal interview between the ________.

(a) Salesperson and the prospect
(b) Salesperson and wholesaler
(c) Salesperson and Marketer
(d) Salesperson and producer

19. Mass production and mass distribution totally depends on all form of ________.

(a) Advertising
(b) Publicity
(c) Both a & b
(d) All the above

20. Advertising by facilitating mass production and mass distribution has provided immense ________.

(a) Profit
(b) Sales
(c) Employment opportunity
(d) Wealth

21. Advertising responsible for creating and rising the ________.

(a) Standard of living
(b) Shares of shareholders
(c) Dividend
(d) Commission

22. Advertising must be carried on by a ________.

(a) Identified seller
(b) Identified sponsor
(c) Identified manufacturers
(d) None of the above

23. Advertising is a paid form of ________.

(a) Remuneration
(b) Communication
(c) Incentive
(d) Publicity

24. In a sense, paid publicity is ________.

(a) Marketing
(b) Administration
(c) Advertising
(d) Sponsor

25. It can make money without advertising ________.

(a) Mint
(b) mass production
(c) Selling
(d) both a and b

26. Mass production and mass distribution totally depends on all forms of ________.

(a) Marketing
(b) buying and selling
(c) Advertising and publicity
(d) wholesaler and retailer

27. Advertising has made ________.

(a) Economics
(b) Economic development in many countries
(c) Profits to buyers
(d) Wealth to shareholders

28. Refrigerators, motor cars, cameras, radio are some of ________.

(a) Modern equipments
(b) Modern amenities
(c) Modern tools
(d) Modern resources

29. Advertising is an indispensable tool supplemented by ________.

(a) Salesmanship
(b) Sales promotion
(c) Both a & b
(d) Sales strategy

30. The wheels of industry & commerce cannot move without power of ________.

(a) Advertising mix
(b) Promotion mix
(c) Marketing mix
(d) All the above

31. The real purpose of advertising is ________.

(a) To buy something
(b) To sell something
(c) To market something
(d) To produce something

32. Advertising helps in promotion of ________.

(a) Market
(b) New product
(c) Prospects
(d) Existing market

33. Advertising helps for actual closing of ________.

(a) Profit
(b) Sales
(c) Market
(d) Wealth

34. Advertising reduces ________.

(a) Selling cost
(b) Marketing cost
(c) Production cost
(d) None of the above

35. Advertising create and retain a ________.

(a) Brand loyalty
(b) Brand preference
(c) Sales
(d) Both a & b

36. We can have advertising relevant to each stage in the ________.

(a) Buying process
(b) Selling process
(c) Marketing process
(d) Advertising process

37. Advertising creates immediate ________.

(a) Buying action
(b) Selling action
(c) Invention of new product
(d) Both a & b

38. Which of the following is the usual medium?

(a) Coupons
(b) Samples
(c) Forms of direct action advertising
(d) All the above

39. Well advertised brands are ________.

(a) Casual goods
(b) Pre-sold goods
(c) Newly introduced goods
(d) None of the above

40. Advertising assures accelerating ________.

(a) Marketing
(b) Storing
(c) Distribution
(d) Selling

41. The transmitted idea is the ________.

(a) Advertising picture
(b) Advertising message
(c) Advertising message
(d) New invention

42. Channels are the advertising media to transmit the messages such as ________.

(a) Radio
(b) Television
(c) Press
(d) All the above

43. They are the target market for advertising ________.

(a) Salesmanship
(b) Advertisers
(c) Audience
(d) None of the above

44. Advertising objectives in terms of communication may be to secure higher and ________.

(a) Higher profit
(b) Higher brand preference
(c) Profit
(d) Lower wealth

45. The ultimate result will naturally be increase in the number of buyers and ________.

(a) Lower market share
(b) Higher market share
(c) High wealth
(d) Low wealth

46. Present predispositions and habits change ________.

(a) Very slowly
(b) Very quickly
(c) Normally
(d) None of the above

47. The total objective of marketing programme is increasing ________.

(a) Sales of market share
(b) Profit of market share
(c) Cost of production
(d) Both a & b

48. The main objective of advertising is to ________.

(a) Produce goods
(b) Increase market
(c) Produce sales
(d) Decrease cost

49. Advertising is an element of marketing mix and ________.

(a) Communication tool
(b) Promotional tool
(c) Processing tool
(d) Selling tool

50. Russell colley in 1961 pioneered ________.

(a) Agmar
(b) Dagmar
(c) Dagar
(d) None of the above

51. The ultimate purpose of most advertising is to help the profitability of ________.

(a) Sales of a product or service
(b) Sales of scrap
(c) Both a & b
(d) None of the above

52. The base minimum goal of advertising is ________.

(a) Comprehension
(b) Awareness
(c) Conviction
(d) Action

53. Which of the following shows brand preference and intention to buy the product in near future?

(a) Conviction level
(b) Non-conviction level
(c) Profit level
(d) Sales level

54. Which of the following moves a prospect through the entire cycle of communication spectrum?

(a) Internet advertising
(b) Telephone advertising
(c) Mail order advertising
(d) Mobile advertising

55. In industrial goods it is a complementary force of communication ________.

(a) Marketing
(b) Distribution
(c) Advertising
(d) Selling

56. In industrial goods which of the following is the dominating force of Communication?

(a) Advertising
(b) Personal selling
(c) Personal distribution
(d) None of the above

57. The advertising has no role of promotion in ________.

(a) Door- to-door selling
(b) Wholesale selling
(c) Retail selling
(d) All the above

58. Personal - selling can sell the products to consumers in a few minutes of ________.

(a) Persuasive selling
(b) Non-persuasive selling
(c) Productive selling
(d) Profitable selling

59. Advertising is used to develop ________.

(a) Objectives
(b) Corporate goals
(c) Marketing goals
(d) Marketing strategies

60. An advertising campaign is a series to ________.

(a) Achieve profit
(b) Achieve goals
(c) Introduce brand loyalty
(d) None of the above

61. All promotional efforts are directed towards ________.

(a) Maximum sales
(b) Maximum sales and service
(c) Maximum profit
(d) Maximum wealth

62. Planning and execution of our advertising and sales promotion campaign can be entrusted to ________.

(a) Organizations
(b) Firms
(c) Advertising agency
(d) Both a and b

63. Which of the following has a general and wide appeal?

(a) Magazine
(b) Banners
(c) Pamphlets
(d) Newspaper

64. Which of the following has long life?

(a) Outdoor advertising
(b) Press advertising
(c) Television advertising
(d) Personal selling

65. Which of the following are not welcome today on the highways due to adverse public opinion?

(a) Bill boards
(b) Hoardings
(c) Both a and b
(d) Banners

66. Which of the following is the advertising suitable for only literate people?

(a) Newspaper
(b) Personal selling
(c) Radio
(d) Television

67. The expiry of newspapers are ________.

(a) 12 hours
(b) 24 hours
(c) 36 hours
(d) 2 hours

68. Mural advertising ________.

(a) Transit advertising
(b) Newspaper advertising
(c) Direct mail advertising
(d) Outdoor advertising

69. Commercial advertising includes ________.

(a) Trade advertising
(b) Industrial advertising
(c) Form advertising
(d) All the above

70. Which of the following is most expensive medium of advertising?

(a) TV
(b) Radio
(c) Newspaper
(d) Magazines

Answers for MCQ

1.	(d)	13.	(b)	25.	(a)	37.	(a)	49.	(a)	61.	(b)
2.	(a)	14.	(b)	26.	(c)	38.	(d)	50.	(b)	62.	(c)
3.	(a)	15.	(a)	27.	(b)	39.	(b)	51.	(a)	63.	(d)
4.	(a)	16.	(c)	28.	(b)	40.	(c)	52.	(b)	64.	(a)
5.	(c)	17.	(b)	29.	(c)	41.	(b)	53.	(a)	65.	(b)
6.	(d)	18.	(a)	30.	(b)	42.	(d)	54.	(c)	66.	(a)
7.	(c)	19.	(c)	31.	(b)	43.	(c)	55.	(c)	67.	(b)
8.	(d)	20.	(c)	32.	(b)	44.	(b)	56.	(a)	68.	(d)
9.	(c)	21.	(a)	33.	(b)	45.	(b)	57.	(a)	69.	(d)
10.	(d)	22.	(b)	34.	(a)	46.	(a)	58.	(a)	70.	(a)
11.	(d)	23.	(b)	35.	(d)	47.	(a)	59.	(b)		
12.	(b)	24.	(c)	36.	(a)	48.	(c)	60.	(b)		

MATCH THE FOLLOWING

1.	Personal selling	(a)	Advertising within buses, railway compartments
2.	Advertising	(b)	Sales promotion
3.	Transit advertising	(c)	Commercially significant news
4.	Branch of marketing	(d)	Outdoor advertising
5.	Publicity	(e)	Non-personal communication
6.	Long life	(f)	Two-way communication

Answers for Match the Following

1.	(f)	2.	(e)	3.	(a)	4.	(b)	5.	(c)	6.	(d)

Chapter 19

Managing Distribution Channels (Part - I)

SUMMARY

Distribution decisions focus on establishing a system that, at its basic level, allows customers to gain access and purchase a marketer's product. However, marketers may find that getting to the point at which a customer can acquire a product is complicated, time consuming, and expensive. The bottom line is a marketer's distribution system must be both effective, i.e.. delivers a good or service to the right place, in the right amount, in the right condition and efficient, i.e., delivers at the right time and for the right cost.

Distribution decisions are relevant for nearly all types of products. While it is easy to see how distribution decisions impact physical goods, such as laundry detergent or truck parts, distribution is equally important for digital goods, e.g., television programming, downloadable music and services, e.g., income tax services. In fact, while the Internet is playing a major role in changing product distribution and is perceived to offer more opportunities for reaching customers, online marketers still face the same distribution issues and obstacles as those faced by offline marketers.

Physical distribution is the set of activities concerned with efficient movement of finished goods from the end of the production unit to the consumer. The physical distribution considers many sales distribution channels such as wholesale and retail, and includes critical decision areas which include customer service, inventory, materials, packaging, order processing, and transportation and logistics.

Function of Physical Distribution Systems

(i) **Customer Service:** The customer service function is a strategically designed standard for consumer satisfaction which the business intends to provide its customers. As an example, a customer satisfaction approach for the handbag business may be that 75% of all custom handbags are delivered to the customer within 72 hours of ordering. An additional approach might include that 95% of custom handbags be delivered to the customer within 96 hours of purchase. Once these customer service standards are set, the physical distribution system is then designed to attain these goals.

(ii) **Order Processing:** Order processing is designed to take the customer orders and execute the specifics the customer has purchased. The business is concerned with this function because it directly relates to how the customer is serviced and attaining the customer service goals. If the order processing system is efficient, then the business can avoid other costs in other functions, such as transportation or inventory control.

(iii) **Inventory Control:** Inventory control is a major role player in the distribution system of a business. Costs consider investment into current inventory, loss of demand for products, and depreciation. There have been inventory control systems implemented such as first in-first out (FIFO) and flow through, which are methods for businesses to handle products.

(iv) Transportation and Logistics: Transportation and logistics costs are a large component of the marketing budget for a product. The system is what moves the products from the production line to the end consumer. This system includes transportation of over the land, sea, and air and the storage and processing of goods through warehouses and distribution centres.

(v) Packaging: Packaging is the technology of enclosing or protecting products for distribution, storage, sale, and use. Packaging is to the process of design, evaluation and production of packages. This can be described as a coordinated system of preparing goods for transport, warehousing, logistics, sale and end use.

Factors Affecting Channels of Distribution

1. **Product Characteristics:** The product characteristic plays an important role in influencing the channel selection. The marketing executive must study the uses of a product, its frequency of purchase; perish ability, rapidity of fashion change, the service required, and its bulkiness.

   (a) Purchase Frequency: The more frequently purchases are made, more feasible it is for the manufacturer to use direct distribution. This requires extensive distribution which involves a financial consideration.

   (b) Perishability: Perishable products like, bakery products, fruits and vegetables, sea food must be placed in the hands of the final consumer as soon as possible after production. These require more of direct marketing because of the risk associated with repeated handling and delays.

2. **Markets Factors/Consumer Factors:** The following market or supply characteristics influence the channel decision:

   (a) Consumer or Industrial Market: The producer of consumer product may choose a long channel involving wholesalers and retailers depending upon the nature of product. In case of industrial product the channel is comparatively short because retailer's services are required in such cases.

   (b) Number of Purchasers: Where number of consumers is large, the channel may be indirect and services of wholesalers and retailers become necessary. But, if customers are few, direct sale can be entertained through representatives.

3. **Company Characteristics:** This choice of channel is also influenced by company characteristic such as its financial position, size, and product mix, morale, of its employees, past channel experience and executive prejudices and overall marketing policies:

   (a) Financial Resources: The financial strength of the company determines which marketing tasks, it can handle efficiently and which ones are to delegate to the middlemen. A company having good financial resources may engage itself in direct marketing in a profitable manner. A weak financial position may force a company to use financially strong intermediaries even if this is not profitable.

   (b) Size of the Company: A large company already handling a wide line of products may be in good position to take an additional product of the same line and handle it in the same way, usually directly. But a smaller firm or one with narrow lines would find middlemen practical.

4. **Middlemen Consideration:** The choice of channel also depends upon the strengths and weakness of various types of middlemen performing various functions. Their behavioural differences, product lines, the number, location, size differ and affect the design of the channel.

   (a) **Attitude of the Middlemen:** The attitude of the middlemen towards the company's policies may affect the channel decision. For example, some middlemen desire to fix their own price for the product the company agrees to allow them to do so, they can very happily agree to sell the products of the company. On the other hand if the company likes to follow the Resale Price Maintenance Policy, the choice is limited.

   (b) **Service Provided by Middlemen:** Services provided by the middlemen may affect the choice of the channel. If the middlemen can provide the services to the customers who the company requires to provide, the middlemen can be appointed; otherwise company will sell the product directly to the consumer.

5. **Environment:** The environmental factors such as economic, ethical, and social conditions and law of the land also influence the channel decision.

   (a) **Economic Conditions:** When economic conditions are depressed the producers prefer shorter channels to cut costs.

   (b) **Social and Ethical Considerations:** Social and ethical considerations such as distribution through black marketing involves question of ethics and injurious to society.

Different Channels of Distribution

The most common routes used for bringing the products in the market from producer to consumer are as follows:

Channel-1: Under the channel-1, the manufacturer directly selles goods to the consumers or end users. There are three alternatives in direct sale to consumers: (a) Sales through advertising and direct methods (b) Sales through travelling sale force (c) Sales through factory outlet of manufacturer. This is the shortest channel a product can follow to the market.

Channel-2: Under the channel-2, the manufacturer sales goods to big retailers and retailers sales goods to the consumers or end users. This channel option is preferable when buyers are large retailers, e.g., a departmental store.

Channel-3: Under the channel-3, the producer sells goods to wholesalers, wholesalers sells to retailers and then retailers sells goods to the consumers or end-users.

Channel-4: Under this channel of distribution, the producer sells goods to the agents, agents sells to the wholesalers, wholesalers sells to retailers and then retailers sells goods to the consumers or end-users. This channel involves selling the product overseas through an agent, who sells them to wholesalers on behalf of the company.

FILL IN THE BLANKS

1. The public and private goods and services can be made available for use of consumption through ________.

2. The emergence and arrangement of the wide variety of distribution-oriented institutions and agencies are called as ________.

3. Intermediaries help in ______ and ______.
4. Channels of distribution are mainly concerned with the ______.
5. A flow of goods is a set of functions performed by ______.
6. In the flow process ______, ______, ______ and ______ are linked.
7. After a producer is selected the next step is to choose ______.
8. Distribution intensity is frequently modified as a product progresses through its ______.
9. Marketers have basic levels of intensity to choose from ______, ______ and ______.
10. ______ and ______ frame work introduces a range of tools available to assist managers in the finalization of a channel plan.
11. The primary participants of channel plan are ______, ______ and ______.
12. Manufacturing activity creates ______.
13. The process in which materials & components are joined into products is typically called ______.
14. Manufacturing in combination with agriculture and mining serves to generate a flow of ______, ______ and ______.
15. Manufacturers take a significant risk with the creation of their ______.
16. Manufacturers of ______, ______ and ______ are not visible to the consumers.
17. The product life cycle is useful for planning the ______ and ______ strategy.
18. ______ initiatives represent the primary focus of the revitalization drive.
19. The general concept of total quality focus managerial attention on ______, ______ and ______.
20. The popular manufacturing strategies are ______ and ______.
21. The goal of flexible manufacturing is to increase responsiveness of ______.
22. To succeed this strategy the manufacturers must have an efficient ______.
23. The goal of focused manufacturing is the lowest possible ______ and ______.
24. Focused manufacturing requires building significant inventories in anticipation of ______.
25. The basic idea is to adopt leading edge manufacturing technology and utilize to the ______.
26. The operation trick is to plan manufacturing schedules to keep anticipatory inventories balanced to ______.
27. ______ and ______ expect manufacturers to maintain a high quality product.
28. ______ enables meeting or matching the supply with consumer demand.
29. Marketing channel decisions influence marketing decisions such as ______, ______ and ______.
30. People with money and willing to purchase want-satisfying goods is called ______.
31. ______ will influence our channel choice.
32. The retailer encounters ______ and ______ difficulty in holding large stocks.
33. The wholesaler supplies to ______.
34. The wholesaler helps retailer in ______.
35. The wholesaler does not grant credit in some cases to ______.
36. Goods are supplied for distribution with in the country by ______, ______ and ______.
37. Physical distribution looks after ______.
38. ______ buy and sell goods their own account and at their own risk and loss.
39. ______ do not take ownership title to goods but actively negotiate the transfer of ownership from seller to buyer.

40. ________, ________ and ________ facilitating agencies were excluded from channel concept.

41. Business goods may be sold directly to ________.

42. ________, ________ and ________ are example of institutional buyers.

43. An agent middleman sells on commission basis directly to ________.

44. ________ have sole agents for distribution.

45. ________ is the large national distributor acting as sole sales agent for many manufacturers

46. Automobiles, appliances, men's and women's clothing, shoes are sold directly to ________.

47. Department store, discount house, chain stores, supermarket, big mail order house are examples of ________.

48. ________ is an agent who does not have direct physical possession of goods in which he deals.

49. Brokers may be organized as ________, ________ and ________.

50. The clients of brokers are ________, ________ and ________.

51. The produce brokers offer services of expert middlemen between ________ and ________.

52. Brokers are experts in ________, and ________.

53. ________ convert commodities into consumer goods.

54. Commission agents play an important role in ________.

55. ________ are important in central markets for purchases on behalf of distance buyers.

56. ________ sell the entire output of their principals or all of given lines of goods.

57. All the commission agents work for a ________.

58. ________ are great risk bearers in the physical or spot markets.

59. In the market dealers act as a ________.

60. Dealers act as the risk-bearing middlemen between ________ and ________.

61. The commodity dealer voluntarily absorbs ________ and ________ in the expectation of making profits.

62. An established firm of good reputation operating in each area may be appointed as ________.

63. The selling agents in each market are able to arrange for his goods to be ________, ________ and ________.

64. The minimum period of an agency should be ________ years.

65. For agency termination notice period on either side is ________.

66. ________ will mention the maximum amount of stock to be held by the agent at a time.

67. Under a consignment sale, the goods are consigned to the selling agent called the consignee on a ________.

68. When the goods are sold, the agent prepares ________ and forwards it to the seller.

69. ________ is deducted from the total sale proceeds and the net amount due is remitted by cheque along with the account sale.

70. ________ are given reasonable areas for exclusive selling rights.

71. ________ should not rely upon his agent for demand creation.

72. In India distributiorship is regarded as restrictive trade practice, subject to approval under the ________.

73. The specialized marketing function are ________, ________ and ________.

74. ________ create time, place, possession and information utility.

75. By practicing specialization and division of labour, ________ and ________ reduce their operating expense ratio.

76. ________ and ________ are the most important marketing intermediaries.

77. ________ is primarily interested in relative efficiency and effectiveness.

78. ________ are individuals or business firms who will sell products to be used primarily for resale or for industrial use.

79. Wholesalers operate on a large-scale in the central market and act as the ________.

80. ________ operate on a small-scale and in the local markets, selling directly to the consumers a variety of goods.

81. ________ are independently owned, buying outright, offering full service and may have general-line or engage in speciality goods.

82. ________ have independent ownership, but taking no title to goods and only actively negotiating sale/purchase of goods.

83. For the manufacturers the wholesalers act as ________ and ________ agency.

84. The manufacturer on manufacturing goods is free from bearing of ________.

85. The manufacturer enjoys ________.

86. There is elimination of wholesalers from channel of distribution by the growth of ________, ________ and ________.

87. If the middlemen is eliminated in the machinery of distribution there is saving of ________.

88. The shorter the chain of middlemen, the smaller will be the gap of prices between the ________.

89. The manufacturer or the retailer will have to perform functions and services ________.

90. Wholesaler supplies to ________.

91. Expand ATM

92. ATM enable customers to do their banking for ________.

93. Expansion of E.C.S is ________.

94. Computer on the counter of a bank offer cashless facilities like ________, ________ and ________.

95. Expansion of PoP is ________.

96. The bank will allow customers to serve themselves ________ and ________.

97. ________ has to forego cash discount when he accepts credit from the wholesaler.

98. Inventory control is a major role player in the distribution system of a ________.

99. ________ and logistics costs are a large component of the marketing budget for a product.

100. ________ is the technology of enclosing or protecting products for distribution, storage, sale, and use.

Answers for Fill in the Blanks

1.	Distribution	11.	Manufacturers; wholesaler; retailers
2.	Intermediaries	12.	Utility
3.	Searching process; sorting process	13.	Manufacturing
4.	Physical distribution of goods	14.	Product; services; commodities
5.	Channel members	15.	Product
6.	Producers; wholesalers; retailers; consumers	16.	Automobiles; appliances; food
7.	Type of channel	17.	Marketing; distribution
8.	Life cycle	18.	Total quality
9.	Intensive; selective; exclusive	19.	People; process; design
10.	Planning; analysis	20.	Flexible; focused

21.	Production	**61.**	Market; credit risks
22.	Marketing channel	**62.**	Sole agent
23.	Per unit cost; fair quality	**63.**	Advertised; packed; warehoused
24.	Future sales	**64.**	Three to five
25.	Maximum capacity	**65.**	Three months
26.	Market demand	**66.**	Agency agreement
27.	Consumers; trading partners	**67.**	Sale or return basis
28.	Sorting	**68.**	Account sale
29.	Pricing; promotion; policy	**69.**	Selling expenses
30.	Market	**70.**	Sale agents
31.	Buying habits of customers	**71.**	Manufacturers
32.	Dearth of capital; lack of space	**72.**	M.R.T.P. Act 1969
33.	Pulse of market	**73.**	Buying; selling, transporting
34.	Window display	**74.**	Middlemen
35.	Retailer	**75.**	Wholesalers; retailers
36.	Manufacturers; producers; importers	**76.**	Wholesalers; retailers
37.	Physical handling of goods	**77.**	Middlemen
38.	Merchant middlemen	**78.**	Wholesalers
39.	Agent middlemen	**79.**	First outlet in distribution
40.	Banks; advertising agencies, warehousing companied	**80.**	Retailers
		81.	Merchant wholesalers
41.	Business buyers	**82.**	Wholesale commission agents
42.	Business buyers; government; hospitals	**83.**	Collecting; marketing
43.	Wholesalers	**84.**	Risk of loss
44.	Textile mills	**85.**	Financial relief
45.	Voltas	**86.**	Departmental; co-operative stores; multiple shop system
46.	Retailers		
47.	Large retailers	**87.**	Middlemen's profit
48.	Brokers	**88.**	Producer's and consumer's
49.	Individuals; partnership; companies	**89.**	Wholesaler
50.	Producers; dealers; manufacturers	**90.**	Retail trade
51.	Sellers; buyers	**91.**	Automatic telling machines
52.	Grades; qualities; trade terms	**92.**	24 hours
53.	Commission agents	**93.**	Electronic credit system
54.	Agricultural markets	**94.**	E.C.S. payment; credit cards; debit cards
55.	Buying agents	**95.**	Point of purchase
56.	Selling agents	**96.**	Anytime; anywhere
57.	Commission	**97.**	Retailer
58.	Dealers	**98.**	Business
59.	Warehouse keepers	**99.**	Transportation
60.	Produce; manufacturer	**100.**	Packaging

TRUE / FALSE

1. The public and private goods and services can be made available for use of consumption through promotion. (True / False)
2. The emergence and arrangement of the wide variety of distribution oriented institutions and agencies are called as intermediaries. (True / False)
3. Intermediaries help in searching and sorting process. (True / False)
4. Channels of distribution are mainly concerned with the physical distribution of goods. (True / False)
5. A flow is a set of functions performed by advertisers. (True / False)
6. In the flow process producers, wholesalers, retailers and consumers are linked. (True / False)
7. After a producer is selected the next step is to choose the product. (True / False)
8. Distribution intensity is frequently modified as a product progresses through its product cycle. (True / False)
9. Marketers have basic levels of intensity to choose from intensive, selective and exclusive. (True / False)
10. Planning and analysis framework introduces a range of tools available to assits managers in the finalization of a channel plan. (True / False)
11. The primary participants of channel plan is the advertiser and consumer. (True / False)
12. Manufacturing activity creates from utility. (True / False)
13. The process in which materials and components are joined into products is typically called as advertising. (True / False)
14. Manufacturing in combination with agriculture and mining serves to generate a flow of product services and commodities. (True / False)
15. Manufacturers take a significant risk with the creation of their product. (True / False)
16. Automobiles appliances and food manufacturers are visible to the consumers. (True / False)
17. The product life cycle is useful for planning the marketing and distribution strategy. (True / False)
18. Total quality initiatives represent the primary focus of the revitalization drive. (True / False)
19. The general concept of total quality focus managerial attention on people, process and design. (True / False)
20. The popular manufacturing strategies are flexible and focused. (True / False)
21. The goal of flexible manufacturing is to increase profit. (True / False)
22. To succeed this strategy the manufacturer must have an efficient market. (True / False)
23. The goals of focused manufactured is the lowest possible per unit cost and fair quality. (True / False)
24. Focused manufacturing requires building significant inventories in anticipation of future shares. (True / False)
25. The basic idea is to adopt leading edge manufacturing technology and utilise it to the minimum capacity. (True / False)
26. The operation trick is to plan manufacturing schedules to keep anticipatory inventories balanced to market demand. (True / False)
27. Consumers, trading partners expect manufacturers to maintain a high quality product. (True / False)

28. Sorting enable meeting or matching the supply with advertisers demand. (True / False)

29. Marketing channel decisions influence marketing decision such as pricing, promotion and policy. (True / False)

30. People with money and willing to purchase want satisfying goods is called as market. (True / False)

31. Buying habits of customers will influence our advertisers. (True / False)

32. The retailers encounters dearth of capital and lack of space difficulty in holding large stocks. (True / False)

33. The wholesalers supplies to retailers. (True / False)

34. The wholesaler helps retailer in window display. (True / False)

35. The wholesaler does not grant credit in some cases to retail. (True / False)

36. Goods are supplied for distribution with in the country by Exports. (True / False)

37. Physical distribution looks after physical handling of goods. (True / False)

38. Merchant middlemen buy and sell goods on their own account and at their own risk and loss. (True / False)

39. Agent middlemen do not take ownership title to goods but actively negotiate the transfer of ownership from seller to buyer. (True / False)

40. Banks, advertising agencies and warehousing companied facilitating agencies were excluded from channel concept. (True / False)

41. Business goods may be sold directly to farmers. (True / False)

42. Business buyers, government and hospitals are example of institutional buyers. (True / False)

43. An agent middlemen sells on commission basis directly to retailers. (True / False)

44. Textile mills have sole agents for distribution. (True / False)

45. Voltas is the large national distributor acting as sole sales agent for many manufacturers. (True / False)

46. Automobiles, appliances, men's and women's clothing, shoes are sold directly to retailers. (True / False)

47. Department stores, discount house, chain stores, supermarket, big mail order house are examples of small wholesalers. (True / False)

48. Brokers is an agent who does not have direct physical possession of goods in which he deals. (True / False)

49. Brokers may be organized as individuals, partnership and companies. (True / False)

50. The clients of brokers are retailers. (True / False)

51. The producer brokers offer services of expert middlemen between advertisers. (True / False)

52. Brokers are experts in grades, qualities and trade terms. (True / False)

53. Commission agents convert commodities into electronic items. (True / False)

54. Commission agents play an important role in buying and selling of goods. (True / False)

55. Buying agents are important in central markets for purchases on behalf of distance buyers. (True / False)

56. Selling agents sell the entire output of their principles or all of given lines of goods. (True / False)

57. All commission agents work for a discount. (True / False)

58. Dealers are great risk bearers in the physical or spot markets. (True / False)

59. In the market, dealers act as a warehouse keepers. (True / False)

60. Dealer act as the risk bearing middlemen between produce and manufacturers. (True / False)

61. The commodity dealer voluntarily absorbs commission in the expectation of making profit. (True / False)

62. An established firm of good reputation operating in each area may be appointed as middlemen. (True / False)

63. The selling agents in each market are able to arrange for his goods not to be advertised. (True / False)

64. The minimum period of an agency should be ten years. (True / False)

65. For agency termination notice period on either side is one month. (True / False)

66. Agency agreement will mention the maximum amount of stock to be held by the agent at a time. (True / False)

67. Under a consignment sale, the goods are consigned to the selling agent called the consignee on a sale or return basis. (True / False)

68. When the goods are sold, the agent prepares cost budget and forwards it to the seller. (True / False)

69. Selling expenses is deducted from the total sale proceeds and the net amount due is remitted by cheque along with the account sale. (True / False)

70. Sole selling agents are given reasonable areas for exclusive selling rights. (True / False)

71. Manufacturers should not rely upon his agent for demand creation. (True / False)

72. In India distributionship is regarded a restrictive trade practice, subject to approval under the M.R.T.P. Act 1920. (True / False)

73. The specialized marketing function are buying, selling and transporting. (True / False)

74. Middlemen create time, place, possession and information utility. (True / False)

75. By practicing specialization and division of labour middlemen reduce their operating expense ratio. (True / False)

76. Wholesalers and retailers are the most important marketing intermediaries. (True / False)

77. Middlemen is primarily interested in relative efficiency and effectiveness. (True / False)

78. Wholesalers are individuals who sell products to be used finally for resale. (True / False)

79. Wholesalers operate on a large-scale in the central market and act as the retailer. (True / False)

80. Retailers operate on a small-scale and in the local markets, selling directly to the consumers a variety of goods. (True / False)

81. Merchant wholesalers are independently owned, buying out right, offering full service and may general line goods. (True / False)

82. Wholesale commission agents have independent ownership, but taking no title to goods and only actively negotiating sale/purchase of goods. (True / False)

83. For the manufacturers the wholesalers act as trading agency. (True / False)

84. The manufacturer on manufacturing goods if free from bearing of profit. (True / False)

85. The manufacturer enjoys financial relief. (True / False)

86. There is elimination of wholesalers from channel of distribution by the growth of advertisers. (True / False)

87. If the middlemen are eliminated in the machinery of distribution there is saving of insurance. (True / False)

88. The shorter the chain of middlemen, the smaller will be the gap of prices between the producer's and consumers. (True / False)

89. The manufacturer or retailer will have to perform the wholesalers' functions. (True / False)

90. Wholesaler plays an important role in distribution. (True / False)

91. Expansion of ATM is any time money. (True / False)

92. ATM enables customers to do their banking only during night time. (True / False)

93. Expansion of E.C.S. is Elector credit system. (True / False)

94. Computer on the counter of a bank offer cashless facilitie like credit card. (True / False)

95. Expansion of PoP is point of purchase. (True / False)

96. The bank will allow customers to serve themselves anytime and anywhere. (True / False)

97. Retailer has to forego cash discount when he accepts credit from the wholesaler. (True / False)

98. As marketing intermediaries, there are no differences between distributors and wholesalers. (True / False)

99. Retailer sells to ultimate consumers for personal and non-business use. (True / False)

100. Franchise means exceptional right given to a person (dealer) (True / False)

Answers for True / False

1.	False	21.	True	41.	True	61.	False	81.	True
2.	True	22.	False	42.	False	62.	False	82.	True
3.	True	23.	True	43.	True	63.	False	83.	False
4.	True	24.	False	44.	False	64.	False	84.	False
5.	False	25.	False	45.	True	65.	False	85.	True
6.	True	26.	True	46.	True	66.	True	86.	False
7.	False	27.	True	47.	False	67.	True	87.	False
8.	False	28.	False	48.	True	68.	False	88.	True
9.	True	29.	True	49.	True	69.	True	89.	True
10.	True	30.	True	50.	False	70.	True	90.	True
11.	False	31.	False	51.	False	71.	True	91.	False
12.	True	32.	True	52.	True	72.	False	92.	False
13.	False	33.	True	53.	False	73.	True	93.	False
14.	True	34.	True	54.	False	74.	True	94.	True
15.	True	35.	True	55.	True	75.	False	95.	True
16.	False	36.	False	56.	True	76.	True	96.	True
17.	True	37.	True	57.	False	77.	True	97.	True
18.	True	38.	True	58.	True	78.	False	98.	False
19.	True	39.	True	59.	True	79.	False	99.	True
20.	False	40.	True	60.	True	80.	True	100.	True

MULTIPLE CHOICE QUESTIONS

1. The public and private goods and services can be made available for use of consumption through ________.

(a) Storing
(b) Distribution
(c) Advertising
(d) Marketing

2. The emergence and arrangement of the wide variety of distribution-oriented institutions and agencies are called as ________.

(a) Intermediaries
(b) Distributors
(c) Marketers
(d) Ultimate consumers

3. Intermediaries help in ________.

(a) Searching process
(b) Sorting process
(c) Manufacturing process
(d) Both a & b

4. Channels of distribution are mainly concerned with the ________.

(a) Physical distribution of goods
(b) Personal selling
(c) Wholesale selling
(d) None of the above

5. A flow is a set of functions performed by ________.

(a) Manufacturers
(b) Channel members
(c) Resellers
(d) Retailers

6. In the flow process they are linked ________.

(a) Producers, wholesalers, retailers and consumers
(b) Producers to consumers
(c) Producer, wholesaler & consumer
(d) Wholesaler to ultimate consumer

7. After a producer is selected the next step is to choose ________.

(a) Type of channel
(b) Market
(c) Target people
(d) Consumers

8. Distribution intensity is frequently modified as a product progresses through its ________.

(a) Product cycle
(b) Life cycle
(c) Manufacturing cycle
(d) None of the above

9. Marketers have basic levels of intensity to choose from ________.

(a) Intensive
(b) Selective
(c) Exclusive
(d) All the above

10. This frame work introduces a range of tools available to assist manageress in the finalization of a channel plan ________.

(a) Planning of a channel plan
(b) Analysis
(c) Both a & b
(d) Organizing

11. The primary participants of channel plan are ________.

(a) Manufacturers
(b) Wholesaler
(c) Retailers
(d) All the above

12. Manufacturing activity creates from ________.

(a) Utility
(b) Place
(c) Time
(d) Location

13. The process in which materials and components are joined into products is typically called as ________.

(a) Manufacturing
(b) Seller
(c) Distributor
(d) Marketer

14. Manufacturing in combination with agriculture & mining serves to generate a flow of ________.

(a) Product
(b) Services
(c) Commodities
(d) All the above

15. Manufacturers take a significant risk with the creation of their ________.

(a) Products
(b) Market
(c) Consumers
(d) None of the above

16. These manufacturers are not visible to the consumers ________.

(a) Automobiles
(b) Appliances
(c) Food, clothing
(d) All the above

17. The product life cycle is useful for planning the ________.

(a) Marketing strategy
(b) Marketing strategy
(c) Both a & b
(d) All the above

18. Which of the following initiatives represent the primary focus of the revitalization drive?

(a) Total quantity
(b) Total quality
(c) Total market
(d) Total producers

19. The general concept of total quality focus managerial attention on ________.

(a) People
(b) Process
(c) Process
(d) All of them

20. The popular manufacturing strategies are ________.

(a) Flexible
(b) Design
(c) Sign
(d) Both a & b

21. The goal of flexible manufacturing is to increase responsiveness of ________.

(a) Advertising
(b) Marketing
(c) Production
(d) Distribution

22. To succeed this strategy the manufacturer must have an efficient ________.

(a) Marketing mix
(b) Marketing channel
(c) Promotion mix
(d) Advertising channel

23. The goal of focused menu factored is the lowest possible ________.

(a) Per unit cost
(b) Fair quality
(c) Both a & b
(d) Inventories

24. The basic idea is to adopt leading edge manufacturing technology and utilize it to the ________.

(a) Minimum capacity
(b) Maximum capacity
(c) Both a & b
(d) Maximum quality

25. Focused manufacturing requires building significant inventories in anticipation of ________.

(a) Demand
(b) Profit
(c) Future sales
(d) None of the above

26. The operation trick is to plan manufacturing schedules to keep anticipatory inventories balanced to ________.

(a) Market demand
(b) Production
(c) Advertising
(d) Globe

27. They expect manufacturers to maintain a high quality product ________.

(a) Consumers
(b) Trading partners
(c) Sellers
(d) Both a & b

28. Which of the following enables meeting or matching the supply with consumer demand?

(a) Sorting
(b) Matching
(c) Quantity
(d) None of the above

29. Physical distribution looks after ________.

(a) Physical handling of goods
(b) Advertising the product
(c) Storing facility
(d) Distribution facility

30. They buy and sell goods on their own account and at their own risk of loss ________.

(a) Wholesaler
(b) Retailer
(c) Merchant middlemen
(d) Both a & b

31. They do not take ownership title to goods but actively negotiate the transfer of ownership from seller to buyer ________.

(a) Agent middlemen
(b) Merchant middlemen
(c) Both a & b
(d) All the above

32. These facilitating agencies were excluded from channel concept ________.

(a) Banks
(b) Advertising agencies
(c) Warehousing
(d) All the above

33. Business goods may be sold directly to ________.

(a) Globe
(b) Business buyers
(c) Businessmen
(d) Firms

34. Example of institutional buyers ________.

(a) Business buyers
(b) Government
(c) Hospitals
(d) All the above

35. An agents middleman seller on commission basis directly to ________.

(a) Consumers
(b) Retailers
(c) Market
(d) Wholesalers

36. They have sole agents for distribution ________.

(a) Textiles industries
(b) Textile mills
(c) Garments
(d) Organizations

37. Which of the following is the large national distributor acting as sole sales agent for many manufacturers?

(a) Voltas
(b) Aiwa
(c) Onida
(d) All the above

38. Automobiles, appliances, men's and women's clothing, shoes are sold directly to ________.

(a) Wholesalers
(b) Retailers
(c) Consumers
(d) Consumers

39. Department store, discount house, chain stores, super market, big mail-order house are examples of ________.

(a) Large retailers
(b) Large wholesalers
(c) Large resellers
(d) None of the above

40. Marketing channel decisions influence marketing decisions such as ________.

(a) Pricing
(b) Promotion
(c) Policy
(d) Both a & b

41. People with money and willing to purchase want- satisfying goods is called as ________.

(a) Market
(b) Consumers
(c) Globe
(d) Product

42. Which of the following will influence our channel choice?

(a) Buying habits of customers
(b) Dealers
(c) Manufacturer
(d) Both a & b

43. The retailer encounters difficulty in holding large stocks ________.

(a) Dearth of capital
(b) Lack of space
(c) Both a & b
(d) All the above

44. The wholesaler specializes in one line of goods and called as ________.

(a) Plus of market
(b) Minus of market
(c) Pulse of market
(d) Impulse of market

45. The wholesaler helps retailer in ________.

(a) Advertising
(b) Buying products
(c) Window display
(d) Both a & c

46. The wholesaler does not grant credit in some cases to ________.

(a) Consumers
(b) Resellers
(c) Retailers
(d) All the above

47. Goods are supplied for distribution with in the country by ________.

(a) Manufacturers
(b) Producers
(c) Importers
(d) All the above

48. Who is an agent who does not have direct physical possession of goods in which he deals?

(a) Brokers
(b) Commission agents
(c) Dealers
(d) Wholesalers

49. Brokers may be organized as ________.

(a) Individuals
(b) Partnership
(c) Companies
(d) All the above

50. The clients of brokers are ________.

(a) Producers
(b) Dealers
(c) Manufacturers
(d) All the above

51. The produce brokers offer services of expert middlemen between ________.

(a) Manufacturers & wholesalers
(b) Wholesalers & retailers
(c) Sellers & buyers
(d) Management to consumers

52. Brokers are experts in ________.

(a) Grades
(b) Qualities
(c) Trade terms
(d) All the above

53. They convert commodities into consumer goods ________.

(a) Brokers
(b) Agents
(c) Commission Agents
(d) Dealers

54. Commission Agents play an important role in ________.

(a) Agricultural markets
(b) Consumable goods
(c) Electronic items
(d) Perishable goods

55. They are important in central markets for purchases on behalf of distance buyers ________.

(a) Buying agents
(b) Selling agents
(c) Commission agents
(d) Brokers

56. Who sell the entire output of their principals or all of given lines of goods?

(a) Selling agents
(b) Dealers
(c) Wholesalers
(d) Retailers

57. All commission agents work for a ________.

(a) Salary
(b) Bonus
(c) Remuneration
(d) Commission

58. Who are great risk bearers in the physical or spot markets?

(a) Dealers
(b) Manufacturers
(c) Sellers
(d) Re-sellers

59. In the market dealer's act as a ________.

(a) Distributors
(b) Warehouse keepers
(c) Storekeepers
(d) Both a & c

60. Dealer act as the risk bearing middlemen between the ________.

(a) Producer & seller
(b) Producer & manufacturer
(c) Producer & wholesaler
(d) Producer & marketer

61. The commodity dealer voluntarily absorbs both in the expectation of making profits ________.

(a) Market
(b) Credit risks
(c) Credit risks
(d) Both a& b

62. An established firm of good reputation operating in each area may be appointed as ________.

(a) Agent
(b) Commission agent
(c) Sole agent
(d) Advisor

63. The selling agents in each market are able to arrange for his goods to be ______.

(a) Advertised
(b) Packed
(c) Warehoused
(d) All the above

64. The minimum period of an agency should be ________.

(a) Six to nine years
(b) Three to five years
(c) Two to four years
(d) One to seven years

65. For agency termination notice period on either side is ________.

(a) Six months
(b) Three months
(c) Nine months
(d) Five months

66. Which of the following will mention the maximum amount of stock to be held by the agent at a time?

(a) Promissory note
(b) Agency Agreement
(c) Bonds
(d) Negotiable instrument

67. Under a consignment sale, the goods are consigned to the selling agent called the consignee a ________.

(a) Sale or return basis
(b) Buy basis
(c) Creation basis
(d) Both a & b

68. When the goods are sold, the agents prepare it and forward it to the seller?

(a) Sale proceeds
(b) Cost sheet
(c) Account sale
(d) Budget

69. Which of the following is deducted from the total sale proceeds and the net amount due is remitted by cheque along with the account sale?

(a) Selling expenses
(b) Commission
(c) Discount
(d) Both a & b

70. Who are given reasonable areas for exclusive selling rights?

(a) Sale agents
(b) Sale marketers
(c) Businessman
(d) All the above

71. Which of the following should not rely upon his agent for demand creation?

(a) Wholesalers
(b) Distributors
(c) Manufacturers
(d) Resellers

72. In India distribution ship is regarded as restrictive trade practice, subject to approval under the ________.

(a) M.R.T.P.. Act 1950
(b) M.R.T.P. Act 1969
(c) M.R.T.P. Act 1960
(d) M.R.T.P. Act 1979

73. The specialized marketing functions are ________.

(a) Buying
(b) Selling
(c) Transporting
(d) All the above

74. They create time, place, possession and information utility ________.

(a) Dealers
(b) Brokers
(c) Middlemen
(d) Agents

75. By practicing specialization and division of labour, they reduce their operating expense ratios ________

(a) Wholesalers.
(b) Retailers
(c) Resellers
(d) Both a & b

76. They are the most important marketing intermediaries ________

(a) Manufacturer and reseller
(b) Wholesalers and retailers
(c) Both a & b
(d) None of the above

77. Who is primarily interested in relative efficiency and effectiveness?

(a) Manufacturer
(b) Marketer
(c) Retailers
(d) Middlemen

78. Who are individuals or business firms who will sell products to be used primarily for resale or for industrial?

(a) Importers
(b) Exporters
(c) Wholesalers
(d) Consumers

79. Wholesalers operate on a large-scale in the central market and act as the ________.

(a) First outlet in distribution
(b) First input in marketing
(c) First input in marketing
(d) Last output in marketing

80. They operate on a small-scale and in the local markets, selling directly to the consumers a variety of goods ________.

(a) Retailers
(b) Marketer
(c) Manufacturer
(d) Exporter

81. Who are independently owned, buying outright, offering full service & may have general-line or engage in speciality goods?

(a) Merchant wholesalers
(b) Trading wholesalers
(c) Both a & b
(d) None of the above

82. Who have independent ownership, but taking no title to goods and only actively negotiating sale purchase of goods?

(a) Wholesale commission agents
(b) Merchant wholesalers
(c) Both a & b
(d) All the above

83. For the manufacturers the wholesalers act as ________.

(a) Collecting agency
(b) Marketing agency
(c) Selling agency
(d) Both a & b

84. The manufacturer on manufacturing goods is free from bearing of ________.

(a) Profit
(b) Risk of loss
(c) Voting
(d) None of the above

85. The manufacturer enjoys ________.

(a) Profit
(b) Capital
(c) Financial relief
(d) Shares

86. There is elimination of wholesalers from channel of distribution by the growth of ________.

(a) Departmental stores
(b) Multiple shop system
(c) Co-operative stores
(d) All the above

87. Which of the following middlemen is eliminated in the machinery of distribution there is saving?

(a) Wholesaler's profit
(b) Middlemen's profit
(c) Retailer's profit
(d) Manufacturer's profit

88. The shorter the chain of middlemen, the smaller will be the gap of prices between the ________.

(a) Wholesaler's & retailer's
(b) Producer's & consumer's
(c) Retailer's & consumer's
(d) Producer's & retailer's

89. The manufacturer or the retailer will have to perform his functions and services ________.

(a) Wholesaler
(b) Middlemen
(c) Resellers
(d) Marketer

90. Wholesaler plays an important role in ________.

(a) Foreign trade
(b) Domestic trade
(c) Distribution
(d) None of the above

91. Expand ATM ________.

(a) All time money
(b) Anytime money
(c) Automatic telling machines
(d) Auto time machine

92. ATM enable customer to do their banking for ________.

(a) Day time
(b) Night time
(c) 24 hours
(d) All the above

93. Expand E.C.S. ________.

(a) Euro cash system
(b) Electronic credit system
(c) Electric cash system
(d) Electronic computer system

94. Computer on the counter of a back offer cashless facilities like ________.

(a) E.C.S payment
(b) Credit cards
(c) Debit card
(d) All the above

95. Expand PoP ________.

(a) Point of production
(b) Point of processing
(c) Point of purchase processing
(d) Point of processing purchase

96. The bank will allow customers to serve themselves ________.

(a) Anytime
(b) Anywhere
(c) Everywhere
(d) Both a & b

97. Who has to forego cash discount when he accepts credit from the wholesaler?

(a) Middlemen
(b) Retailer
(c) Banker
(d) Customers

98. Who receives higher percentage of discount?

(a) Retailer
(b) Distributor
(c) Commission agent
(d) Broker

99. MacDonald food chain has _______.

(a) Retailers
(b) Wholesalers
(c) Franchise for selling their product

100. Direct selling includes the following

(a) Mail order sale
(b) In home selling
(c) Direct response marketing
(d) All the above

Answers for MCQ

1.	(b)	**18.**	(b)	**35.**	(c)	**52.**	(d)	**69.**	(a)	**86.**	(d)
2.	(a)	**19.**	(d)	**36.**	(b)	**53.**	(c)	**70.**	(a)	**87.**	(b)
3.	(d)	**20.**	(d)	**37.**	(a)	**54.**	(a)	**71.**	(c)	**88.**	(b)
4.	(a)	**21.**	(c)	**38.**	(b)	**55.**	(a)	**72.**	(b)	**89.**	(a)
5.	(b)	**22.**	(b)	**39.**	(a)	**56.**	(a)	**73.**	(d)	**90.**	(c)
6.	(a)	**23.**	(c)	**40.**	(d)	**57.**	(d)	**74.**	(c)	**91.**	(c)
7.	(a)	**24.**	(b)	**41.**	(a)	**58.**	(a)	**75.**	(d)	**92.**	(c)
8.	(b)	**25.**	(c)	**42.**	(a)	**59.**	(b)	**76.**	(b)	**93.**	(b)
9.	(d)	**26.**	(a)	**43.**	(c)	**60.**	(b)	**77.**	(b)	**94.**	(d)
10.	(c)	**27.**	(d)	**44.**	(c)	**61.**	(d)	**78.**	(c)	**95.**	(c)
11.	(d)	**28.**	(a)	**45.**	(c)	**62.**	(c)	**79.**	(a)	**96.**	(d)
12.	(a)	**29.**	(a)	**46.**	(c)	**63.**	(d)	**80.**	(a)	**97.**	(b)
13.	(a)	**30.**	(c)	**47.**	(d)	**64.**	(b)	**81.**	(a)	**98.**	(a)
14.	(d)	**31.**	(a)	**48.**	(a)	**65.**	(b)	**82.**	(a)	**99.**	(c)
15.	(a)	**32.**	(d)	**49.**	(d)	**66.**	(b)	**83.**	(d)	**100.**	(d)
16.	(d)	**33.**	(b)	**50.**	(d)	**67.**	(a)	**84.**	(b)		
17.	(c)	**34.**	(d)	**51.**	(c)	**68.**	(c)	**85.**	(b)		

MATCH THE FOLLOWING

1.	Intermediaries	**(a)**	Trade practices
2.	Manufacturing activity	**(b)**	Time, place and possession
3.	Utility	**(c)**	Point of purchase
4.	Retailer	**(d)**	Channels of distribution
5.	M.R.T.P. Act	**(e)**	Production
6.	PoP	**(f)**	Consumer sale

Answers for Match the Following

1.	(d)	**2.**	(e)	**3.**	(b)	**4.**	(f)	**5.**	(a)	**6.**	(c)

Chapter 20

Managing Distribution Channels (Part - II)

SUMMARY

Distribution is a very important component of Logistics and Supply Chain Management. Distribution in supply chain management refers to the distribution of a good from one business to another. It can be factory to supplier, supplier to retailer, or retailer to end customer. It is defined as a chain of intermediaries; each passing the product down the chain to the next organization, before it finally reaches the consumer or end-user. This process is known as the 'distribution chain' or the 'channel.' Each of the elements in these chains will have their own specific needs, which the producer must take into account, along with those of the all-important end-user. Distribution channels may not be restricted to physical products from producer to consumer in certain sectors, since both direct and indirect channels may be used. Hotels, for example, may sell their services typically rooms directly or through travel agents, tour operators, airlines, tourist boards, centralized reservation systems, etc. process of transfer the products or services from producer to customer or end-user.

Distribution is one of the four elements of the marketing mix, the other three being product, pricing and promotion. This marketing mix is also referred to as the four Ps of marketing; distribution is here called physical distribution or place. Simply put, distribution is the process of delivering the products manufactured or service provided by a firm to the end-user. Various intermediaries are involved in this process. This chain of intermediaries which helps in transferring the product from one intermediary to the next before it reaches the end-user is called the Distribution Chain or Distribution Channel. Each intermediary has a specific role and need which the marketer caters to.

Distribution channels are not limited to products only even the services provided by a producer may pass through this channel and reach the customer. Both direct and indirect channels come into use in this case. For instance, the hotel industry provides facility for lodging to its customers, which is a non-physical commodity or a service. The hotel may provide rooms on direct booking as well as through indirect channels like tour operators, travel agents, airlines etc. Distribution chain has seen several improvements in the form of franchising. Also there has been link ups between two service sectors like travel and tourism which has made services available more accessible to the customer. For instance hotels also provide cars on rent.

Functions of a Distribution Channel

(i) The primary function of a distribution channel is to bridge the gap between production and consumption.

(ii) A close study of the market is extremely essential. A sound marketing plan depends upon thorough market study.

(iii) The distribution channel is also responsible for promoting the product. Awareness regarding products and other offers should be created among the consumers.

(iv) Creating contacts or prospective buyers and maintaining liaison with existing ones.

(v) Understanding the customer's needs and adjusting the offer accordingly.

(vi) Negotiate price and other offers related to the product as per the customer demand.

(vii) Storage and distribution of goods.

viii) Catering to the financial requirements for the smooth working of the distribution chain.

(ix) Risk taking for example by stockholding.

Channel Strategy

Channel Strategy is the decision about the allocation of roles within a channel of distribution, and the way in which the channel is formally or informally managed and administered.

Different Channel Strategies

(i) Push Strategy: Push strategy is a manufacturing strategy aimed at other channel members rather than the end consumer. The manufacturer attempts to entice other channel members to carry its product through trade allowances, inventory stocking procedures, pricing policies, etc. Under this strategy the communications and promotional activities by the marketer to persuade wholesale and retail channel members to stock and promote specific products.

(ii) Pull Strategy: A manufacturing strategy aimed at the end consumer of a product. The product is pulled through the channel by consumer demand initiated by promotional efforts, inventory stocking procedures, etc. Under this strategy the communications and promotional activities by the marketer to persuade consumers to request specific products or brands from retail channel members.

Channel Management

Channel management is a term that refers to the way that a business or supplier of products uses various marketing techniques and sales strategies to reach the widest possible customer base. The channels are all of the various outlets by which the product is marketed and sold to customers. When done properly, channel management motivates those channels to sell the product and ultimately develops a better relationship between customer and product. This is achieved by identifying the goals for each distinctive channel and then implementing various marketing strategies to make sure that those goals are attained, all while staying consistent to the overall brand of the business.

Channel management, as a process by which a company creates formalized programs for selling and servicing customers within a specific channel. The customize a channel management program that includes:

(i) Goals: At first define the specific goals for each channel segment. Consider the goals for the channel as whole as well as individual accounts. And, remember to consider the goals for both acquisition and retention.

(ii) Policies. Construct well defined polices for administering the accounts within this channel. Be sure to keep the unique characteristics of each segment in mind when defining policies for account set up, order management, product fulfillment, etc.

(iii) Products. Identify which products in offering are most suited for each segment and create appropriate messaging. Also, determine where the sell opportunities lie.

(iv) Sales/Marketing Programs. Design support programs for the channel that meet their needs, not what idea of their needs are. The standard considerations are product training, co-op advertising, seasonal promotions, and merchandising.

Physical Distribution Management

Physical Distribution Management (PDM) is concerned with ensuring that the individual efforts that go to make up the distributive function are optimized so that a common objective is realized. This is called the 'systems approach' to distribution management and a major feature of PDM is that these functions be integrated.

There are two central themes that should be taken into account:

(i) The success of an efficient distribution system relies on integration of effort. An overall service objective can be achieved, even though it may appear that some individual components of the system are not performing at maximum efficiency.

(ii) It is never possible to provide maximum service at a minimum cost. The higher the level of service required by the customer, the higher the cost. Having decided on the necessary level of service, a company must then consider ways of minimising costs, which should never be at the expense of, or result in, a reduction of the predetermined service level.

The Physical Distribution Process

The distribution process begins when a supplier receives an order from a customer. The customer is not too concerned with the design of the supplier's distributive system, nor in any supply problems. In practical terms, the customer is only concerned with the efficiency of the supplier's distribution. That is, the likelihood of receiving goods at the time requested. Lead-time is the period of time that elapses between the placing of an order and receipt of the goods. This can vary according to the type of product and the type of market and industry being considered. Lead-time in the shipbuilding industry can be measured in fractions or multiples of years, whilst in the retail sector, days and hours are common measures. Customers make production plans based on the lead-time agreed when the order was placed. Customers now expect that the quotation will be adhered to and a late delivery is no longer acceptable in most purchasing situations.

Physical Distribution process consists of the following elements:

1. **Order Processing:** Order processing is the first of the four stages in the logistical process. The efficiency of order processing has a direct effect on lead times. Orders are received from the sales team through the sales department. Many companies establish regular supply routes that remain relatively stable over a period of time providing that the supplier performs satisfactorily. Very often contracts are drawn up and repeat orders are made at regular intervals during the contract period. Taken to its logical conclusion this effectively does away with ordering and leads to what is called 'partnership sourcing'. This is an agreement between the buyer and seller to supply a particular product or commodity as a when required without the necessity of negotiating a new contract every time an order is placed. Order-processing systems should function quickly and accurately. Other departments in the company need to know as quickly as possible that an order has been placed and the customer must have rapid confirmation of the order's receipt and the precise delivery time. Even before products are manufactured and sold the level of office efficiency is a major contributor to a company's image.

2. **Inventory:** Inventory, or stock management, is a critical area of PDM because stock levels have a direct effect on levels of service and customer satisfaction. The optimum stock level is a function of the type of market in which the company operates. Few companies can say that they never run out of stock, but if stock-outs happen regularly then market share will be lost to more efficient competitors. Techniques for determining optimum stock levels are illustrated later in this chapter. The key lies in ascertaining the re-order point. Carrying stock at levels below the re-order point might ultimately mean a stock-out, whereas too high stock levels are unnecessary and expensive to maintain. The stock/

cost dilemma is clearly illustrated by the systems approach to PDM that is dealt with later.

3. **Warehousing:** Marketing texts tend to pay more attention to warehousing. This is mainly because of the relatively longer distances involved in distributing in India, where it can sometimes take days to reach customers by the most efficient road or rail routes. The logistics of warehousing can, therefore, be correspondingly more complicated in India than in the UK. However, the principles remain the same, and indeed the European Union should be viewed as a large 'home market'. Currently, many companies function adequately with their own on-site warehouses from where goods are dispatched direct to customers. When a firm markets goods that are ordered regularly, but in small quantities, it becomes more logical to locate warehouses strategically around the country. Transportation can be carried out in bulk from the place of manufacture to respective warehouses where stocks wait ready for further distribution to the customers.
4. **Transportation:** Transportation usually represents the greatest distribution cost. It is usually easy to calculate because it can be related directly to weight or numbers of units. Costs must be carefully controlled through the mode of transport selected a mongst alternatives, and these must be constantly reviewed. During the past 50 years, road transport has become the dominant transportation mode in India. It has the advantage of speed coupled with door-to-door delivery. The patterns of retailing that have developed, and the pressure caused by low stockholding and short lead times, have made road transport indispensable. When the volume of goods being transported reaches a certain level some companies purchases their own vehicles, rather than use the services of haulage contractors.

Logistics

Logistics is the management of the flow of goods between the point of origin and the point of use in order to meet the requirements of customers or corporations. Logistics involves the integration of information, transportation, inventory, warehousing, material handling, and packaging, and often security. Logistics is a channel of the supply chain which adds the value of time and place utility. Today the complexity of production logistics can be modeled, analyzed, visualized and optimized by plant simulation software, but is constantly changing. This can involve anything from consumer goods such as food, to IT materials, to aerospace and defense equipment.

The Oxford English Dictionary defines logistics as "the branch of military science relating to procuring, maintaining and transporting materiel, personnel and facilities." Another dictionary definition is "the time-related positioning of resources." As such, logistics is commonly seen as a branch of engineering that creates "people systems" rather than "machine systems". When talking in terms of human resources management, logistics means giving inputs, i.e., "recruiting manpower", which ultimately work for the final consumer or to delivery.

Main Logistics Targets

Logistics is one of the main functions within a company. The main targets of logistics can be divided into performance related and cost related. They are high due date reliability, short delivery times, low inventory level and high capacity utilization. But when decisions need to be made, there is always a trade-off between these targets. This is what makes being a logistician challenging and interesting.

Logistics Viewpoints

Inbound logistics is one of the primary processes and it concentrates on purchasing and arranging inbound movement of materials, parts and/or finished inventory from suppliers to manufacturing or assembly plants, warehouses or retail stores.

Outbound logistics is the process related to the storage and movement of the final product and the related information flows from the end of the production line to the end user.

Logistics Fields

1. **Procurement Logistics:** Procurement Logistics consists of activities such as market research, requirements planning, make or buy decisions, supplier management, ordering, and order controlling. The targets in procurement logistics might be contradictory - maximize the efficiency by concentrating on core competences, outsourcing while maintaining the autonomy of the company, and minimization of procurement costs while maximizing the security within the supply process.
2. **Production Logistics:** Production Logistics connects procurement to distribution logistics. The main function of production logistics is to use the available production capacities to produce the products needed in distribution logistics. Production logistics activities are related to organizational concepts, layout planning, production planning, and control.
3. **Distribution Logistics:** Distribution Logistics has, as main tasks, the delivery of the finished products to the customer. It consists of order processing, warehousing, and transportation. Distribution logistics is necessary because the time, place, and quantity of production differ with the time, place, and quantity of consumption.
4. **Disposal Logistics:** Disposal Logistics' main function is to reduce logistics cost(s), enhance service(s), and save natural resources.

Business Logistics

Logistics as a business concept evolved in the 1950s due to the increasing complexity of supplying businesses with materials and shipping out products in an increasingly globalized supply chain, leading to a call for experts called supply chain logisticians. Business logistics can be defined as "having the right item in the right quantity at the right time at the right place for the right price in the right condition to the right customer", and is the science of process and incorporates all industry sectors. The goal of logistics work is to manage the fruition of project life cycles, supply chains and resultant efficiencies.

In business, logistics may have either internal focus (inbound logistics), or external focus (outbound logistics) covering the flow and storage of materials from point of origin to point of consumption. The main functions of a qualified logistician include inventory management, purchasing, transportation, warehousing, consultation and the organizing and planning of these activities. Logisticians combine a professional knowledge of each of these functions to coordinate resources in an organization. There are two fundamentally different forms of logistics: one optimizes a steady flow of material through a network of transport links and storage nodes; the other coordinates a sequence of resources to carry out some project.

Logistics Management

Logistics is that part of the supply chain which plans, implements and controls the efficient, effective forward and reverse flow and storage of goods, services and related information between the point of origin and the point of consumption in order to meet customer and legal requirements. A professional working in the field of logistics management is called a logistician.

Logistics Outsourcing

Logistics outsourcing involves a relationship between a company and an LSP which, compared with basic logistics services, has more customized offerings, encompasses a broad number of service activities, is characterized by a long-term orientation, and, thus, has a rather strategic nature.

1. **Third-party Logistics:** Third-party logistics (3PL) involves using external organizations to execute logistics activities that have traditionally been performed within an organization itself. According to this definition, third-party logistics includes any form of outsourcing of logistics activities previously performed in-house. If, for example, a company with its own warehousing facilities decides to employ external transportation, this would be an example of third-party logistics. Logistics is an emerging business area in many countries.
2. **Fourth-party Logistics:** The concept of Fourth-party Logistics (4PL) provider was first defined by Andersen Consulting (Now Accenture) as an integrator that assembles the resources, capabilities and technology of its own organization and other organizations to design, build, and run comprehensive supply chain solutions. Whereas a third party logistics (3PL) service provider targets a function, a 4PL targets management of the entire process. Some have described a 4PL as a general contractor who manages other 3PLs, truckers, forwarders, customs house agents, and others, essentially taking responsibility of a complete process for the customer.

FILL IN THE BLANKS

1. ________ is a trading activity directly related to the sale of goods or services to the ultimate consumer.
2. The retailer alone can offer ________ to the consumers.
3. One of every six is employed in ________.
4. They have full set of retailers to satisfy our daily wants in every ________.
5. A retailer aims at giving consumers ______.
6. Daily demands of consumers are like ________, ________ and ________.
7. A retailer attracts customer's attention to new goods through _______ and ________.
8. Specialized retailers offer durable and costly consumer goods on ________.
9. A retailer is the connecting link between ________ and ________.
10. Retailers have personal contact with ______.
11. ________, ________ and ________ are example for retail stores in Mumbai.
12. ________ and ________ is an own brand retail stores in India.
13. ________ can have the greatest market appeal at the time of inflation.
14. All sales efforts are useless if the retailing does not cross ______.
15. Right time and money can make effective ________.
16. ________ is a test of retail success for consumer's satisfaction.
17. Mobile retailers and fixed retail shops are independent retailers are based on ______ and ________.
18. ________, ________ and ________ have an unfavorable effect on the profits of the retailers.
19. Example of perishable article is ________, ________ and ________.
20. Operating profits is ________.
21. Sales are influenced by management decisions on ______, ________ and ________.
22. ________ and ________ retailers offer a very keen competition to small-scale fixed retail shops.
23. Example of electronic goods is ________, ________ and ________.

24. Limited line of rapidly turnover items are ________, ________ and ________.

25. Books and magazines, utensils & jewellery are ________.

26. ______ offers great shopping convenience to customers.

27. Convenience stores are in each locality like ________ and ________.

28. ________ requires limited amount of capital, organizing power and limited.

29. Wholesalers sell at lower prices instead of offering ________.

30. ________ can take full advantage of the specialized services of the wholesaler.

31. ________ is a self-service food store with grocery and produce department.

32. Super market has a minimum selling area of ________.

33. The sales of grocery in U.S.A. were done by supermarket in 1990, more than ______.

34. Combination stores is a combination of complementary namely ______, ______ and ________.

35. ________ is a network of a members of branches situated at different parts of the country.

36. Retailer's organization buys in bulk and performs the work of the wholesaler like ________, ________ and ________.

37. Chain stores are strictly the retailer's enterprise to eliminate ______.

38. Multiple shops are the manufacturer's enterprise to eliminate ______, ______ and ______.

39. Retailing came into existence since ______.

40. Discount selling has killed ______.

41. ________ have home shopping network, a retail T.V media for 24 hrs per day.

42. Electronic kiosks sell goods through video catalogues kept in ______, ______ and ______.

43. ________, ________ and ________ are the examples of mobile retailers.

44. ________ and ________ is given as additional attraction to consumers.

45. Direct marketing cannot displace ________.

46. ________, ________ and ________ are popular retail organization.

47. A super market also sells non food lines like ________, ________ and ________.

48. ________, ________ and ________ are products sold by vending machines.

49. Organised retail stores are also known as ________.

50. Hyper market combines the principles of supermarket, department store, speciality shop and service shop in ________.

51. Apparel, housewares, hardware items and hobby items are examples of ________.

52. ________ and ________ classes constitute the hyper market.

53. Expansion of USP is ________.

54. Consumer prefer ________, ________ and ________.

55. ________, ________ and ________ is the primary patronage appeal of customers.

56. Discount retailing also have prevalent in ________, ________ and ________.

57. Consumers of middle income group of people, who were price minded emerged after the ________.

58. ________ and ________ were more suitable for middle income group of people.

59. ________, ________ and ________ required little sales efforts and local sales promotion.

60. ________ examine samples and make the orders.

61. The customer is given the delivery of goods at the ________.

62. Order is checked and then sent to ________ for filling.

63. Repeat customers may be nailed a copy of _____ as they can make the order at home.

64. Customers get well-known brands at _____.

65. An example for branded retail outlet is _____.

66. Factory outlets are owned and operated by manufacturers to sell _____ goods.

67. Factory outlet stores prices of retail on a broad range of items below _____.

68. Off-price retailers buy from producers their excess output at the end of a _____.

69. Shopping centre concept represents a natural evolution of _____.

70. Shopping center may consist of numerous _____.

71. Shopping centres are drawing away the retail trade from central metropolitan cities to _____.

72. Chain store idea is very popular in the _____ and _____ in India.

73. _____ is a big retailing institution in Chennai.

74. Co-operative store is an organization owned, managed and controlled by consumers to reduce the _____ and _____ of middlemen.

75. The minimum members required registering a society or store is _____.

76. Members of the store make joint _____ among themselves at the current market prices.

77. _____ is preferred to avoid unhealthy competition with other retailers.

78. Every person of co-operative store has to pay _____.

79. A definite percentage of profits is utilized for _____ and _____ purposes.

80. Profits after payment of limited interest on capital are utilized for the distribution of _____.

81. Personal security is the best security honoured in _____.

82. Before declaration of dividend, at least 25% of the net profit must be credited to _____ for social benefits of members.

83. In general marketing, marketer depends upon _____, _____ and _____ to promote their products to bring mass distribution.

84. _____ is used for awareness, interest and to build the brand image.

85. Merchandise can be displayed and sold through _____ and _____.

86. _____ has assumed greater importance than even mail-order sale.

87. In Nutrela, 8000 good demonstrations were held in _____.

88. The growing satellite networks can create _____ and _____.

89. The mail order method is firmly established in all markets through _____.

90. A distributor buys goods directly from _____.

Answers for Fill in the Blanks

1.	Retailing	10.	Consumers
2.	Safe and reliable goods	11.	Benzer; sheetal; amarsons
3.	Retailing	12.	Kid's kemp in bangalore; big jo's
4.	Residential locality	13.	Price strategy
5.	Discounts	14.	3 feet
6.	Fresh food stuffs; vegetables; fruit	15.	Promotion
7.	Window display; demonstration	16.	Acid test
8.	Instalment sale basis	17.	Sole trader; partnerships
9.	Wholesaler; consumer	18.	High taxes; competition; increased cost of sales

19.	Vegetable; fruits; eggs	55.	National brand; heavily advertised; low priced
20.	Sales- operating costs	56.	Sporting goods; electronic goods; bookselling
21.	Location; marketing mix; inventory	57.	Second world war
22.	Street; pavement	58.	Supermarkets; discount houses
23.	Freeze; washing machines; furniture	59.	Branding; Packaging; Advertising
24.	Food; beverage; common drugs	60.	Shoppers
25.	Speciality stores	61.	Showroom
26.	Convenience stores	62.	Warehouse
27.	Grocery shops; provision stores	63.	Catalogue
28.	Unit stores	64.	Discount price
29.	Credit to retailers	65.	Nike
30.	Small shop keepers	66.	Irregular goods
31.	Super market	67.	50 %
32.	3600 sq. metres	68.	Irregular goods
33.	75 per cent	69.	Urban expansion
34.	Grocery; drugs; perishable goods	70.	Retail stores
35.	Multiple shops	71.	Sub-urban regions
36.	Transport; ware housing; financing	72.	Metros; class one towns
37.	Wholesalers	73.	Stop and shop chain store ltd.
38.	Small retailers; middlemen; wholesaler	74.	Commission; number
39.	1960	75.	Ten members
40.	Unfair trade practice	76.	Purchases and Sales
41.	Indonesia	77.	Sale of market price
42.	Airports; railway stations; stores	78.	Entrance fee
43.	Hawkers; peddlers; pavement sellers	79.	Social; educational
44.	Trading stamps; gift coupons	80.	Dividends
45.	Retail stores	81.	Co-operative organization
46.	Chain stores; supermarkets; discount houses	82.	General Reserve
47.	Drugs; hardware; utensils	83.	Advertising; sales promotion; personal selling
48.	Cigarettes; cold drinks; newspaper	84.	Advertising
49.	Modern trade	85.	Vending machines; electronic kiosks
50.	One giant size store	86.	Telemarketing
51.	Consumer needs	87.	Five years
52.	Middle; upper	88.	brand awareness; facilitate phone buying
53.	Unique selling point	89.	Direct marketing
54.	Low price; limited service; free delivery	90.	Manufacturer

TRUE / FALSE

1. Retailing is a trading activity directly related to the sale of goods or services to the ultimate consumer. (True / False)
2. The retailer alone can offer safe and reliable goods to the consumers. (True / False)
3. One of every six is employed in retailing. (True / False)
4. They have full set of retailers to satisfy our daily wants in every residential locality. (True / False)
5. A retailer aims at giving consumers commission. (True / False)
6. Daily demands of consumers are like fresh foodstuffs, vegetables and fruits. (True / False)
7. A retailer attracts consumer attention to new goods through demonstrations. (True / False)
8. Specialized retailers offer durable and costly consumer goods on installment sale basis. (True / False)
9. A retailer is the connecting link between advertisers. (True / False)
10. Retailers have personal contact with advertisers. (True / False)
11. Benzer, sheetal and Amarsons are example for retail stores in Dubai. (True / False)
12. Kid's Kemp in Benglure is an own-brand retail store in Australia. (True / False)
13. Price strategy can have the greatest market appeal at the time of inflation.(True / False)
14. All sales efforts are useless if the retailing does not cross 8 feet. (True / False)
15. Right time and money can make effective sales. (True / False)
16. Acid test is a test of retail success for consumer's satisfaction. (True / False)
17. Mobile retailers and fixed retail shops are independent retailers. (True / False)
18. High taxes have an unfavourable effect on the profits of the retailers. (True / False)
19. Example of perishable article is vegetable (True / False)
20. Operating profit is sales + operating cost. (True / False)
21. Sales are influenced by management decisions on location, marketing mix. (True / False)
22. Street and garment retailers offer a very keen competition to small-scale fixed retail shops. (True / False)
23. Example of electronic goods is washing machine. (True / False)
24. Limited line of rapidly turnover items is food and common drugs. (True / False)
25. Books and jewellery are regular stores. (True / False)
26. Convenience stores offer great shopping convenience to manufacturers. (True / False)
27. Convenience stores are in each locality like grocery shops. (True / False)
28. Unit stores requires limited amount of capital, organizing power and limited marginal skill. (True / False)
29. Wholesalers sell at lower prices instead of offering credit to retailers. (True / False)
30. Small shopkeepers can take full advantage of the specialized services of the wholesaler. (True / False)
31. Supermarket is a self-service food store with grocery and produce department. (True / False)
32. Supermarket has a minimum selling area of 2400 sq. metres. (True / False)

33. The sales of grocery in U.S.A were done by supermarkets in 1990, more than 80 percent. (True / False)

34. Combination stores is a combination of complementary namely grocery, drugs and perishable goods. (True / False)

35. Multiple shops are a network of a number of branches situated at different parts of the country. (True / False)

36. Retailer's Organization buy in bulk and perform the work of the wholesaler like transport, warehousing & financing. (True / False)

37. Chain stores are strictly the retailer's enterprise to eliminate retailers. (True / False)

38. Multiple shops are the manufacturer's enterprise to eliminate small retailers, middlemen and wholesaler. (True / False)

39. Retailing came into existence since 1930. (True / False)

40. Discount selling has killed fair trade practice. (True / False)

41. Indonesia have home shopping network a retail T.V media for 24 hrs per day. (True / False)

42. Electronic kisosks sell goods through video catalogues kept in airports, railway stations and stores. (True / False)

43. Hawkers is not an example of mobile retailers. (True / False)

44. Trading stamps, gift coupons is given as additional attraction to consumers. (True / False)

45. Direct marketing cannot displace wholesalers. (True / False)

46. Chain stores, supermarkets and discount houses are popular wholesaler organizations. (True / False)

47. A supermarket also sells non-food lines like drugs, hardware and utensils. (True / False)

48. Cigarettes are products sold by personal selling. (True / False)

49. Organised retail stores are also known as modern trade. (True / False)

50. Hypermarket combines the principles of supermarket, department stores in one giant size store. (True / False)

51. Apparel, house ware are example of electronic items. (True / False)

52. Middle and lower classes constitute the hyper market. (True / False)

53. Expansion of USP is Unit System Process. (True / False)

54. Consumer prefers low price and limited service. (True / False)

55. National brand, heavily advertised and low price is the secondary patronage appeal of customers. (True / False)

56. Discount retailing also have prevalent in sporting goods. (True / False)

57. Consumers of middle income group of people who were price minded emerged after First World War. (True / False)

58. Supermarkets are not suitable for middle income group of people. (True / False)

59. Branding packing and Advertising requires lot of sales efforts. (True / False)

60. Shoppers examine samples and make the orders. (True / False)

61. The customer is given the delivery of goods at godowns (True / False)

62. Order is checked and then sent to market for filling. (True / False)

63. Repeat customers may be mailed a copy of catalogue as they can make the order at home. (True / False)

64. Customers gets well-known brands at discount price. (True / False)

65. Authorized textile showrooms are common in rural areas. (True / False)

66. Factory outlets are owned and operated by manufacturers to sell regular goods. (True / False)

67. Factory outlets stores prices of retail on a broad range of items below 10%. (True / False)

68. Off-price retailers buy from producers their excess output at the end of a irregular goods. (True / False)

69. Shopping centre concept represents a natural evolution of rural expansion. (True / False)

70. Shopping centre may consist of numerous retail stores. (True / False)

71. Shopping centres are drawing away the retail trade from central metropolitan cities to sub-rural regions. (True / False)

72. Chain store idea is very popular in India. (True / False)

73. Stop & shop chain store ltd, is a big retailing institution in Mumbai. (True / False)

74. Co-operative store is an organization owned and managed by consumers. (True / False)

75. The minimum members required to register a society is 8 members. (True / False)

76. Members of the store make joint purchase and sale among themselves at the current market prices. (True / False)

77. Sale at market price is preferred to avoid unhealthy competition with other retailers. (True / False)

78. Every person of co-operative store has to pay commission. (True / False)

79. A definite percentage of profits are utilized for educational purposes. (True / False)

80. Profits after payment of limited interest on capital are utilized for the distribution of shares. (True / False)

81. Personal security is the best security honoured in co-operative organization. (True / False)

82. In general marketing, marketer does not depend on advertiser to promote their product. (True / False)

83. Before declaration of dividend, at least 25% of the net profit must be credited to general reserve. (True / False)

84. Advertising is used for awareness, interest and to build the brand image. (True / False)

85. Merchandise can be displayed and sold through vending machines. (True / False)

86. Tele marketing has assumed greater importance than even mail-order sale. (True / False)

87. An effective product demonstration can convince a customer (True / False)

88. The growing satellite networks can create brand awareness. (True / False)

89. The mail order method is firmly established in all markets through direct marketing. (True / False)

90. Outbound logistics is the process related to the storage and movement of the final product and the related information flows from the end of the production line to the end user. (True / False)

Answers for True / False

1.	True	6.	True	11.	False	16.	True	21.	True
2.	True	7.	True	12.	False	17.	True	22.	True
3.	True	8.	True	13.	True	18.	True	23.	True
4.	True	9.	False	14.	False	19.	True	24.	True
5.	False	10.	False	15.	False	20.	False	25.	False

26.	False	**39.**	False	**52.**	False	**65.**	False	**78.**	False
27.	True	**40.**	False	**53.**	False	**66.**	False	**79.**	True
28.	True	**41.**	True	**54.**	True	**67.**	False	**80.**	False
29.	True	**42.**	True	**55.**	False	**68.**	True	**81.**	True
30.	True	**43.**	False	**56.**	True	**69.**	False	**82.**	False
31.	True	**44.**	True	**57.**	False	**70.**	True	**83.**	True
32.	False	**45.**	False	**58.**	False	**71.**	False	**84.**	True
33.	False	**46.**	False	**59.**	False	**72.**	True	**85.**	True
34.	True	**47.**	True	**60.**	True	**73.**	False	**86.**	True
35.	True	**48.**	False	**61.**	False	**74.**	True	**87.**	True
36.	True	**49.**	True	**62.**	False	**75.**	False	**88.**	True
37.	False	**50.**	True	**63.**	False	**76.**	True	**89.**	True
38.	True	**51.**	False	**64.**	False	**77.**	True	**90.**	True

MULTIPLE CHOICE QUESTIONS

1. Which of the following is a trading activity directly related to the state of goods or services to the ultimate consumer?

(a) Retailing
(b) Retailer
(c) Wholesaler
(d) Selling

2. The retailer alone can offer it to the consumers________.

(a) Safe and reliable goods
(b) Industrial goods
(c) Consumable goods
(d) Machinery

3. One of every six are employed in________.

(a) Wholesale
(b) Retailing
(c) Organization
(d) Industry

4. They have full set of retailers to satisfy our daily wants in every________.

(a) Location
(b) Residential locality
(c) Both a & b
(d) None of the above

5. A retailer aims at giving consumers ________.

(a) Quality products
(b) Quality products
(c) Quantity products
(d) Discounts

6. Daily demands of consumers are like________.

(a) Fresh foodstuffs
(b) Vegetables
(c) Fruit & milk
(d) All the above

7. A retailer attracts customer's attention to new goods through________.

(a) Window display
(b) Demonstration
(c) Both a & b
(d) Advertising

8. Specialised retailers offer durable & costly consumer goods on________.

(a) Hire basis
(b) Installment sale basis
(c) Discount basis
(d) Free-delivery basis

9. A retailer is the connecting link between________.

(a) Manufacturer & Consumer
(b) Wholesaler & Consumer
(c) Retailer & Consumer
(d) Wholesaler & retailer

10. Retailers have personal contact with________.

(a) Consumers
(b) Users of products
(c) Sellers of products
(d) Both a & b

11. Which of the following is an example for retail stores in Mumbai?

(a) Benzer
(b) Sheetal
(c) Amarsons
(d) All the above

12. Which of the following is an own-brand retail stores in India?

(a) Kid's kemp in Bangalore
(b) Big Jo's
(c) Voltas
(d) Both a & b

13. Which of the following have the greatest market appeal at the time of inflation?

(a) Price strategy
(b) Pricing policy
(c) Pricing objective
(d) None of the above

14. All sales efforts are useless if the retailing does not cross________.

(a) 3 feet
(b) 2 feet
(c) 4 feet
(d) 5 feet

15. Right time and money can make effective________.

(a) Sales
(b) Distribution
(c) Promotion
(d) Profit

16. Which of the following is a test of retail success for consumer's satisfaction?

(a) Product test
(b) Acid test
(c) Market test
(d) Research & development

17. Mobile retailers and fixed retail shops are independent retailers based on________.

(a) Sole trader
(b) Partnerships
(c) Joint stock company
(d) Both a & b

18. Which of the following have an unfavourable effect on the profits of the retailers?

(a) High taxes
(b) Competition
(c) Increased cost of sales
(d) All the above

19. Which of the following is an example of perishable article?

(a) Vegetable
(b) Fruits
(c) Eggs
(d) All the above

20. Operating profit is________.

(a) Sales + Operating costs
(b) Sales + Profit

(c) Sales – Operating costs
(d) Both a and b

21. Sales are influenced by management decisions on________.

(a) Location
(b) Marketing mix
(c) Inventory
(d) All the above

22. They offer a very keen competition to small-scale fixed retail shops ________.

(a) Street retailers
(b) Parement retailers
(c) Provision stores
(d) Both a & b

23. Example of Electronic goods is__________.

(a) Freezers
(b) Washing machines
(c) Furniture
(d) All the above

24. Limited line of rapidly turnover items are________.

(a) Food
(b) Beverage
(c) Common drugs
(d) All the above

25. Books and magazines, utensils and jewellery are ________.

(a) Mobile retailers
(b) Convenience stores
(c) Speciality stores
(d) Both a & b

26. It offers great shopping convenience to customers________.

(a) Retailers
(b) Convenience stores
(c) Speciality stores
(d) Speciality stores

27. Convenience stores are in each locality like________.

(a) Grocery shops
(b) Grocery shops
(c) Both a & b
(d) Convenience stores

28. Which of the following requires limited amount of capital, organizing power and limited marginal skill?

(a) Unit stores
(b) Grocery shops
(c) Speciality stores
(d) Convenience stores

29. Wholesalers sell at lower prices instead of offering________.

(a) Cash to retailers
(b) Credit to retailers
(c) Discounts
(d) Commission to agents

30. Which of the following take full advantage of the specialized services of the wholesaler?

(a) Retail shops
(b) Small shopkeepers
(c) Provision stores
(d) None of the above

31. Which of the following is a self- service food store with grocery and produce departments?

(a) Large- scale retail organization
(b) Supermarket
(c) Big retailers
(d) Combination stores

32. Supermarket has a minimum selling area of________.

(a) 2.400 sq. metres
(b) 1,400 sq. metres
(c) 3,600 sq. metres
(d) 1,000 sq. metres

33. The sales of grocery in the U.S.A were done by supermarkets in 1990, more than ________.

(a) 60 per cent
(b) 70 per cent
(c) 75 per cent
(d) 50 per cent

34. Combination stores is a combination of complementary namely ________.

(a) Grocery
(b) Drugs
(c) Perishable goods
(d) Both a & b

35. Which of the following is a network of a member of branches situated at different parts of the country?

(a) Chain stores
(b) Multiple shops
(c) Retail shops
(d) Department stores

36. Retailer's organization buys in bulk & performs the work of the wholesaler namely ________.

(a) Transport
(b) Ware housing
(c) Financing
(d) All the above

37. Multiple shops are the manufacturer's enterprise to eliminate all ________.

(a) Small retailers
(b) Middlemen
(c) Wholesaler
(d) Both a & b

38. Chain stores are strictly the retailer's enterprise to eliminate ________.

(a) Retailers
(b) Middlemen
(c) Wholesalers
(d) None of the above

39. Retailing came into existence since ________.

(a) 1930
(b) 1960
(c) 1990
(d) 2000

40. Discount selling has killed ________.

(a) Unfair trade practice
(b) Fair trade practice
(c) Hypermarket
(d) Competition

41. In which country they have home shopping network, a retail T.V media for 24 hrs per day?

(a) Indonesia
(b) China
(c) U.S.A.
(d) Japan

42. Electronic kiosks sell goods through video catalogues kept in________.

(a) Air ports
(b) Railway stations
(c) Stores
(d) All the above

43. Which of the following is an example of mobile retailers?

(a) Hawkers
(b) Peddlers
(c) Pavement sellers
(d) All the above

44. Which of the following is given as additional attraction to consumers?

(a) Trading stamps
(b) Gift coupons
(c) Both a & b
(d) Gift cheque

45. Direct marketing cannot displace ________.

(a) Wholesale stores
(b) Retail stores

(c) Provision stores
(d) Department stores

46. Which of the following is a popular retail organization?

(a) Chain stores
(b) Supermarkets
(c) Discount houses
(d) All the above

47. A super market also sells non- food lines like ________.

(a) Drugs
(b) Hard ware
(c) Utensils
(d) All the above

48. Which of the following is a suitable products sold by vending machines?

(a) Cigarettes
(b) Cold drinks
(c) Newspaper
(d) All the above

49. Large scale retail outlets include ________.

(a) Departmental store
(b) Shopping centre
(c) One price shop
(d) All the above

50. Hypermarket combines the principles of supermarket, department store, speciality shop and service shop in ________.

(a) One giant six store
(b) Two giant size store
(c) Thousand giant size store
(d) Multiple store

51. Apparel, housewares, hardware items and hobby items are examples of ________.

(a) Consumer needs
(b) Wholesaler needs
(c) Manufacturers needs
(d) None of the above

52. They constitute the hyper- market ________.

(a) Middle classes
(b) Upper classes
(c) Lower classed
(d) Both a & b

53. Expand U.S.P.________.

(a) Unique selling point
(b) Unit system point
(c) Unit selling process
(d) Unique system process

54. Consumers prefer________.

(a) Low price
(b) Limited service
(c) Free delivery
(d) Both a & b

55. Which of the following is the primary patronage appeal of customers?

(a) National brand
(b) Heavily advertised
(c) Low priced
(d) All the above

56. Discount retailing also have prevalent in________.

(a) Sporting goods
(b) Electronic goods
(c) Bookselling
(d) All the above

57. Consumers of middle income group of people, who were price minded, emerged after the________.

(a) First world war
(b) First world war
(c) Second world war
(d) Third world war

58. These were more suitable for middle income groups of people ________.

(a) Supermarkets
(b) Discount houses
(c) Multiple shop
(d) Both a & b

59. Which of the following is required little sales efforts and local sales promotion?

(a) Branding
(b) Packaging
(c) Advertising
(d) All the above

60. They examine samples and make the orders ________.

(a) Shoppers
(b) Manufacturers
(c) Wholesaler
(d) Marketer

61. Many consumers buy from the same provision store because ________.

(a) Fair price
(b) Courteous service
(c) Credit facilities
(d) All the above

62. Order is checked and then sent to for filling ________.

(a) Store room
(b) Warehouse
(c) Godowns
(d) Provision ships

63. Repeat customers may be mailed a copy of it, as they can make the order at home ________.

(a) Account sales
(b) Catalogue
(c) Budget sheet
(d) Cost sheet

64. Customers get well known brands at ________.

(a) Cost price
(b) Market price
(c) Discount price
(d) Manufacturers price

65. People visit authorized showrooms because ________.

(a) Genuine product
(b) Fair price
(c) Product variety
(d) All the above

66. Factory outlets are owned and operated by manufacturers to sell ________.

(a) Surplus goods
(b) Irregular goods
(c) Discontinued goods
(d) All the above

67. Factory outlet stores prices of retail on a broad range of items below ________.

(a) 20 %
(b) 40 %
(c) 50 %
(d) 60 %

68. Off- price retailers buy from producers their excess output at the end of a ________.

(a) Irregular goods
(b) Regular goods
(c) Wastage goods
(d) Partly used goods

69. Shopping centre concept represents a natural evolution of ________.

(a) Rural expansion
(b) Urban expansion
(c) Local- market area
(d) None of the above

70. Shopping center may consist of numerous ________.

(a) Wholesale stores
(b) Retail stores

(c) Agents
(d) merchandise

71. Shopping centres are drawing away the retail trade from central metropolitan cities to ________.

(a) Rural regions
(b) Urban regions
(c) Suburban regions
(d) Sub-rural regions

72. Chain store idea is very popular in the ________.

(a) Metros in India
(b) Class one town in India
(c) Silicon city in India
(d) Both a & b

73. Which of the following is a big retailing institution in Chennai?

(a) Stop & shop chain store ltd.
(b) Shop chain store ltd.
(c) Shoppers shop chain store ltd.
(d) None of the above

74. Co-operative store is an organization owned, managed and controlled by consumers to reduce the ________.

(a) Member of middlemen
(b) Commission of middlemen
(c) Both a & b
(d) Departmental stores

75. The minimum members required registering a society or store is ________.

(a) Ten members
(b) Twelve members
(c) Seven members
(d) Fifteen members

76. Members of the store make it among themselves at the current market price ________.

(a) Joint- purchases
(b) Joint- sales
(c) Both a & b
(d) None of the above

77. Which of the following is preferred to avoid unhealthy competition with other retailers?

(a) Sale at cost price
(b) Sale at market price
(c) Sale at profitable price
(d) Sale at reasonable price

78. Every person of co-operative store has to pay________.

(a) Commission
(b) Brokerage
(c) Entrance fee
(d) Exit fee

79. Income companies a percentage of profits is utilized for ________.

(a) Social purposes
(b) Educational purposes
(c) Both a & b
(d) Travelling purpose

80. Profits after payment of limited interest on capital are utilized for the distribution of ________.

(a) Dividends
(b) Shares
(c) Profits
(d) None of the above

81. Personal securing is the best security honoured in a________.

(a) Co-operative organization
(b) Banks
(c) Mutual funds
(d) Financial institutions

82. Before declaration of dividend at least 25 % of the net profits must be credited to it for social benefits of members ________.

(a) Shareholders account
(b) General Reserve

(c) Revenue Reserve
(d) Capital Reserve

83. In general marketing, marketer depends upon it to promote their products to bring mass distribution ________.
(a) Advertising
(b) Sales promotion
(c) Personal selling
(d) All the above

84. Which of the following is used for awareness, interest & to build the brand image?
(a) Advertising
(b) Marketing
(c) Personal selling
(d) Reselling

85. Merchandise can be displayed & sold through________.
(a) Vending machines
(b) Electronic kiosks
(c) Both a & b
(d) None of the above

86. It has assumed greater importance than even mail- order sale________.
(a) Telemarketing
(b) Tele- conference
(c) Both a & b
(d) All the above

87. Product demonstration is one of the effective methods for selling ________.
(a) Computer
(b) Soup
(c) Ice cream
(d) Instant coffee
(d) All the above

88. The growing satellite networks can create ________.
(a) Brand awareness
(b) Facilitate phone buying
(c) Both a & b
(d) None of the above

89. The mail order method is firmly established in all market through ________.
(a) Indirect marketing
(b) Direct marketing
(c) Telephone marketing
(d) Personal selling

90. The customize a channel management program that includes________.
(a) Goals
(b) Policies
(c) Products
(d) All the above

Answers for MCQ

1.	(a)	**10.**	(d)	**19.**	(d)	**28.**	(c)	**37.**	(d)	**46.**	(d)
2.	(a)	**11.**	(d)	**20.**	(c)	**29.**	(b)	**38.**	(c)	**47.**	(d)
3.	(b)	**12.**	(d)	**21.**	(d)	**30.**	(a)	**39.**	(b)	**48.**	(d)
4.	(b)	**13.**	(a)	**22.**	(d)	**31.**	(b)	**40.**	(a)	**49.**	(d)
5.	(d)	**14.**	(a)	**23.**	(d)	**32.**	(c)	**41.**	(c)	**50.**	(a)
6.	(d)	**15.**	(c)	**24.**	(d)	**33.**	(c)	**42.**	(d)	**51.**	(a)
7.	(c)	**16.**	(b)	**25.**	(c)	**34.**	(d)	**43.**	(d)	**52.**	(d)
8.	(b)	**17.**	(d)	**26.**	(b)	**35.**	(b)	**44.**	(c)	**53.**	(a)
9.	(b)	**18.**	(d)	**27.**	(c)	**36.**	(a)	**45.**	(b)	**54.**	(d)

55.	(d)	**61.**	(d)	**67.**	(c)	**73.**	(a)	**79.**	(c)	**85.**	(c)
56.	(d)	**62.**	(c)	**68.**	(a)	**74.**	(c)	**80.**	(a)	**86.**	(a)
57.	(c)	**63.**	(b)	**69.**	(b)	**75.**	(a)	**81.**	(a)	**87.**	(a)
58.	(d)	**64.**	(c)	**70.**	(b)	**76.**	(c)	**82.**	(b)	**88.**	(c)
59.	(d)	**65.**	(d)	**71.**	(c)	**77.**	(b)	**83.**	(d)	**89.**	(b)
60.	(a)	**66.**	(b)	**72.**	(d)	**78.**	(c)	**84.**	(a)	**90.**	(d)

MATCH THE FOLLOWING

1.	Distribution Channel	**(a)**	Self service food store
2.	Factory outlets	**(b)**	Mail order
3.	Mobile Traders	**(c)**	Order processing, transportation
4.	Supermarket	**(d)**	Hawkers
5.	Direct marketing	**(e)**	Irregular goods
6.	Distribution logistics	**(f)**	Bridge between production and consumption

Answers for Match the Following

1.	(f)	**2.**	(e)	**3.**	(d)	**4.**	(a)	**5.**	(b)	**6.**	(c)

Chapter 21

Marketing of Services

SUMMARY

Service refers to an act or performance that one party can offer to another that is essentially intangible and does not result in the ownership of anything.

Characteristics of Services

The services have unique characteristics which make them different from that of goods. The most common characteristics of services are:

1. **Intangibility:** Services are activities performed by the provider, unlike physical products they cannot be seen, tasted, felt, heard or smelt before they are consumed. The marketer of service cannot rely on product-based clues that the buyer generally employs in alternative evaluation prior to purchase.

   Example: Teaching, Consulting, Legal advices are services which consider the intangibility in nature.

2. **Inseparability:** Services are produced and consumed simultaneously. In case of physical goods, they are manufactured into products, distributed through multiple resellers and consumed later. But, in case of services, it cannot be separated from the service provider. Thus, the service provider would become a part of a service.

   Example: Doctor and Patient, Taxi operator drives taxi and the passenger uses it. The presence of taxi driver is essential to provide the service. To use the services of an airline, hotel, etc., customer must be physically present.

3. **Perish Ability:** The service relevant resources, processes and systems are assigned for service delivery during a definite period in time. Hence, services cannot be stored. The services go waste if they are not consumed simultaneously, i.e., value of service exists at the point when it is required. A marketer should effectively utilize the capacity without deteriorating the quality to meet the demand.

   Example: An empty seat on a plane can never be utilized and charged after departure.

4. **Variability:** Services are highly variable, as they depend on the service provider and where and when they are provided. Service buyers are aware of this variability. So, the service firms should make an effort to deliver high and consistent quality in their service and this is attained by selecting good and qualified personnel for rendering the service.

   Example: Variability of services means that services are not uniform in quality. One doctor's service will be different from another doctor's service. One teacher's teaching is different from another teacher.

5. **Non-ownership:** Ownership is never transferred in the case of services. A lot of the implications of ownership depend on how the service providers perform while delivering the service. The ownership criteria come after the service product has been delivered to the customer and not before.

Importance of Services Marketing

The Importance of Services can be summarized as follows:

1. **Generation and Expansion of Employment and Business Opportunities:** The components of the service sector are wide and varied. For example, the service sector includes personal care services, education services, medicare services, communication services, tourism services, hospitality services, banking services, insurance services, transportation services, consultancy services, etc. The organized and systematic development of the service sector would create enormous employment opportunities. Application of marketing principles in the service sector is instrumental to the development of the economy. However, it is appropriate to mention that India has not been successful in utilizing the potential of the service sector. The significance of the service sector lies in its capacity to create job opportunities. If the service sector is properly developed, it will solve the problem of unemployment in India to a great extent. After liberalization policy, the service sector in India has been emerging as a dominant component in the economy.
2. **Optimum Utilization of Resources:** India is bestowed with rich resources. The human resources available in India favour the growth of the service sector. While the labour content in most manufacturing activities is dropping steadily with use of technology, the labour content in the service sector is comparatively high. As India is rich in human resources, service sector can grow steadily. Moreover, service sector offers excellent export opportunities too. In fact, the important agenda of the World Trade Organization (WTO) is opening up of market for services. Though its performance in the export of computer software is quite commendable already, it should concentrate on other areas as well. Service firms such as personal care services, the entertainment services, tourism services, hotel service contribute to the growth of the economy without consuming any natural resources.
3. **Capital Formation:** There are indications that services will grow more rapidly in the near future. Economic, social and political factors signal an expansion of the service sector. Investments and job generations are far greater in the service sector compared to manufacturing. It is estimated that telecom alone will account for an investment of ₹ 150,000 crores in the coming years. Investment encourages capital formation. For the development of a nation, the flow of capital should be directed towards the most productive uses. If investments are made in the service sector, it will contribute to the nation-building process. With increased developmental activities, the per capita income increases which, in turn, facilitates capital formation. Performance of profitable services can absorb higher investments, thereby accelerating the rate of capital formation.
4. **Increasing the Standard of Living:** The standard of living of the people in any country would be decided on the basis of quality and standard of products consumed or services availed in the day to day living. Any development is transparent only when the living conditions of the masses improve. When compared with developed countries, the standard of living in India is far from satisfactory. Standard of living cannot be improved by offering more opportunities for earnings. On the other hand, the standard of living is determined by the availability of goods and services for

citizens and a wise spending on them. The development of services industry is sure to promote the standard of living of the people.

5. **Use of Environment-friendly Technology:** Nowadays, almost all services are found technology-driven. Developed countries are making full use of latest technology while rendering services. Technologies used by service generating organizations such banks, insurance companies, tourism, hotel services, Eco-friendly services. Technologies used in manufacturing organizations may have harmful effects on the environment. So, services industry does not pollute the environment which is indeed creditable.

Services Management refers to the total organizational approach that makes quality of service as perceived by customer. It is the process of monitoring and optimizing a service to ensure for meeting the critical outcomes of the customer values.

Reasons for the Growth of Service Sector

1. **Economic Prosperity:** One of the key factors for the growth of demand for services is the economic prosperity. The rural households in the upper income category are growing at a much faster pace than the urban households in the corresponding categories. The Economic liberalization process has a positive impact on the Indian households. Their income as well as their expenditure has been pushed, creating a demand for many goods and services.
2. **Changing Role of Women:** Traditionally the Indian woman was confined to household activities. But with the changing time there has been a change in the traditional way of thinking in the society. Women are now allowed to work. They are employed in defence services, police services, postal services, software services, health services, hospital services, entertainment industries, business process outsourcing and so on. The percentage of working women has been growing rapidly. The changing role of women has created a market for a number of product and services.
3. **Cultural Changes:** Change is the underlying philosophy of culture but place of change in Indian culture is not uniform. However, during the last century the factors of change are prominent. The emergence of the nuclear family system in place of the traditional joint family system creates a demand for a host of services like education, health care, entertainment, telecommunication, transport, tourism and so on. There has been a marked change in the thought processes relating to investment, leisure time perception and so on which has created a huge demand for services.
4. **I.T. Revolution:** For the last 15 years India is occupying a vital position in the area of Information Technology. Information Technology became one of the key service businesses of the country. India has the largest software skilled population in the world. The domestic market as well as the international market has grown substantially. Realizing the potential for this area many state governments have made IT as their most, prioritized segment. States such as Karnataka, Andhra Pradesh, Madhya Pradesh Maharashtra and Delhi have already achieved substantial progress in information technology.
5. **Development of Markets:** During the last few decades the wholesaler and the retailer population has grown in the country. Urban India has become a cluster of wholesaling and retailing business. In the semi–urban areas, retailing has spread to the nooks and

corners of the streets and in the rural areas retail business is significantly present. A new kind of organizations, offering marketing services has come up. The government also offers marketing services to the small-scale agricultural farmers, artisans and other traditional business sectors such 'as promotion of regulated markets, export promotion councils, development boards etc.

6. **Market Orientation:** The changing competitive situation and demand supply positions has forced the manufacturing organization to shift their philosophy from production orientation to market orientation. Market is a service function that has been added in the organization. The pressures in the market has further forced the manufacturing organizations to have marketing research, accounting, auditing, financial management, human resource management and marketing research divisions – all of which are services functions.

7. **Health Care Consciousness:** In India, the health care market has grown substantially. The increased life expectancy is the result of the consciousness of the people regarding the health issues. The growth of fitness clubs, diagnostic centres, medical counseling and health-related information sites are the reflections of the growing demands for health care services. The government as well as the social organizations has taken up the mass campaigns in order to create awareness among the illiterate persons and the rural population on health service.

8. **Economic Liberalization:** The economic liberalization of the 1991 has brought many changes in the Indian scenario. With the disinvestment and the privatization policies the state owned monopolies in many service areas came to an end multinationals were permitted to enter the Indian market. Liberal lending policies and lower interest rates motivated many people to become self-employed. Different sectors like Banking, Insurance, Power projects, Tele-communication, Hospitality sector, Health Services, Entertainment, Air transport, and Courier services witnessed intense competition, due to the entry of multinationals. The flow of time-tested service technology from various parts of the world changed the attitude of the Indian consumer towards sources.

Marketing Mix in Service Industry

Marketing mix refers to the blend of ideas, concepts and features which the marketing management put together to achieve market targets. The marketing mix of services have be extended beyond 4Ps and three additional Ps *viz.*, people, physical evidence and process have been added to meet the challenges posed by the special characteristics of services.

The following are the 7Ps of marketing mix components in service marketing:

1. **Product:** In service marketing mix product refers to the service offered. Though service products are essentially intangible, there are certain physical characteristics which consumers will assess in their evaluation of the service product choice. They include attractiveness of the terms of physical features like good accommodation, suitability of climate etc., in case of tour operation, introduction of new product modifying or deleting the old product, making continuous efforts to design qualitative service products that provide maximum consumer satisfaction, branding etc.,

   Examples: Credit card facility providers include coverage of risk due to accident tour operators providing good lodging facility, guides to tourists, private players in telephones are offering number of service products to suit different types of customers like student connection, airlines are charging lower rates to senior citizens etc.

2. **Pricing:** Pricing is an important element of the marketing mix that brings in revenues and profits. The success of a service depends on the pricing strategy developed or adopted by the company. However, it is easier for customers to evaluate the value derived from goods, when compared to services. There are four ways in which prices of services are perceived to be different from those of goods.

   Service customers perceive the price as an indicator of the quality offered and they include non-monetary costs like time costs, search costs, convenience costs, and psychological costs involved in consuming the services, while estimating their value. There is difficulty in comparing the prices of services due to their specific characteristics such as intangibility. Finally, prices vary with fluctuations in demand.

   Example: Interest rate on fixed deposit or on loan depends on 'time factor', price discrimination also takes place in services, banks offer additional 0.5% or 1% interest on deposits of senior citizens. A transport operator may offer lower price to a regular commuter and a different price to a casual traveler. Similarly if the objective of service provider is market penetration prices may be fixed lower to attract large number of consumers. On the other hand if the firm is targeting high income group and providing exclusive luxury service, price will be higher. Since services are perishable and intangible good pricing policy will contribute to the success of the organization.

3. **Promotion:** Service organizations can retain existing customers, attract new customers, increase brand awareness, build business, reduce their perceived risk and finally, gain the trust of their customers through promotional campaigns. Service companies should first understand the importance of communication in an organization with its internal and external customers.

   These are personal selling, advertising, sales promotion, publicity, public relations and direct marketing. A service company should also have knowledge about the basic differences between packaged goods and service industries to design effective promotional techniques. The service personnel play a more important role in service delivery when compared to packaged goods.

   Example: In tourism industry, hotel owners and airline and other transport operators need to promote their services to tour operators as well as to end users.

4. **Place:** The fourth element of the marketing mix, namely, 'place', involves various efforts made by the service organizations to make the services accessible and available to the customers. Service location plays an important role in service delivery. Further, it conveys the service quality provided by the service provider and stamps an image of the service company in the customer's mind.

   In case of direct distribution where service personnel are also involved in the service delivery, the behavior of service personnel towards with customers also creates an image of the service provider in the customer's mind. Service organizations aim to deliver services through direct distribution, where a service provider visits the customer or a customer visits a service provider. When service providers cannot deliver services through direct distribution, they opt for various forms of intermediaries.

Example: Hotels, ATMs, bank branches, insurance branches, travel agents, educational institutions, shopping malls, etc., have to be placed in such a way to provide convenient accessibility, safety and protection; availability of infrastructural facilities, etc.

5. **People:** This element of service marketing mix is very important because almost all the services are delivered by one human being to another. The person delivering the service creates customer satisfaction and the perception of the service depends on their interaction. Service personnel can be classified in different ways depending on the level and nature of interaction that they have with customers-low-contact and high contact service personnel; consumer-service and professional service employees; and contact personnel, moderate contract personnel, back-office staff, support staff and management.

6. **Physical Evidence:** Customers in the service sector attempt to take cues about the service provider's capabilities and the quality of service offered from physical evidence. The major elements of physical evidence include the physical environment, the modes and content of communication, service personnel, the tangible elements accompanying the service and the brand.

   Example: Prospectus of college can give the college profile, faculty data, laboratories, office set up, etc. Brochure of tour organizer can give physical evidences like pictures of hotel rooms and resorts and details of tour guides transport facility etc. Fast food outlets use good colour schemes and display of pictures to convey an image of good quality service.

7. **Process:** Process is an important element of the marketing mix that determines how a service should be created and delivered to the customer. The characteristics of service process include complexity, divergence, service location, customer participation and the service itself – whether it is technology-based or process-based. The types of process include line or flow operations and job shop process. The elements of service blueprint include customer actions, onstage and backstage employee actions, and support processes to their minutest detail. Further, the interaction among these elements is explained through the line of interaction, line of visibility and line of internal interaction. These will help a service provider to clearly read a blueprint and identify the activities that add value to the customer so that he can concentrate on such activities.

   Example: In a self-service hotel, consumer is contributing in his role in the production of service process by going to the counter and getting the food to the table. In recent years efforts are being made by service providers to involve consumers more in the production process.

Meaning of Service Marketing

Service marketing is a branch of marketing that involves distribution of fast moving consumer goods and durable goods. This field refers to both businesses to consumer as well as business to business services. The marketers and managers need to be more customers oriented in addition to being concerned about priced realistically, distributed through convenient channels and actively promoted to customers.

Factors for Designing Service Process

The following are the factors to be considered in the design and implementation of service process:

1. **The Service Itself:** The service is a dependent factor, which should be understood before it is processed and most of the services are equipment based like laundry services, upkeeping of lawn and services with highly intangible attributes like banking, legal services, medical services, etc., are process dependent.
2. **Customer Participation:** Customer participation will increase the degree of customization; the customer represents productive labour just at the moment it is needed. The degree of customer involvement depends on the wide range of service delivery system from serf-service to complete dependence on a service provider. E.g., the room services in a hotel depends on the type of room the customer has availed like deluxe room, air conditioned room, suite, etc.
3. **Degree of Customer Contact:** A system should be designed for high volumes and should be focused. It should also be flexible while perform the service activities. In the process of delivering the service, the provider will have to come into contact with the customer and proper care should be taken to provide best service, by which the customer derives satisfaction. This will help the management to take correct decisions at the correct time.
4. **Location of Service Delivery:** The service provider should ensure whether the service is to be provided in his premises or it should be provided at the customer's place. E.g., bridal make-up can be done at the customer's place or at the beauty parlour also, medical services in case of emergency is done at the customer's place itself.
5. **Complexity of Service:** It refers to the number of processes involved in the delivery of the service irrespective of whether it is high or low services. E.g., service in a hotel are high in complexity but low in divergence (a variation that deviates from the standard or norm). The deviation/divergence can be determined by looking at the blue print of service processes.

FILL IN THE BLANKS

1. ________ has become a powerful economic engine in its own right.
2. ________ is an example of a pure tangible article.
3. ________ is an example for tangible goods with a few supplementary after- sale services.
4. The attention will be on the services sold by business and professional concerns with ________.
5. The activities, benefits or satisfactions which are offered for sale are called as ________.
6. The major services employing service personnel is ________, ________ and ________.
7. The types of organization are ________ and ________ organization.
8. ________ is now regarded as a reward for creating a satisfied customer.
9. ________ and ________ identification receive great emphasis.
10. The primary function of service is ________.
11. The service market consists of providers of ________, ________ and ________ service.

12. The example of personal care service is ________ and ________.

13. The example for labour service is ________.

14. The example for professional service is ________.

15. ________ and ________ is the unique feature of industrialization.

16. Services cannot be seen, tasted or felt and this feature of services in known as________.

17. The services sold in the consumer market and business market ________, ________ and ________ service.

18. ________, ________ is the example of food services.

19. ________ offer simple and cheaper meals to customers.

20. ________ offers elegant and costly food but with superb services and royal comforts to the customers.

21. ________ has boosted the development of hotel industry.

22. ________ is the best example of scientific commercialization of marketing of customer services.

23. ________ is considered as a source of foreign exchange in all countries.

24. Modern hotels provides ________.

25. In a five star hotel room accommodation range is between ________.

26. ________ is the magic word means a great deal in a super deluxe hotel.

27. A customer is willing to pay ₹ 30 for the soft drink and ₹ 10 for a papad, because of ________, ________ and ________.

28. ________ is thriving only on the customer services and satisfaction.

29. ________ is an example for personal care services.

30. ________ brought about development in the personal care services.

31. ________ is growing popularly in all countries due to ever- increasing demand for improving individual personality.

32. ________ are called as service stations for mechanical road transport.

33. The garages and repair shops are specialized in repairs and maintence of ________, ________ and ________.

34. ________, ________ and ________ is an example for entertainment services.

35. ________ is responsible for the steady growth of entertainment services.

36. A person can have round- the- world trip just in ________.

37. ________ is very popular in international tourism.

38. The means of communication is ________, ________ and ________.

39. We have communication all over the world through ________.

40. Insurance gives protection against risk like ________, ________ and ________.

41. To facilitate the business operations, industry wants the service of ________, ________ and ________.

42. Business purchases some of the specialized services like ________ and ________.

43. ________ is the lifeblood of business.

44. ________ is required for fixed capital.

45. To ensure sound investment portfolio, investment companies guide business about the purchase of ________, ________ and ________.

46. Flow of goods in the process of marketing is facilitated through ________.

47. Expansion of FIEO ________.

48. e-Mail cellular phone enables ________, ________ and ________.

49. The charge for master health check up range is ________.

50. Unutilized services are ________.

51. Fluctuations in demand take place ________ and ________.

52. ________ are unused in the rainy season.

53. The burden of selling an intangible product like services falls mainly on the ________.

54. Expansion of TSRP is ________.

55. ________ is the latest and advanced service rendered by banks to its customers.

56. The Apollo – Hospital, Chennai, has adopted a strategy of circulating a twelve page quarterly tabloid called ________.

57. Bank advertisement takes places through ________, ________ and ________.

58. Along with ATM's the bank also offers 24 hours a day of ________.

59. The marketing of health care is done through means of ________.

60. ________ and ________ are assertively promoting and marketing the concept of packaged health care.

61. Many hospitals are holding ________ activities to spread awareness about health care.

62. The main objective of hospitals is ________ and ________.

63. Corporate hospitals focus on patient care and ________.

64. ________ is the hi- tech health services centre in Asia for all health care amenities and facilities.

65. Gronroos's model is an important contribution to the marketing strategy in ________.

66. The External marketing concentrates on ________, ________ and ________.

67. Internal marketing deals with ________ and ________ of employees.

68. Gronroos's added the "people" as the fifth 'P' in ________.

69. People include ________, ________ and ________ marketing.

70. Heterogeneity means ________.

Answers for Fill in the Blanks

1.	Service	12.	Beauty parlours; laundries
2.	Soap; salt	13.	Domestic workers
3.	Television set; computer	14.	Accountant
4.	Profit seeking motive	15.	Division of labour; work specialization
5.	service	16.	Intangibility
6.	Telecommunication; railway; defence	17.	Financial; insurance; transport
7.	Profit; non-profit	18.	Restaurants; cafeterias
8.	Profit	19.	Small eating places
9.	Market segmentation; market demand	20.	Five star hotels
10.	Marketing	21.	Tourism
11.	Personal; professional; industrial	22.	McDonald service

23.	Tourism	47.	Federation of Indian Export Organization
24.	Numerous amenities	48.	Online banking; online shopping; ticket reservation
25.	₹ 5,000 to ₹ 10,000 and above	49.	₹ 1000 to ₹ 5000
26.	Image	50.	Economic losses
27.	Product; taste; service rendered	51.	Seasonally or weekly; days or hours
28.	Hotel industry	52.	Cricket fields
29.	Beauty parlours	53.	Promotion mix
30.	Rising standards of living	54.	Technical Assistance Research Program
31.	Health and fitness organizations	55.	Internet banking
32.	Petrol pumps	56.	Heart beat
33.	Cars; trucks; motor cycles	57.	Radio; T.V.; newspaper
34.	Amusement parks; cricket; movies	58.	Phone banking
35.	Rising purchasing power	59.	Promotion
36.	One fortnight	60.	Private hospital; medical centres
37.	Air transport	61.	Public lectures
38.	e-Mail; telex; postal services	62.	Service motive; earring profit
39.	Satellite	63.	Profits
40.	Accident; death; sickness	64.	Chennai
41.	Storage; transport; finance	65.	Service marketing
42.	Merchant banking; Advertising	66.	Preparation; pricing; promotion
43.	Finance	67.	Training; motivating
44.	Long- term finance	68.	Marketing mix
45.	Shares; bonds; property	69.	Internal; External; interactive
46.	Transport and ware housing services	70.	Quality of services cannot be standardised

TRUE / FALSE

1. Service has become a power full economic engine in its own right. (True / False)

2. Soap, salt is an example of a pure tangible article. (True / False)

3. Television set is not an example for tangible goods. (True / False)

4. The attention will be on the services sold by business and professional concerns with developing motive. (True / False)

5. The activities, benefits or satisfactions which are offered for sale are called business. (True / False)

6. The major services employing service personnel are telecommunication. (True / False)

7. The profit & non- profit are the benefits of organization. (True / False)

8. Profit is now regarded as a reward for creating a satisfied customer. (True / False)

9. Market segmentation and market demand receives less emphasis. (True / False)

10. The primary function of service is advertising. (True / False)

11. The service market consist of providers of nonpersonals. (True / False)

12. The example of personal care service is perishable goods. (True / False)

13. One of the examples for labour service is accountant. (True / False)

14. One of the examples for professional serve is domestic workers. (True / False)

15. Division of labour is an unique feature of industrialization. (True / False)

16. Twenty to thirty kinds of services are sold by departmental stores. (True / False)

17. The services sold in the consumer market and business market is financial service. (True / False)

18. Restaurants is one of the examples of food services. (True / False)

19. Small eating places offer simple and cheaper meals to customers. (True / False)

20. Five star hotels offers elegant and costly food. (True / False)

21. Tourism has boosted the development of hotel industry. (True / False)

22. Mc-Donald service is the best example of scientific commercialization of marketing of customer services. (True / False)

23. Tourism is not considered as a source of foreign exchange. (True / False)

24. Modern hotels provide numerous amenities. (True / False)

25. In a five star hotel the discounted room accommodation range between ₹ 5000 to ₹ 10000. (True / False)

26. Image, Atmosphere, locality is the magic word means a great deal in a super- deluxe hotel. (True / False)

27. A customer is willing to pay ₹ 15 for the soft drink and not ₹ 50 for a paped for service rendered (True / False)

28. Hotel industry is thriving only on the customer services and satisfaction. (True / False)

29. Beauty parlours is not an example for personal care services. (True / False)

30. Rising standards of living brought about development in the personal care services. (True / False)

31. Health and fitness organization is growing popularly in all countries (True / False)

32. Petrol pumps are called as service stations for mechanical road transport. (True / False)

33. The garages and repair shops are specialized in repairs and maintenance of cars and trucks. (True / False)

34. Amusement parks is a best example for entertainment services. (True / False)

35. Rising purchasing power is responsible for the steady growth of entertainment services. (True / False)

36. A person can have round- the -world trip in a month. (True / False)

37. Air transport is very popular in international tourism. (True / False)

38. One of the latest disposal means of communication is mobile. (True / False)

39. We have satellite communication all over the world. (True / False)

40. Insurance gives protection against risk like accident, death. (True / False)

41. To facilitate the business operations, industry wants the service of storage, transport and finance (True / False)

42. Business purchases some of the specialized services. (True / False)

43. Finance is the lifeblood of business. (True / False)

44. Long- term finance is required for fixed capital (True / False)

45. To ensure round investment portfolio, investment companies guide business about purchase of cars. (True / False)

46. Flow of goods in the process of marketing is facilitated through transport service. (True / False)

47. FIEO stands for Federation of Indian Export Organization. (True / False)

48. e-Mail cellular phone enables in-line banking. (True / False)

49. The charger for master health check up range is ₹ 1000 to ₹ 5000. (True / False)

50. Unutilized services are economic losses. (True / False)

51. Fluctuations in demand takes place seasonally. (True / False)

52. Cricket fields are unused in the rainy season. (True / False)

53. The burden of selling an intangible product will fall on advertising mix. (True / False)

54. Expansion of TARP is Technical Assistance Research Program.(True / False)

55. Internet banking is the latest and advanced service rendered by banks to its customers. (True / False)

56. The Apollo hospitals, Chennai, has adopted a strategy of circulating a twelve page quarterly tabloid called heart beat. (True / False)

57. Bank advertisements take place through radio. (True / False)

58. Along with ATM's the bank also offers 24 hours a day of phone banking. (True / False)

59. The marketing of health care is done through means of advertisement. (True / False)

60. Private hospitals are assertively promoting and marketing the concept of packaged health care. (True / False)

61. Many hospitals are holding public lecturers to spread awareness about health. (True / False)

62. The main objective of hospitals is service motive. (True / False)

63. Corporate hospitals focus on patient care and profit. (True / False)

64. Chennai is the hi- tech health services centre in Asia for all health care amenities. (True / False)

65. Gronroos's model is an important contribution to the marketing strategy in profit. (True / False)

66. The external marketing concentrates on preparation. (True / False)

67. Internal marketing deals with training of employees. (True / False)

68. Gronroons's added the "people" as the 1st P is marketing mix. (True / False)

69. People includes internal, external and interactive marketing. (True / False)

70. Quality of services cannot be standardised. (True / False)

Answers for True / False

1.	True	7.	False	13.	False	19.	True	25.	True
2.	True	8.	True	14.	False	20.	True	26.	True
3.	False	9.	False	15.	True	21.	True	27.	False
4.	False	10.	False	16.	True	22.	True	28.	True
5.	False	11.	False	17.	True	23.	False	29.	False
6.	True	12.	False	18.	True	24.	True	30.	True

31.	True	**39.**	True	**47.**	True	**55.**	True	**63.**	True
32.	True	**40.**	True	**48.**	True	**56.**	True	**64.**	True
33.	True	**41.**	True	**49.**	False	**57.**	True	**65.**	False
34.	True	**42.**	True	**50.**	True	**58.**	True	**66.**	True
35.	True	**43.**	True	**51.**	True	**59.**	False	**67.**	True
36.	False	**44.**	True	**52.**	True	**60.**	True	**68.**	False
37.	True	**45.**	False	**53.**	False	**61.**	True	**69.**	True
38.	False	**46.**	True	**54.**	True	**62.**	True	**70.**	True

MULTIPLE CHOICE QUESTIONS

1. Which of the following has become a powerful economic engine in its own right?

(a) Service
(b) Commodity
(c) Market
(d) Advertisement

2. Which of the following is an example of a pure tangible article?

(a) Soap
(b) Salt
(c) Radio
(d) Both a & b

3. Which of the following is an example for a tangible good with a few supplementary after - sales services?

(a) Television set
(b) Computer
(c) Both a & b
(d) Cosmetics

4. The attention will be on the services sold by business and professional concerns with________.

(a) Service motive
(b) Profit seeking motive
(c) Wealth
(d) None of the above

5. The activities, benefits or satisfactions which are offered for sale are called as________.

(a) Goods
(b) Commodity
(c) Service
(d) All the above

6. The major services employing service personnel are________.

(a) Telecommunication
(b) Railway
(c) Defence
(d) All the above

7. The types of organizations are________.

(a) Profit organization
(b) Non-profit organization
(c) Both a & b
(d) Service organization

8. Which of the following is now regarded as a reward for creating a satisfied customer?

(a) Service
(b) Profit
(c) Organization
(d) Goodwill

9. This identification receive great emphasis ________.

(a) Market segmentation
(b) Market demand
(c) Market policies
(d) both a & b

10. The primary function of service is ________.

(a) Production
(b) Marketing
(c) Profit
(d) Policies

11. The service market consists of providers of ________.

(a) Personal service
(b) Professional service
(c) Industrial service
(d) All the above

12. The example of personal care service is ________.

(a) Beauty parlours
(b) Countries
(c) Both a & b
(d) None of the above

13. Which of the following is the example for labour services?

(a) Domestic workers
(b) Office workers
(c) Factory workers
(d) All the above

14. The example of professional services is ________.

(a) Accountant
(b) Lawyer
(c) Engineer
(d) All the above

15. Which of the following is the unique feature of industrialization?

(a) Division of labour
(b) Work specialization
(c) Both a & b
(d) Providing time for leisure

16. How many kinds of services are sold by departmental stores?

(a) Twenty to thirty
(b) Ten to twenty
(c) Fifty to sixty
(d) Thirty to fifty

17. The services sold in the consumer market and business market is________.

(a) Financial service
(b) Insurance service
(c) Transport service
(d) All the above

18. Which of the following is the example of food services?

(a) Restaurants
(b) Cafeterias
(c) Hotels
(d) All the above

19. Which of the following offers simple and cheaper meals to customers?

(a) Small eating places
(b) Three star hotels
(c) Five star hotels
(d) Restaurants

20. Which of the following offers elegant and costly food but with super services and royal comforts to the customers?

(a) Restaurants
(b) Five star hotels
(c) Small eating place
(d) None of the above

21. Which of the following has boosted the development of hotel industry?

(a) Transport
(b) Tourism
(c) Service
(d) All the above

22. Which of the following is the best example of scientific commercialization of marketing of customer services?

(a) Food service
(b) Professional service
(c) McDonald service
(d) Communication service

23. Which of the following is considered as a source of foreign exchange in all countries?

(a) Tourism
(b) Hospital
(c) Stockbrokers
(d) State transport

24. Modern hotels provide________.

(a) Numerous amenities
(b) Comforts
(c) Refined services
(d) All the above

25. In a Five star hotel the discounted room accommodation range between ________.

(a) ₹ 2,000 to ₹ 4,000
(b) ₹ 3,000 to ₹ 6,000
(c) ₹ 5,000 to ₹ 10,000
(d) ₹ 10,000 and above.

26. Which of the following is the magic word means a great deal in a super - deluxe hotel?

(a) Image
(b) Atmosphere
(c) locality
(d) Both a & b

27. A customer is willing to pay ₹ 30 for a soft drink & ₹ 10 for a papad, in a restaurant because of________.

(a) Product
(b) Taste
(c) Atmosphere/Image
(d) All the above

28. Which of the following is thriving only on the customer services and satisfaction?

(a) Tourism industry
(b) Banking industry
(c) Hotel industry
(d) Transportation

29. Give example for personal care services________.

(a) Health and fitness centres
(b) Beauty parlours
(c) Dry cleaners
(d) All the above

30. Which of the following brought about development in the personal care services?

(a) Income of the people
(b) Rising standards of living
(c) Quality of service
(d) Rising service centres

31. Which of the following is growing popularly in all countries due to ever-increasing demand for improving individual personality?

(a) Banking
(b) Health and fitness organizations
(c) Income of dieticians
(d) None of the above

32. Which of the following are called as service stations for mechanical road transport?

(a) Petrol pumps
(b) Mechanic shops
(c) Showrooms
(d) Both b & c

33. The garages and repair shops are specialized in repairs and maintenance of ________.

(a) Cars
(b) Trucks

(c) Motorcycles
(d) All the above

34. Give example for entertainment services ________.

(a) Amusement parks
(b) Cricket
(c) Movies
(d) All the above

35. Which of the following is responsible for the steady growth of entertainment services?

(a) Rising purchasing power
(b) More leisure time
(c) Both a & b
(d) Standard of living

36. A person can have round the world trip just in ________.

(a) One fortnight
(b) One week
(c) Two days
(d) Four weeks

37. Which of the following is very popular in international tourism?

(a) Water transport
(b) Land transport
(c) Air transport
(d) Railway transport

38. The latest means of communication is ________

(a) e-Mail
(b) Telex
(c) Postal services
(d) All the above

39. We have this communication all over the world ________.

(a) Radio
(b) Television
(c) Satellite
(d) All the above

40. Insurance gives protection against risk like ________.

(a) Accident
(b) Death
(c) Sickness
(d) All the above

41. To facilitate the business operations, industry wants the services of ________.

(a) Storage
(b) Transport
(c) Finance
(d) All the above

42. Business purchases some of the specialized service like ________.

(a) Merchant banking
(b) Advertising
(c) Both a & b
(d) None of the above

43. Which of the following is the life blood of business?

(a) Employees
(b) Finance
(c) Business plan
(d) CEO

44. Which of the following is required for fixed capital?

(a) Short-term finance
(b) Medium-term finance
(c) Long-term finance
(d) None of the above

45. To ensure sound investment portfolio investment companies guide business ________.

(a) Shares
(b) Bonds
(c) Property
(d) All the above

46. Flow of goods in the process of marketing is facilitated through ________.

(a) Financial service
(b) Insurance service
(c) Transport and warehousing service
(d) Office service

47. Expand FIEO________.

(a) Federation of Indian Export Organization
(b) Federation of Industrial Export Organization
(c) Firm of Industrial Entrepreneur Organization
(d) First - In Employment office.

48. e-Mail cellular phone enables ________.

(a) Online banking
(b) Online shopping
(c) Online shopping
(d) All the above

49. The charges for master health check up range is ________.

(a) ₹ 150 to 1,500
(b) ₹ 250 to 2500
(c) ₹ 350 to 3500
(d) ₹ 1000 to 5,000

50. Unutilized services are ________.

(a) Economic losses
(b) Economic gains
(c) Both a & b
(d) None of the above

51. Fluctuations in demand take place ________.

(a) Seasonally or weekly
(b) Days or hours
(c) Both a & b
(d) Yearly once

52. They are unused in the rainy season ________.

(a) Buses
(b) Tourism
(c) Cricket fields
(d) Stadium

53. The burden of selling an intangible product like services falls mainly on the ________.

(a) Promotion mix
(b) Advertising mix
(c) Marketing mix
(d) Marketing strategy

54. Expansion of TARP________.

(a) Training Assistance Research Programme
(b) Technical Assistance Research Programme
(c) Transfer Acknowledgment Report Process
(d) Telephone Acknowledgment Research Process

55. Which of the following is the latest and advanced service rendered by banks to its customers?

(a) ATM
(b) Tele-banking
(c) Internet banking
(d) All the above

56. The Apollo Hospital, Chennai, has adopted a strategy of circulating a twelve page quarterly tabloid called________.

(a) Heart beat
(b) Diabetics
(c) Thyrolysis
(d) Heart surgery

57. Bank advertisements take places through ________.

(a) Radio
(b) T.V
(c) Newspaper
(d) All the above

58. Along with ATM's the bank also offers 24 hours a day________.

(a) Phone banking
(b) Mobile banking

(c) SMS banking
(d) Tele banking

59. The marketing of health care is done through means of________.

(a) Marketing
(b) Promotion
(c) Advertising
(d) Medical camps.

60. They are assertively promoting and marketing the concept of packaged health care________.

(a) Private hospitals
(b) Private medical centres
(c) Private medical camps
(d) Both a & b

61. Many hospitals are holding these activities to spread awareness about health care________.

(a) Public lecturers
(b) Seminars
(c) Workshops
(d) All the above

62. The main objectives of travels is________ and tourism.

(a) Customer service
(b) Earning profit
(c) Both a & b
(d) Wealth maximization

63. Corporate hospitals focus on________.

(a) Patient care
(b) Profits
(c) Goodwill
(d) All the above

64. Which of the following is the hi-tech health services centre in Asia for all health care amenities of facilities?

(a) Mumbai
(b) Bangaluru
(c) Chennai
(d) Hyderabad

65. Gronroos's model is an important contribution to the marketing strategy in________.

(a) Service marketing
(b) Advertising
(c) Manufacturing
(d) Trading

66. The external marketing concentrates on________.

(a) Preparation
(b) Pricing
(c) Promotion
(d) All the above

67. Internal marketing deals with________.

(a) Training of employees
(b) Motivating employees
(c) Both a & b
(d) Guiding employees

68. Gronroos's added the "people" as the 5th 'p' in the service market in________.

(a) Advertising mix
(b) Marketing - mix
(c) Promotion mix
(d) Marketing strategy

69. People includes________.

(a) Internal marketing
(b) External marketing
(c) Interactive marketing
(d) All the above

70. Which of the following is the first company to offer 'Freight collect' to the customer________.

(a) Elbee courier
(b) Private courier service
(c) Freight courier pvt. ltd.
(d) None of the above

Answers for MCQ

1.	(a)	15.	(c)	29.	(d)	43.	(b)	57.	(d)
2.	(d)	16.	(a)	30.	(b)	44.	(c)	58.	(a)
3.	(c)	17.	(d)	31.	(b)	45.	(d)	59.	(b)
4.	(b)	18.	(d)	32.	(a)	46.	(c)	60.	(d)
5.	(c)	19.	(a)	33.	(d)	47.	(a)	61.	(d)
6.	(d)	20.	(b)	34.	(d)	48.	(d)	62.	(c)
7.	(c)	21.	(b)	35.	(c)	49.	(d)	63.	(d)
8.	(b)	22.	(c)	36.	(a)	50.	(a)	64.	(c)
9.	(d)	23.	(a)	37.	(c)	51.	(c)	65.	(a)
10.	(b)	24.	(d)	38.	(a)	52.	(c)	66.	(d)
11.	(d)	25.	(c)	39.	(d)	53.	(a)	67.	(c)
12.	(c)	26.	(d)	40.	(d)	54.	(b)	68.	(b)
13.	(d)	27.	(d)	41.	(d)	55.	(c)	69.	(d)
14.	(d)	28.	(c)	42.	(c)	56.	(a)	70.	(a)

MATCH THE FOLLOWING

1.	Tangible good	(a)	Fluctuations in demand.
2.	Restaurants	(b)	Television set.
3.	Marketing	(c)	Personal car.
4.	Beauty parlor	(d)	Entertainment services.
5.	Movies	(e)	Primary function of service.
6.	Pricing of services	(f)	Food services.

Answers for Match the Following

1.	(b)	2.	(f)	3.	(e)	4.	(c)	5.	(d)	6.	(a)